Home-Grown Hate

Perspectives on Gender

Series Editor: Myra Marx Ferree, University of Wisconsin, Madison

Home-Grown Hate
Gender and Organized Racism

Edited by **Abby L. Ferber**

ROUTLEDGE
NEW YORK AND LONDON

Published in 2004 by
Routledge
270 Madison Ave,
New York NY 10016
www.routledge-ny.com

Published in Great Britain by
Routledge
2 Park Square, Milton Park,
Abingdon, Oxon, OX14 4RN
www.routledge.co.uk

Library of Congress Cataloging-in-Publication Data

Home-grown hate : gender and organized racism / Abby L. Ferber, editor.
      p.   cm.—(Perspectives on gender)
   ISBN 0-415-94414-7 (Hardcover : alk. paper)—ISBN 0-415-94415-5
(Paperback : alk. paper)
    1. White supremacy movements—United States—History—20th century.
2. Racism—United States—History—20th century.   3. Sexism—United
States—History—20th century.   4. United States—Race relations.   5. Hate—United
States.   6. United States—Social conditions—1980–   I. Ferber, Abby L., 1966–   II. Series.
   E184.A1H65   2003
   305.8′00973—dc21   2003011935

Publisher's Note
The publisher has gone to great lengths to ensure the quality of this reprint
but points out that some imperfections in the original may be apparent.

For Joel, my partner in life
and for my grandmother, Esther, and mother, Shelly, who taught me what is
most important in life—and to stand up for it

Contents

Acknowledgments

I am sincerely indebted to each of the contributors to this volume. My own understanding of this movement has expanded in new directions thanks to their work. Through ongoing dialogues occurring across publications, conversations, conferences, and e-mails, I was inspired to assemble this volume and widen the discussion.

Just as we know the pivotal role of the surrounding culture in fostering or discouraging involvement in organized racism and hate crimes, my own cultural milieu has been pivotal in enabling me to accomplish this work. I wish all of my academic peers were as fortunate as I have been, surrounded, as I am, by supportive and engaging colleagues in the Department of Sociology and the many faculty affiliated with Women's Studies and Ethnic Studies at the University of Colorado at Colorado Springs. And my students are equally important to me. I have worked with an amazing, very diverse group of students this year in my seminar on privilege and power: Amanda, Angie, Annette, Charles, Jaimie, John, Kimberly, Ruth, Leisa, Linda, Regina, Tara, and Tracy. Their willingness to challenge themselves both intellectually and emotionally and the supportive community they have provided for each other have been wonderful to experience. They give me hope for the future. Such an open, caring, supportive academic environment makes all the difference in the world.

Were it not for the tremendous logistical and editorial support of Shari Patterson and Amanda Terrell-Orr, this book would have taken another year to complete. Their careful work and dedication to this project has been invaluable. I am also appreciative of the assistance of John McLay and Kristina

Haley. Working with series editor Myra Marx Ferree and Routledge editor Ilene Kalish has been wonderful. They have been patient, supportive mentors throughout the long process of bringing this manuscript to publication. I also appreciate the thorough work of Production Editor, Donna Capato, and Copy Editor, Gill Kent.

I also want to specifically thank a few of the many other colleagues who continue to inspire me: Becky Thompson, Michael S. Kimmel, Peggy McIntosh, and Sociologists for Women in Society, whose meetings energize so many of us. And Andrea Herrera, my good friend, collaborator, and coconspirator (and very possibly my long-lost twin sister from whom I was separated at the hip at birth).

Finally, the support of my family is crucial. I want to acknowledge my mother, my sister, Darcy, and my entire extended family, who continue to take an interest in my work; I love and appreciate you all. And most important, Joel and Sydney, "my dear ones."

Foreword

MICHAEL S. KIMMEL

I recently saw a cartoon in which a hooded member of the Ku Klux Klan is explaining the politics of today's Klan to a potential female recruit. "Actually, I'm more of an off-white supremacist," he explains.

While the cartoonist obviously meant this cartoon to suggest that the white-supremacist movement, taken as a whole, might need to tone down its misogyny to enable its nativism, racism, and anti-Semitism to appeal to younger white women, the articles in this book suggest that such soft-pedaling may not be necessary—or at least not as much as we might have thought.

Taken together, the articles in this stimulating collection have made me more aware of the many different facets of the white-supremacist movement, both between women and men within particular branches of the movement, and among the various branches of the movement themselves. It may make more sense, following Chip Berlet's lead here, to speak of white-supremacist *movements*—making the movement itself plural to encompass the various strands of the movement from traditional "old school" neo-Nazis, Klan, and far-right extremists to the more recent skinheads, militias, and Aryan youth groups.

One can see a variety of views, for example, of women—of women's "proper sphere," her "nature," and her mission in life: to make white babies, to raise and nurture young racists, or to stand alongside their men as street-fighting skinheads, ready and willing to use violence against those they feel are stealing their birthright. Some strands of the movement emphasize a recharged, ultratraditional image of women, maximizing gender difference in a fantasy of return to nineteenth-century separation of spheres; others offer a toughened angry vision, minimizing gender difference to stand united as a race.

And one can see the appeal of both visions to different groups of women. To some, the traditional patriarchal bargain—he works outside the home, soberly and responsibly bringing home his paycheck, and forswears drinking, gambling, carousing, and womanizing, while she stays at home, raises the children, and maintains the home—might seem a far sight better than the deal they presently have. (Such a model might also explain the popularity of the Promise Keepers to many women, despite their antediluvian view of women's sphere.) To others, of course, the image of kick-ass street-fighting "women warriors" appeals to a feisty postfeminist notion that women can also "do" masculinity and feel strong and empowered in the process.

And yet, despite all these differences, they remain differences within a unity—a general unity about their vision of the future and a general unity in their analysis of their present predicament. And it is the single strength of these essays that they make it clear that one cannot fully understand either their analysis of their situation or their vision of the future without understanding how these movements are gendered.

Of course, that is not to say that once one understands the gender of these social movements—both the gendered identities of the participants and the gendered nature of the organizations themselves—one has adequately explained the movements. Far from it. One must also continue to explore the fate of different classes, ethnic groups, and geographic regions within a general pattern of globalization. One must continue to explore the meaning of American religiosity, local cultural traditions, and the dynamic intersections of race and class in American history. No, one cannot understand these movements fully just by holding them up to a gender lens. Nor, however, can one pretend to fully understand these movements without holding them up to a gender lens.

The elements of this gendered lens have to do with the way class, race, and gender combine and collide into a sense of racial entitlement, class-based anger, and gendered sense of emasculation. The white-supremacist movement is animated by and populated by downwardly mobile lower-middle-class men (and their female counterparts)—men who grew up believing that this was "their" country and that all they had to do was to follow the same rules their fathers and grandfathers did and they too could reap the rewards of their entitlement. Many followed those rules: they served in the military, invested their life savings into small shops or farms, voted, and worked hard at whatever jobs they could find. And then, just when they felt they should reap the rewards they were promised and to which they felt entitled, the government jumped in to hand these rewards to undeserving others, especially black people and immigrants. What they want, says one member, is to "take back what is rightfully ours."

In many cases it was their fathers who lost the farm to foreclosure, who had to close the ma-and-pa grocery store when Wal-Mart moved in a few miles up the road, who got laid off from their high-skilled and high-paying manufacturing job when the company decided to relocate in the Philippines or Mexico. And the rage of the sons is fueled by those three entangled streams: racial entitlement, class-based rage, and the shame of emasculation. It is a lethal brew.

Let me illustrate this by referring to two famous cases. The two most devastating terrorist attacks ever accomplished on American soil were the bombing of the federal office building in Oklahoma City in 1995 and the attacks of 9/11. The former was undertaken by Timothy McVeigh and several associates; the second was masterminded and commanded by Mohammad Atta, the pilot of the first plane to hit the towers.

To see these as completely disparate acts committed by two entirely differ-ent types of individuals would miss the ways that McVeigh and Atta shared these qualities of rage, entitlement, and emasculation. On his return from the Gulf War in 1992, McVeigh wrote a letter to his hometown newspaper in Lockport, New York, complaining that the legacy of the American middle class had been stolen by an indifferent government. "The American dream," he wrote, "has all but disappeared"; "most people are struggling just to buy next week's groceries."[1]

Atta was slim, sweet-faced, neat, meticulous, a snazzy dresser. The youngest child of an ambitious lawyer father and a pampering mother, Atta grew up shy and polite, a mama's boy. "He was so gentle," his father said. "I used to tell him, 'Toughen up, boy!'"[2]

Both failed at their professions, sending them into a spiral of downward mobility. McVeigh dropped out of business college and found his calling in the military during the Gulf War, where his exemplary service earned him commendations; but he washed out of Green Beret training—his dream job—after only two days. Both of Atta's sisters were doctors—one a physician and one a university professor. His father constantly reminded him that he wanted "to hear the word 'doctor' in front of his name. We told him, your sisters are doctors and their husbands are doctors and you are the man of the family."

Defeated, humiliated, emasculated, a disappointment to his father and a failed rival to his sisters, Atta retreated into increasingly militant Islamic theology, and McVeigh drifted further and further to the extreme right. Despite the chasms of difference between the two, those emotions were similar—and similarly gendered. McVeigh and Atta, like their compatriots, needed to prove their masculinity, to prove that they were "real men" after all. And real men don't get mad; they get even.

The events of 9/11 also revealed many of the differences among the various white-supremacist groups and organizations. Some were infuriated by the immigrant invasion and urged their members to take up arms against all aliens and immigrants as the beginning to the final racial holy war. Others, however, could only stand by in awe as Islamic fundamentalists struck a blow against the corrupt and feminizing American government—a blow that they were still too weak, emasculated, and disorganized to pull off themselves. "We could work with those Islamic guys," one Klansman from Alabama told a journalist. "Those Islamic guys all feel the same way we do about who controls the world."[3] "It's a disgrace that in a population of at least 150 million White/Aryan Americans, we provide so few that are willing to do the same [as the terrorists]," bemoaned Rocky Suhayda, the chairman of the American Nazi Party. "A bunch of towel head/sand niggers put our great White Movement to shame."[4]

Among the intellectual virtues of this collection is that it enables us to see the many different ways that such shame is experienced—as gendered, raced, classed. And among its political virtues, then, is that it reminds us that any efforts to struggle against the far right's vision of racial, sexual, and ethnic purity will always inevitably revolve around a struggle over what it means to be a man.

Introduction

ABBY L. FERBER

Recently surfing the Web, I came across these two illustrations on the White Aryan Resistance's "Racist Cartoon Gallery" (Figs. I.1 and I.2). The first image, a caricature of a pregnant African-American woman, poses the racist joke: "Q: What do you call a black woman who has three or more abortions? A: A Crimefighter." The second illustration depicts a pregnant female fetus within the womb of its mother and reads: "... THIS REMARKABLE REVELATION JUST IN! ... FINALLY, AN ANSWER TO THE AGEOLD SCIENTIFIC MYSTERY, "HOW DO MEXICANS MANAGE TO REPRODUCE SO RAPIDLY?" ... RESEARCH HAS NOW REVEALED THAT THEIR FEMALE OFFSPRING ARE ACTUALLY BORN PREGNANT!"

As these disturbing yet not uncommon images reveal, women's bodies and control over reproduction are central to white supremacy. These two images stand in sharp contrast to the many real photos of white women I found. For example, one photo of an angelic blond woman cradling an infant at her breast, reads: "MOTHER AND CHILD—What White person who has healthy instincts and spiritual attitudes could fail to be moved by this photograph? Yet if this woman doesn't have three or more children during her lifetime she is helping to speed her Race along the road to extinction."[1] As these images argue, reproduction is essential to issues of racial preservation. White supremacists believe the white race faces the threat of genocide due largely to white women's low birthrates and interracial mixing, paired with the higher birthrates of African-American and Hispanic

1

Fig. I.1 Cartoon of a pregnant African-American woman from the White Aryan Resistance Web site's "Racist Cartoon Gallery."

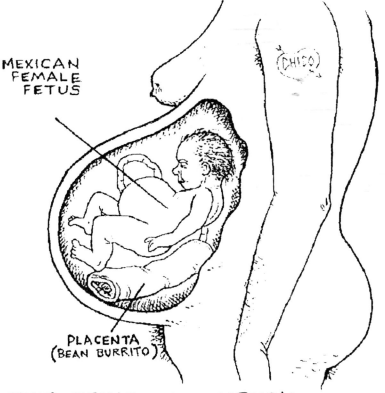

Fig. I.2 "Beans … Beans … Beans" from the White Aryan Resistance's "Racist Cartoon Gallery."

women. Leaf through any white-supremacist publication or Web site, and one will find numerous images and articles addressing this "dire" issue.

These images are even further revealing. The first two cartoons present women of color as ugly, hairy, tattooed stereotypes. Images of white women, on the other hand, tend to emphasize both their beauty and nurturing qualities. Overwhelmingly, women of color and Jewish women are drawn and caricatured, while white women are exclusively photographed. These varied illustrations highlight the intersections of race and gender in white supremacist logic. White women are argued to be the epitome of beauty and gentle, kind, caring, nurturing sexual objects adored by men of all colors, while women of color are invariably depicted as masculinized, beastly-looking, drug-addicted welfare dependents. And as their articles and books attest, the beauty of women is assumed to be a sign of the advancement of the race; hence white women's supposed beauty is taken as a sign of the naturalness of white supremacy and is used to rationalize the racial order.

Looking beyond the ideology, recent real-life violent attacks also highlight the politics of gender and reproduction in the movement:

> In California, Benjamin Matthew Williams, a devotee of the anti-Semitic Christian Identity religion who teamed with his little brother to firebomb three California synagogues and an abortion clinic, killed himself in Shasta County Jail on Nov. 17. His trial for murdering a gay couple—a crime he said was "God's will" in a confession to newspaper reporters—had been scheduled to start this January.... In Georgia, white supremacist Tracy Hampton was recently convicted and sentenced to death for two murders; he targeted Tanya Ramsdell because he believed her unborn baby had been fathered by a black man.[2]

White-supremacist violence frequently targets mixed-race couples, gays and lesbians, and others blamed for contributing to the disappearance of the white race. On abortion, the movement takes a more complex position, supporting abortion for women of color but attacking the option for white women.

An analysis of gender is essential to understanding these images and actions, yet until very recently, one would have been hard-pressed to find research on the white-supremacist movement that provided any discussion of gender. Kathleen Blee's work was one of the first analyses of women in the movement and the role of gender in the belief system. Since writing *White Man Falling: Race, Gender and White Supremacy,* I have witnessed an exciting outpouring of gendered analyses, and I conceived of this project to bring together the very interesting yet sporadic research being conducted on the various gendered dimensions of this movement. These various projects, taken together, significantly contribute to our understanding of the contemporary movement and gender and social movements more generally. The various chapters focus on a wide array of gender issues, ranging from the composition of the movement to its ideology, tactics, beliefs, and activities of members, the recruitment of individuals into and out of the movement, and the role of the researcher in constructing and defining social movements. Together, these pieces significantly enhance our understanding of the movement and highlight that issues of gender cannot be solely the domain of the feminist scholar.

Too often the issue of gender in white supremacism is reduced to a question of women's involvement in the movement, yet, as this collection documents, the entire movement should be explored through a gendered lens. We cannot understand this social movement without examining it through a gendered lens. That does not mean that gender is the primary concern of this movement. In many respects the issues of gender within the movement mirror the issues of gender found in the broader culture. However, rather than leading us to ignore gender, because it permeates all of society and is thus not unique to this movement, this volume demonstrates that we cannot understand this movement without understanding its gender dimensions. Valerie Jenness explores this issue more fully in her chapter, examining the exclusion of gender from many hate crime statutes. Jenness argues that gender has generally been excluded precisely because gender-based hate crimes are so common and pervasive. This exclusion further contributes to the invisibility of violence against women. Indeed, gender inequality is so pervasive in part because it still so often remains invisible. Our analyses need to make gender visible.

A Glimpse at the Movement

While there are hundreds of white-supremacist groups in the United States, the movement is not a new phenomenon. The Ku Klux Klan, historically the most influential white-supremacist organization in the United States, was founded in 1865. It is difficult to estimate the membership in organized racist groups. In 2002, the Southern Poverty Law Center counted 708 active hate groups in the United States, including a wide variety of white-supremacist organizations ranging from neo-Nazis and Klan groups to Christian Identity adherents and skinheads. While some organizations are attempting to move into the political mainstream, others have become increasingly violent (see Chapter 5 by Dobratz and Shanks-Meile).

While the movement seemed to be growing strong early in 2002, riding a wave of increased anti-Semitism following 9/11, a rash of arrests, legal attacks, and deaths have recently left the movement in disarray. Matthew Hale, a key member on the far right, was recently arrested on charges of obstruction of justice and solicitation to murder the federal judge presiding over his copyright trial over the use of the name World Church of the Creator (WCOTC). Hale is a law school graduate denied admission to the Illinois bar and was closely linked to Benjamin Smith, his follower who subsequently embarked upon a three-day shooting rampage, killing two and injuring nine. Hale was particularly powerful within the movement. He built the WCOTC from fourteen chapters in 1996 to eighty-eight in 2002, one of the most widespread neo-Nazi organizations. He was also responsible for greatly increasing the presence of the organization on the Web.

David Duke, America's most mainstream white supremacist, who in 1991 garnered 670,000 votes—close to 55 percent of Louisiana's white ballots—in the race for governor, recently pleaded guilty to charges of tax evasion and mail fraud. He allegedly spent thousands of dollars donated by fellow white supremacists gambling in casinos rather than trying to "save the race."

William Pierce, the inspirational leader of the neo-Nazi National Alliance and author of important white-supremacist publications, including *Hunter* and *The Turner Diaries* (recognized as the model for the Oklahoma City bombing), died unexpectedly in July, 2002. Pierce was the mastermind who had acquired the racist Resistance Records label and turned it into a huge moneymaker for his organization as well as a new recruitment tool to reach young people, and his writings have inspired the broader movement. With the immediate losses of these three significant leaders (although it may not be the end for Hale and Duke), in addition to the loss of the Aryan Nations compound as a result of a lawsuit brought about by the Southern Poverty Law Center, movement organization has been set back.

The three leaders above tell us something about the range of individuals attracted to the movement. All three were college educated, one with a law degree, another with a Ph.D. in physics. In contrast to our stereotypes of crazy, down-and-out, marginal men, members of white-supremacist organizations tend to resemble the general population in terms of education, occupation, and income.[3] Hate groups are especially successful recruiting in communities suffering from economic downturns; however, the movement attracts people from every class. Due to the increasing wealth gap and declining real wages in the United States, everyone but the very wealthy face downward mobility and may perceive themselves as doing poorly.

While far more people read white-supremacist publications than participate in movement activities, this is increasingly the case due to the Internet. Much has changed within the white-supremacist movement in the past decade. The movement's use of the Internet to reach a wider audience makes it increasingly difficult to measure its audience, breadth, and influence. In 2002, the Southern Poverty Law Center counted 443 hate-based Web sites. These sites allow the movement the ability to reach a wide audience with little money or effort and provide viewers with seemingly intellectual material as well as privacy, and anonymity. Over the past decade, the Internet has facilitated the forging of a well-connected, international movement that was never before possible.

New technology, in conjunction with an increasing promotion of the lone wolf philosophy, has shifted the emphasis of the movement. The lone wolf philosophy encourages individuals to carry out acts of violence alone or in small cells without implicating larger organizations, in order to avoid the legal consequences of promoting violence. In *White Man Falling* I argued that the boundaries of the movement were ambiguous and that the movement overlapped tremendously with what we call the "mainstream." This point is now even more important. If anything, the borders of the movement have further dissipated. It is increasingly difficult to tell who is or is not a member of the movement. Indeed, traditional notions of "membership" are becoming outdated. The movement's goals of spreading white-supremacist ideology and encouraging violent acts designed to provoke a race war no longer require building groups with large membership rosters. With the Internet providing the primary means of communication and facilitating a sense of identity and community among previously isolated pockets of people around the world, it may be time to rethink what constitutes the "movement."

In addition to the rise of new technologies, the movement has expanded its focus, attempting to reach out to women and youth. While organizations historically recruited and attracted primarily men, many groups have recently targeted women. The changing composition of the movement is addressed most thoroughly by Kathleen Blee in her recent book, *Inside Organized Racism*, and in her chapter in this volume. And women are not just serving cookies; they are increasingly joining men in acts of violence:

> In 2002, active neo-Nazi Christine Greenwood and boyfriend John Patrick McCabe, members of Blood and Honor, were charged with possessing bomb-making materials. Greenwood founded Women for Aryan Unity, a group closely affiliated with the neo-Nazi World Church of the Creator, and launched an "Aryan Baby Drive" to distribute food and clothing to poor white families. . . . Former Army intelligence officer Rafael Davila and his ex-wife Deborah Davila were arrested . . . after a grand jury indicted them for unlawfully possessing top-secret military documents. Deborah Davila, who has ties to the neo-Nazi Aryan Nations, was also charged with attempting to disseminate the documents for profit. . . . Two members of a neo-Nazi terror cell, Leo Felton and Erica Chase, were convicted . . . in a conspiracy to bomb Jewish and African-American landmarks and leaders. . . . [Chase] had ties to the neo-Nazi World Church of the Creator and the Outlaw Hammerskins gang.[4]

Efforts aimed at young whites have also increased, utilizing not only the Web but the white-power music industry and enabling the movement to reach middle- and upper-class educated teens and college students.

White-power music has increased its following, bankrolled many white-supremacist activities, and facilitated the development of a strong, racist, youth culture.

These modern tools of recruitment, in conjunction with a shifting attempt to make the movement more palatable to women and youths, represent the most significant and potentially powerful changes I have witnessed since I first began following this movement. A number of chapters in this volume argue that these shifts lend an aura of legitimacy to the movement and its ideology. These new technologies and the growing presence of women and families convey a sense of normalcy to movement activities and goals and contribute to a sense of belonging to a larger, legitimate community (see Chapter 2 by Blee and Chapter 3 by Perry).

And yet the more things change, the more they remain the same. In *White Man Falling* and *Hate Crime in America*, I outlined the basic beliefs that have remained constant. The white-supremacist worldview is remarkably flexible, capable of explaining just about any contemporary social/political issue or problem. Despite the wide differences among many organizations and individuals, the movement remains united by a shared system of beliefs. White supremacists believe that racial and gender differences are essential and unchanging, given by either God or biology. Social inequality is seen as a reflection of the natural order. This naturalized hierarchy places white men securely on top. Jews, defined as a nonwhite race, are constructed as the ultimate enemy, trying to race-mix the white race into oblivion. People of color and women are defined as inferior to white men, and it is believed to be white men's duty to protect innocent white women and children from the brainwashing Jews who control the world and from the criminal, animal-like blacks and other people of color. For white supremacists, the only way to secure the future of the white race is through the creation of a racially pure homeland or the elimination of all nonwhites.

These assumptions underlie the movement's critique of contemporary America—if things are falling apart all around us, it is because we are trying to change people's essential nature. White-supremacist ideology hence offers itself as the antidote to America's current social problems by promising to empower individuals, especially men, who feel they no longer have any power. The movement seems to offer white men the chance to prove their masculinity (see Chapter 6 by Ferber and Kimmel). White men are repeatedly attacked by the movement for becoming feminized (and unsettling the natural order), and are encouraged to become "real" men by standing up and protecting white women, reasserting their place in the natural hierarchy, and taking over the world. Furthermore, the movement's fear of white genocide leads to an obsession with controlling white women's sexuality and reproduction.

White supremacists recruit new members based on the assumption that the white race is under attack. American society has experienced tremendous social change in recent decades, sparked by the civil rights, women's, and gay and lesbian movements. More recently, debates over affirmative action, multicultural curricula, welfare, and other contentious topics have been perceived by many white men as attacks against them, against not only their racial privilege but their identity *as men* as well. Organizing against the real and perceived advances of the civil rights, women's, and gay and lesbian movements, white-supremacist organizations seek to reassert white, male, heterosexual hegemony. While the tactics of the white-supremacist movement are extreme, including their encouragement of violence, they are part of a broader cultural backlash against movements for equality.

The white-supremacist movement draws upon historically mainstream views about race and gender. Research reveals that many Americans share the views of white supremacists, even if they are not members of the movement. For example, Joe Feagin and other sociologists have documented that the majority of whites embrace stereotypes that blacks are inferior and lazy, that Jews are moneygrubbing, and that discrimination against people of color is a thing of the past.[5] Less than 10 percent of hate crimes are actually committed by members of white-supremacist organizations. The presence of the movement nevertheless serves to encourage hate-motivated violence, providing a voice, community, and even a sense of legitimacy for a wider audience. As survey research reveals, white-supremacist organizations articulate the wider concerns shared by many Americans as well as a comprehensive ideology that enables a broader audience to interpret their own experiences and concerns. The white-supremacist movement and the broader white-supremacist culture have a symbiotic relationship, each contributing to the strength of the other. In conjunction with the rise of new technologies and expanded recruitment, this belief system is now reaching wider and wider audiences, and the lines between white-supremacist and other right-wing views on race and gender are further blurring.

Through the Prism of Gender

Rachel L. Einwohner, Jocelyn A. Hollander, and Toska Olson observe that, despite the growth of literature on both gender and social movements, the two are rarely addressed together. Until very recently, "scholars have paid relatively little attention to how gender affects social movement structures and processes and how social movements, in turn, affect gender."[6] Thanks to the work of feminist sociologists, we have witnessed the growth of research on gender and social movements; however, this research has most often focused on women's movements and social movements concerned primarily with gender issues. Recent work, however, argues that it is time we extend our analysis of gender and social movements to the study of social movements which are not, on the surface, about women or gender.[7] This collection speaks to that goal.

As Bahati Kuumba argues, "gender is a basic organizing principle in human society and . . . gender roles, relations, and inequalities impact social problems in complex ways."[8] Feminist research can contribute to a deeper comprehension of social movements and social problems far beyond the first simple step of bringing women into the picture. As feminist scholars have long argued, a feminist approach cannot just "add women and stir." Adding women to the picture changes the entire picture.

Because our entire social world is gendered, gender comprises a set of cultural tools or cultural resources that all social movements draw upon, whether deliberately or unconsciously. Einwohner and colleagues identify five specific ways in which social movements may be gendered. At the most obvious level, they may be *gendered in composition.* Historically, gendered analyses have been applied to movements of women, reflecting our cultural assumption that only women are gendered, whereas men reflect universal, nongendered interests. In *White Man Falling,* however, I argued that the fact that the organized racist movement was made up primarily of men was also an issue of gendered interests. Like the Promise Keepers and the Million Man March, the organized white racist movement has traditionally attracted and represented the position and interests of men.

In Chapter 7, Randy Blazak argues that both microlevel psychological and macrolevel sociological reasons attract men to the movement, and most of these revolve around issues of masculinity. For example, at the microlevel, in response to a "complex worldview based on moral relativism . . . hate groups provide a simplistic worldview." This strain is particularly gendered in the white-supremacist emphasis upon strict, dichotomized sex roles. One is either a man and must behave masculinely, or one is born a female and must behave femininely. Any aberration is seen as a threat to the natural order.[10] Similarly, the "inability to express aggression in a culture that decries violence causes strain. Hate groups provide an outlet for aggression." This strain is also gendered, as men join the movement to prove their masculinity by talking about and occasionally acting out a violent masculinity. The macrolevel forms of strain are more overtly gendered by Blazak, including changing constructions of masculinity and femininity, loss of social status by white males, and the lack of advocacy groups or movements representing white men. Each of the forms of micro- and macrolevel strain identified by Blazak are highly gendered, emphasizing that individuals are attracted to the movement for gender-based reasons.

As Kathleen Blee points out, women's "experiences in organized racism, no less than those of men, are highly gender-specific. Women enter racist groups because of contacts and issues that reflect their places as women in the larger society." In Chapter 2, Blee explores the various factors precipitating the increased recruitment of women into certain white-supremacist organizations. The homegrown nature of the movement is due in large part to the activities of women. Women are responsible for the bearing and rearing of children—fulfilling their duty to reproduce the white race and also educating and socializing their children into racist beliefs, thereby reproducing the movement.)

According to Eihnwohner and colleagues, movements may also possess *gendered goals.* Despite the fact that the movement voices primarily racialized concerns, gendered goals pervade its literature and language. In fact, these gendered goals are interwoven with racial goals. For example, in order to secure the existence of the white race, the central gendered goal that white women's primary duty is to bear pure white children is embraced. The racial goal here is dependent upon the gender goal. In Chapter 3, Barbara Perry explores the particular "politics of reproduction" so central to the movement, focusing specifically on abortion, homosexuality, and miscegenation, three highly gendered issues that preoccupy white-supremacist discourse and are central to the goal of preserving the white race.

Tactics may also be gendered. Movement tactics, behaviors, displays, and activities can all take gendered forms. For example, the men of the movement adopt highly masculinized wardrobes, tattoos, boots, and so on. While these vary among the specific organizations, the images and performances are often highly masculine and warrior-like. Chapter 6, by Kimmel and Ferber, explores this. For women involved in the movement, the gendered tactics vary. For example, in some of the organizations, women are encouraged to adopt an overly traditional, feminine role, serving refreshments at meetings and taking care of the men. Within other groups, however, this feminine image is questioned, and women seek to participate in heretofore masculine tactics. For example, on the www.resist.com Web site, their "positions" section presents a "Declaration of White Womanhood." The declaration states:

> It has come to the attention of several White racist females . . . [that some men in the movement yearn] for a return to the days when women were submissive and silent and tolerant of the intolerable. . . . it disgusts me that you would use our movement as a means of muddying White women by urging them to act like mindless breeeders with the brains of a sub-Saharan nigger. . . . We are proud White women, not puny, weak, submissive, Asian geisha girls. . . . Stop whining about strong White women and look to them as partners in the Struggle, rather than just ovaries with tits.[11]

Chapters in this volume by Kathleen Blee, Betty Dobratz and Stephanie Shanks-Meile, Barbara Perry, and JoAnn Rogers and Jacquelyn Litt explore what are often conflicting views within the movement regarding women's place. The greater participation of women in the contemporary movement has brought many of these issues to the fore. Nevertheless, the issue of gendered tactics is central to the roles played by both men and women in the movement, and the movement is being forced to respond to changing notions of appropriate gendered tactics for women as broader social constructs of womanhood have changed. While this "declaration" attempts to redefine women's place in the movement, it ends with this remarkable statement: "In closing, I warn you all that White racist women have a little network independent of men and we have begun taking notes. Those who treat us like common mud whores will soon learn that bad treatment equals fewer dates." Ironically, the authors conclude by employing traditionally feminine gendered tactics, limiting their power as women to objects of sexual desire.

In many ways women are now the glue that holds the movement together, forming and strengthening the social ties among members, helping individuals to feel apart of a larger "family," and helping to forge a sense of collective identity (see Chapter 2 by Blee). Women also make the movement more accessible and less threatening to the mainstream by creating Aryan coloring books for kids and women's Web sites, and home-schooling their children. They contribute to the seeming ordinariness of life in the movement.

Women are rarely found in actual positions of leadership in the movement. Nevertheless, a gendered lens shifts our understanding of leadership activities. Blee argues that we must focus on leadership practices rather than simply leadership titles. Feminist analyses of leadership in social movements has revealed that those in less visible roles are often providing "group cohesion, mediating conflict, developing political strategies, and nurturing collective identity." Exploring this middle layer of leadership activities reveals the important roles women play in leading and coalescing the movement and also makes visible an entire range of more informal activities essential to the success of any social movement.

Gendered tactics such as these are connected to the construction of *gendered identities* by the movement. Movement members select and perform specific gendered identities (not necessarily traditional ones, but gendered nonetheless). The previous example demonstrated this well in not only arguing that women ought to engage in tactics similar to the men of the movement but also claiming a specific gendered identity for women in the movement. Throughout the publications of organized racist groups, there is much discussion of white women's roles as mothers and breeders of the race, and chapters by Blee, Dobratz and Shanks-Meile, Perry, and Rogers and Litt examine these. On the other hand, Chapter 6 by Kimmel and Ferber explores the particular gendered identity for men constructed throughout the movement's literature. As Einwohner and colleagues surmise, "regardless of whether a movement supports or resists gender stereotypes ... it cannot avoid responding to them."[12]

Finally, *gendered attributions* come into play. Outsiders to the movement attribute certain gendered attributes to movement members.) For example, members of organized racist movements are often overly simplified by outsiders, and women are often dismissed as simply meek, submissive followers in the movement. As the passage from the declaration shows, this is often not the case. Blee's life histories of thirty-four women in the movement more fully dispel this myth. (The movement itself also constructs gendered attributes *for others*) In *White Man Falling*, I explored in detail the gendered and racialized identities constructed within the movement of people of color and Jews. The gendered white identities constructed by the movement for its members is in direct opposition to the identities the movement constructs for African-Americans, Jews, and other nonwhites. The images I began this introduction with exemplify the ways gender is attributed to different women across race.

It is also important to emphasize that movements can be gendered even when gender is not an intentional focus for a movement. Hence, while Dobratz and Shanks-Meile present the explicit views of organized racists themselves, who frequently see the movement in nonsexist terms, their views can be contrasted with the highly gendered imagery employed by the movement. ("Gender is thus contested terrain: something to be struggled over through the claiming of identities and the attribution of characteristics."[13])

Finally, (Einwohner and colleagues emphasize that gender is also key to the success of a movement. Literature on social movements has revealed "that strategies using frames that 'resonate' with preexisting belief systems will be more effective.... Frames that are consonant with the ideas that are already widespread in society may be more effective because they evoke ideas that are familiar and compelling to the society's members."[14] The chapters by Kimmel and Ferber, Rogers and Litt, and Blee support this contention. Each demonstrates, in a different manner, the ways in which the gendered narratives and activities employed by the movement may facilitate recruitment and normalize movement activities. As Blazak's research highlights, gender composition and gendered issues may also contribute to the recruitment of individuals *out* of the movement.

(The future of the movement is to a large extent dependent upon women. Women clearly play a significant role in holding organized groups together and recruiting future generations and newcomers to the movement, yet, as Blee surmises, "the interpersonal conflicts and political disillusionment" experienced by so many women in the movement may instead herald its downfall.)

In addition to the realms discussed by Einwohner and colleagues, Myra Marx Ferree and David Merrill raise yet another important dimension of a feminist analysis of social movements: the role of the researcher-activist. Central to the emergence of a gendered analysis of social movements is the questioning of the goal of value-neutrality in science. As feminist science studies have argued, objectivity is impossible, and "evade[s] fundamental questions about whose perspectives and needs shape its particular relevances."[15] We, as researchers, are involved in a framing process as well—that of framing the movement for our readership.

When I wrote *White Man Falling*, this was a central concern for me. What role do we, as scholars, play in defining and producing this movement? To what extent do the predominant characterizations of the movement as "extremist" contribute to the invisibility of privilege and of far more invidious forms of white supremacy which pervade our culture? Throughout that book I explored the points of ideological overlap and similarity among white-supremacist and mainstream constructions of race and gender, arguing that the white-supremacist movement draws upon and is fueled by mainstream racisms and gender constructs. Since then, I have engaged in an ongoing dialogue with Chip Berlet, senior researcher for Political Research Associates. Our conversations have helped me to sharpen and clarify my own position and to learn from his. I am pleased to be able to include some of that debate in this volume, as it remains a central concern for me and a significant issue for anyone interested in this movement and right-wing politics. Our discussions have revolved around two issues in particular, both of which he addresses in Chapter 1: our disagreement over the significance of gender to this movement; and his emphasis upon the uniqueness of this movement and its differences from other movements and the mainstream, as opposed to my own emphasis on the similarities and points of connection.

What constitutes the right? What divisions and classifications among the right are appropriate? Berlet presents his own set of categorizations and argues that careful and precise classifications are necessary to understand and strategize against the right. I hope to make visible this role that we play in defining the right and its divisions. Is it more important to focus on the similarities or the differences? Both can be productive, and we should not be compelled to take only one approach. In my own work, I have wanted to focus primarily on the similarities because I found that the majority of the research to date had been preoccupied with the differences. In fact, the differences are often assumed and taken for granted, with no attention to the similarities, especially the similarities between that which we define as the "far right" and the "mainstream."

One of the central insights of sociology is that reality is socially constructed and that we actively create and maintain those constructions.

Members of the movements themselves are involved in constructing the movement (as we witness in recent declarations that the movement is really about love and not hate, or really about separation and not supremacy), and we, as academics, activists, teachers, citizens, also construct the movement in specific ways tied to our own interests and priorities. There will never be one agreed-upon way of defining the movement, nor should there be. Social constructs are always shaped by political interests. Each one of us approaches the subject with varying agendas, and the classifications one develops or employs often reflect that agenda.

Berlet's goals and mine differ at times. As someone whose job it is to track and follow the wide range of actors and organizations on the right, it is obviously important for him to be able to make sharp distinctions between the various segments of the movement. In my own work, it is my goal to explore the ways in which race and gender are intricately interconnected and constructed across our culture; therefore I am much more interested in highlighting the similar ways in which the various groups along the spectrum of the right engage in similar processes of race and gender construction. I am interested in revealing those underlying narratives and constructs which undergird not only far-right but mainstream understandings of race and gender. I hope that by examining the points of overlap, we can be moved to interrogate further those race and gender ideologies labeled "mainstream" and see the dangers lurking in our own often unquestioned assumptions which help to legitimate and bolster the white-supremacist movement and perpetuate institutional racism and sexism throughout our culture. We both approach the subject with different goals and often speaking to different audiences, and therefore it makes sense that our classifications vary to support those goals.

Ferree and Merrill emphasize that a feminist approach to social movements requires an examination of the researcher-activist as someone with values and politics that necessarily and rightly shape the research process. Reflecting this fact, the authors in this volume use their own terminology for referencing the movement. The labels range from hate groups to white nationalist, white separatist, white supremacist, and others. Berlet's chapter provides a foundation for defining and conceptualizing the movement. The debate over proper terminology is not an insignificant matter. I use the terms white-supremacist movement or organized racism (following Blee), although neither of these terms is ideal. The term white-supremacist may obscure the fact that American society is itself white-supremacist, while the term organized racism is so broad that it is often used to include black racist separatist groups (for example, by the Southern Poverty Law Center). Terminology is never simple; labels carry political consequences and highlight the significant role that we as researchers, activists, and onlookers play in constituting the movement itself. For example, while some scholars employ the term white separatist, I believe this term obscures the racist, supremacist nature of the movement and downplays the threat of these organizations.

While members of the movement themselves may prefer the term white separatist, this is part of the larger reframing of the movement as a movement about love and preservation of the white race rather than about racism and hatred. As I argued in *White Man Falling,* the ideology of separation assumes, indeed requires, a notion of white supremacy. There is a starting assumption that there are inherent and essential racial differences and that racial groups are inherently hierarchized, with whites being by nature superior. It is this underlying foundation of racism and white supremacy that justifies their attempts to separate and preserve the white race. Additionally, despite attempts to present a kinder, gentler face as racial preservationists, any quick glance through movement Web sites and publications immediately reveals the overtly hateful and racist rhetoric which pervades their mission. As researchers and activists, I believe, we make a mistake when we present the movement as its members wish to be presented and thereby facilitate their attempt to reframe the movement and attract new recruits. Instead, it is our task to critically interrogate the movement itself. White separatism and white supremacy are intricately bound together in the same project; however, the choice of terminology is a political, value-laden decision.

This book, with its central focus on gender, represents a purposeful reframing of the movement in order to enable and encourage broader collaborative activism against the right-wing politics of racism and sexism. The focus on gender does not imply that gender is more central to the movement than the politics of race. Instead, it follows the lead of many women of color who have argued that race and gender are inseparable and cannot be understood in isolation. This is the important insight of recent "intersectional" analyses: race and gender (and class, and sexuality) are interlocking, they shape each other, and we cannot fully comprehend one without attention to the others because one is never present alone.[16]

Following a path very different from Berlet, Rajani Bhatia, in her contribution to this volume, explores the points of overlap in contemporary environmentalist discourses and traditional Nazi as well as contemporary white-supremacist ideology, particularly around issues of population and the environment. She highlights not only the ideological similarities but, frighteningly, the actual connections in terms of key individuals and organizations. Revealing the gendered nature of the discourse, she explores both movements' attempts to colonize the bodies of poor women of color. These movements are collapsing many right/left boundaries, creating new configurations that require new responses. Recognizing the dramatic impact of these movements on women should lead to more openly profeminist and antiracist coalitions, such as the Committee on Women, Population, and the Environment formed to provide a feminist analysis of population and environment issues and to reveal the racist, eugenic foundations of the population-environment issue.

Revealing the gender politics of these movements broadens the opportunities for forming coalitions to work together to counter this right-wing threat to the lives of women, the poor, and people of color. Even though race is the primary, central concern of the white-supremacist movement, we cannot understand the racism of the movement without understanding its gendered nature; gender is central to the particular constructions of whiteness, blackness, and Jewishness that pervades the discourse.[17] Race and gender cannot be easily separated.

Intersectional theory has forcefully demonstrated that race cannot be neatly separated from gender. To do so maintains the invisibility of whiteness and of masculinity. All people have both racial and gender identities that shape their lives simultaneously. As Elizabeth Spelman highlighted in her book, *Inessential Woman,* the pop-bead theory of race and gender does not work. Race and gender are not simply different beads on a string that can be popped off one at a time. So to ask which is more primary to a movement, race, or gender misses the point.

For example, in *White Man Falling* I analyzed the white-supremacist obsession with race-mixing. If we ignore the issue of gender, we cannot comprehend just why miscegenation is such a threat to white supremacy. Gender shapes this obsession. It is only white women who are obsessed over. Images of white women and black men fill the publications and Web sites of white-supremacist groups, and in the final scenes of *The Turner Diaries,* white women who had been involved in interracial relationships are hung during the bloody "Day of the Rope," yet the issue of white men in relationships with women of color is rarely ever discussed, and when it is, excuses are made for their actions, blaming white women for becoming too feminist. If we ignore gender, we cannot understand the various reasons why men and women are attracted to and drawn out of this movement. As participants in this movement, men and women are gendered beings; they do not leave their gender at the door when they join up. As volumes of feminist research now attest, gender shapes most realms of behavior. The fact that gender is ubiquitous should tell us that we cannot understand any social movement without exploring its gender dynamics.

To bring gender into the picture does not mean one implies that a movement is sexist or that sex and gender are the primary nor only concern of a movement. To bring gender into the picture means that we cannot fully understand what motivates individuals to join a movement, to stay in a movement, to leave a movement, to understand its ideology, its imagery, its mission and goals, without paying attention to gender.

As Kuumba argues, "gender, on both objective and subjective levels, significantly impacts social movement recruitment and mobilization, roles played and activities performed within movements, resistance strategies and organizational structures, and the relevance and impact of movement outcomes. As a result, taking gendered patterns into account opens up a Pandora's box of previously unasked questions and concerns."[18]

Once we begin thinking about gender in relationship to this movement, indeed a Pandora's box of questions arise: Are men and women recruited into the movement in the same ways? Do men and women join the movement for the same reasons? To what extent does gender impinge upon men and women's motivations for joining the movement? Are they equally committed to the movement? Do they equally identify with and support the goals of the movement? Does the movement play the same role in male and female members' lives? Do they leave the movement for the same reasons? Has the recent growth in numbers of women in the movement changed the ideology of the movement or movement tactics? Has the greater involvement of women changed the movement's level of legitimacy and respectability among outsiders? What is the relationship between the movement and the societal gendered division of labor? To what extent are changing gendered roles and identities in the broader culture shaping the politics of gender within the movement? How are gender relations produced within the movement and how do they vary among different sectors and organizations? How are members' experiences within the movement differentiated by gender?

As Kuumba observes: "At every turn, these questions and their answers reveal relationships to gendered structures, ideologies, symbols, and roles."[19] The chapters in this volume provide some answers, but they simultaneously open up new realms for investigation. It is my hope that this volume will intervene in the ongoing dialogue and research agenda on the white-supremacist movement and also encourage other scholars and activists to explore other social movements through the prisms of gender and race. Race is similarly necessary to our understanding of movements that on the surface seem to be primarily about gender. Until we fully appreciate the extent to which gender and race intertwine to shape all of our lives and the society we participate in, our analyses and our forms of resistance will be limited.

1

Mapping the Political Right: Gender and Race Oppression in Right-Wing Movements

CHIP BERLET

(Right-wing hate groups do not cause prejudice in the United States—they exploit it.)What we clearly see as objectionable bigotry surfacing in extreme-right movements is actually the magnified form of oppressions that swim silently in the familiar yet obscured eddies of "mainstream" society. (Racism, sexism, heterosexism, and anti-Semitism are the major forms of supremacy that create oppression and defend and expand inequitable power and priv-ilege; but there are others based on class, age, ability, language, ethnicity, immigrant status, size, religion, and more.[2] (These oppressions exist inde-pendent of the extreme right in U.S. society.)

Bigotry and prejudice are easy to find in the texts of various right-wing movements in the United States, but they occur in varying degrees in differ-ent groups and can change over time. Between the hate-mongering groups of the extreme right and the reform-oriented groups in the conservative right are a series of dissident-right social movements. Examples include the Christian right and the patriot movement (which includes the armed citizens' militias).

Some scholars study the dissident right and extreme right and treat them as a single entity for analytical purposes. In one sense this is fair: both the dissident right and the extreme right have stepped away from politicians, elections, and legislation where the political movements and institutions of the conservative right are most active. Many scholars and activists refer to all right-wing movements outside the electoral system as the far right or the hard right. This chapter will use the term hard right in this manner, to cover both the dissident right and the extreme right.

While it is sometimes appropriate to discuss similarities in the various movements in the hard right, too often very real differences are minimized, ignored, or dismissed. The terminology and definitions used to describe hard-right groups are sometimes applied in an overbroad or confusing manner. Some of the work conflating the dissident right with the extreme right uses guilt by association or fallacies of logic in ways that would be more obvious (and raise more objections) if the groups being examined were not held in such low esteem in academia and the general public.

This is not to apologize for supremacist bigotry in the U.S. political right, but to argue that the specific ideology and the types and degrees of prejudice, supremacy, and oppression are important distinctions to be observed, since they vary greatly depending on the sector of the hard right under inspection. This variance is so significant that the Christian right, patriot movement, and extreme right should be studied as autonomous social movements. Later in this chapter, the commonalities and differences among these three sectors of the right will be examined in detail, along with critical comments concerning previous research, including my own.

Coming to Terms with Right-Wing Movements

It is not useful to lump together all right-wing dissident groups outside the mainstream as "far-right hate groups" or "religious-political extremists." If scholars presume to study demonization as socially dysfunctional, we should scrupulously avoid it in our own work. Not all forms of prejudice rise to the level of hate. Not all scapegoating calls for genocide. Not all forms of sexism qualify as misogyny. Not every group that defends heterosexism is a hate group. To some observers the Christian right, the patriot movement, and the armed militias may seem far to the right; but it is neither accurate nor fair to claim they are identical to neo-Nazis or other race-hate terrorists.

When talking about the hard right, we need to discuss as shared attributes only those attributes that are actually shared by *all* the different sectors. It is true that scholars often can find some similarity in the ideologies, styles, tools, frames, narratives, or targets utilized across the hard right. What is neither useful nor accurate is the tendency to discover a distinct aspect of one movement, such as the extreme right, and then extrapolate it across all movements in the hard right. If the same features are identical in the extreme right, patriot movement, or the Christian right, then some evidence needs to be presented. In addition, all sorts of people occasionally make prejudiced statements. Locating one prejudiced statement by an individual is not convincing evidence that the statement represents the ideological worldview of the individual. In the same way, finding a member of a movement or group who utters prejudiced or hateful statements is not convincing evidence that the member's view represents the ideological worldview of the group itself or even most of its members. Maybe it does, maybe it does not—evidence is required.

When writing about the social evils of prejudice and oppression, the devil is in the details. Many older studies of prejudice had a "tendency to collapse distinctions between types of prejudice" observes Elisabeth Young-Bruehl. They assumed "that a nationalism and racism, an ethnocentric prejudice and an ideology of desire, can be dynamically the same." Furthermore, she writes, "there is a tendency to approach prejudice either psychologically or sociologically without consideration for the interplay of psychological and sociological factors."[3] In a complementary fashion, Steven Buechler notes that issues of class, race, and gender are "omnipresent in the background of all forms of collective action" and reflect "institutional embeddedness within the social fabric at all levels." But he adds that these are distinct yet overlapping structures of power that need to be assessed both independently and jointly. To do this, it is important "to theorize the different, specific, underlying dynamics that distinguish one structure from another."[4] Ultimately, the successful assertion of "collective human rights" or "group rights" depends on the "linking of ethnicity/race, class, gender, and sexuality," argues William Felice, because this linkage "mutes supremacist tendencies by denying the right of any one group to assert supremacy over a different group."[5] For brevity, this constellation of identities is sometimes referred to as race, gender, and class.

To unravel systems of oppression involving race, gender, and class, we need a more complex formula that is better at mapping out the dynamics of societal oppressions in ways that resonate with the everyday experiences of our colleagues, students, neighbors, and families. This is especially important in an era of open hostility to discussions of supremacy, domination, and oppression. Developing a concept of "racial formation," Michael Omi and Howard Winant argue that "racial projects" that are "racist" entail a linkage between "essentialist representations of race and social structures of domination."[6] They further argue that "racial ideology and social structure" act in an interconnected and dialectical manner to shape racist projects. Applying these concepts to racism, sexism, and heterosexism, I think it is useful to define societal oppression as the result of a dynamic process involving ideas, acts, and a hierarchical position of dominance that is structural. The dominance enshrined in "social structures of domination" involves both unequal power and privilege. The resulting formula is as follows: supremacist ideology + discriminatory acts + structural dominance = oppression.[8]

In studying groups that promote oppression, scholars need to identify discrete components of ideology, methodology, and intent in order to classify and explain more accurately how different social movements function. Increased attention to specificity in language, categorization, and boundaries can assist our analysis of oppressions promoted by the hard right. By tracing the similarities and differences among hard-right movements and charting the dynamic relationships among the various sectors, we not only better understand movement dynamics but also learn how to construct a more effective counterstrategy to defend and extend freedom and equality.[9]

Terminology and Boundaries

A number of scholars who have studied the contemporary hard right already use a range of careful distinctions.[10] However, Martin Durham has called for scholars to pay even greater attention to precision in terminology when analyzing right-wing political groups.[11] Many analysts, especially in Europe, see the landscape of the political right as involving three major sectors, with some sort of dissident (often populist) sector between the conservative right and the extreme right.[12] Figure 1.1 shows how these sectors interact.

Note that Christian nationalists are closer to the conservative right (an example would be the legislation-oriented Free Congress Foundation), as opposed to Christian theocrats (such as the group Concerned Women for America), who promote more antidemocratic agendas. The most militant and doctrinaire Christian-right groups, such as those that embrace Christian Reconstructionism, actually fit best under the banner of the extreme right.[13]

The term extreme right refers to militant insurgent groups that reject democracy, promote a conscious ideology of supremacy, and support policies that would negate basic human rights for members of a scapegoated group. The terms extreme right and racist right are often used interchangeably, although for some groups on the extreme right gender is also a major focus, and racism exists in various forms and degrees in all sectors. Extreme-right ideologies of overt white supremacy and anti-Semitism envision a United States based on unconstitutional forms of discrimination. Extreme-right groups are implicitly insurgent because they "reject the existing political system, and pluralist institutions generally, in favor of some form of authoritarianism."[14] In contrast, dissident-right groups still hope for the reform of the existing system, even when their reforms are drastic and the dissidents are skeptical that their goals will be reached. The term "hate group" describes an organization in any sector that overtly and aggressively demonizes or dehumanizes members of a scapegoated target group in a systematic way.[15] The term "extremist" is of dubious value and not used in

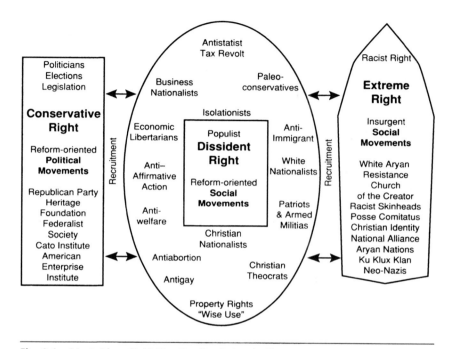

Politicians
Elections
Legislation

**Conservative
Right**

Reform-oriented
**Political
Movements**

Republican Party
Heritage
Foundation
Federalist
Society
Cato Institute
American
Enterprise
Institute

Recruitment

Antistatist
Tax Revolt

Business
Nationalists

Paleo-
conservatives

Isolationists

Economic
Libertarians

Populist
**Dissident
Right**

Anti-
Immigrant

Anti–
Affirmative
Action

Reform-oriented
**Social
Movements**

White
Nationalists

Anti-
welfare

Christian
Nationalists

Patriots
& Armed
Militias

Antiabortion

Christian
Theocrats

Antigay

Property Rights
"Wise Use"

Recruitment

Racist Right

**Extreme
Right**

Insurgent
**Social
Movements**

White Aryan
Resistance
Church
of the Creator
Racist Skinheads
Posse Comitatus
Christian Identity
National Alliance
Aryan Nations
Ku Klux Klan
Neo-Nazis

Fig. 1.1 Adapted from *Right-Wing Populism in America* (Berlet and Lyons, 2000)

this chapter. As Jerome Himmelstein argues, "At best this characterization tells us nothing substantive about the people it labels; at worst it paints a false picture."[16]

When analyzing a movement or group, we must ask a whole series of questions: What are the main public issues and what are the subtexts? What is overt and what is covert? What is intentional and what is unintended? What is conscious and what is unconscious? What are the degrees of prejudice and what are the degrees of discrimination? How different are the ideologies and actions from those of "mainstream" society? This last question is especially important when looking at historic movements because, while it is fair to judge these earlier movements by today's standards, it also is necessary to locate the group in its historic context.

Commonalities

(One reason that differences and boundaries within the hard right are often overlooked is that hard-right groups not only can share the same targets for scapegoating but also can use common styles, frames, and narratives) In addition, since the late 1970s, mobilization by the hard right in the United

States has been assisted by a widespread heteropatriarchal identity crisis. Before I argue the differences, I need to examine the commonalities.

Common Styles and Frames

Particular styles of expressing ideology are used in creating collective-action frames used by movements to mobilize support.[17] Styles used frequently by U.S. right-wing movements include the following.

Dualism

Dualism is a form of binary thinking that divides the world into good versus evil, with no middle ground tolerated. There is no acknowledgment of complexity, nuance, or ambiguity in debates, and hostility is expressed toward those who suggest coexistence, toleration, pragmatism, compromise, or mediation. Dualism generates three related processes: demonization, scapegoating, and conspiracism.[18] Demonizing or scapegoating a subordinated "Other" is one way to defend white and male privilege.[19]

An Apocalyptic Style

The word "apocalypse" refers to an approaching confrontation, cataclysmic event, or transformation that marks the end of an epoch. A handful of people have been given a warning so they can make appropriate preparations. Apocalyptic (and millennialist or millenarian) social movements often combine demonization, scapegoating, and conspiracism with a sense that time is running out, so quick action is needed.[20]

Conspiracism

Robert Goldberg traces the concept of conspiracy thinking back to the "Latin word *conspirare*—to breathe together," which implies a dramatic scenario.[21] Conspiracism is a particular narrative form of scapegoating that frames demonized enemies as part of a vast insidious plot against the common good, while it valorizes the scapegoater as a hero for sounding the alarm.[22] Apocalyptic conspiracism across the hard right is a masculinist narrative that engenders confrontation. Damian Thompson argues that the conspiracy theories that Richard Hofstadter described as the "paranoid style" in right-wing movements are really derived from apocalyptic beliefs.[23] According to Mark Fenster, conspiracy theories are a misdirected attempt to figure out how power is exercised in a society.[24] Exposing alleged conspiracies of elites is one way to gain status in certain sectors of the hard right. There are real conspiracies whereby groups of people secretly organize to enforce or challenge the status quo, but in the long run, these conspiracies do not control the broad sweep of history.[25] Governments can engage in conspiracism as well, which often leads to political repression by state agencies.[26]

Populist Antielite Rhetoric

Populism is a rhetorical style that seeks to mobilize "the people" as a social or political force. Populism appears in both left-wing and right-wing movements. It can challenge or defend the status quo. It can promote or undermine democratic civil society.[27] The central motif of many historic right-wing dissident movements is a form of populist antielitism that portrays the current government regime as indifferent, corrupt, or traitorous.[28] These episodes of right-wing populism are often generated by economic, social, or cultural stress that assists right-wing organizers in the mass mobilization of alienated cross-class sectors of a population.[29] Populism plays different chords in each sector of the right—but the recurring melody is a particular form called producerism. Producerist narratives portray a noble middle class of hardworking producers being squeezed by a conspiracy involving secret parasitic elites above and lazy, sinful, and subversive parasites below.[30] Producerist white supremacy helped fuel the attack on newly gained black rights after the Civil War.[31] Producerist anti-Semitism was central to the success of German Nazi ideology in attracting an alienated audience for a mass base.[32] With the collapse of Communism in Europe, the hard right turned its attention to generating populist resentment over federal government policies.[33]

Authoritarian Assertion of Dominance

Assertion of dominance refers to the relative perceived need for authoritarian enforcement of hierarchical and hegemonic control. Dominance involves both power and privilege. Dominant power need not require a majority in a population, such as in white control of colonial India or South Africa. Groups that lack dominance can still see it as their ultimate goal. The justification for asserting dominance is frequently based on the self-perceived supremacy of the group making the assertion. This supremacy can be articulated in biological or cultural terms.

These four styles often appear like a nested set of Russian dolls. Dualistic demonization, scapegoating, and conspiracism are regular components of the apocalyptic style. Apocalyptic dualism is a common component of populist antielitism. And antielite conspiracism, apocalyptic dualism, and populist rhetoric are often found in the most extreme-right insurgent groups in which dominance is asserted in an authoritarian manner. According to Lee Quinby, among some hard-right groups "the reassertion of masculinist hierarchy is being cast in terms of apocalyptic avowals of (heterosexist) family values and the New World Order."[34] Linda Kintz notes that this "linkage between God, the Constitution, and masculinity provides a powerful foundation of emotion."[35]

Common Sparks: Alienation and Identity Crisis

The dissident right and extreme right were able to exploit the same historic economic, cultural, and political opportunities in the 1980s and 1990s. A significant factor in shaping these movements was alienation generated by a gender- and race-driven identity crisis.[36] Women certainly can play significant roles in hard-right movements.[37] Yet, when placed in a larger context of economic, social, cultural, and political grievances, it is angry, straight, white, Christian men who seem to comprise a large pool of potential recruits for right-wing movements.[38]

Social movements are built around some claim or grievance.[39] The various segments and groups of the hard right in the United States embrace a core narrative that argues that straight white Christian men have been "dispossessed" from their proper place in the nation.[40] Several questions immediately arise: Who are the agents of dispossession? From whom is America to be taken back? To whom is it to be restored? We can easily round up the usual suspects: blacks, Jews, immigrants, liberals, welfare mothers, secular humanists, corrupt politicians, government bureaucrats, feminists, gays and lesbians, and so on. These suspects populate a producerist frame that paints a picture of betrayal and subversion of the "American Dream" by parasites above and below.[41] Some mainstream politicians have been eager to exploit these scapegoats to attract votes.

People from all walks of life seem to be active in hard-right movements, but most of the participants seem to be in the middle class or working class. Of course, that is also a picture of the general population in the United States. There are far more people angry with big government, bloated corporate leaders, and blustering politicians than participants in the hard right.[42] In fact, much of the middle class has been primed to be what Barbara Ehrenreich has called a "bludgeon for the right."[43] More research in the area of demographics is needed.

Differences

Despite the many commonalities among the branches of the hard right, we cannot lose sight of the significant differences. When any social movement is observed closely, there is usually some central villain that emerges or at least some hierarchy to the alleged villainy. This is certainly true when studying the hard right.[44] Figure 1.2 examines the extreme right, patriot movement, and Christian right, and lists their primary targets, secondary targets, major methodologies, and major styles ranked by hypothetical relative importance.

Both the patriot movement and the Christian right are sectors of the dissident right, yet they have differences between them; and they both

Movement Sector	Primary Target	Secondary Targets	Methodologies	Major Styles Listed by Hypothetical Rank
Extreme Right	Race	Government, Gender	Insurgency: Exclusion, Violence	Domination Conspiracism Apocalypticism Populist Antielitism
Dissident Right Patriot Movement & Armed Militias	Government	Gender, Race	Reform: Defensive Vigilantism	Populist Antielitism Conspiracism Apocalypticism Domination
Dissident Right Christian Right	Gender	Government, Race	Reform: Electoral, Regulatory	Apocalypticism Conspiracism Domination Populist Antielitism

Fig. 1.2 Examining Different Sectors of the U.S. Political Right

have differences from the extreme right. All three sectors cobble together their ideologies, styles, and frames from the same basic materials but using slightly different priorities. While there are subtle forms of Eurocentric white supremacy in the Christian right, for example, its major form of supremacy is founded upon heteropatriarchal hegemony. In the extreme right, populist antielitism is a merely a rhetorical style used to mask underlying elitist and authoritarian goals; for the patriot movement, however, populist antielitism is both the primary frame and a major ideological premise. Figure 1.2 is not meant to be exclusive. Each sector has many different targets, styles, and methods. In addition, each sector also produces print publications, Web sites, videos, radio programs, and other propaganda materials used in outreach projects seeking to mobilize support.

Methodologies

In establishing analytical boundaries for any set of movements it helps to separate ideology from methodology and then examine how they interact.[45] Methodologies used or promoted by social movements range from passive to active. In the civic sphere, these methodologies include electoral reform and traditional lobbying, dissident mobilization and organizing to force reform outside of elections and legislation, civil disobedience, vigilantism and violence (both aggressive and defensive), and insurgency (up to and including attempts to overthrow the government).[46] Violence can—and has—been generated from within each of the sectors listed in figure 1.2. Sometimes violence is a conscious strategy of propaganda or provocation and it can extend to the formation of underground revolutionary cells and insurgent armed struggle.[47] While many social movements are reformist rather than insurgent, violence can occur even in movements that reject it. Unintended violence sometimes happens, for example, when a small affinity group reacts to a precipitating event.[48] An unprovoked police attack is an example.

Nicholas Kittrie observes that not all participants in social movements break laws or engage in violence and that in democratic societies such distinctions are important.[49] Separating ideology from methodology has important public policy considerations, because law enforcement under the U.S. Constitution is supposed to be concerned primarily with criminal acts, not dissident beliefs. To label all militia groups as "hate groups" or to lump the entire movement together with insurgent neo-Nazi groups is not just analytical oversimplification, it implies a potential for violence that has consequences for law enforcement. This is especially true in post-9/11 reality, in which Attorney General John Ashcroft and the Justice Department have pursued policies that make little or no distinction among nonviolent civil disobedience, vandalism, terrorism, and armed revolution. Scholars need to be aware that the government frequently justifies surveillance and infiltration of dissident groups and detention of dissidents by blurring the lines between ideology and methodology.[50]

Figure 1.2 makes a set of claims about the priorities and practices of the extreme right, patriot movement, and Christian right. Let us examine each sector in detail to see what evidence exists to support this view.

The Extreme Right

The extreme right in the United States is comprised primarily of groups overtly promoting white supremacy, anti-Semitism, and heteropatriarchy. Even within the extreme right there is some differentiation.[51] Indeed, even among scholars and antiracist activists there is differentiation involving analytical models.[52] There is little disagreement, however, about the basic supremacist themes of most groups on the extreme right. Nonetheless, a brief overview is needed to set a baseline to compare with the other sectors in the hard right.

The white supremacy in the extreme right is rooted in pseudoscientific theories of the biological superiority of a (socially constructed) White "race."[53] Key seminal texts include Arthur de Gobineau's 1853-to-1855 *The Inequality of Human Races,* Francis Galton's 1870 *Hereditary Genius: An Inquiry into Its Laws and Consequences,* and Madison Grant's 1916 *The Passing of the Great Race.* Core ideas include the essentialist claim that heredity, not environment, "is the controlling factor in human development"; that dysgenic "primitive elements" in a society have always slowly "reasserted their physical type and have gradually bred out their conquerors"; and that "the more primitive strata of the population always contain physical traits derived from still more ancient predecessors."[54]

[White-supremacist ideology continues to develop rhetorical frames that facilitate aggression, violence, and murder.]In the late 1990s there were several horrific acts of violence. The Oklahoma City bombing, the dragging murder of James Byrd, Jr., and a shooting spree in Illinois and Indiana by Church of the Creator devotee Benjamin Nathaniel Smith provide vivid examples.[55] [The apocalyptic race war envisioned by Christian Identity theology probably helped motivate Buford O'Neal Furrow, Jr., who in 1999 wounded several people in an attack on a Jewish institution in California, then killed a Filipino-American postal worker.[56] Christian Identity accentuates "racist and anti-Semitic motifs," envisioning a "militarized apocalypse" pitting godly, white, Christian men against traitorous government officials, manipulative evil Jews, and subhuman people of color.[57]]

Richard Kelly Hoskins is a well-known white-supremacist ideologue. Hoskins' book *War Cycles, Peace Cycles* was found among Furrow's belongings.[58] In 1958, Hoskins wrote *Our Nordic Race,* in which he claimed: "The history of our [Nordic] race is an epic story which should thrill the hearts of our youth."[59] According to Hoskins: "Today the entire world is seething with unrest. The line of conflict is found wherever the protective ring of outposts of our western civilization comes in contact with the now belligerent and aggressive nations of the colored world."[60] Hoskins identifies the villains as a "group of 'agitation Jews,' in close co-operation with a group of Nordic Race Traitors, [who] are almost wholly responsible for the destructive 'one race, one creed, one color' Marxist campaign that has brought strife and disunity to our country and to the rest of Western Civilization."[61]

Hoskins also proposes some solutions, a tactical reform agenda, and a strategic plan that implies a more aggressive methodology. Hoskins calls for passing more "laws prohibiting racial interbreeding" to keep from being "destroyed by Marxist mongrelism from within."[62] In order to ensure "Nordic preservation," Hoskins suggests cooperation with white allies and "kinsmen" around the world to "crush beneath the heel the traitors within, and stalwartly meet the tidal wave of colored fanaticism that is rapidly approaching our shores."[63] For Hoskins, the primary focus is on white supremacy, but a secondary focus for him is on the issues of race traitors, Marxists, and "agitation Jews." He also is critical of the role of government in aiding "mongrelism from within." [Since contemporary white supremacy is based on pseudoscientific racialism, Jews are considered to be part of the Semitic race, even though not all Jews are Semitic, and many people who consider themselves Semites are Arab, and some are Muslim.]

The 1980s and 1990s saw innovation in the extreme right. Some leaders sought a new sanitized image.[64] Some groups spun off underground cells, while others acted as "Lone Wolves," as suggested by Klan leader Louis Beam in a 1983 essay titled "Leaderless Resistance."[65] At the same time, some Ku Klux Klan (KKK) groups shifted their focus to new immigrants.[66] Other white supremacists began to promote the idea of racial separatism.[67] The Internet opened up new vistas for publicizing extreme-right texts.[68] Within the ideological insurgency of the extreme right, actual activities range from meek to murderous, and proposed acts include discrimination, separation, exclusion, intimidation, violence, expulsion, and genocide.[69] The demographics of the extreme right remain difficult to ascertain for a variety of reasons. James Aho found that in Idaho, members of the extreme right seemed to reflect the demographics of the communities in which they were operating.[70] Kathleen Blee found diversity in her interview subjects, including persons who were college-educated or came from financially secure backgrounds.[71]

Looking for Sex under the Sheets

While the main focus in the extreme right is on race, the idea of proper breeding to preserve the genetic heritage of the "White race" obviously involves gender roles and reproduction. The twin threads of miscegenation and emasculation weave strands of gender into masculinist white-supremacist discourse. Abby Ferber and Michael Kimmel have convincingly explored this idea in several studies,[72] as do other chapters in this volume.

One significant difference in the ways racism, anti-Semitism, heterosexism, and sexism operate, however, can be seen in the "final solutions" of the most extreme supremacist groups. While many groups in the extreme right have no qualms about calling for the extermination of Jews, blacks and other people of color, or gay men and lesbians, there is no visible extreme-right group (or any hard-right group) that calls for the extermination of *all* women.[73] Indeed, white women are seen as essential to the propagation of the white race.

Gender issues in the extreme right revolve around control over reproduction. The extreme-right group White Aryan Resistance (WAR) supports abortion for women of color but opposes it for white women because it is seen as a form of race suicide. In the view of WAR, black women are lazy parasitic sluts, while white women are energetic warrior goddesses. The exception would be white women who are "race traitors," who then drop perilously down below black women in WAR's implicit rating system.[74] In a disturbing way, this buttresses the arguments of Ferber and Kimmel that the racism of the extreme right is tied to the gendered issue of white men needing to control and conserve "their" white women.

The Patriot Movement and the Armed Militias

The citizen's militias emerged as an armed wing of the patriot movement in the mid-1990s. Composed of independent units, the militias developed into an autonomous movement combining the conspiracist suspicion of big government typical of the patriot movement with a form of defensive vigilantism. The central narrative of the militia movement was that the U.S. government had been hijacked by a vast secret conspiracy of globalist evil elites plotting to construct a tyrannical New World Order run by the United Nations as a police state and using foreign troops transported by black helicopters. They feared an impending wave of government repression, starting with a roundup of weapons and culminating in totalitarian tyranny on behalf of a one-world government.[75]

Rural areas suffered greatly in the 1980s and 1990s. Farm and ranch economies essentially collapsed, with transnational agribusiness swooping in to buy out thousands of family-owned operations. Suicide rates in the farm belt rose, along with reports of abuse and mental illness. Hard-right groups spread conspiracy theories in this region, while corporate media and policy-makers for the most part ignored the plight of the residents who saw their way of life devastated.[76] As one song sung to raise funds for Farm Aid put it, these families were being "weeded out."[77] Extreme-right groups such as the Posse Comitatus laid part of the groundwork for the militias during this period.[78]

Patriot social movements in the mid-1990s involved as many as five million Americans who believed that the government was manipulated by subversive secret elites and was planning to use law enforcement or military force to repress political rights. Durham observes that "the movement is divided in strategy and exhibits both authoritarian and libertarian impulses" and that "aspects of each have the potential to bring its adherents into conflict, sometimes bloodily, with a federal government that they see as a threat to their rights and a servant of their enemies."[79] Government analytical errors and abuses of power during just such confrontations resulted in needless deaths at the Weaver family cabin in Ruby Ridge, Idaho, and the Branch Davidian compound in Waco, Texas. Spurred by anger over these events, the patriot movement spun off the militia movement as an armed wing.[80] Armed citizens' militias quickly emerged in all fifty states, and according to a tally kept by the Southern Poverty Law Center (SPLC), there were 224 militia units in 1995.[81] At its peak during this period there were between 20,000 and 60,000 active participants.

The main factors behind the growth spurt of the militias were government missteps during the Weaver and Waco confrontations and fears generated by proposed federal gun-control legislation.[82] The government is central to these factors. Sarah Mahan, who conducted a content analysis of four

Militia of Montana videotapes, found that the central narrative was to use insinuation and intimation in an "attempt to 'prove' the presence of a grand conspiracy to which the viewers, as American citizens, must be alerted." The videos cited "instances of injustice" to "weave a web of suggestive rhetoric designed to make the viewers afraid of their own government."[83] The antigovernment ideology of the militias is part of a long history of similar right-wing movements in the United States.[84]

John Akins likened militia conspiracy theory to an ideological octopus: "In this analogy, the body of the octopus represents the New World Order theory; each tentacle represents a specific concern, such as firearm ownership, abortion, or prayer in schools. Each tentacle of this ideological octopus reaches into a pre-existing social movement, yet each connects with the others at the body, the New World Order."[85] The armed citizens' militias drew recruits with these and other concerns from a broad range of preexisting movements and networks throughout the dissident right and extreme right.[86] Recent social-movement theory argues that it is face-to-face recruitment through preexisting relationships—family, friends, and coworkers—that draws people into an activist group. People join groups because they have some grievance or fear, but they are seldom attracted by the specific ideology of the group they join and in fact tend to learn and adopt the ideology only after joining the group. This is true with the hard right.[87]

Early studies of some patriot movement participants, such as members of the John Birch Society, show a similar demographic to that of the Christian right.[88] There is, however, research suggesting that the patriot movement in the United States may involve two demographic groups. While Birchers are more upscale, many participants in the citizens' militias (the armed wing of the patriot movement) seem to have a shaky socioeconomic status, have been downsized, or are experiencing an economic reversal.[89] Joshua Freilich, on the other hand, found that gender-driven cultural factors were more important than economic factors in predicting the number of militia units in a state. He found militias most active in states where female empowerment was low and masculinist paramilitary culture was widespread.[90] Carolyn Gallaher argues that the patriot movement is predominantly white working-class men facing a loss of both racial dominance and economic security.[91] Hans-Georg Betz found that right-wing populist parties in Europe drew from two distinct sectors. People in the working class focused on resentment of immigrants, while more upwardly mobile entrepreneurial libertarians focused on resentment of government bureaucrats. Betz also found that these European right-wing populists attracted a disproportionate number of men, persons employed in the private sector, and younger voters.[92] It is likely that gender, race, and class all play some role in mobilizing right-wing populist groups in complicated ways that have not as yet been fully explored.

Masculinism and Militias

Kimmel and Ferber argue persuasively that right-wing militias are seeking "Restoration of Rural American Masculinity."[93] This is true even for suburban and urban participants in the militia movement, since one aspect of their identity is bound up in longing for the romanticized terrain of rural Frontier America. According to Kimmel and Ferber, militias are:

> both fiercely patriotic and simultaneously anticapitalist and antidemocratic government or, more accurately, anticorporate capitalist and antifederal government. To negotiate that apparent contradiction, the militias, like other groups, employ a gendered discourse about masculinity, to both explain the baffling set of structural forces arrayed against them and to provide a set of "others" against which a unifying ideology can be projected.[94]

Alienation among men is especially obvious in the patriot movement and its armed wing, the citizens' militias. Daniel Junas, in one of the earliest published reports on the movement, observed that the:

> predominantly white, male, and middle- and working-class sector has been buffeted by global economic restructuring, with its attendant job losses, declining real wages and social dislocations. While under economic stress, this sector has also seen its traditional privileges and status challenged by 1960s-style social movements, such as feminism, minority rights, and environmentalism. Someone must be to blame.[95]

Arrington studied patriot groups in North Carolina and concluded that the patriot movement "is made up mainly of alienated white men who yearn for their lost dominance." According to Arrington, "The working guy hasn't seen his lot improved in a long time. He feels betrayed. The American Dream doesn't include him. It's a myth so far as he is concerned. Something's gone wrong."[96]

Ehrenreich argues that warrior culture originally developed from the need to defend the tribe from external threats. Now, at a time when some men feel unable to fulfill what they see as traditional roles as provider and defender, a reversion to aggressive paramilitary behavior is not surprising.[97] James Gibson writes about a broader paramilitary culture that emerged in the early and mid-1970s.[98] In a later article Gibson points out that the militias grew "at the same time that a series of social changes involving race and gender shook the foundations of male dominated American society."[99] Part of this narrative of alienation was a story of betrayal by government leaders of the foot soldiers in Vietnam (and later, working stiffs back home).[100] This in part accounts for the fixation of many veterans on locating soldiers missing in action and still supposedly being held captive in Vietnam.[101] This suspicion of elite manipulation and betrayal fueled the popularity of the *Rambo* genre of films, in which callous government elites use soldiers as pawns, and the antihero has to fight both internal and external enemies.[102] So while issues of race and gender prompted the backlash, an additional target was a conspiracist caricature of the government that acts as a distorted class/less analysis.

The priapic masculinist rhetoric in the following statement from the Militia of Montana is typical:

> ONE BULLET AT A TIME
> THAT'S HOW YOU'LL GET OUR GUNS
> You Treasonous Bastards that ask for our vote, swore an oath, took our money, then do a job "on us" instead of "for us." BACK OFF NOW before you cause a revolution. We at M.O.M. are not alone. People within your own ranks are on our (America's) side. We are everywhere. YOU leaders of each and every branch of this federal government are guilty of TREASON. If you have the audacity to even ask why, read on.[103]

As a masculinist movement, the militias can certainly be said to privilege certain traditional male gender roles, despite the participation of women in the militias. There does not seem to be persuasive evidence, however, that in other ways the militia movement is any more sexist or patriarchal than large sectors of "mainstream" U.S. society. One should ask: Masculinist compared to what? Cynthia Enloe asks several questions that help apply a feminist approach to the analysis of what constitutes a masculinist model:

> Are any of the key actors motivated in part by a desire to appear "manly" in the eyes of their own principle allies or adversaries? What are the consequences? Does the alleged reasonableness of any . . . policy choice rest on the unexamined assumption that women's issues . . . can be addressed "later," that it is men's anxieties that must be dealt with immediately?[104]

Clearly the militia movement would be a masculinist movement using these criteria. But here is the catch. Enloe is writing an article on "Masculinity as Foreign Policy Issue." She argues that American culture ("assigns high value to masculinized toughness" and that the "conventional notion of manliness" is a "major factor shaping U.S. foreign policy choices." She refers to "America's conventional, masculinized political culture" and points out that many negative consequences of widespread macho politics appear throughout U.S. society.[105]

So the masculinist nature of the militia movement is a hyperbolic version of preexisting masculinist norms in "mainstream" society. At the same time, the masculinist attributes of the militias are different from those of the Christian right or the extreme right. While the militia movement uses a masculinist methodology and gendered discourse, its *primary* ideological target is not gender. Establishing the undeniable hyperbolic masculinist narrative in the militia movement does not *automatically* prove the presence of specific forms of sexism, antifeminism, patriarchy, misogyny, or heterosex-ism that are different from mainstream societal norms. These claims need to be documented and placed in perspective.[106]

Militias and the Extreme Right

Some scholars identify the militias as having similarities to "other far-right hate groups."[107] Kimmel and Ferber argue that "far-right groups are in-tricately interconnected, and share a basic antigovernment, anti-Semitic, racist and sexist/patriarchal ideology."[108] Many antiracist activists portray the militia movement as largely indistinguishable from the extreme right.[109]

Just how much of the militia movement is dominated by the extreme right? Is militia movement racial prejudice identical to that found in neo-Nazi groups in the extreme right? Are the militias a hate group? Do most militia members "hate" blacks, Jews, and the government equally? Do they actually "hate" women? It might help to flip the political chart around and look at the political left. Would it be useful for a sociologist to argue that progressive, socialist, communist, and Stalinist groups of the "far left" are "intricately interconnected" and "share a basic anti-government" extremist outlook?

How can we explain the genesis of this disagreement? After the Oklahoma City bombing in 1995, some analysts who studied the U.S. political right pointed at the militia movement as the source of the attack.[110] Many also argued that the militia movement was essentially a front for extreme-right groups.[111] In retrospect, neither assertion stands up to close scrutiny. Mark Pitcavage notes that: "People who were monitoring hate groups were among the first analysts to have discovered the militias."[112] So it was predictable that some watchdog groups would see the militias merely as extensions of existing hate groups in the United States.

Pitcavage argues that from the very beginning there was a lack of appreci-ation that "the militia movement was a different movement from the white supremacist movement." There was a tendency to "claim that the conspiracy theories in the militia movement were just a ruse" for recruitment by the extreme right and that "eventually people in the militia movement would be introduced to intolerance," especially through anti-Semitic conspiracism.[113] In some cases this is just what happened, but it was not a universally suc-cessful endeavor.

The Southern Poverty Law Center (SPLC), the Anti-Defamation League (ADL), and Political Research Associates (PRA) currently describe the patriot movement and militias in terms different from those they use to describe extreme-right groups such as the KKK and neo-Nazis. All three watchdog groups note that the extreme right played a role in the spread of the militias. The SPLC, for example, agues that while only some in the militia movement "were explicitly racist many of the key militants and ideologues of the movement had long histories of involvement in white supremacist groups."[114]

How close are militias to the white supremacy of the extreme right? Pitcavage points out that a key early leader in the militia movement, Linda Thompson, "had no apparent racist motivations. Thompson was part of the patriot movement, and introduced the idea of the militias" to a wide audience in the summer of 1993 over shortwave radio and her computer bulletin board system (BBS).[115] Kenneth Stern notes that Thompson identified herself as a libertarian and social-justice activist.[116] She and her husband repeatedly sought to distance themselves from racism and anti-Semitism.[117] The Thompsons and many other militia and patriot movement leaders openly fought against recruitment efforts by the extreme right. A series of debates and splits demonstrated that there was a struggle within the militia movement between those comfortable with overt racism and anti-Semitism and those who opposed those tendencies.[118] There were even some in the patriot movement who opposed Christian patriot theories about sovereign citizenship based on claims that white men had "natural" citizenship rights that were allegedly superior to the citizenship guaranteed to blacks under amendments to the Constitution.[119]

Durham agrees that the militia movement should not be defined primarily by anti-Semitism or white supremacy. He argues that "Patriot conspiracy theory is [not] always undisguised or even disguised anti-Semitism."[120] This is a crucial point that is easily misunderstood. There *are* elements of white supremacy and anti-Semitism in the patriot movement but not in the same form or force as in the extreme right and in some cases barely distinct from prejudice found in sectors of "mainstream" society. As John Green explains: "A lot of negative ideas are picked up from the common experience, and sometimes people pick them up without knowing their pedigree."[121]

Some analysts trace the birth of the militia movement to a 1992 Estes Park, Colorado, meeting of antigovernment activists. Stern argues that while the meeting was significant, it "may be an overstatement to say that this Colorado gathering was the birthplace of the American militia movement."[122] The Estes Park meeting:

> may have laid some of the groundwork for the militias' formation, not only in suggesting structure, but also in solidifying connections between longtime white supremacists and Identity followers, on the one hand, and others such as Larry Pratt of Gun Owners of America. Yet its importance should not be overrated. Meetings happen every day. In order to have an impact they must plug into a social fabric that is ready to receive the meeting's message.[123]

The "1992 meeting at Estes Park was not the birth of the Militia movement," asserts Pitcavage even more firmly. "What Larry Pratt was talking about was militias in the sense of the Guatemalan death squads, not in the ideological sense of the militia as a movement" as it materialized in the United States. And "none of the major early militia leaders appear to have had strong ties to white supremacist groups or the Estes Park meeting."[124] One attendee, however, was John Trochman, who had espoused the white-supremacist and anti-Semitic theology of Christian Identity. Trochman founded the influential Militia of Montana.[125]

Pitcavage does see Christian Identity as playing an important role for some key militia leaders such as Trochman in which it serves as "a medium that allows for bridging anti-government viewpoints with intolerance."[126] Pitcavage, however, argues that while Trochman is personally involved with Christian Identity, as a militia movement leader, Trochman "does not actively promote it [and] it is the government that is his primary focus. With Pete Peters it is the reverse. Intolerance is his main focus, and he promotes that, along with anti-government ideas," which are his secondary focus.[127] Pitcavage says that for the average member of the patriot movement, "the basic problem is with the legitimacy of the system—in part or in whole. They are anti-government, and this then manifests itself as tax protest, sovereign citizenship, and the militia."[128]

Kimmel and Ferber have analyzed both extreme-right race hate groups and the militia movement. They write that while "the militias may be less overtly racist and anti-Semitic than some other groups of white supremacists . . . many researchers have documented the extensive links between" militias and "other fringe groups on the far right."[129] Kimmel and Ferber begin and end their paper on the militias with a quote and a cartoon from the neo-Nazi group White Aryan Resistance (WAR).[130] Throughout their paper, they attempt to demonstrate attributes of the militia movement by citing material from extreme-right neo-Nazis. This skates close to guilt by association, and sometimes falls through the ice. Yet their analysis would be entirely appropriate if aimed solely at extreme-right groups or if they more carefully discussed the differences between the extreme-right neo-Nazis and the dissident-right militias while demonstrating that both these sectors of the hard right have elements of male supremacy, white supremacy, and anti-Semitism.

Are Militias Really Hate Groups?

Rebecca Katz and Joey Bailey have developed an analytical framework to study the militias that postulated two kinds of militia groups: those based primarily on constitutionalist legal arguments and those influenced primarily by prejudice and supremacy. While their study is actually very useful and informative, I find problematic the decision of the authors to use the umbrella term "militia hate group." According to the authors, they developed the "definition of a militia hate group" in part by borrowing from "the 1990 law identifying hate crimes as 'crimes that manifest evidence of prejudice based on certain group characteristics.'" They then offer the definition:

> A militia hate group is: A group manifesting evidence of prejudice based on certain group characteristics; it focuses on the individual need for weapons ownership; professes suspiciousness regarding the government without specific deeds in mind; calls for more loyalty to the organization of the militia than to the nation itself; and holds the first ten amendments and the history of the development of the Constitution as more important than the rest of the Constitution or the Supreme Court's interpretations of the Constitution.[131]

For the most part, this list of characteristics provides an accurate picture of what constitutes an armed citizens militia. But how did the term "militia hate group" get concocted? First, the authors take a nonscholarly definition from criminal law that defines a hate crime as a crime based on prejudice. Even if we accept that a crime based on prejudice equals a hate crime (and I do), prejudice alone is not hate. The authors assert that the militia movement is a hate group without following the formula of the criminal definition they cite. The statute says a hate crime mixes crime with prejudice. The authors offer no evidence that a majority of militia members, even in the more overtly prejudiced units, routinely commit crimes based on prejudice. They have simply redefined prejudice (absent evidence of discriminatory acts or crimes) as hate.

Furthermore, if a hate group were defined as a "group manifesting evidence of prejudice based on certain group characteristics," then the Republican Party would qualify as a hate group, especially since the adoption of the "Southern Strategy." According to Dan Carter, the Southern Strategy of the Republicans was based on research conducted by political analyst Kevin Phillips, who "bluntly recognized the critical role fear in general, and white fear of blacks in particular, would play in guaranteeing the emerging Republican majority."[132] Racist and anti-Semitic views are repugnant—even when unintentional or unconscious—but they are frequently not criminal and are protected by the First Amendment. Jeffrey Kaplan has warned of the tendency to lump right-wing organizations together, especially by watchdog groups monitoring the right.[133] He argues that "the right wing talks a better revolution than it is prepared to fight."[134]

At the same time, there *is* overlap between the patriot movement (and the militias) and the extreme right. Mary Rupert's description of the patriot movement as "A Seedbed for Fascism" is especially useful.[135] In *Right-Wing Populism in America* Matthew Lyons and I describe the militia movement as a right-wing populist movement "with important fascistic tendencies.... Like the America First movement of the early 1940s, the Patriot Movement and the militias represented a large-scale convergence of committed fascists with nonfascist activists."¹³⁶

(The patriot movement, like other populist movements on the dissident right, is in a constant state of tension—being pulled toward reform by the conservative right and toward insurgency by the extreme right. The extreme right uses populist and producerist rhetoric to attract recruits from dissident-right populist movements)(see figure 1.1). In the 1980s, sectors of the patriot movement were much closer to the extreme right. Examples would be groups such as the Christian Patriots Defense League and the Posse Comitatus, with leaders such as James Wickstrom, William Potter Gale, and Gordon Kahl.¹³⁷ According to Pitcavage, "the philosophy of the 1980s patriot movement was closer to half-and-half antigovernment and intolerance." In the 1990s, however, "the patriot movement was much closer to libertarianism, and the major leaders mostly were not overtly racists" but were more concerned with the government imposing a New World Order.¹³⁸ Barbara Perry observes that the militias have changed over time and have shifted toward the extreme right: "Given the broader appeal, audience, and membership of the militia movement, it is alarming that hate activists are beginning to infiltrate these organizations, where they can add their racial and sexist animosities to the militia's distrust of the state."¹³⁹ As the movement dwindled, overt and covert racists and anti-Semites achieved dominance in an increasing number of militia units.

The Christian Right

Unlike the militias, most sectors in the contemporary Christian right have resisted the overtures of their most insurgent compatriots and moved instead toward the conservative right and participation in the electoral system. While they often complain about the government and political system, the primary focus of the Christian right is gender. Christian political activism reaches back to the early settlers and has always had a profound effect on the U.S. political scene.¹⁴⁰ Christian political and social movements have oscillated between progressive and reactionary poles. The mobilization of Christian activists during the civil rights movement of the 1960s echoed the progressive reform aspects of abolitionism, the Social Gospel movement, and the Temperance movement.¹⁴¹ Right-wing Christian activism is no less creative and adaptive than that of its progressive siblings.

The Christian right is a series of groups that compose both a social movement and a political movement. It has components that stretch from the conservative right to the hard right. Here we concentrate on that sector of the Christian right that is part of the dissident right. A number of studies have found that increasingly, people with above-average income, education, and social status populate the organizations of the Christian right in the United States.[142] Many are managers and small business owners.[143] When studying the contemporary Christian right, it is easy to find evidence of apocalypticism, conspiracism, and populist antielitism.[144] Much of the populist rhetoric reflects alienation caused by the shifting sands of gender, sexual identities, and class positions.[145] "The rise of the Christian right, with its emphasis on 'family values,' gender roles, and a muted, cultural form of Eurocentric racism, was one of the most significant features of politics in the 1980s and 1990s."[146] Nonetheless, the Christian right should not be lumped together with the militias or the extreme right.[147]

Starting in the early 1900s, the major scapegoat for the Christian right was godless communism.[148] After the collapse of European communism, around 1990, a new scapegoat was found.[149] The new mobilizing focus for the Christian right was an umbrella concept called the Culture War, launched against the scapegoat of secular humanism.[150] For the Christian right, the apocalyptic demon of secular humanism had three heads: liberal moral relativism; the feminist movement and its demands for reproductive rights; and the gay and lesbian rights movements. As a result of this analysis, the Christian right launched campaigns aimed at policing "traditional" gender roles.[151] According to Clarkson, abortion and homosexuality are together a "permanent, defining issue for the movement."[152] In part as a payback for Christian right voter turnout and in part due to ideological and theological agreement, George W. Bush has embraced several items from the Christian right agenda on gender. Wendy Kaminer warns that the "current regime envisions an ideal world in which heterosexual couples can't divorce and gay couples can't marry, women cannot get an abortion, and even contraception is scarce, especially for teens."[153]

Gender is not the only issue for the Christian right but it is often the prism through which other issues are surveyed. Linda Kintz develops the idea of "structures of resonance" that span different sectors of the Christian right, link it to free-market capitalism, but ultimately embed it in the idea of "natural" roles for women and men.[154] This essentialist determinism of gender roles is a central feature of the rhetoric of the Promise Keepers movement.

The Promise Keepers (PK) is an evangelical Christian men's movement that in 1995 hosted thirteen major events drawing over 725,000 men; within a year, the group's annual budget was $115 million, with a staff of over 400.[155] Despite periodic serious organizational and financial setbacks, the group continues to hold meetings nationwide. Early appraisals of the movement by progressive analysts were dire.[156] Many of the leaders of the PK were tied to overtly politicized Christian right parachurch ministries and conservative legislative and electoral campaigns. Critics pointed out that James Dobson's Focus on the Family—a major Christian-right institution—published much of the PK's literature, including various key books.[157] In 1994, one leader of the PK, Rev. James Ryle, warned: "America is in the midst of a cultural revolution, which has poised our nation precariously on the brink of moral chaos, which is caused by what I am referring to as the crisis of homosexuality."[158] Other PK leaders spoke of men taking back control of their families.[159] One report called PK "The Third Wave of the Religious Right."[160]

In an article on white men and the feminist movement, Newton criticized what she called "sinister conspiracy" predictions of where the PK was heading.[161] Although I was one of those who had jumped on the early bandwagon spreading dire warnings, in retrospect I now see that Newton's criticism is accurate. The PK did not march men into the reactionary wing of the Republican Party; and if that was the intent of some leaders, it failed. Some of our early analysis of the PK was overly simplistic. It emphasized worst-outcome scenarios based on two false assumptions: that followers in a movement always adopt the full range of ideological and methodological demands of the leaders; and that leaders in one movement automatically impose on that movement all the ideological and methodological demands of the other movement in which they are active.[162]

Newton, however, went further, noting that:

> It is interesting how eager some progressive men have been to dismiss any liberatory potential in organizations like the Promise Keepers, which in fact make sustained efforts to retrain men in their relationships with women, children, and other men and in directions which feminists might approve. I often like to imagine a football stadium full of progressive, white, heterosexually identified men repeating one of the Promise Keepers' ritual mantras: "I was wrong. I am sorry. Can you forgive me?"[163]

Newton also suggested that Colburn and Rogers might be right when they wrote: "we need a progressive version of the Christian Coalition."[164] Newton is correct that progressives could learn from the PK's strong organizational skills as well as their skillful framing of messages. However, Newton conflates the aggressive electoral partisanship of the Christian Coalition—primarily a political movement—with the millennialist and revivalist PK—primarily a social movement. One does not see groups of weeping, hugging men at Christian Coalition meetings.[165] On the other hand, as part of routine religious practice, many evangelical men regularly hug each other during church services as part of "sharing the peace," and they are generally encouraged to ask publicly for forgiveness for their sins and transgressions, making those aspects of the PK unremarkable in the evangelical world.

Here we see also overt methodology masking underlying ideology. Men who learn to get in touch with their own feelings can still oppress women, especially when they are being taught to reclaim dominion over their wives and children. Newton is not alone in this type of analysis. When journalist

Donna Minkowitz discovered to her surprise that conservative Christian men attending huge rallies could be likeable (and, like her, be passionate about their concerns), she checked her usually perceptive progressive political critique at the ticket counter.[166] PK men certainly are open in their emotion, but as Schindler points out, the emotion-filled "religious ecstasy" in PK events is used to "assert and to sanctify the primacy of Christian men in the matrix of class, race and gender."[167]

Both Newton and Minkowitz are correct, however, in pointing out that there is something different going on inside PK from old-fashioned women-bashing. PK men *are* being asked to modify their behavior somewhat. Connie Anderson found that men in PK are trying to construct a form of "involved fatherhood" that is dramatically different from what they experienced with their own fathers.[168] This awareness of traditional sexism is a conscious aspect of PK. The cover story of the November/December 1997 issue of the group's magazine *New Man* was "Sexism: What Are the Feminists Trying to Tell Us?"

Some have complained that the critics of PK often fail to understand how the evangelical concept of "submission" is negotiated within families.[169] This is tricky terrain. PK president Randy Phillips talked about the need to "listen [to] and honor and respect our wives."[170] Yet when confronted on a TV interview program by a Unitarian-Universalist religious leader, Rev. Meg Riley (representing the activist group Equal Partners in Faith), Phillips was forced to admit that "we talk about ultimately the decision lying with a man."[171] Women in evangelical subcultures, however, are not docile and helpless and they frequently find ways to exercise power.[172] Christian Smith has studied the notion of male leadership and submission in the Christian evangelical subculture and has found a diversity of interpretations that often undercut the overt patriarchal statements by leaders.[173] Here is evidence of a division between leaders' ideals and followers' actual practice.

Both Diamond and Kimmel call the PK ideology a "kinder, gentler" form of sexism and patriarchy.[174] This is a useful concept, because there do seem to be some concessions being made by men to accommodate the demands of contemporary women evangelicals, but they are made to retain a diminished yet still dominant role for men.[175] And they are concessions—as in revocable grants. Some aspects of the early criticisms of the PK were correct—the ideology of the group does have a political component.[176] Brickner points out that the PK honestly does not see itself as political, but it is apolitical only if one uses the narrowest definition of what constitutes politics.[177] Schindler concludes: "the discourse of masculinity found within conservative religious movements, such as the Promise Keepers and the Victorian era movement 'muscular Christianity,' is inherently political. Any masculinity project aimed at restoring or reclaiming a 'traditional' male role for privileged white heterosexual males has a political impact within the tapestry of class, race, and gender power."[178]

The PK's stance on homosexuality reflects the trend in the Christian right to refrain from nasty demonization and return to the common evangelical stance of hating the sin but loving the sinner. This is a shift from hate to prejudice but is a far cry from embracing equality.[179] Lee Quinby criticized the PK vision of "apocalyptic masculinity," which, she argued, rejected gender equality and scapegoated homosexuals and feminists "as a threat to the pure community."[180]

The Subtext of Race

Many authors have pointed out that the mobilization of the Christian right as a component of the New Right in the late 1980s was built on a preexisting Christian right countermovement opposing "the Equal Rights Amendment (ERA), legally sanctioned abortion, and gay rights initiatives."[181] Yet while the central focus of the PK and the Christian right is on gender and sexuality, there has long been a subtext of race. There was also a preexisting Christian right countermovement opposing federal attempts to remove tax-exempt status from historically segregated white Christian private schools.[182] Mild white-supremacist themes in the form of white, Eurocentric cultural standards were common fare in Christian-right groups in the 1960s and 1970s.[183] Bivouacked just behind the front lines in the Culture War, with its assumptions about a natural hierarchical gender order, are troops defending white, middle-class, "family" values, which are seen as under attack.[184] The PK movement is one in which gender appears to trump race. White men seem to drop the color line and ask black men to help them erect a gendered Maginot Line against sharing power equally with women. But scratch the surface, and mild elements of white-supremacist privilege appear.

According to Heath, collective identity is constructed in the PK movement in a way that rearranges the boundaries of hegemonic forms of normative white masculinity. It does this in a contradictory way. The group allows men to interact in a more open and emotionally demonstrative way and raises awareness of racism and sexism, yet it does not address (and may reinforce) the structural and institutional systems of oppression that underpin race and gender privilege available to white men.[185] With the PK, just as in the broader Christian right, the main goal is reinforcing heteropatriarchal gender norms, but reinforcement of racialized white middle-class norms is a secondary target. This white Eurocentrism is mild in comparison to the overtly supremacist white racial ideologies of the extreme right, and the implicit Christian nationalist anti-Semitism in the Christian right is very different from the overt genocidalist anti-Semitism in the extreme right.[186]

A racial reconciliation movement within the Christian right gained strength in the mid- to late 1990s.[187] As part of this process, Eurocentric white supremacy in the PK does not appear to be either conscious or intentional, and expressions of racist prejudice are sincerely discouraged. Issues of the PK's *New Man* magazine regularly feature covers with black men portrayed as leaders and role models.[188] A number of progressive critics, however, have pointed out the difference between racial reconciliation (seeking healing of wounds and changes in individuals) and racial justice (seeking equality and changes in social systems).[189] Andrea Smith, for example, criticizes how racial reconciliation fails to inspect or challenge systems and institutions of racial oppression that generate dominant power and privilege for white people.[190] Narratives in PK literature and speeches by its leaders promote a mild white-supremacist discourse that is evidenced through hegemonic white middle-class cultural assumptions of what constitutes "proper" ideas and behavior. This is typical of the rhetoric of many black conservatives.[191] The conundrum of claiming that black leaders in PK can promote mild white supremacy is explained by their use of deterministic *cultural* forms of racism rather than essentialist *biological* forms of racism. This shift from biological to cultural is part of a trend within white supremacy.[192]

Theologically the PK represents a type of Calvinist, white, middle-class, evangelical Protestantism that views the Apocalypse as God's battle against the evil agents of the Antichrist.[193] This implicitly pressures black participants to abandon the traditions of African-American evangelical Protestantism, with its view of Apocalypse as part of a prophetic struggle of egalitarianism against the evil of oppression. Mild white supremacy in the PK intersects with both race and class politics. The apocalyptic vision of the PK facilitates attempts to shift traditionally Democratic-voting black evangelicals to support Republicans who claim to be battling the same forces of evil identified by the PK: abortion, feminism, and homosexuality. Kintz describes how this politicization has been formalized within the PK.[194]

Clearly, observers of the Christian right have substantial disagreements. Gardiner has suggested that caution is required when analyzing the Christian right. National organizations often do not act like local groups; rhetoric and publicity claims often outdistance fact; schisms and transformation sometimes cause collapse, but sometimes new formations and new energy; it is hard to predict which groups will rise, and if they do, how far.[195] Rhys Williams addressed the contentious and contending views of the PK by explaining that:

> the disparity of perspectives on PK reflects, in large part accurately, the wide diversity of PK as a social phenomenon. It really is all of the things that various observers have attributed to it. It is a disparate movement, made up of many

men and with a vast array of motives, ideologies, and outcomes. In that way, PK reflects the reality, maintained by a growing number of scholars in the sociology of social movements, that social movements and collective action are disparate phenomena.[196]

In 1999, an edited collection by Claussen raised the standard for discussing the PK. Both supporters and critics contributed articles with complex and nuanced analyses. In one chapter, Newton offers a sophisticated evaluation of complexities in the PK, including evidence that: "The shift within PK discourse toward a more structural reading of racism owes much to the fact that men of color in the PK leadership have agendas of their own just as PK's effort to make antiracism a central feature of godly masculinity owes much to the way progressive men of color have traditionally defined what it means to be 'a man.'"[197] She notes that: "Despite PK's generally conservative politics, its definition of masculinity represents a considerable intervention into far Right and conservative understandings of masculinity in the past."[198] Andrea Smith urges activists to take notice of the openings that the racial reconciliation movement provides for discussion.[199] This highlights the potential that progressive critics could open a dialogue with some sectors of the Christian right such as the PK in a way that would, if nothing else, promote the values of civil society.[200]

Conclusions

Joe Feagin points out that it does not matter if racism is conscious or unconscious, verbal or violent: "oppression is not less serious because it is more subtle."[201] This holds true for sexism, heterosexism, anti-Semitism, and all forms of oppression. Even if an organized hate group is small in number, or an act of ethnoviolence is carried out by a handful of unaffiliated vandals, the direct victims feel the same pain, and the whole community in which the attack took place suffers. The negative outcome of a public act or utterance that spreads prejudiced or hateful ideas is the same, no matter what the motivation or intent. This is why there is a need for visible and forceful public displays of disapproval and attempts at healing by leaders in political, religious, ethnic, business, and labor sectors.

Scholars, activists, and government officials, however, need to maintain their own perspectives, even if at times it is appropriate to work in concert. A high level of analytical nuance may not seem necessary to many activists and policy-makers constructing a public frame. Sometimes activists or government officials make political decisions about language and categorization that may not be appropriate for use by scholars. Oversimplification might help create catchy poster slogans, but it encourages faulty scholarship. Furthermore, in the long run, activists can use complex analytical research to develop more effective strategies to challenge oppression as it appears in a variety of forms.

In *Racism, Sexism, Power and Ideology*, Colette Guillaumin argues that the great irony of the rise of modern egalitarianism and democracy was the ascendance of the idea that "human groups were no longer formed by divine decree or royal pleasure, but an irreversible diktat of nature." This "served to justify the system of oppression which was being built at the same time. By proposing a scheme of immanent physical causality (by race, colour, sex, nature), that system provides an irrefutable justification for the crushing of resourceless classes and peoples, and the legitimacy of the elite."[202]

In analyzing the oppression of women, she calls for consideration of the material fact of the power relation between men and women, as well as the ideological effect of the idea that nature "is supposed to account for what women are supposed to be."[203] It is in the teasing apart of the ideological and material practice that Guillaumin finds the most revealing critique of the essentialist naturalism that is the bulwark of many oppressive ideologies:

> [I]t is very necessary to do this, for naturalism is the only mode of thought that allows the binding together in an intangible way of characteristics which if analysed—that is, forcefully dissociated—would as a matter of fact cause *their relationship* to become obvious. In other words, the fact would become obvious that they have a history, that they are born of specific relationships, of the links which exist between mental activities and material activities; between slavery (a material practice) and skin colour (a mental practice), between domestic exploitation (a material practice) and sex (a mental practice). From the moment that the mechanisms which *create* the one (mental practices) *from* the other are made visible, these revealed links make obvious the syncretism which merges the relationships into the deeds and shatters the affirmation that the deed and the discourse on it are one and the same thing.[204]

According to Guillaumin, "introducing the wedge of doubt into this tight block of 'law immemorial' is no small matter." She says we must "shatter the notion of instinct" that creates the syncretism of "body/slave/property" named "black" and the syncretism of "body/domestic work/property" named "women."[205] When we look at the densely interwoven forms of oppression, subordination, and exploitation in the United States, our task is to explore the links between the ideological and the material practice, not merely as an intellectual exercise that increases the subtlety of our analysis but as a way to rip away the curtain to reveal the unfair power and privilege hiding backstage.

When analyzing the political right, we must move to a more detailed and sophisticated level of work where the establishment of boundaries, categories, and terminology that map differences of degree allows us to increase the nuance in our analysis. Blee makes a similar argument about studying the racist movement: "We need to go further, to lay aside untested assumptions" about beliefs and attitudes of activists and ideologies of groups "and begin to systematically catalog the ideological frictions" so that "we can discern—and exploit—its weaknesses."[206] This challenge awaits us whether we are studying the race hate groups of the extreme right, the antielite, antigovernment conspiracism of the patriot movement, or the gender-driven campaigns of the Christian right.

In doing so, we must always recognize that theories, acts, and systems of oppression based on gender, race, sexuality, class, ethnicity (and much more) exist throughout our society, not just in dissident or insurgent movements of the political right.

2
Women and Organized Racism

KATHLEEN M. BLEE

Women hold a perplexing role in modern organized racism. Historically, racist groups in the United States, with only sporadic exceptions, have been the province of white men. This is not surprising, given the deep misogyny and exultation of white-male privilege that underlies much racist rhetoric. Yet in recent years, organized racist groups in the United States have increasingly recruited white Aryan women as members. It is difficult to ascertain the exact membership of the racist movement, but it is likely that women are between 25 and 50 percent of the new recruits in a number of prominent racist groups. Women are sought as members to bolster the size of floundering racist groups. A number of male racist leaders also regard women as safer recruits than men, less likely to commit nonracist crimes or to have past criminal records that would draw them and the group to the attention of the police.

In this chapter, I discuss the role of women in contemporary racist groups and the new tensions that the inclusion of women has produced within the racist movement. I draw on my observation of racist group events, analysis of documents published and/or distributed by racist groups, interviews with male racist leaders and in-depth, unstructured life-history interviews with thirty-four women who were active members of a racist group in the United States during the mid-1990s. These women were selected from a variety of racist groups, including Ku Klux Klan, neo-Nazi, Christian Identity, white-power, skinhead, and other white-supremacist groups. They lived in every region of the country, with nine from the South, ten from the West Coast, eight from the Midwest, and three from the East Coast and in fifteen

49

different states, with the greatest concentrations in Georgia (4), Oklahoma (3), Oregon (4), and Florida (4).

To explore whether women at different levels of racist group hierarchies vary in their racist identification or commitment, I searched for women in various positions in their groups. I selected four who were leaders known both in the movement and outside, ten who were leaders but who were not known publicly, and twenty who were rank-and-file members of racist groups. I also sought women of disparate ages in an effort to assess whether the appeal of racist groups might be understood differently by very young women and by their older counterparts or by women unencumbered by family responsibilities as compared to women with minor children.

The women in the study ranged in age from sixteen to ninety, with a median age of twenty-four. Characteristic of the racist movement as a whole, the majority (20 interviewees) were in their twenties. In general, members of the Ku Klux Klan groups were older and skinheads younger, but one adherent to racist skinhead politics was in her eighties, and several Klan women were in their early twenties. Most had a boyfriend or husband, although several were divorced or never-married and claimed not to be interested in a long-term relationship with a man. Despite the virulent homophobia of most racist groups, one woman identified as lesbian, and several others mentioned having short-term sexual relationships with women in their past. About one third were raising minor children and the vast majority of those without children anticipated having babies in the future.

Gathering accurate information about members of organized racist groups is difficult. Racist activists tend to be disingenuous, secretive, intimidating to researchers, and prone to give evasive or dishonest answers. Standard interviews are often unproductive, yielding little more than organizational slogans repeated as personal beliefs. Typical interviews also collect information in such a way that makes it impossible to disentangle cause and effect. For example, women racial activists often identify their boyfriend or husband as part of the racial movement, reinforcing the perception that women are recruited into racist groups as the girlfriends or wives of male activists. Yet it is equally plausible that some intimate relationships between women and men racist activists are formed in racist groups, that women get involved with men who share their existing ideas. Also, standard interviews also tend to assume that extremist attitudes precipitate involvement in extremist politics. However, it may be the case that the causal direction is reversed, that attitudes become more extreme by virtue of association with an extremist group.

To overcome the limitations of standard interviews, I use a life-history approach, eliciting from each woman an unstructured account of her life story rather than asking questions about beliefs or commitments. Each life-history interview followed a similar format. The woman was asked to tell the story of her life, how she came to be where and who she is today. In order to observe how each woman would compose her own life story— how she would select and causally connect the events that she regarded as most significant—I did not intervene to suggest particular directions in the narrative but only to encourage a full exposition of her life.

At the conclusion of the life narratives, I asked each woman a series of open-ended but structured questions to collect comparable background data on individuals and their groups. These questions asked about support networks, organizational policies and activities, personal racial practices and contacts, recruitment and entry into racist politics, her role in the racist movement and in her group, education, work history, family background, religion, husbands, and intimate partners. Below, I examine the role of women in contemporary racist groups and the effects that the inclusion of a significant number of women has had on organized racism in the United States.

Women in Racist Groups

Women's activities in organized racism differ considerably across groups. In general, Christian Identity and Klan groups tend to emphasize women's familial and social roles, while women in some white-power skinhead and other neo-Nazi groups are involved in more direct action, playing what I term "operative" roles. But these distinctions are often blurred. Groups overlap in their memberships, and women move between groups. Even groups that share a similar racist philosophy vary in their treatment of women members, reflecting their different histories, their leaders' ideas, and their balance of male and female members. In general, the roles of racist women fall into three categories: familiar, social, and operative.

Familial Roles

The most common activities for women in organized racism are racial elaborations of the domestic roles to which women are traditionally assigned.[1] Racist activist women are expected to assume tasks associated with creating and nurturing a racist family. Because some segments of organized racism, especially Ku Klux Klan groups, emphasize that organized racism is "like a family," the scope of those tasks is not clear. Sometimes the racist family is invoked to refer to women's responsibilities to their husbands and children. At other times, it denotes women's obligation to sustain a collective "family" of organized racists. Many racist leaders try to create a familial atmosphere by stitching together political and recreational activities that promote loyalty and commitment from their followers. As Robert Miles of Aryan Nations told one reporter: "No one who joins these circles is ever without family. Each of us is the father and the mother, the brother and the sister of every white child who's within our ranks."[2]

Nearly every Klanswoman I interviewed framed her discussion of organized racism partly in terms of family, claiming that organized racism promoted "family-like" qualities of caring and mutual responsibility among its members. Although, as I show later, many Klanswomen have specific criticisms of their groups, on an abstract level they insist that the Klan's ideal follows a family model. "Everyone's real supportive and, naturally you're going to have your little arguments here and there, but ... basically, they're all real supportive, just like a big family," concluded a Klanswoman. An Aryan supremacist claimed that her racist colleagues were "part of my life, like family." A Nazi said that the thing she liked best in the group was "the camaraderie and the sense we get of having an extended family. The kinship we feel is probably the most important thing to all involved." Another claimed that "the unity between people who live so far apart is amazing. It is its own family." A Southern woman made a Klan rally sound like a family reunion: "We'd all be together. The guys would play football. And it was like a big family, togetherness. It was the perfect utopia." Just as threats and conspiracies are understood by racist women largely in terms of their impact on immediate family and on daily life, so too the "virtue" of being in a racist group is often expressed in terms of its impact on self and family. A member of a violent Aryan group summarized how she felt about the group by saying: "It's given me more purpose and commitment in my life and I think it's helped me get closer to ... my family, my friends. It's strengthened bonds of commitment."

The family sought by the racist community is more than just a metaphor. European fascism was built on existing cultural practices and norms, including those that governed family life.[3] Similarly, modern organized racism is based in part on familial expectations and ideologies, however distorted.[4] This invocation of family life also enables those within the racist movement to draw on codes of behavior and understandings by which personal relationships are fashioned and judged. As they learn to understand organized racism in terms of familial qualities, recruits to racist groups apply their expectations of familial relationships to those within racist groups. For some members, this analogy is positive, bolstering their commitment to organized racism. But for others, including many women, the equation of family life and racist group life exposes painful conflicts. Women whose experience in racist groups does not measure up to idealized portraits of family life— those who find racist groups oppressively male-dominated or male leaders patronizing or dismissive of women—feel cheated and resentful. Others find that the emphasis on family life contradicts the demand that they sever relationships with family members outside the racist movement.

Families are expected to serve as platforms for racist recruitment efforts. Modern neo-Nazi and some Klan groups enlist women and adolescent girls, hoping to absorb entire families. In a Nazi publication a reporter described a rally to which "many brought their families. Loving fathers and mothers watched their children play all across the compound with the pure Aryan children from other families. I saw with my own eyes what we all are working so hard to achieve in microcosm. A pure White nation made up of happy, successful White families working and playing together under the protection of the Swastika."[5] A Klan leader commented that "you couldn't join the Klan unless your whole family came in at the same time. It was truly a family of families."[6]

In most racist groups, women are expected to mother their immediate families as well as the larger racist "family." Except in a few racist skinhead and neo-Nazi groups, women racists are told to fulfill their obligations to male intimates and to the racist movement by bearing Aryan babies. Cautioning racist men that "selecting a proper mate is the only way to give us the possibility in life to improve the heritary [sic] makeup of the coming generation," racist groups make it clear that racial obligation includes racial procreation. Such pronouncements are particularly frequent in Christian Identity and neo-Nazi groups that emphasize long-term planning for a racist future. This maternal responsibility is made explicit in the recruiting efforts of some groups that seek to win the "birth-rate war" by enlisting race-conscious white Aryan women who will give birth to a large number of children.[7]

In reality, the childbearing patterns and expectations of racist activist women are more mixed than the glorification of fertility in racist propaganda might suggest. On the one hand, several women I interviewed spoke with enthusiasm about their potential or actual contributions to increasing the white population, including one neo-Nazi who described being in a racist recruitment video "pregnant and strolling down the street with my baby and [being] so proud." Similarly, a skingirl interviewed by sociologist Mark Hamm commented that "what people don't know is that the [skinhead group] are strong into family values and strong anti-drug. There are eleven women in our group and eight are pregnant. This is the most important way we can carry on with the white power tradition."[8] An eighteen-year-old woman interviewed by a reporter at an Aryan Fest prided herself on supporting the white movement even before she had her own babies by contributing toward movement drives for "cribs, baby clothes, [and] diapers" for "white families starting out."[9]

On the other hand, many women in my study who were childless at the time of their interview expressed a desire to have no more than three or four children. Although a few predicted vaguely that they would have "a big white family" or that they wanted "as many [children] as possible," most were like a neo-Nazi who alluded to pressure in the movement to have many babies, commenting that she would have "of course more than the typical one or two that the women of today want" but insisting that she was "not really aiming for ten either." A skinhead said that she supported the idea of having a lot of children—"at least four"—but that she was not willing to begin having babies until she and her boyfriend were financially and geographically stable and "prepared to raise her children in a decent environment." Another, an aspiring racist, told a reporter that the emphasis on babies—the insistence of male skinhead leaders that "the purpose of intercourse is to have as many white Christian babies as possible"—made her and her girlfriends reluctant to pursue their involvement in the racist movement.[10]

Women with children and those older than thirty tended to be the most conservative in their childbearing goals. Most claimed that they did not want any additional children beyond the one or two they already had. One Klanswoman lowered her voice as she confided: "My husband wanted seven kids. I had two. I don't want any more." A skinhead, pregnant with her first child, concluded that she would have "only as many [children] as we can afford. I wouldn't want to deprive children of what they need just to have more." Some women even elaborated medical steps they had taken to ensure that they would not again become pregnant.

Racist women are also held responsible for socializing their children into racial and religious bigotry. They often provide verbal instruction in the norms of racist living, such as direct admonitions "to stay away from nigger children." Sometimes their cautions are more indirect. For example, a skinhead mother recounted a conversation she had had with her elementary-school-aged daughter, a story oddly preceded by the mother's assurance that "I don't push her to believe any beliefs." "My daughter understands," the mother insisted. "She knows she's a special person. . . . It's the little things, [like] when she didn't know what a black kid was, I explained that she's different because of color, to let her know that she shouldn't be involved with nonwhite."

The children are ushered into a world of racial and religious hatred at a very early age. Homes are strewn with drawings, photos, flyers, videos, and pamphlets filled with vicious lies and threats against racial and religious enemies. In one house, a child's high chair featured a hand-scrawled swastika on the back. In another, children's crayons lay on flyers denouncing Jews as inhuman. Still others displayed pictures of lynchings on living-room walls or newspaper clippings about the bombing of the Oklahoma City federal building on refrigerator doors. Male leaders of racist groups, too, are involved in efforts to socialize youths as racist activists. A particularly pernicious means of targeting the very young is the racist comic book, such as the *New World Order Comix* published by the National Alliance and distributed by skinhead groups.

Children have easy entry into the spectacle of organized racism. Toddlers learn that Jews are the offspring of Satan. Their older siblings learn to call nonwhites "mud people" as readily as other children learn the names of video games. From birth, some Klan children are installed in a "Klan Kid Korp," preparing them for a life of racist activism.[11] Garbed in miniature Klan robes and flaunting imitation torches and guns, they are introduced to racist activism as fun and frolic. One woman told me: "At night, the lighting of the crosses, that is a big to-do. The men, of course, were in the front lines, the women were there, and there were lots of children, too, lots of children running around and they were just so happy." Racist women extend this socializing further, creating networks of like-minded families in which their children can find assurance that their views are correct, even typical. Some children of racist families attend Aryan-only schools, where they can find white supremacist friends. Others are home schooled, a method that almost all racist groups promote if not require to prevent children from becoming "double-minded" as they learn different racial values at home and in school (even in Christian schools).[12]

Some children are assigned minor tasks in racist groups; hence in one Klan chapter, "the kids fold the pamphlets and put them in plastic bags and then take them at night and throw them onto lawns." They also are prompted to secure children in other white-supremacist groups as pen pals, an effort intended to deepen their racist identity and create a network of future activists. One such letter, credited to "Jessica," aged six and in the first grade, starts out with the neutral statement that she likes "to skate and play with my best friend," but it ends with a message that seems to have been fed to her by an adult: "I love the white race and I want to keep my race alive." Similarly, "Kimberly," a thirteen-year-old, describes her "red hair" and her interests in "TV, roller blades, talking on the phone," and then adds, "I am proud to be white." Writings purportedly by racial-activist children, though perhaps actually penned by adults, are found both in newsletters aimed at the young (e.g., *Little Aryan Warriors*) and in propaganda issued from adult women's racist groups. An eight-year-old girl asks other children: "Are you tired of... sitting on your butt, watching the Cosby Show? Letting other kids make fun of you? Then do something about it NOW!"[13] A twelve-year-old girl is presented as the author of a poem titled "Being White Is Not a Crime," which reads in part:

> White and proud
> That's what I am
> Storming the streets
> Getting rid of the trash.
> What's wrong with knowing your race is strong?[14]

The extent to which parents succeed in transmitting racial hatred and racial activism across generations is unclear.[15] Some women—especially women who grew up in Christian Identity (CI) households, married CI men, and are home-schooling their children in CI philosophies—claimed that they learned racism in their families. A female founder of a skinhead gang credited her Klan mother for her political "consciousness." Another woman recalled that her father had warned he would kill her himself if she was ever involved with an African-American boy. Another woman said that her schoolteacher mother "raised us to be aware that even though all people are in fact people, there are differences between the races." A CI adherent said that she suspects that during her childhood her uncle was a member of the Klan:

> I remember going to a situation that they call a rally. Now I know what it is. When I was little, going to where I remember all these men talking and I remember my dad saying, "Be well behaved" and so forth. And I remember other kids. I got to play with other kids. It took many years before I realized that my uncle took me to a Ku Klux Klan meeting. I didn't even know what it was. It was a giant picnic, is what I thought. But when the men talked, I remember that you had to be hush-hush and you can go out and play with the other kids but don't disturb the meeting.

But socialization from adult relatives is not the only or even the most likely route into adult racist activism. More than half of the women I interviewed had no immediate or extended family members who were racist activists or held strongly racist views. Some women insisted, in the words of one, that their parents "secretly agreed" with their racist views or might be "closet racists," but many admitted that their parents' racial views were much opposed to their own; their mothers, fathers, or both "believed that everyone's equal" and had even played some small part in civil rights or other progressive movements. One said her father was victimized by the Klan when he was sexually involved with a nonwhite woman, another that "my parents would have a massive stroke if they found out that I was a racist." Only logical contortions enabled one skinhead to reconcile her views with her upbringing:

> The whole time I was young I was taught that racism was awful, that you just weren't racist, you just didn't judge someone on the basis of skin color. And I still believe that way. . . . I don't care about skin color. It's just that I don't agree with multiculturalism and I know that race-mixing hurts society.

Moreover, the claims of those women who told me that they came from a family of racists need to be treated skeptically. Some seemed to identify a continuous strain of racism in their families only in retrospect, after they themselves had become racist activists. Women would present themselves in their life stories as descended from a proud line of white racist warriors, but when I asked for more details, they could not name any specific racist forebear. One white supremacist did admit, with chagrin, that both her parents were racially tolerant; still, she insisted, "I haven't met any of them, but somewhere down the line in my family there are some grand dragons or grand wizards [of the Klan] or something." Similarly, other women mentioned cousins, uncles, or distant relatives who were reputed to be in racist groups.[16]

A less obvious but also important role played by women racists within the family pertains to their control of family consumption. Just as some progressive movements have struggled to politicize consumers' choices, so too racist groups try to channel the money they spend into sympathetic hands.[17] Some urge their members to boycott products certified as kosher.[18] Several women I interviewed claimed to avoid these foods, though most could not identify the symbols that marked rabbinical endorsement (a recent inventory of such symbols posted on a white-supremacist women's group's Web page may increase their awareness). Other groups encourage the bartering or trading of goods and services among racist activists and support vendors who sell racial paraphernalia.

At least a few women use their positions in racist groups or those of their husbands to benefit from racist purchasing. Some try to support themselves through their racist activities. A widow of a prominent racist activist sells "Aryan crafts"; Aryans, her advertisements claim, should buy from her rather than purchasing goods from major corporations ("who knows where the money is spent!") or frequenting "the mud [i.e., minority] infested, Jewish inspired shopping malls."[19] Another woman runs an enterprise called "Cathie's Celtic Corner," and yet another hawks racist gear in ads in racist magazines.[20] One woman sells "hand crafted N.S. [National Socialism] banners" along with Viking statues, etched glass, and other wares.[21]

Social Roles

Women must also act as the social facilitators of racist groups, an expectation nearly as deep-seated as that making them responsible for bearing white children and raising them as racists. The importance of this role has grown in recent years as racists have sought to increase the longevity of their groups.[22] When social ties are strengthened, members who have individual identities as racist activists come to view themselves as part of a larger social movement, developing a "collective identity" of racist activism. In describing an "incubation period during which new collective identities are formed . . . in submerged social networks out of view of the public eye," the sociologist Carol Mueller captures how social networks among its members support organized racism.[23] Social ties strongly influence people to join racist movements; in addition, as members of racist groups come to know each other in social as well as activist settings, they reinforce one another's commitment to the goals of organized racism. They create the "oppositional subculture" by which organized racism is sustained over time.[24]

Racist groups have proven remarkably successful in structuring the social lives of their adherents around movement activities. When I asked racist women how much of their socializing takes place with others in the racist movement, their estimates ranged from 50 to 100 percent, with most guessing 85 to 90 percent. As a Klanswoman told me: "Once you get into the Klan, it becomes your whole family, all your socializing, all your parties." Racist women give a variety of explanations for their predilection for spending free time among fellow racists. These include mutual protection ("a lot of people like us are afraid we will be hunted"; "we look out for one another when one is in trouble") and loyalty ("I'm totally secure in my trust in everyone in [her group]"). They also cite reinforcement of their beliefs ("I like being with people who share my beliefs"; "you do not need to defend your beliefs to anyone because they already share your views"), lack of access to other sets of friends ("when I decided I was going to be a skinhead, I lost a lot of friends, but I gained friendships I can count on"), and a perceived need for rapid and accurate sources of information ("everyone just updates on events that I should know about that are excluded from normal papers"). It is women who are responsible for making racist group life work, for creating rallies and meetings that leave people with a positive feeling. They often succeed; a skinhead remembered that her first Klan rally "was just like a big reception; it was a lot of fun." A neo-Nazi similarly recalled being surprised to find that a racist event was "kind of like a big powwow or something. There was no cross burnings or screaming."

A flyer advertising a neo-Nazi event promises a day of fellowship and racist learning, along with a social time of music and meals at a local banquet hall—meals served, of course, by "the ladies." Such gendered division of labor is common among racist groups; hence, for the social hour following a strategy meeting at the Aryan Nations' racist compound in Idaho, a sixty-year-old woman played the organ and baked cookies.[25] Although women remain in charge of providing meals for racist events in many groups, some leaders deny that such gender-specific assignments demonstrate women's marginality to racist operations. In the *Aryan Research Fellowship Newsletter*'s report on the Aryan Nations Youth Conference, a spokesman for the group claimed that women prepared meals on-site only to protect the gathered male racists, who otherwise would have had to buy meals in town (where they might fall into the hands of local police or antiracist activists).[26]

The emphasis on survivalism and self-sufficiency in the racist movement may heighten this gendered division of labor in the future.[27] One racist women's group sees its responsibility as "first aid, child safety, [and organizing an] emergency information guide, maternity clothes exchange, Aryan Alphabet Coloring book, Aryan Parents Newsletter, [racist] P.O.W. art collection and fund."[28] Christian Identity women are organized as "White Nurses," preparing to heal the broken bodies of Aryan (male) combatants in the coming race war."[29] Another group defines women's roles in the racist movement as midwifery, child care, and survival cooking.[30] Barb, an Aryan supremacist, instructs new women recruits that "woman's big responsibility is to be ready to fight to raise children (no drop-off day camps), and be ready to offer other women a shoulder to cry on. Many young women today didn't have a parent to teach them to cook from scratch (even the generation past had that problem and turned to TV dinners); or to hand sew, and now women must learn it themselves and teach their children." The wife of a prominent Aryan supremacist was described to me by one racist skinhead woman, without intended irony, as "like Donna Reed...a very nice, wonderful, matronly woman." Barb is a model racist social facilitator. Her role is doggedly maternal, coaching younger skingirls in "how to make our men happy and the importance of being good parents, and make sure we're eating nutritionally, and does anyone need vitamins?" At the racist compound where she lived, this model homemaker would "have us stay and make muffins and coffee and bring them out to our men [but] she'd go through the roof if a man stepped in our flowers' cause she had these gardens all around the place."[31]

Acting as social facilitators, women are central to efforts to create links between organized racist groups and outsiders. Indeed, women's greater participation and visibility in the racist movement are probably responsible for making it more accessible to mainstream populations. Because women seem incongruous in organized racism, they lend an air of placidity to racist gatherings and seem to lessen the threat that such groups pose. Women holding babies, schooling children, or serving chicken at buffet tables can to some degree "normalize" racial politics. A journalist recounts: "I see a Nazi sitting with a latte at an outdoor bistro table. This Nazi has no swastikas, no tattoos, no combat fatigues. Instead, she has a chic red bob, blue tinted sunglasses and a small son. If I hadn't seen her heil the Nazis at noon, I would only see a pretty mother in her early 20s enjoying the late evening sun."[32]

Racist women acknowledge their role in this effort, noting that their involvement helps racist groups convey a sense of the ordinariness of racist activism; in the words of one woman, they "portray a positive image [of] honor and integrity."[33] After several members of his group appeared on a TV talk show, one male racist leader commented: "the women did quite well, dressing modestly, using proper makeup and proper arguments. The men should have stayed at home."[34]

Racist women also take more deliberate steps to gain entree into mainstream populations, seeking connections with sympathetic outsiders and attempting to recruit new members into the movement; they act as the racist equivalents of what, in her study of the African-American civil rights movement, Belinda Robnett calls "bridge leaders."[35] A Nazi group declares its members "advocates [of] a community form of activism" and urges them to get out and meet people, so that they might show by example "the society that we would like to see." In so doing, "we will do much to break the image that the Zionist controlled news media portrays about white nationalists." Among the varieties of community involvement suggested are "running for public office, engaging in business, and generally acting as responsible citizens, all while being openly known as National Socialists."[36]

Many neo-Nazi and Klan groups practice some form of community "outreach." One woman described the work of women in her group on behalf of animal protection, which they support as an affirmation of "mother nature" against the masculine "cowardly excuse for power called 'sport killing,' . . . the need in their pitiful lives to establish a sense of dominance." Some go further, claiming environmentalism and animal rights as issues for white racist activists since "it is not necessary to carry on a race if there is not a world to live in."[37] Such efforts, along with programs in self-education, first aid, and survival cooking, are described by a member as "projects that bring respect in the community so they'll listen."[38]

Racist women understand that groups of women who seem innocuous can attract people into racist politics. They are fully aware that most people enter the racist movement through personal contacts with existing members, and they work to create the opportunities that make such recruitment possible. Bible study groups bring ordinary women into contact with hard-core racists. Animal rights turn into Aryan rights. One recruit told of attending a women's meeting billed as a Christian apocalyptic "preparation for end times"; she thought that "it would be boring—but it turned out to be excellent and exciting, with all the women who participated (and most did) taking part and exchanging ideas, really great." Although she expressed disappointment that "many things listed were not covered in depth due to time running down," the list of topics shows a strategic mixture of fundamentalist Christianity, self-sufficiency, and racism, with lessons on women in Scriptures, home birthing, healing with herbs, and home schooling tucked between workshops on "how to use the system" and revelations about domestic spy satellites and secret inoculations with microscopic "transformers" meant to "track our people."[39] Perhaps the greatest threat posed by modern organized racism is seen not in the highly visible parades of middle-aged Klan members, who are inevitably far outnumbered by anti-Klan demonstrators, but in the mundane advertisements for toddler car seats and Aryan cookbooks that appear in white-power newsletters and on Aryan electronic bulletin boards.

Operative Roles

The operative roles taken by women in organized racism range from routine clerical tasks to informal (and very occasionally formal) leadership and paramilitary activities.[40] Most racist groups allow women to take part in public activities, though such participation is less common in Christian Identity and some Klan groups.

Women are found as formal leaders in only a handful of groups, but they often exercise informal leadership. Recognizing women's importance as informal leaders challenges the common assumption that all racist leaders are men.[41] That erroneous impression is created by the extreme difficulty of gathering information about the racist movement; most scholars and journalists rely on the public statements of self-appointed racist spokesmen such as David Duke. Moreover, the ostentatious organizational titles that racist men customarily bestow on each other—Grand Dragon, Imperial Wizard, Commander—misleadingly imply a hierarchical structure of authority. Though their titles suggest that they command the obedience of hundreds of followers, these men may in fact enjoy little more than token allegiance from a handful of marginally committed group members. Conversely, those who actually lead racist groups may have no titles.

If we focus on the practices of leadership rather than on self-enhancing claims or titles, the picture we see is different and more complex. "Leadership," in the sense of providing group cohesion, mediating conflict, developing political strategies, and nurturing collective identity, is often concentrated in the middle and less visible layers of racist organizations. These leaders, though not always women, are the right-wing equivalent of what the anthropologist Karen Brodkin Sacks terms "centerwomen": those who maintain and strengthen social groups.[42] Racist centerwomen command racist groups very differently from male racist leaders. Men's leadership in racist groups is typically described as manipulative, distant from followers, and simultaneously contemptuous of racist group members and dependent on their adoration and respect for self-aggrandizement.[43] In contrast, women's informal racist leadership is more elusive, indirect, and personal. It may also be more effective and more dangerous. One woman noted that the male leaders "think of me as being all for people on their side. That's how they look at it, too. 'On our side.' (Laughs) No, no complexities involved, right. They think of me as one of them, but yet not one of them. I know they have a hard time accepting me the way I am." Another distinguished herself from male leaders by noting, "I don't go for titles or offices or anything. I don't care about them." And a third downplayed her influence in the organization, saying that she was interested only in "routing the sociopaths out of the movement."

One way of exploring such differences in racist leadership style is suggested by Dick Anthony's and Thomas Robbins's distinction between "norm-rejecting" and "norm-affirming" religious groups.[44] Norm-rejecting groups, like male racist leaders, favor heroic uniqueness and individual enlightenment over conventional behavior. Norm-affirming groups, in contrast, are formed around strong beliefs and strict rules. Women racist leaders who operate in the fashion of norm-affirming groups may be able to nurture more sustained commitment to their groups, have more success in recruiting new members, and be less likely to alienate potential recruits. As one woman recounts of members of her group: "The girls look up to me. They're still going to dress their way, the way they do and I only suggest. I suggest you don't have your hair this way [she used her hand to demonstrate the very short hair of 'skinheads']. I suggest you grow your hair out. . . . If there's a little bit of hair you get along in the world much better." Another notes the problems faced by young recruits, which need to be addressed by older members such as herself: "[Her group]'s gonna have to work on these young people. And show exactly what's gonna happen, that you're all right."

Priscilla, a Klanswoman who declined to describe herself as a leader because she had no official title but who nonetheless admitted that her work was vital to her group, similarly nurtured activism. She recounted her efforts gently to persuade recruits to attend public marches, an escalation of their engagement that entails greater personal danger and risk of exposure than do private rallies or meetings. While male leaders make harsh demands, insisting that recruits risk everything for the movement, Priscilla uses a subtler and more personal appeal. "I've been on rallies. I've been on marches," she informs me. "All they have to do is send a flyer and I will have everybody show up. That makes me feel good because they respect me that much. I don't tell them, 'Hey, you have to take your last dime and spend it on gas and starve to death to get there.' . . . I'm not like that. I'd say, 'Hey, it'd be great to have you.' "

Several women, in describing recruitment efforts, make it clear that they are practicing leadership indirectly and through social ties. One tells me: "I have a way of speaking in grocery stores, department stores. I approach people out of the blue, not as a [racist group] person. But if they look at something, I make a comment and that leads into something else. 'Cause they get into a conversation with me and then I try to explain some things. I don't bring up [her group] or nothing. No, I don't do that. But I try to educate them, I try to throw out little things that might make them think." Other women dismiss their male comrades' attempts to thrust racist literature and flyers into the hands of potential recruits as 'ineffective."[45] One woman insists that her low-key approach is more productive, especially for recruiting women: "I'd say, 'Come over. We'll get together, we'll talk, we'll have some fun.' I mean, we have picnics where all the kids play together, all the women get together. We cook our meals, you know, we sit around, we talk about how the kids are progressing, what they want in their lifetime, in their lifestyle."

Women's informal leadership does not stop with recruitment. Racist women also play an important part in creating the social community of racism and in easing new recruits into that social world. A white supremacist tells of her efforts to guide young women in the practices of racist activism: "I've got girls that tell me, 'Lookit, I got a new tattoo,' and I'm, like, 'That's nothing to be proud of, that's stupid. It'll poison your blood and when the race war comes you can't give blood. . . . Don't go out and get tattoos and shave your head 'cause nobody's gonna listen to that.' To me I think they're a lot better if they get themselves an education, a steady job, a nice place to live, than think about having tattoos." Such instruction in daily life as a racial activist suggests a form of leadership quite different from that provided by the battle-worn male warrior glorified in racist literature. Women like this white supremacist mediate between the proclaimed goals of racist groups (for example, to foment a race war) and the actions that bolster such goals. When she instructs "her" girls to avoid tattoos and shaved heads and to pursue education and jobs, she is creating an organizational space in which complex personal identities can be configured as personal and collective identities of racist activism. Perhaps even more frightening, she is attempting to make possible something heretofore unknown: a long-term and intergenerational racist movement. In nudging her young charges to become more effective and dedicated racist activists, this middle-aged woman illustrates how women's practices of informal leadership can secure racist goals.

Women's operative roles in organized racism are not limited to private acts of leadership. At least some women participate fully in direct action. A Norwegian racist women's group, Valkyria, uses a paramilitary approach to organize against prostitution and pornography. Its members take part in strategy meetings with men and train with weapons.[46] Terrorist actions by women racists, though still uncommon in the United States, are on the rise.[47] Among the women I interviewed, about one third reported that they had been arrested for violent acts in connection with racist activism, usually for assault; more than three quarters claimed to have been in a physical fight with members of minority groups.[48] One woman, notorious for her public role at the helm of a major Nazi group, proudly described her physical prowess on behalf of white supremacy in a 1994 interview with *Mademoiselle*. As the "three-year reigning champion" of the hammer toss, she and her husband-to-be, the male champion, won the honor of "getting to light the ceremonial swastika"—a startling outcome for the daughter of wealthy parents who had earlier studied photography at the Art Institute in Chicago.[49]

Women's public activism can serve strategic goals for racist groups. When racists confront antiracist protestors, the participation of women can discourage retaliation. A journalist watching a Nazi "flag parade" in Idaho observed: "Three young women with babies in strollers salute the Nazis. Immediately, they are surrounded by screaming protesters. One young Nazi mother cradles a baby in one hand and uses the other to punch a young man repeatedly in the face until he is bloody. A young Nazi man who is with her stands back and lets her be the warrior. The strategy works: The man who has been beaten will not hit a woman."[50]

Women usually take operative roles that are less public. Some work to support racist prisoners. A number of racist publications carry letters purporting to be from the wives and families of men imprisoned for racist activities, decrying the conditions in which their menfolk are forced to live or lamenting their difficulties in visiting the prison. In a typical example, the wife of a man apparently imprisoned for racist terrorism writes:

> Our life changed dramatically...when my husband was arrested, stood trial, and was convicted...we were expecting the birth of our son.... After our son's birth, I relocated to where we now live, and I became a welfare recipient. What a colossal nightmare! [My husband] got moved...farther and farther away from us and deeper and deeper into the more violent penitentiaries. Our visits stopped as the costs of visiting were way out of sight.... [Then] people found out and some support began coming in. From that time on, two groups have sent regular support and best wishes, one group was you [Bounties Bestowing...Blessings Bequeathed] folks.[51]

Racist prisoner support groups maintain lists of prisoners seeking correspondents. They claim to screen them all to ensure that those on their pen-pal list are white and Christian, but they note that not all are "political" (i.e., racist activist) prisoners hoping to communicate with racist comrades; some are potential recruits. Although such groups claim to do nothing more than give a prisoner "the security that someone cared enough to assist with his/her family needs," their real purpose clearly is to distribute the racist writings of imprisoned racist leaders, to free racist prisoners, and to supply racist propaganda to prisoners. Under innocuous names such as "Bounties Bestowing...Blessings Bequeathed," they link racist activists outside and inside prison walls and may help strengthen racist networks in prisons, such as the notorious Aryan Brotherhood.[52]

Most of women's—and men's—actions in racist groups are more mundane, although not inconsequential. The women I interviewed described hours spent photocopying literature, making flyers, distributing propaganda, spraying racist graffiti on buildings and highways, writing to current and potential racist activists, promoting and managing white-power bands, stamping public-library books with racist messages and phone numbers, and tucking racist literature under windshield wipers and house welcome mats, in grocery bags, and in racks of restaurant menus. Others work the Internet, seeing it as a way for racist women of all ages and levels of experience to recruit others "without ever leaving home or taking away from their families."[53] These actions are largely ineffectual as means of recruiting new members to the racist movement, but they help spread a message of intimidation to the potential targets of racist groups.

In her study of women in the late-twentieth-century Italian underground, Luisa Passerini observes that "the discovery of a specific female identity—beyond the illusory mimicking of male models, in the organization and in the armed struggle—comes later than the fundamental decision to get involved."[54] Those in modern organized racism have no specific female identity as yet. Women's roles are in flux, neither submissive (as tradition demands of women) nor clearly activist (as racist propaganda suggests). But we should not see women in today's organized racism as simply mimicking male models. Their experiences in organized racism, no less than those of men, are highly gender-specific. Women enter racist groups because of contacts and issues that reflect their places as women in the larger society. And once inside organized racism, women find themselves pushed to follow several and sometimes conflicting paths: to shape the racial family, to bolster its social networks, and to assert themselves as leaders and activists.

Conflicts over Women's Role

The introduction of women into the racist movement has not been without controversy. Many men are hostile toward women members and unsure what role women should play in a movement that has historically characterized itself in idioms of fraternalism: as a clan, a brotherhood, a community of like-minded men.[55] Moreover, the effort to create a "racist family" has been hampered by a disinclination to interfere in the private lives of members, particularly in the power of men over their wives and children. And although a few women and groups describe themselves as "white-supremacist feminist" or insist that it is possible to combine "white power with Women power," organized racism has found it difficult to incorporate issues of women's rights.[56] As a result of these problems, many women members become dissatisfied, sometimes openly unhappy, about life in white-supremacist groups even as they continue to support racist and anti-Semitic goals.

Conflicts within Racist Groups

(In public, racist leaders often insist that women are treated as men's equals in the racist movement.)Indeed, it is increasingly common for women to be a focus of racist speeches and propaganda. One neo-Nazi group proclaims: "We believe that without our women the movement will never achieve victory. [Our group] supports the equality of the sexes. We encourage the men of all political organizations to start showing more respect for the ladies. Our women should stand and fight with us."[57] However, this verbal support for women's rights does not imply any sympathy for feminism, which most male racist leaders routinely blame for deforming Aryan women. Racist propaganda decries the feminist movement as Jewish-controlled, as a conspiracy led by such women as Gloria Steinem and Betty Friedan to alienate white Aryan women from their male counterparts, and as an assault on the masculine strength necessary for white victory.[58] One racist newsletter put it bluntly: "feminism is the means to weaken Aryan masculinity, promoted by the international Jew. . . . [T]he Jews started this emasculation with the young intending that they never become real men who, someday, could challenge their worldwide supremacy."[59]

Many racists leaders encourage their female recruits to hold good jobs. But some groups, especially those associated with Christian Identity, see the employment of women outside the home as part of a Jewish plot.(They argue that Jews use their economic dominance to force Aryan women to work, and then gain control over the Aryan children left unsupervised by at-work mothers.) For them, Aryan women who work for wages, or even those in college, are racial enemies: they further Jewish goals."[60]

Most of the women I interviewed were highly critical of the feminist movement.(They saw it as controlled by Jewish women and lesbians and as proabortion and antifamily. They characterized feminism as "disgusting" or "a bunch of ugly women trying to get the spotlight," and made such statements as "Gloria Steinem should be shot.")However, some women did not share this blanket condemnation. One dedicated Nazi credited feminism with indirectly strengthening the racist movement,("because, before women's lib came about, our movement was ten years lacking [behind]. We [women] wasn't able to do anything and now we can hold office . . . we can have authority where before we had none." Other women racist activists drew on the rhetoric of feminism to demand rights for Aryan women and to decry the misogyny of contemporary society.)When a skinhead publisher spoke of the "male-dominated society" in which she "had the [work] experience [while] the men had the power and the salaries," she echoed the frustrations of many progressive women. It is the perceived cause of the problem—in this case, Jewish control of the economy—that sharply distinguishes her racist ideas about male domination from nonracist ones.

A few male leaders even admit openly that men have found it difficult to regard women's issues as important to racist agendas. One, commenting on television coverage of gang rapes, claims to be frustrated by the cavalier response of fellow racist activists: "When I discussed this matter with several racialist friends (all male) over the next few days, I encountered a disheartening reaction. They all agreed that rape was a bad thing [but that] it was essentially a 'woman's problem' and that as such it fell outside the overall scope of racialist interests." Such attitudes, he continues, reflect a narrow view of women that could cause additional problems for the racist movement.

> Any discussion of women's rights and feminism within the Movement usually ends abortively with the unchallenged assertion that the whole topic is an artificial one concocted by Jewish communist lesbians to further divide and weaken the White race. Such an attitude is fundamentally un–National Socialist.... Too many male racialists live in a dream world of their own fantasies when it comes to women. Home is the only place they should be, it is felt, and cooking dinner and having babies are the only things that they should be doing.[61]

Another male leader, discussing the formation of a neo-Nazi women's group, traces its problems to the reluctance of racist men to accept women as their comrades:

> The biggest problem the [group] has with recruiting is the men not accepting their women as counterparts in this race struggle, therefore pushing their women into the closet when racial matters and confrontations arise [because] most men have chosen dainty little dormice as mates who will kiss their ass and give them no feedback at all ... [M]ost men in this situation are afraid that if their mate gets involved with other women, she will become even more harsh.... White racially conscious women are most beautiful when they are in battle. Any man who feels threatened by his woman if she wages a few battles of her own might as well hang it up because he is no man at all, let alone a White Warrior! Men who enslave and oppress their women are egotistical losers and "boyish" inside.

His earlier fears about women activists, he concludes, were misplaced: "I was predicting gossip and ceaseless nonsense.... It was not happening like that at all. The gossiping, glamour girls weeded themselves out ... were excommunicated and could not reap the harvest of victory and/or glory."[62]

Ku Klux Klan groups in particular, have hotly contested the place of women in the racist movement. On the one hand, some male Klan leaders have been among the most outspoken in their desire to recruit women into the racist movement. For the most part, however, those Klanswomen have been seen as a means of bringing into the movement more men—their husbands and boyfriends. This approach is the reverse of earlier efforts, whereby women were recruited through boyfriends and husbands already active in the Klan. But the underlying premise remains the same—the Klan is an organization of men) As one Klan leader told me:

> A lot of [racist] men today, and this is true . . . a lot of men are a bunch of woosies. OK, I'll put it that way. Their women, girlfriends, and wives wear the pants in the family and in the relationship now. . . . So, in order to bring in men, the men will follow the women. It's sort of a reversal. If a wife is against the husband's being involved, you can just about forget the husband's hanging around for long once the wife starts complaining about the lack of attention she's getting. . . . The other way, if the wife is into it, she'll drag the husband along. I've seen that too many times to ignore it, so we don't hold women back from promotions or climbing the ladder We can't afford to not let them have whatever positions they want to work for.

Despite his protestations that the Klan is an "equal opportunity" promoter of its female and male members, (very few women have been given positions of power in any Klan groups. In fact, the Klans may have more gender inequality within their organizations than any other groups in the racist movement, with the exception of Christian Identity sects (with which many Klan leaders are affiliated))

Klanswomen are acutely aware of gender inequities in the organization. One woman said that she was not interested in recruiting her grown daughter, because if her daughter joined the Klan, there "wouldn't be anything for her to do. She could go to a few rallies or picnics, but wouldn't be allowed to go to the real meetings. There would be basically nothing." Another made a similar point, telling me that "the Klan is male-oriented, totally sexist. The men still run it, as far as the offices go." Yet another woman, who had been in the Ku Klux Klan a little more than three years, expressed her disillusionment with the gender politics of the group, saying that "they acted as if women were equal [to men] but once you are inside the Klan, women are not equal at all."

[White-supremacist skinhead groups present more varied and more extreme gender practices.[63]) Many skin groups are intensely male-dominated and violently misogynist: skinhead boys and men refer to their female comrades as "boy toys" and feel it is their privilege to dominate and exploit their girlfriends, wives, and female comrades.[64] A Klan leader cast himself as an advocate of women's rights by pointing out to me how he differed from skinheads:

> I've noticed [the skins] have a different attitude. Their men regard the women as sort of a biking attitude, you know, they're there to serve the man and they keep 'em off the front. Sort of on a pedestal, but yet they can look down on them at the same time. . . . In fact, one woman told me that the skinheads from Pennsylvania, this is what she said, at least one group look upon women as cattle. . . . So I think it's a false sense of protecting the women. They won't have them out on the front lines. They're going to keep them behind the scenes, so they can have the refreshments ready when they get back from the demonstration.

Almost all racist skinhead propaganda projects images of extreme masculinity as central to racial activism. The pamphlet *The Code of the Skinhead,* for example, begins with a quotation from the philosopher Friedrich Nietzsche predicting that "a more manly, war-like age is coming, which will bring valor again into honor!" and movement 'zines commonly define skinheads as young men "that love to have fun, beer, and girls (not necessarily in that order)."[65] A statement titled "I Am the Wife of a Warrior" makes it clear that women belong distinctly in the background when racial warfare is being waged by skinhead men:

> My vows to my warrior-husband are as strong as fine tempered steel. . . . I am subject to long, lonely nights of worry and tears, while my warrior-husband fights our battles. I suffer his defeats, as I celebrate his victories. . . . Should he be wounded, I nurse him back to health, so that he can return to the forefront of the battle. I support my warrior-husband in all ways and through all circumstances [because] my warrior husband fights for me.[66]

Oddly, however, skinhead women are often the racist movements' most physically aggressive women, and at least some prominent skinhead women publicly confront the sexism of male skinhead culture.[67] As the message on one hate line asked: "Why do so many male skinheads and other males in the white resistance simply degrade women, get drunk, yell 'white power' and little else? Well, the answer is these are not Aryan warriors. . . . These are punks who use race as an excuse to be antisocial."[68]

Even skinhead women who are not physically combative may not conform to the image purveyed in skinhead propaganda. A twenty-two-year-old skinhead, living with and supported by her skinhead boyfriend, was nevertheless willing to challenge him when her relationships outside the skinhead world conflicted with the beliefs of her group. Her mother's sister was openly lesbian, and she commented that she "didn't really mind . . . [to me] it wasn't really a big issue, [although] to some skins it was a huge issue." Specifically, she recalled that her boyfriend was "appalled" when he found out that she had been frequenting a local gay and lesbian dance club. "I had gone in there a few times and when he found out he went nuts. But it wasn't that big of an issue at all for me. . . . Hey, to each their own. It's not something I'd be into."

Conflicts within Personal Relationships

In a treatise on recruitment, a women's neo-Nazi group argues that it is difficult to recruit women into "our movement" because of the personal behavior of male racist activists toward their female partners and wives. Warning that "the poor treatment that Whites of the opposite sexes give each other these days [and the resulting] deep emotional scars inside our kin" have political consequences, it urges movement men to recognize the political "dangers of promiscuity" and stop "discard[ing] partners like garbage."[69]

Such sentiments are not unusual among racist activist women. In his study of racist skinheads, the sociologist Mark Hamm found a good deal of conflict over issues of sexual promiscuity. For example, a Texas skinhead and high school honor student reported that "this guy [who was married] got caught sleeping with another girl [and] she got her ass kicked."[70] On national television, Moli, a self-described Nazi, boasted: "I don't have a man in my life right now because I don't want one right now. The one who I choose is going to have the same beliefs as myself or I won't want him at all. I'm very proud of myself and I'm not giving up my beliefs for no one."[71]

In an appeal that is titled "A Woman's Opinion: (Scary Thought, Guys?),", members of a neo-Nazi women's group ponder how to recruit more "solid women" (those who "think for themselves") into the racist moment. They assemble the following quiz for men:

> You are at a gig. You see a beautiful Aryan Woman. What do you do? A) Go over and talk to her and try to score before your girlfriend returns from getting you yet another beer. B) Stare and make crude comments to your buddies about how you would like to get her into bed. C) Get your girl & then go meet this other woman and her boyfriend. It is always great to meet Racial Kin—especially another Sister!

After a complaint that ironically draws on racist propaganda about Aryan women as goddesses ("We are just sick and tired of seeing our Sisters and potential sisters degraded and insulted when we know we deserve so much more since we are the ultimate symbol of love and beauty"), women are presented with the following scenario:

> You are arguing with your boyfriend because you believe that he doesn't show you the respect that you, as an Aryan Woman, deserve. He claims that he has the utmost respect & would die for any Aryan Woman yet, the night before he was with the waitress at the bar doing . . . well, you know! Does this sound familiar? I think it is time to re-evaluate your "meaningful" relationship with this so-called Man![72]

The struggle over gender roles in racist activists' personal relationships is evidenced in many women's gripes about being dominated by their male partners. They complained that male intimates wanted to control their every action, often in the name of racist solidarity:

> He didn't want me working. I wanted to work I wanted to go to school. So I took part-time classes at [the local] community college and I worked part-time. He chose my friends. Almost all my friends from high school I was not allowed to see. In fact, there are three friends that I still remain close with that he will just go bonkers if he knew.
> I remember one time [a friend] came over to the house and Jerry did not care for her, didn't want me hanging out with her. It must have been my birthday or something, that would have been the only reason why she would have

been allowed to be there. And she and Jerry got into a heated argument about something and she ended up swearing at him and telling him exactly what she thought about the whole white-power movement and this and that. And he just looked at me. And he said, 'Get her out of here.' Not in those words. And she got out of there. And I only called her from work from that point on.

In their conversion stories, the women tied their fears mostly to male members of minority groups. Some described the danger they felt from hostile men at public racist events; one recalled: "[Anti-racist activists] got a hold of me and almost killed me literally had to run my life.... All I remember is all of a sudden, whoom, all these people are running from here and there, not far from me. [I thought] 'Oh shit, they're gonna kill me if they get a hold of me.' They're yelling, 'Kill the Nazi kill the bitch.'... I was scared for my life." When pressed to describe their private lives, however, some talked about feeling threatened by their male racist comrades. Several told of being beaten by racist boyfriends or husbands. Indeed, racist women are often stereotyped as victims of domestic violence, though it is unclear whether they are more likely to suffer violence from their male intimates than are women in the general population. But the problem is serious enough that male racist leaders were forced to act publicly against one prominent leader after he was arrested for battering his girlfriend. Moreover, battered racist women have few avenues for help. As members of racist groups, they distrust and fear the police; and few believe that their networks of racist comrades are likely to prevent further occurrences or punish the perpetrators.

Almost all women racists spoke of difficulties in their personal lives caused by their activism, difficulties that are compounded by a lack of support from their male partners. Despite the racist imperative to produce many white babies, some said they had trouble juggling commitments to children and to racism. One woman noted: "I used to sit for hours and hours and fold literature. I'm into being mom now. I don't care. Let the literature pile up." A Klanswoman complained bitterly about her husband: "He's been at more rallies than I have. But you know I have to work and I can't really be there and work at the same time. And the bills have got to be paid." A male Klan leader confirmed these rigid gender expectations in his uncritical explanation of his inability to maintain a stable relationship with a woman: "Girls that will put up with this [Klan life] are hard to come by. You know, I thought I had one, this girl here I dated for about two and a half years. She was a good girl, but, you know, when she'd want to do something on the weekend, I'd say, 'Well, we got a rally.' "[73]

In recent years, the racist movement's emphasis on becoming a surrogate family for its members has further complicated women's lives. In an interview with a reporter, a twenty-two-year-old woman who wanted to be a nurse to aid white people points to the personal costs of the pressure on women to have many white babies: "Reproducing a white child is a great thing. . . . But it's the thing to do, especially with a lot of skinhead girls, to have white children when they are very young. A lot of the girls quit high school."[74] Another woman decries what she regarded as the limited scope allowed women in the Klan: "Klan men see women as breeders, and most women in the Klan feel they should produce babies for the white race."

Gender differences are seen clearly in pen-pal columns designed for Aryan singles. Hence the White Aryan Resistance offers the "Aryan Connection," a personals column for those seeking racially suitable dates and marriage partners, which encourages "sports, camping, dancing or whatever Aryans would aspire to"; and on the Internet, racist women and men can use "White Singles" to advertise for politically like-minded partners and spouses.[75] Ads from racist women request men who are stable and family-oriented; almost none refer directly to racial beliefs or practices. They seek "a hardworking skinhead who wants a family," or "a responsible, respectable, and active male," or "a serious relationship/ husband to settle down with and have a big family." These criteria are consistent with the personal dreams that racist women narrated in their life stories, which almost exclusively envisioned interpersonal harmony, a happy family life, and a stable marriage. In contrast, racist men advertise for women with explicitly political requirements, searching for a Klan "anti–women's libber" who is free of any and all nonwhite influences, or someone "who loves and fights for her racial survival."[76]

Studies of successful social and religious groups find that members often have a deep emotional attachment to, even love for, their groups.[77] Such attachments are rarely seen among women in the racist movement. One Klanswoman could recall no names of those in a group to which she had previously belonged and had described as "like family." Another said that the Klan "seemed like the perfect utopia at the time, but now looking back, I remember other things." Still others found themselves depressed at the nature of their groups, which they viewed as self-defeating and fractionalized by "squabbles about petty ideological differences." "The picture I had in my mind was a lot different than it finally turned out," commented an eighteen-year-old who had moved to Idaho to enter into a polygamous relationship with a white supremacist.[78] Indeed, it is hard not to notice the air of forced conviviality at racist gatherings; there is likeness and common purpose, but little sign of the intimacy, excitement, and spontaneity from which deeper social ties are fashioned. While its agenda of racial terrorism and vicious Aryan supremacism puts the racist movement chillingly far from the mainstream of American political life, the hollowness at its core mirrors obstacles to social connection that are widespread in modern America.

A deep sense of resignation colors many racist women's life stories, a sense of obligation rather than passion for racist activism. They talk of finding themselves in a racist movement that they support but that does not always support them, and they hesitate to involve their children, particularly their daughters, in the life of organized racism. Some women do describe feeling empowered by being a racist activist. But others paint a more negative picture. They rarely see themselves as racist heroes or warriors, talking instead of having made great sacrifices to be in a movement that has given them little in return. The image of women's activism projected in racist propaganda and in the speeches of racist leaders does not match the daily experiences of the average woman in a racist movement that remains very ambivalent about its female members.

Racist women react to this gap between their expectations and reality by tempering their involvement with racist life in various ways. Despite intense pressure, racist women resist severing connections with friends and family from the outside. Publicly they concur with racist ideas, but privately they refuse to enact those that intrude too deeply on their personal relationships. They proclaim their undying zeal for racism, but they search for boyfriends and husbands who are responsible and stable rather than politically inspiring. They work to recruit others, but their support of even the main tenets of organized racism is less than wholehearted.

The experiences of racist women in many ways resemble those of women in other social movements. In progressive groups, women often find themselves expected to perform maternal and wifely roles: they are usually responsible for nurturing a family feeling among activists, sustaining family life, socializing children, and ensuring that purchasing decisions reflect the movement's goals, and they bear the burden of creating and maintaining social ties among members. There, too, women are often found in middle-level and informal leadership positions. Racist groups are also like other groups in failing to provide their women members with a sense of satisfaction to compensate for the group's internal shortcomings. It is not difficult to find progressive women echoing the despondency expressed by racist women who think their movement will never become more accommodating to them or to other women.

But in other ways, women in racist groups are in a very different situation. Organized racism, perhaps more than any other social movement, is intensely concerned with biological reproduction. Racist groups are obsessed with ensuring the purity of racial bloodlines, determining race from racial markings, and increasing white birthrates. To racists, reproduction can never be left to chance. It is the racial destiny and obligation of Aryan women to produce large numbers of children. The centrality of biological reproduction overshadows other roles for women in racist groups and it is a particular source of discontent among women.

Moreover, unlike those in more mainstream social movements, racial activists differ greatly from the larger white society from which they seek recruits. Their commonly held ideas about race, religion, and government seem bizarre and frightening to outsiders. To recruit members, racist movements must make themselves appear more normal, less threatening. Presenting women in the movement as fulfilling traditional gender roles is key to achieving that end. When racist women take part in everyday activities such as food preparation or child care, they can seem reassuringly similar to women in the rest of society. The very ordinariness of their tasks can disguise the racist and anti-Semitic goals at which they aim. Hence racist groups favor positioning women members where they will come into contact with outsiders while engaging in the most normal-seeming and gender-traditional functions possible, even when women want—and are promised—a broader set of roles within the movement.

Finally, like other extremist and marginal groups, racist groups embrace conspiratorial ideas, which are wedded to strict internal hierarchies of authority meant to shield members from outside influences and dangers. Racist groups teach their members that they are the targets of attacks from the government and racial minorities. They teach them to depend on the group for protection. This mind-set favors tightly controlled groups with minimal input from rank-and-file members, perpetuating male leadership.

These features suggest that the road to gender inclusion in racist groups will be a rocky one. Plans to fuel a sustained revival of white supremacism in the United States by recruiting many women are not likely to be successful.[79] The number of women members may increase, but there is no certainty that women will be central figures within racist groups or even remain in them for long. A more likely outcome is that the interpersonal conflicts and political disillusionment experienced by racist women may contribute to the demise of organized racism.

3
"White Genocide": White Supremacists and the Politics of Reproduction

BARBARA PERRY

"We must ensure the existence of our people and our future for White children."

Such are the fourteen words by which many white supremacists live and act. Contained in this mantra is the central motivation of the movement: the perpetuation of a pure, all-white race, which they see as currently threatened by the politics of multiculturalism and tolerance. The contemporary hate movement, then, is grounded in a profound sense of dislocation shaped by a perceived crisis of identity spawned by the civil rights movements of the late twentieth century. As the People's Resistance Movement sees it, "political moves and social changes are now taking place which . . . are rapidly weakening our institutions and threaten to end in chaos and anarchy."[1] Jared Taylor, founder of the virulently racist *American Renaissance* magazine, is similarly explicit about the source of his hostility. Traditional arrangements in racial and gender relations, he argues:

> served the country well, so long as . . . the two traditional minorities, Blacks and Indians, did not have voices. All this changed, beginning in the 1960s. The civil rights movement gave voices to Blacks and Indians, and changes in immigration law brought a massive influx of non-whites. It was the end of a certain kind of America.[2]

The "American" is no longer (as if it ever was) an uncontested vision. Instead, the very meaning of American identity, and especially the meaning of whiteness and masculinity, have been thrown seriously into question by the politics of diversity and tolerance. Hate groups have mobilized in an effort to reassert a narrow, exclusive understanding of the national identity.

Perhaps not surprisingly, scholars have focused almost entirely on the racial agenda of the white-supremacist movement. For good reason, attention has been paid to the racist, anti-Semitic, and xenophobic leanings of the movement.[3] Only with the recent work of scholars such as Kathleen Blee, Abby Ferber, and Jesse Daniels have we begun to understand the ways in which this racialized rhetoric is inextricably bound up with particular notions of gender and sexuality. This new and exciting scholarship is drawing attention to the fact that the white-supremacist movement's racial project is simultaneously gendered. As Ferber's extensive work in this area attests, racial purity cannot be sustained without strict adherence to rigid constructions of appropriate gender and sexual behavior. All white women must fulfill their role as procreators of the race, all white men must fulfill their role as white saviors, all white people must be protected from the evils of nonwhite, non-Christian, nonheterosexual Others. For example, Ferber articulates the simultaneous construction of race and gender as follows: "Responding to what is perceived as a threat to both racial and gendered certainties, the contemporary white supremacist movement is primarily concerned with rearticulating white, male identity and privilege."[4]

The intersections of the discourses of race, gender, and sexuality are taken up in this paper, as I explore how the movement's politics of reproduction seek to ensure the perpetuation and purity of the white race. To do so, I closely examined the white-supremacist Web sites identified on the Hate Directory.[5] I paid particular attention to rhetorical constructions of race and gender that gave some indication of the sponsoring group's positions on the "rightful" relationships between men and women, and between people (especially men) of color and white people. While multiple ideological themes emerged, in this paper I am concerned with the convergence of race and gender talk in the context of abortion, miscegenation, and homosexuality.[6]

What emerges from consideration of this rhetoric is the extent to which the politics of reproduction and hence the control of women are deemed so crucial to maintaining racial purity. As I argue in the following section, what is curious about this very traditional rhetoric is the fact that it retains its centrality within the white-supremacist movement at the same time as the movement is undergoing a significant transformation toward "mainstreaming" in terms of demographics and presentation. I follow this introductory discussion with an analysis of the ways in which "discourses of difference"—as found in reflections on abortion, miscegenation, and homosexuality—reinforce white, heterosexual, male supremacy.

The More Things Change...

As I noted above, the remarkable thing about the contemporary "politics of reproduction" is that it remains true to age-old canons of the white-supremacist movement, in spite of the dramatically shifting demographics of its membership. The history of the hate movement is undoubtedly lengthy. It finds its very roots in racist and misogynistic theories, ideologies, and practices that are centuries old. However, the contemporary hate movement faces something of a dilemma. The legacy of the civil rights movement means that both the vicious rhetoric and historically effective means of responding to the threat of Otherness—lynching, genocidal practices, and legal exclusion—have less resonance today. They are as likely to be condemned as applauded. To a certain extent, this is a "kinder, gentler nation" than it was at the beginning of the twentieth century. Consider the public outcry and condemnation of the murderers of James Byrd and Matthew Shepard. The savvy, organized hate-mongers of today are not ignorant of this limitation and hence are forced to alter their tone and tactics. If they are to recruit, if they are to establish public credibility, they must distance themselves from the likes of John William King—as the Klan did when it too denounced the lynching of Byrd in Jasper, Texas. This does not mean that racist or misogynistic sentiment is no longer a part of their arsenal. Rather, it means that such narrow visions of identity are increasingly contextualized within a more contemporary, sanitized "look" and "feel," intended to render the appearance of moderation. In short, the hate movement is in the midst of a metamorphosis.

In dramatic ways, hate groups threaten to extend their impact beyond their immediate membership. Their mantra of intolerance is gaining considerable legitimacy in light of the changing messengers and media that carry their message. The uncertainty that characterizes contemporary identity politics leaves the most fearful and most alienated elements of society vulnerable to the recruitment efforts of the hate movement, which provides "easy answers" to America's woes. They share with white-supremacist organizations one of the elements McAdam insists is crucial to the development and cohesiveness of any social movement: a shared consciousness or perception of unjust conditions.[7] Dobratz and Shanks-Meile, for example, found the "white man's struggle" and "fear of falling" to be important bases for white supremacists' decisions to become part of the movement.[8] Significantly, an increasing proportion of the hate movement's membership seems to be characterized by nontraditional demographics, as more middle-income, white-collar workers become drawn to the message of salvation.[9] The hate movement represents a beacon, since:

> it is diverse in its expression, which can provide a haven for those seeking an explanation of the social conditions of white disenfranchisement along with a call to action. The "new rural ghetto" consists of formerly middle-class people who had achieved "American cultural goals" and lost it. Often forgotten, they are filled with rage as they "watch in hunger" as others eat at tables that not long ago were their own.[10]

Moreover, slight modifications in the presentation of intolerance have made the contemporary hate movement more palatable, more acceptable to a public sensitized by a generation of discourse of equality, multiculturalism, and diversity. In a word, hate is increasingly "mainstream" and hence increasingly legitimate. In part this has been accomplished by toning down the rhetoric and engaging in symbolic racism. This "new racism" couches the old hostilities in abstract, ideological terms or "code words" that appear to have rational rather than emotive connotations.

The Ku Klux Klan (KKK) has been at the forefront of the movement towards a more moderate appearance. Grand Wizard Thomas Robb, for example, asserted that Klan leaders would be "taught to avoid statements that sound hateful and turn people off."[11] He and others of like mind speak of love of the white race rather than hatred of others, of preservation of a way of life, and other such mantras. In their search for respectability, some hate groups have rejected explicitly racist terms for more "subtle" code words which act as proxies for traditional rhetoric. Primary among these is the assurance that they don't hate blacks, or Jews, or gays; rather they love their own white race. The Zionist Occupied Government (ZOG) becomes "government interference"; white Christian becomes "average citizen"; cross burnings become "illuminations"; African Americans become "welfare cheaters."

Whatever the rhetoric, the message remains the same as it has been for a century and a half: the "other" is not to be trusted; the "other" threatens the white, Christian, heterosexual hegemony. Nowhere has this "sanitization" been more evident than in the political success enjoyed by David Duke, former Louisiana KKK grand wizard. Duke's recognition that legitimacy could come only with moderation and respectability is apparent in his exhortation for Kluxers to "get out of the cow pasture and into hotel meeting rooms."[12] To further solidify his new identity, Duke publicly disavowed his Klan membership in 1980, only to reemerge as the founder of the National Association for the Advancement of White People (NAAWP). Through this "white rights" organization Duke continued to promote racial segregation. His efforts to mainstream his racist visions are apparent in his exhortations—similar to Robb's—"never [to] refer to racial superiority or inferiority; only talk about racial differences, carefully avoiding value judgements."[13]

Moreover, it is not just "angry white men" who fill the ranks of movement membership. As Blee's work makes abundantly clear, women are an increasingly integral part of many hate groups.[14] They have grown in strength both quantitatively and qualitatively: "women constitute a significant component of the membership, and a small but important part of the leadership, in today's organized racist groups."[15] Moreover, as with men, the majority of the women interviewed by Blee could be considered middle class by virtue of their own professional status as nurses or teachers, for example, or by virtue of their husbands' steady income.

The presence of women in the movement—especially professional women—seems puzzling at first glance. Given the overtly patriarchal structure and beliefs of most white-supremacist groups, one might expect relatively independent, educated women to be deterred from entry into the membership. Blee's work demonstrates how women negotiate the apparent schism between their personal self-interests and the contrary agenda of the movement. While Blee's interviews suggest most strongly that women actively seek a "fit" between themselves and movement ideologies, she also raises the possibility that "the organizing momentum of the racist movement in recent years, and its ability to attract substantial numbers of women recruits, may reflect its ability to accommodate some measure of ideological dissension within its ranks even while maintaining a facade of political unity."[16]

In addition to expanding their membership bases through "softening" their rhetoric, hate groups have also sought to recruit from the growing militia movement. Given the broader appeal, audience, and membership of the militia movement, it is alarming that hate activists are beginning to infiltrate these organizations, where they can add their racial and sexist animosities to the militia's distrust of the state. Recognizing a golden opportunity to extend their rhetoric of hate beyond traditional hate-group membership, some leading hate activists have quickly joined ranks with the growing militia movement. Morris Dees provides a rough estimate that there are over 440 active militia groups and over 360 patriot groups nationwide, with cells in every state.[17] The Center for Democratic Renewal (CDR) suggests that by 1995, the militia movement boasted at least 100,000 members. Ironically, events like the Waco and Ruby Ridge sieges and the Oklahoma City bombing seem to have stimulated membership.[18] However, much of the recent growth can also be attributed to the movement of supremacists from traditional hate groups into the militia. The CDR claims that while militias are not exclusively made up of supremacists, "the line becomes blurred as one out of five active white supremacists have not only become involved but have become national leaders" in the movement."[19]

[Increasingly, the distinctions between the two types of organizations are becoming muted in terms of membership and ideology.]Louis Beam, a long-time Klansman and virulent racist, is the architect of the militia movement's strategy of "leaderless resistance." Beam learned from his experiences with the Klan the danger of traditional lines of leadership and communication. "Leaderless resistance" advocates phantom cells and individual action as a means of defeating state tyranny. Beam hosts an annual Aryan World Congress, where he takes the opportunity to encourage the formation of militias and to encourage Aryan Nation members to join these antigovernment organizations. Ongoing dissemination of information through newsletters, computer on-line services, and leaflets keeps members informed and allow them to design viable strategies for attack.

Beam is not alone in his exploitation of the Internet. While many purveyors of hate are content to spread their rhetoric of intolerance in the "real" community, there are those who prefer to hold their conversations in "cyberspace" or in the context of "virtual communities."(Consistent with the shifting demographics (i.e., middle-class) and sophistication of the hate movement is an increasing willingness to take advantage of the Internet as a tool for both recruitment and unification.)Traditionally, the primary means by which hate groups recruited members or spread their message of intolerance have been by word of mouth or by pamphleteering. However, several current factors have combined to change this. (On the one hand, cheaper, faster, and more accessible means of transmission and communication have emerged—telephone messaging and computer messaging, to name just two. On the other hand, hate-group leadership has become much more sophisticated to the extent that they are in a position to take advantage of these developing technologies.)

Tom Metzger, founder and continued leader of White Aryan Resistance (WAR), has a particular genius for exploiting new, high-tech, communication options. He and his counterparts in other hate groups have been blessed with a novel marketing gift in the form of the Internet.(This particular form of communication is superior to all others as a means of widely and quickly disseminating hate propaganda. Computers are increasingly affordable. At the very least, they can be easily accessed through work, local schools, universities, and colleges. Web sites are easily and cheaply maintained. Best of all, from the perspective of hate groups, the Net remains unregulated. In short, readiness and ability to exploit the Internet ensures effective communication between current and potential movement membership, which, according to McAdam, is also vital to movement solidarity.[20])

Young people are especially vulnerable to the lure of the Internet.(It is largely high school and college students, along with young professionals, who take advantage of the Net.) Anti-Defamation League (ADL) national director Abraham Foxman notes that "high tech haters are all the more pernicious because they are targeting the television-reared, multi-media, computer literate generation: our youth."[21]

There are in fact many sites that seem to be especially alluring to the MTV generation—those sites that feature music. Resistance Records is North America's largest distributor of white-power music. Its Web site offers audio excerpts of dozens of such CDs. Moreover, it includes downloadable album covers and on-line ordering. Operation Ghetto Storm goes one step further; in addition to all of the above, this white-power band site provides written lyrics of the band's music.

In short, the hate movement has taken on a new, modern face. It is no longer the preserve of uneducated bigots from the backwoods—if indeed it ever was. On the contrary, as the foregoing analysis suggests, it is now increasingly crossing into the mainstream. (The strength of the contemporary hate movement is grounded in its ability to repackage its age-old messages of white male supremacy in ways that make them more palatable and appealing to a very different population. In spite of these cosmetic changes, white-supremacist rhetoric remains decidedly raced and gendered.

Discourses of Difference

To the extent that hate groups define their collective identity as the norm, they necessarily engage in a politics of difference that seeks to negate, exclude, and repress those groups that are outside the norm, for instance, nonwhites, non-Christians, nonheterosexuals, even nonmales. They do so by invoking ideological claims to superiority and power that represent the ongoing struggle on the part of supremacists for the right to define the limits and boundaries of inclusion within the United States. Goldberg might refer to these mutually reinforcing claims as a "field of discourse" characterized by:

> racist expressions of principles, supposed justifications of difference, advantages, claims to superiority (whether considered "natural" or "developed") and of racist practices and institutions. These expressions have widely divergent forms: scientific, linguistic, economic, bureaucratic, legal, philosophical, religious, and so forth.[22]

It is these discursive forms that have long created a coherent hate movement. In particular, in this chapter, I examine the "supposed justifications" for the regulation of reproduction in the interests of the continuation of the white race. Hence, for example, the National Alliance insists on distinguishing between that which is "wholesome and natural," that is white Christian heterosexuality, and its opposite, that which is "degenerate and alien."[23] As this example illustrates, it is apparent that many of the identified ideologies are constructed upon essentializing dualisms: us versus them; good versus evil; strong versus weak; superior versus. inferior. Moreover, these dualities are interpreted as inherent in the groups in question and therefore a legitimate foundation for the marginalization of the "Other," who is consistently the negative and subordinate half of the equation.

(The secret to the success of these social constructs is that they are virtually invisible to the extent that the divisions appear natural; they are taken for granted] Omi and Winant articulate this notion with respect to race, although it is an equally apt assessment of gender or sexual identity:

> Everyone learns some combination, some version, of the rules of racial classification, and of her own racial identity, often without obvious teaching or conscious inculcation. Thus we are inserted in a comprehensively racialized social structure. Race becomes "common sense"—a way of comprehending, explaining and being in the world.[24]

The systems of classification to which Omi and Winant refer tend to presume essentialist, mutually exclusive categories of belonging. They assume an either/or understanding of identity: one is either a man or a woman; either white or black or Asian or Native; either Christian or Jew or Muslim. (Given this conceptualization of identity, one is forced to choose "a side.") In some contexts, the choice is given, since differences in race or gender, for example, are assumed to be innate, biological, that is, "natural." Whatever the case, discrete boundaries are assumed. One can belong only to one side of the equation; the borders are held to be impermeable. Consequently, identity formation is often concerned with "drawing boundaries, engaging in boundedness, configuring rings around" the categories of difference.[25] There is no room for elision, since this would threaten the "natural" order. The task of the white-supremacist movement in this context, then, is to police the borders between categories.

Associated with these closely guarded divisions are corresponding assumptions about the members within each category. That is, particular traits and abilities are associated with each group. Generally, these traits are posed in oppositional terms, such that the social construction of one group necessarily implies the construction of its opposite. Fine refers to these opposites as "nested," or as forming a "coherent system."[26] Weis, Proweller, and Centri similarly refer to the "parasitic construction" of self and other.[27] Neither could exist independently without the other. In creating the self, in carving out an identity, we necessarily create its antithesis. However, as Frankenberg reminds us, this coconstruction is not symmetrical.[28] It implies dominance, normativity, and privilege on the one hand, and subordination, marginality, and disadvantage on the other.

(Also implicit in this construction of difference is the assumption of a good/bad opposition.)Not only is the Other different; by definition he or she is also aberrant, deviant, inferior. Structures of oppression operate through a set of dualisms—such as good/evil, superior/inferior, strong/weak, dominant/subordinate—wherein the second half of the binary is always marked as deficiency relative to the superior capacities and privileges of the norm. The marking of difference as deficient is a social, political process that creates hierarchies along divisions such as race, sexuality, and class.(Once a group has been defined as inferior, defective, or substandard, it is necessarily assigned a subordinate place in society. This construction of the Other facilitates the unequal distribution of resources and power in such a way that it appears natural and justifiable.)Racism, sexism, and homophobia all are predicated upon such negative valuations of difference. Women, for example, are deemed inferior by virtue of their "weakness" or "irrationality"; Asians by virtue of their "hyperrationality."

The white-supremacist movement epitomizes this raced and gendered project. It is at the forefront of efforts to define the rightful place of women, men, and nonwhites. Members see themselves as saviors of the white race to the extent that they are actively engaged in documenting and responding to the threats posed by such contemporary evils as homosexuality, feminism, multiculturalism, and of course, ZOG. In this paper, I am especially concerned with the ways in which the movement articulates its agenda of racial purity through attacks on abortion, miscegenation, and homosexuality.

Abortion

From the perspective of some white supremacists, women have one function that defines their station in life: childbearing. Extremist conceptions of gender parallel those of race to the extent that gender is also deemed essential. There are two natural and distinct sexes, each with biologically "wired" roles. This basic tenet informs subsequent racist and homophobic ideological stances. Sapp, Holden, and Wiggins cite a right-wing pamphlet on the topic of gender differences: "there is the world of woman and the world of man. Nature has ordained that man should be the guardian of the family and the protector of the community. The world of contented womanhood is made of family: husband, children and home."[29] Hence it falls to the white woman to ensure the physical and social reproduction of the white race. This is her role and responsibility. Any deviation is an inherent threat to the continuation of the race.

However, just as the black civil rights movement led African Americans to "forget their place," so too has the women's movement distorted the proper and natural relationship between men and women. Too many women—especially feminists and lesbians—seem no longer to need or at least depend on men.(This poses a threat to men's masculinity, certainly, but also to the white race as a whole. Women are foregoing childbearing for their careers; abortions reduce the white birthrate; white women are choosing to marry nonwhite men. Women are in the midst of constructing a feminine gender identity that undermines definitions of the natural sex order that white supremacists have crafted) Consequently, white supremacists "want to save the white race by controlling the behavior of white women— they attack interracial couples, lesbians and feminists. They join the antiabortion movement, believing they can prevent white women from getting legal abortions."[30]

For the white-supremacist movement, abortion is an issue of control and autonomy. The denial of women's control over their own bodies becomes an attempt to maintain their subordination to and dependence on men. This is a crucial exercise in the wake of thirty years of the women's movement, during which the gender line was blurred and the hegemony of masculinity questioned. [Antiabortion politics, then, are an important means of reaffirming that essentialist gender line. It reasserts the sanctity of traditional gender relations of power, which places women on the "private," domestic side and men on the "public," political side. In an interview in *Free Speech*, William Pierce, founder of the National Alliance, refers to the sexual division of labor as consisting of "fundamentally different roles for men and women: men are the providers and protectors, and women are the nurturers. Men bring home the bacon and they guard the den; women nourish the children and tend the hearth."[31]

In this conservative vision of woman-as-mother, women are to be fulfilled only through the institution of motherhood. The problem is that: "This image of 'mother' is not an image of a real woman with real children, or of a real woman active in the public world of work—let alone of a real woman who controls her own sexual behavior. It is instead, an objectified image of a 'woman' as a disembodied vessel of domestic nurturance."[32]

But according to hate groups, this is as it should be. Too many women have rejected the responsibility of domestic nurturance. And access to abortion has facilitated this:

> Today greater numbers of White children are being killed in the womb than ever before. And when we are speaking of killing our own offspring, if we are true to the instincts that ensure our survival and make us what we are, we must recognize that we are speaking of a particularly horrifying kind of killing. There is something almost unbelievably depraved about women committing this obscene act for no other reason than convenience.[33]

The depravity referred to by Kevin Alfred Strom of the National Alliance is not to be blamed on individual women. Rather, the culprit behind the loss of traditional gendered identities is feminism. As a philosophy and as a practice, to hate groups, feminism represents, a "destructive aberration," "a sickness with deep emotional roots."[34] It is held to be destructive to the extent that it has contributed to an unnatural racial and gender balance:

> At the racial level it is destructive because it divides the race against itself, robbing us of racial solidarity and weakening us in the struggle for racial survival, and because it reduces the White birthrate.... It also undermines the family by taking women out of the home and leaving the raising of children to television and day-care centers.[35]

Like the militia movement of which Kimmel and Ferber write, white supremacists blame feminism for the erosion of the traditional relationship between men and women, by encouraging women to seek fulfilment outside the family in a "traditionally male role," that includes education, employment, and political activism.[36] Feminism encourages an "arrangement between men and women which goes against Nature. Biologically, a man is a man in every cell of his body and his brain... and a woman is a woman to the same degree."[37] When women go against nature, they upset this delicate balance, assuming "unfeminine" qualities and roles. This is a potent challenge to the assumption of masculine superiority, since feminism constructs women as politically and economically capable in their own right.

Moreover, the perception among white supremacists is that both abortion and feminism are underwritten by Jews.[38] Abortion specifically is but one more cog in the great Jewish conspiracy to undermine the White race. A cartoon featured on the WAR Web site illustrates the perceived role of Jews in encouraging and facilitating white abortions. The cartoon caption reads:

> Did you know that most abortionists are Jewish or other non-whites... and that the pro-abortion movement is headed by unfeminine feminist Jewesses who counsel non-whites to not get abortions.... And did you know that abortionists slaughter nearly one million white babies every year? Jewish ritual murder is alive and well in the United States of America... and is very legal![39]

The message here illustrates another interesting paradox. It implies a singular concern with white abortions: while white supremacists resist abortion by "liberated" white women, they would not generally stand in the way of abortions for women of color. In fact, they are strongly critical of the "unregulated" birthrates among nonwhite communities, wherein "The Brown and Black races are boiling over in every non-White country. There is no shortage of non-White people."[40] As the following WAR statement makes clear, it is not necessarily abortion in general that is problematic. Rather it is abortion by Aryan women—WAR would welcome nonwhite abortions as a "powerful weapon in the limitation of non-White births:"[41]

> WAR supports birth control and abortion for non-whites living in North America. WAR encourages racially conscious White women to produce white children.... As the non-white races continue to breed with little control, White

people have voluntarily destroyed millions of healthy, White babies.... Those who have bought into this suicidal way of thinking must at some point receive future Aryan justice.[42]

White abortion tips the racial balance—this is what white racialists fear. They fear not only the loss of control of "their women" but of their own place in American politics and culture. If nonwhite minorities are allowed to become a mathematical majority, the assumption is that they will also become dominant in sociopolitical terms as well. The hegemonic position of white men would be in question. Consequently, movement members encourage active interventions to increase abortions among nonwhite communities: "Among non-whites, invest in ghetto abortion clinics. Help to raise money for free abortions. Abortion clinic syndicates throughout North America, that primarily operate in non-White areas and receive tax support, should be promoted."[43]

Miscegenation

If white abortion threatens the continuation of the white bloodline, miscegenation threatens its purity and ultimately also its survival. Consequently, it is in the discourse of antimiscegenation that we most readily see the intersection of the racism and sexism inherent in hate groups' rhetoric. For Strom, race-mixing is tantamount to white genocide and hence spells death for the white race.[44] Strictures against interracial unions are an attempt to control and regulate equally those who are not white and not male. The womb of the white woman must be preserved for the bearing of pure, white children. Men of color must not be permitted to defile that vessel.[45] Moreover, white women are held to be especially to blame for racial suicide:

> The nigger can't really help it's [sic] behavior, the white woman can though and it is really her we should condemn. It is the white woman who is going against the work of God. We have to get the message out to these white women. Can you imagine the pain and anguish her parents must feel when she brings home a nigger to meet Mum and Dad? Even more pain when they are presented with half cast [sic] abomination. The end of thousands of years of the families [sic] white gene pool.[46]

Antimiscegenation rhetoric hence seeks to reaffirm the boundaries between genders and between races, to reaffirm the appropriate "place" of white women and nonwhite men.[47]

The hostility toward interracial relationships is ultimately grounded in the essentialist understanding of racial difference. Boundary crossing is thus not only unnatural but threatening to the rigid hierarchies that have been built around these presumed differences. Whether god-given or biologically derived, the white race is deemed inherently superior to all others. The creation of race categories and valuations represents a means of identity construction for both whites and other races. Race is seen as an "essence" that carries with it inherent differences between groups, differences that are claimed as justification for "natural" hierarchies. The National Alliance summary statement of beliefs makes this apparent:

> We see ourselves as part of Nature, subject to Nature's law. We recognize the inequalities which arise as natural consequences of the evolutionary process. . . . We accept our responsibilities as Aryan men and women to strive for the advancement of our race in the service of Life.[48]

They go on to state that:

> (O)ur world is hierarchical. Each of us is a member of the Aryan (European) race, which, like other races, developed its special characteristics over many thousands of years during which natural selection not only adapted it to its environment but also advanced it along its evolutionary path.[49]

A similar claim is made by the longest-lived white-supremacist group, the KKK:

> Our main and fundamental objective is the Maintenance of the Supremacy of the White Race in this Republic. History and physiology teach us that we belong to a race which nature has endowed with an evident superiority over all other races, and that the Maker in thus elevating us above the common standard of human creation has intended to give us over inferior races a domination from which no human laws can permanently derogate.[50]

(Inevitably, the white race is presumed to be at the top of this hierarchy, followed by the Jews and the "mud-people," that is people of color.)For many white supremacists, the focus has historically been on the "inferiority" of the black race.(Whether in Africa or America, blacks are deemed to be incapable of creativity, incapable of intellectual labor, incapable of constructing a "civilization" or "culture.")White racialist Roger Roots offers "proof" of this in his essay "100 Facts About Whites and Blacks," in which he catalogs the "deficiencies" and "threats" posed by blacks.[51] For example, he contends that "throughout 6,000 years of recorded history, the Black African Negro has invented nothing," nor have they cultivated anything, nor have they built anything of lasting value. Roots also devotes considerable attention to another favorite theme among white supremacists—IQ measures. He cites studies showing differences in brain size, intelligence, test performance, and so on, all of which are meant to show that blacks are inherently less intelligent than whites. Roots concludes his survey by favorably citing Robert E. Lee's declaration that "wherever you find the Negro everything is going down around him, and wherever you find the White man you see everything around him improving."

⟨It is these presumed relationships of inferiority and superiority that underlie hostility toward the political, legal, and economic advances of minorities since the civil rights movement.⟩ Why should "inferior" races prosper and compete on the same level with the far more intelligent, moral, and advanced white race? Why should obviously less endowed peoples be privileged by affirmative action policies? Minorities, from this perspective, do not "deserve" to benefit from the labors of the white race, since they are unable to return the favor.

It is also these presumed relationships of inferiority and superiority that underlie the strident calls for "racial purity." Race-mixing inherently taints the white race and infects it with the weaknesses of the other races. Senator Bilbo of Mississippi is often cited as the most articulate defender of this claim:

> But if the blood of our White race should become corrupted and mingled with the blood of Africa, then the present greatness of the United States of America would be destroyed and all hope for civilization would be as impossible for a Negroid America as would be redemption and restoration of the Whiteman's blood which has been mixed with that of the Negro.[52]

Any "contamination" by nonwhite blood introduces into the white bloodline all of those reviled deficiencies characteristic of the "mud-people." Supremacists look with disgust and hostility on those race-traitors who seek out nonwhite mates, as is the case for the Klansman overheard by Raphael Ezekiel at a Klan rally: "What is the worst, to see a couple—to see some white woman and some black man—ugh! It just turns my stomach."[53]

Strom's treatise on miscegenation provides ample evidence of this perspective. The title of the essay, "Racemixing—Worse Than Murder: Murder is Homicide; Racemixing is Genocide," is indicative of the tone of his argument.[54] ⟨Strom fears that the increase in interracial births will ultimately lead to the elimination of the white race, and with it all hope for progress and civilization.⟩ For him and others of like mind, race-mixing constitutes part of the genocidal agenda of nonwhite races. Strom links the rhetoric of white supremacy with that of antimiscegenation, arguing that the white race's:

> continued existence would undoubtedly be assumed by our superior intelligence and unmatched technology, if it were not for those who practice and promote the genocide of our people through racial mixing. By their actions they are killing us.... They kill infinite generations of our future. Their crime—the crime of racial mixture—is far, far worse than mere murder.[55]

Race-mixing is deemed to be yet another symptom of the loss of white power and identity, since it violates the sacred order of the established hierarchy. Moreover, it directly threatens the perpetuation of the white race, since:

> Every White man who commits the crime of marrying a non-White will not be fathering any White children. Every White woman who pollutes her body and her spirit by marrying a non-White will not be giving birth to any White children. And by their actions they will be committing the crime of misleading White boys and girls to follow their example.[56]

Consequently, miscegenation elicits calls for enforced racial purity as a means of correcting the emerging imbalance in the relationship between whites and nonwhites. The latter must be put back in "their place"—by force if necessary.

Such responses are especially encouraged where the "race-mixing" is "involuntary," that is where white women have been forcibly raped by men of color. White supremacists are masters of the perpetuation of controlling images of men of color that portray them as "animal-like" or "less than human" in their sexual appetites. Roots's "100 Facts about Blacks and Whites" makes consistent reference to the "simian-like" nature of Africans, with such phrases as "similar to an ape," "approximating the simian form," "like that of the gorilla," or "thus more characteristic of an ape."[57] These characterizations distance "us" from "them" in a very dramatic way, constituting the "Other" as unhuman and therefore not subject to the same respect, rights, and protections as their white counterparts. It releases the hate activists from the inhibitions and prohibitions that govern interactions between fully human beings.

If these "subhumans" can be shown to be a violent threat to the white race, then the potential white perpetrators can further distance themselves from their potential nonwhite victims. Hence another common theme among hate groups is the inherent criminality of minorities. Nonwhites are portrayed as "egregiously anti-social elements, riot-prone minorities, dastardly criminals, homosexuals, drug-dealers, perverts" who pose a constant threat to the moral, peaceful, law-abiding white race.[58] White nationalist Yggdrasil favorably cites an Australian journalist's claims that crime statistics indicate that "a large segment of black America has waged a war of violent retribution against white America."[59] Confederate White Pride erroneously reports that minorities are responsible for over 85 percent of all violent crime.[60] Strom refers to the unconstrained and ongoing rapes of white women and girls by "Black criminals."[61]

White Western culture has long held to paradoxical controlling images of the sexualities of people of color: ("Typically . . . other men are both 'too masculine' and 'not masculine enough.' . . . (T)he others are seen as too masculine—violent rapacious beasts, with no self control—or not masculine enough—weak, helpless, effete, incapable of supporting a family."[62] Nonetheless, foremost among these has been the tendency to imagine people of color as "excessive, animalistic, or exotic in contrast to the ostensibly restrained or 'civilized' sexuality of white women and men."[63] At different times, in different contexts, most nonwhite groups have been perceived as sexual predators, guided by their animal-like instincts. Since all but the white race were historically held to be subhuman creatures anyway, it was a small step to paint the Others' sexuality in similar terms. Unlike their white superiors, people of color had not learned to tame their sexual desires nor to direct them toward "appropriate" objects, that is, members of their own race.

Nowhere have white fears been more palpable than in whites' historical relationship with black males. No other group has been so narrowly defined by their sexuality than have black males. This was clear under slavery, where "bucks" were valued for their breeding capacity, but also where black male subordination was justified on the grounds of his savage and beastly nature. As Messerschmidt contends, black masculinity was irrevocably defined in terms of black sexuality, which in turn was seen as "animalistic and bestial."[64] Hence the unrestrained instincts and desires of black men could be reined in only through the use or threat of violence.

The sexualized image of black males was reproduced in postbellum culture. In fact, to the extent that black sexual independence was correlated with their economic and political freedom, blacks presented an even greater threat to white masculine superiority. The fact that alleged black rapists were as often castrated as lynched suggests an attempt to emasculate the "savage" by symbolically (and literally) erasing his identity, much as one would control a wild dog. The vicious forms of punishment meted out to black males served to highlight their animal nature at the same time as reinforcing the power and hegemony of white males. Consequently, "both race and masculine difference were reproduced through the practice of lynching and castration and ultimately emasculating the African American male body."[65]

The presumption of black male as sexual predator continues to underlie racial difference and racial violence in the contemporary era. In fact, the myth of lascivious, rapacious, and insatiable black sexuality is perhaps one of the most enduring themes in United States culture. It emerged in the 1988 Willie Horton presidential-election advertisements; it was also evoked even by Clarence Thomas's claim that he was the victim of a "high-tech" lynching; and it ensured Mike Tyson's conviction for sexual assault. The image of the black sexual predator is the cultural lens through which whites perceive blacks. And this is an image that is apparent throughout white-supremacist discourse.

On the basis of these controlling images of people of color, white women and especially white men are fearful and suspicious of the sexualities of the Other. Speaking of the white fear of black bodies in particular, Cornel West contends that this "fear is rooted in visceral feelings about black bodies fueled by sexual myths of black men and women . . . either as threatening creatures who have the potential for sexual power over whites, or as harmless, desired underlings of a white culture."[66]

In this context, white supremacists attempt to reinforce the normativeness of white sexuality while punishing people of color for their real or imagined sexual improprieties. It is a means of degrading the bodies of the Other, with an eye to controlling them. Verbal or even physical attacks on such groups emasculate the sexual threat, thereby firmly establishing the essential boundaries between groups.

The thread that binds these historical processes together is the coconstruction of the black sexual predator and the white savior. At the height of postbellum white resistance to black citizenship, South Carolina senator Bill Tillman expressed the black threat and the white response:

> The white women of the South are in a state of siege. . . . Some lurking demon who has watched for the opportunity seizes her; she is ravished, her body prostituted, her purity destroyed, her chastity taken from her. . . . So far as I am concerned he has put himself outside the pale of the law, human and divine. . . . We revert to the impulse to "kill, kill, kill."[67]

More recently, an advertisement produced by the 14 Word Press contends that: "The highest Law of Nature is the preservation of one's own kind. There is no time remaining for White men to indulge in reality denial or cowardice. If our women are not worth fighting for, then I ask you, 'What is?'"[68]

Only through avenging the "defilement" of the white woman can the white male reclaim his appropriate position as the "protector" and "savior" of white women. (This simultaneously casts the black male in the image of "evil" and the white male in the image of "goodness" (and of course white women as defenseless). In defending their women from the unrestrained sexuality of black men, white supremacists are also defending themselves— that is, the sanctity of their own carefully restrained, "civilized," normative sexuality. And more important, they are defending the white race from defilement and loss of authority.

In contrast to the fearful image of men of color, Jewish men occupy an uncertain place on the racialized hierarchy of sexuality. Kimmel and Ferber highlight this ambivalence within militia discourse, positing that Jews are at once perceived to be both hyper- and hypomasculine.[69] Nonetheless, for the most part, Jews are not regarded as a direct threat in the way black males are. They are, rather, presumed to be asexual—apparently their financial desires overwhelm their sexual desires. However, Jewish men are presumed to represent a more insidious sexual threat. From their positions of cultural and political power, Jews are in fact suspected of encouraging whites to engage in interracial relationships. In fact, like abortion, miscegenation is a key element in the Jewish conspiracy to weaken the white race and its culture: "It is the disruption of the White man's natural environment and the dehumanization of his society and culture, therefore, which the Jews and their collaborators in the news and entertainment media have worked for in order to encourage racial mixing."[70] Miscegenation deprives white men of their sexual rights to white women; but at the same time, it threatens to destroy the white race by introducing "impurities" into the bloodlines.

Homosexuality

It is also the Jews, according to white-supremacist rhetoric, who have spawned the current wave of "degeneracy" and "homosexuality" as yet another means of weakening the hegemony of white, heterosexual, Christian males. Daniels notes that white supremacists refer to this as the "feminizing influence of Jewish men on white men."[71] In so doing, Jews have created a cultural phenomenon that threatens to minimize not only the sexual dominance of heterosexual white men but also their political and economic power.

Just as white supremacists fear that abortion is an act of genocide and miscegenation is an act of racial suicide, so too do they imagine homosexuality to represent a threat to the continued survival of the white race. Since, it is assumed, homosexuals do not reproduce, they too constitute race-traitors: "Those who recruit for homosexual sodomy are a factor in pushing us ever closer to the edge of racial suicide. Every recruit for them is how many White children never born?"[72]

The abhorrence of homosexuality is grounded in the essentialist understanding of gender referred to previously. Gender constitutes a hierarchical structure of domination not only between but within genders. This structure of power is also constitutive of the broader pattern of sexual power relations, in which heterosexual masculinity comes to the fore. The hierarchy of masculinities valorizes this narrow, hegemonic form of masculinity while denying or limiting the power of "lower" forms. Because male homosexuality challenges the fundamental assumption of what it is to "be a man," it is inevitably assigned an inferior—and deviant—status. In fact, according to the Creator's Rights Party, gay men are "manslayers":

> Homosexuals are first and foremost manslayers. . . . To destroy the distinctive activities of the man is to remove the presence of man as surely as if the man himself were literally destroyed. If nobody does what the man is supposed to do,

then the man literally is destroyed, or at least paralyzed and thereby made unfit for any activity except death. Homosexuals and their supporters have literally destroyed the venerable word "man." In this way they have gone a long way toward slaying all men in this generation.[73]

White supremacists support the widespread perception that homosexuality is a wholly aberrant and unnatural phenomenon: "America should not accept homosexual activity as normal behavior. . . . Nature intended for a man and a woman to interact sexually, not members of the same sex."[74] As this quote suggests, the homophobic rhetoric tends to be highly charged, referring to "perversions," "defectives," "nature freaks," and "degeneracy." Like autonomous women, homosexuals are represented as distortions of the natural order. Even more than women, homosexuals challenge essentialist gendered boundaries. They are in fact "gender-traitors," in that they refuse to be forced into the binary categories of feminine or masculine. And, as noted, they are also considered race-traitors by virtue of the threats they pose to the reproduction of the white race.

The rhetoric of many hate groups reaffirms the moral culpability of gays. Just as hate groups vilify nonwhites, they portray gays as a menace to society on many levels. For example, there is a concern that homosexuals seek to pervert white youths by recruiting them to their "lifestyle": "They want to teach that this perversion is proper. They want to teach our kids in school this is normal."[75] More than that, however, gays presumably victimize youth through child pornography or molestation. According to American Christian Nationalist CyberMinistries, "The simple fact is that gays moleste [sic] children much more than straight people. In Maryland state prisons, 70% of the child molesters in prison, molested boys, i.e., *homosexual by definition*" (emphasis added).[76] From this perspective, homosexuality is synonymous with pedophilia.

Additionally, gays are held to blame for the spread of AIDS, a phenomenon equally threatening to their "recruits" and to the white race in general. The Knights of the Ku Klux Klan point to a correlation between the repeal of sodomy legislation and the "plague of AIDS now ravaging our land."[77] Strom proclaims that those who are lured into homosexuality get "anal sodomy, death by infectious disease, and an anti-life philosophy."[78] Given these multiple threats, the ultimate conclusion reached by hate activists is that homosexuality must be eliminated. For some, the answer is to help gays find God so that they might see the error of their ways. For others, however, there is no salvation for gays. They must be physically eliminated. Hence it is not uncommon for hate groups to engage in violence against gays or to call for the death penalty for known homosexuals. In other words, "suffer not the sodomite to live."

Conclusion: Resisting the Tide of Hate

In the preceding pages I have traced the ways in which the simultaneously raced and gendered discourse of the white-supremacist movement attempts to assert reproductive strategies intended to ensure the survival and purity of the white race. What is apparent from this reading is that "the regulation of sexuality is governed not only by a compulsory heterosexuality, but by a compulsory interracial sexuality, which desires to maintain the illusion of racial purity and secure racial boundaries."[79]

What is remarkable about this politics of reproduction is the extent to which it reflects the mainstream. We like to think that the white-supremacist movement is in fact a "lunatic fringe." Yet the vitriol of the hate groups is not so much an aberration as it is a reaffirmation of racist and gendered views that permeate society. Consequently, the political rhetoric of hate does not fall on deaf ears. For example, Feagin and Vera present ample survey data to support the contention that individual Americans subscribe to a range of intolerant and bigoted attitudes and stereotypes that might make them at least sympathetic to the positions of hate groups.[80] Whatever the questions tapped—beliefs about criminal activity, sexualities, interracial marriages—white respondents tend to characterize ethnic and racial minorities in negative terms and to maintain relatively traditional views about the relative roles of men and women. For example, a National Opinion Research Center (NORC) survey in 1990 found that a majority of white respondents evaluated blacks at the high end of the scale with respect to tendencies toward both violence and welfare dependency. A 1993 Gallup poll further confirms this issue. When asked which racial group was responsible for the bulk of crime (among blacks, Hispanics, Asians, and whites), respondents rated blacks at the upper end of the continuum and whites at the lowest end.

Degradation of the Other is on fertile ground in a culture with a history of—indeed origins in—a worldview that sees nonwhites as sexual predators, for example. The United States has a legacy of centuries of persecution of minorities, whether they be Natives, immigrants, women, or sexual deviants. Such a history normalizes the stigmatization and mistreatment of those who do not appropriately conform to the preconceived hierarchies. That leaves us with a culture reflected in bitter letters to the editor and opinion polls that seem to tap deep divisions and resentment—fodder for the hate movement.

The uncertainty that characterizes contemporary identity politics leaves the most fearful and most alienated elements of society vulnerable to the recruitment efforts of the hate movement, which provides "easy answers" to America's woes. Such elements share with white-supremacist organizations one of the elements McAdam insists is crucial to the development and cohesiveness of any social movement: a shared consciousness or perception of unjust conditions.[81]

The white-supremacist movement—and the related militia movement—provides ready answers for why white men feel displaced and defeated.[82] And it presents options for the reassertion of a white masculine identity intended to return Others to their rightful place.

One of the themes that underlies the foregoing conceptualization of the white-supremacist movement is that it is engaged in the process of constructing difference by which Others—white women, gay men, and men and women of color—have been defined negatively in terms of their relationship to some dominant norm; that is, that "black" is defined as inherently inferior to "white," Jewish to Christian, gay to straight. Nonetheless, there is reason for hope. To the extent that difference is socially constructed, it can also be socially reconstructed. In other words, as a society, we can redefine the ways in which difference "matters." We can strive for a just and democratic society in which the full spectrum of diversity addressed here is reevaluated in a positive and celebratory light.

In confronting the raced and gendered rhetoric of the hate movement, we would do well to heed Young's advice that we embrace a positive politics of difference.[83] This would involve much more than efforts to assimilate Others or merely "tolerate" their presence. Rather, it challenges us to celebrate our differences. Of course, this requires that much of our current way of ordering the world would be radically altered. It means that we must cease to define "different" as inferior and see it instead as simply not the same. As Minow states so elegantly: "Changing the ways we classify, evaluate, reward, and punish may make the differences we had noticed less significant . . . irrelevant or even a strength. The way things are is not the only way things could be."[84]

This is doing difference differently, under different ground rules where enacting one's identity is not an occasion for potential rebuke. Rather, doing difference becomes a risk-free expression of one's culture, perspectives, and insights. To engage in such a powerful politics is to resist the temptation to ask all Others to conform to an artificial set of norms and expectations. It is to reclaim and value the "natural" heterogeneity of this nation rather than to force a false homogeneity. It is to refuse to denigrate the culture and experiences of black people, women, or gay men, for example. It is to learn and grow from the strength and beauty that alternate cultures have to offer.

4

Normalizing Racism: A Case Study of Motherhood in White Supremacy

JOANN ROGERS
JACQUELYN S. LITT

As Proud, White Women, we shall create and build a world in which
our White Children will grow up free and strong with their heads held
high, and be [the] powerful and noble warriors Nature intended.[1]

This article examines the meanings of gender and motherhood in the right-wing white-separatist group, the World Church of the Creator (WCOTC). We advance two basic arguments. First, we argue that women in the movement are constructed as arbiters of white supremacy through their labor as mothers of children and managers of households. Second, we argue that through the use of motherhood the extremist discourse normalizes racist activities. WCOTC rhetoric uses motherhood and gender to appeal to potential followers. In valorizing women's traditional roles, the group normalizes its racism into a set of practices and beliefs that draw upon what is acceptable and familiar in dominant codes of gender.

Our interest in examining the role that motherhood plays in right-wing racist ideology is spurred in part because of how this role taps into—and radically simplifies—crises in gender and reproductive politics currently circulating in the United States. We note striking parallels between the white racist motherhood espoused in WCOTC and other contemporary mothering movements, notably the "natural mothers" and "simple livers" that observers such as Chris Bobel and Juliet Schor identify.[2] We believe that the separatism espoused in an array of mothering movements, including extreme racist ones, taps into a profound sense of alienation and uncertainty regarding gender and motherhood, that is, around reproductive politics, work-family conflict, inadequate schools, and environmental danger. We are particularly concerned about the power of right-wing ideologues to racialize these wide-ranging concerns regarding gender and motherhood.

WCOTC Background

> The guiding principle of all your actions shall be: What is best for the White Race.[3]

Leaders of WCOTC portray the white man as having created, molded, and civilized almost every continent in the world. Their view draws upon dominant ethnocentric beliefs and values about the superiority of European cultures over others. The goal of the WCOTC is to formulate all white communities which, in turn, will become all white nations. Although their rhetoric is couched in a language of "separatism," the members of the WCOTC are supremacists because they believe the white race is superior to any other race.[4]

The World Church of the Creator was first introduced to the public in 1973 in Lighthouse Point, Florida, as the Church of the Creator (COTC). The founder, Ben Klassen, was a self-professed white separatist. The establishment of the COTC coincided with the publication of Ben Klassen's first book, *Nature's Eternal Religion*. In 1981 he published his second manifesto, called the *White Man's Bible*. By May of 1982, he had purchased property in North Carolina, three miles from the Georgia state border, where he set up the new headquarters for the COTC. The COTC started with Klassen's ideology of uniting race and religion. Klassen, an atheist, believed that the only way the white race would survive as a pure race in the future was to satisfy the need for religion with that of race.

Klassen's publications helped to attract new members who, according to the Anti-Defamation League (ADL), were the younger and more violent groups of white separatists such as neo-Nazi skinheads. During the 1990s, Ben Klassen initiated weapons-training programs at his Church's headquarters in North Carolina. Klassen was eventually forced to sell his compound to pay off the debts from a lawsuit brought against him by the Southern Poverty Law Center.[5]

Klassen committed suicide by consuming four bottles of sleeping pills after being diagnosed with cancer.[6] He did not seek medical treatment because he disavowed the use of modern medicine and physicians. Klassen believed that cancer, caused by poor dietary habits, was a final stage of the body's attempt to purge itself from toxins.[7]

After Klassen's death, the Guardians of Faith Committee of WCOTC, elders of the Church, elected Matt Hale as the new Pontifex Maximus. Hale holds bachelor's degrees in political science and music from Bradley University and has a law degree from Southern Illinois University. After he was named the head of the Church, Hale moved the headquarters to his home in Peoria, Illinois. Hale changed the name of the Church to the World Church of the Creator (WCOTC) claiming that the Church has members in Canada, South Africa, Sweden, and England as well as the United States.

Matt Hale seemed to be the spark that the COTC needed. According to the ADL, "Matt Hale has been one of the most effective and best-known leaders on the far right since he took over the helm of the World Church of the Creator in 1996."[8] In the summer of 2002, the *New York Times* identified Hale as potentially filling a leadership vacuum in racist organizations in the United States, created by the death that summer of William Pierce, author of the well-known *Turner Diaries* and leader of the National Alliance, another right-wing racist group. The racist leader Richard Butler of the Aryan Nations is seriously ill, which has also left room for Hale to assume dominance in extreme racist movements.

Hale claims that the WCOTC "is the fastest growing and most dynamic and inspiring organization in existence for the survival expansion, and advancement of our beloved White Race."[9] The discourse of the WCOTC holds that "what is good for the White Race is the highest virtue and what is bad for the White Race is the ultimate sin." Matt Hale comes from the new generation of white activists who use the Internet as an organizing tool. The use of the Internet has allowed white separatists to read, join, and organize within the privacy of their own homes. WCOTC Web sites include many branch affiliations and a site targeted to women.

The focus of this chapter is an analysis of the published writings of the Women's Frontier (WF), the WCOTC organization for women. The WF includes a newsletter for women, which was initiated in 1998 by "Sister" Lisa Turner and a Web site containing information for women regarding the WTOTC.[10] Turner continues to edit and produce the *Women's Frontier Newsletter (WFN)* as a tool to recruit white women to the movement. Turner defies the stereotypes of women as secondary or passive players in white racist activism. She is an advocate for advancing the role and significance of women in the church: "White female voices must be heard, if the Church is to truly accomplish its goal of taking back White territory worldwide."[11]

Method

This chapter is based on primary research on the published writings by members and leaders of the WCOTC. The data come primarily from the Web site of WCOTC, which includes the *Women's Frontier Newsletter,* a WF

Web page writings by Turner and other leaders, and chat rooms and resource sites for women.[12] The newsletter was originally distributed in printed form through the mail but has been transferred to electronic distribution.

The first author of this chapter generated the data from newsletters published in the 1999 calendar year, which included eleven issues from Volumes 7 to 18. The typical issue runs to fifteen pages. We also used the WF Web page and primary articles on women in the movement, including Turner's pivotal essay, "The Cooptation of White Women," first published in the *Women's Frontier Newsletter*. Each newsletter takes on a different personality and character of its own, although most contain a "Creativity quote" of the month coined by Ben Klassen or Matt Hale. Some issues contain letters written by male and female members or other visitors to the Web site. With the exception of Turner, who signs her articles, most of the posted commentary is anonymous. Names are typically attached to the letters. We also studied the chat rooms of WF chapter Web sites in Sacramento and Maryland.

We used "grounded theory" to generate the major categories that emerged in the reading. Dominant themes that emerged early in the analysis, such as motherhood, separatism, and nature, were used to refine the general categories into which much of the primary material fitted.

As a study of published writing, this article cannot address the activities and beliefs of rank-and-file women members or followers of WCOTC. Instead, this paper undertakes a close analysis of the discursive uses of gender and motherhood in the published discourse. Our sense is that the Internet allows for a dispersed but vital "imagined community"[13] in which interested women and men can find support for their views, redefine their conceptions of race and gender, and resolve potential feelings of isolation that accompany marginality.

Women in the World Church of the Creator

> Giving women a more active role in the white supremacy movement is a matter of necessity and survival.... Now it's do or die for the white race.... [W]e can't afford to fight with one hand tied behind our back. We won't win while hopping on one leg.[14]

> To attract women, we must speak from a women's perspective. To do anything less at this time in history is to fool ourselves into thinking that somehow, as if by magic, women will flow into the White Cause without specific racial support systems with which to empower their lives, their families, and reflect their unique struggles and challenges as White women who valiantly battle the mud onslaught every day.[15]

> White women engage in a desperate battle for the future of our race, our nation, and our families.[16]

In popular thought as well as much research, the world of white racist activism is a man's world, defined and populated exclusively by white men who perform public acts of racist intimidation and violence. Yet recent research has provided new evidence that women are involved in white-supremacist activities and that they may even constitute one half of new recruits.[17] Moreover, research has begun to document that women's roles in the white-supremacist movement are geared less toward public organizing and displays of hate and more toward family and social roles that uphold white separatism and teach white supremacy in everyday life. The documents we analyzed confirm this picture of mothers as everyday activists who provide what we are calling *activist racist mothering*. The activist rhetoric contains two overarching ideals about women and the racist hate movement. First, mothers' everyday practices and attitudes play a central role in the production of white supremacy. Second, women should be given a more public and visible role in the movement, which would bring them, if not into leadership, at least into public forms of activism. Both approaches hold an ideology that constructs women as purposefully oriented toward and responsible for securing white racial superiority.

It is not surprising that women in the movement use motherhood or "maternalism" as a point of departure for activism, as this has been a strategy employed by women, progressive and reactionary, for centuries in the United States and across the globe. Yet it is precisely in the quotidian that we identify the danger that this activist racist mothering represents. This mothering movement gains legitimacy by transforming the everyday activities of maternal caretaking—health, feeding, cleaning, and educating—into practices that further white racism. Using and appealing to gendered ideology provides a backdrop of normalcy to the extreme racism embraced by this group.[18]

In her historical overview of white supremacist movements in the United States, Kathleen Blee argues that women have always been active in racist hate groups.[19] Women as well as children joined the ranks of the Ku Klux Klan (KKK) in the 1920s and are populating the array of white-power and neo-Nazi groups in the current era of organized racism. Known collectively as the "Fifth Era," the organized racist movement today includes neo-Nazis in major groups such as White Aryan Resistance (WAR), its women's group, Aryan Women's League (AWL), Christian Identity movements, a loose array of white-supremacist groups, and the revivified KKK, which includes a number of racist organizations and boasts a following of over ten to fifteen thousand.[20] Among the many commonalties in these groups is the use of mothering practice as an agent of racial separatism and hatred.

"Sister" Lisa Turner of the WCOTC, the symbol and embodiment of racist mothering, is, like the male leadership, confrontational in her views and ideas about women's roles in forging white supremacy. While we were limited in access to background information on Turner, we are able to glean from sources a picture of committed activism, an awareness of public discourse on feminism and women's studies, and a passionate embrace of separatist and supremacist discourse. Jim Nesbitt's article "The American Scene—White Supremacist Women Push for Greater Role in Movement," published in the *WFN*, identifies Turner as embodying "one of the strongest forces of change buffeting the White supremacist movement." Nesbitt describes Turner as "as a petite, blue-eyed woman of German and Swedish ancestry, with reddish-blond hair" and as "college-educated, savvy about the power of the Internet, adamant about women having a voice in the cause that has captured her passionate commitment and articulate about her core beliefs."[21]

In her own writings, Turner laments the lack of women in the white-separatist movement:

> [P]ro-White organizations are still 90% men and 10% women. This unbalanced situation perpetuates itself, it feeds on itself (which the jews love) and fuels the stereotype that the Movement is full of "women haters," and "misogynists."... The fact remains that we see concrete proof of men's presence in the form of their writings—books, articles, essays, journals, newsletter, magazines, letters to the editor (which are nearly always 99% from men in Movement publications), websites, news groups on the Internet, etc. I'm dismayed by the lack of written racialist expressions from women.[22]

According to Nesbitt, "Turner represents several new trends in the white supremacy movement that experts say are creating an unstable transition period." The new trends include "an increasing number of women [who] are following Turner's lead and demanding a shoulder-to-shoulder role with men." He believes that demands for women's equality represent an important cultural shift away from the traditional, male-dominated view of women as "Aryan breeders" who are assigned a passive role, providing food and comfort to their racial warriors. According to Turner:

> The good news is that activism by women [has] increased due to the efforts of out reach chapters such as the WCOTC Women's Frontier.... This year the WCOTC has seen female membership increase—not because of wishful thinking, or day dreaming that women are going to drift in, because of our women's targeted outreach chapters.[23]

Turner is direct in her attempt to counteract the stereotypes of "trailer trash and dysfunctional people" who the media uses to discredit white extremists. In Turner's words:

> We feel like we're a new wave of pro-white activists, and that we shouldn't be pigeonholed. Pro-white has become synonymous with trailer trash and dysfunctional people, and it's time for us to let people know that we're your neighbors, we're your co-workers, we're educated, we're professionals.[24]

Turner's admonition about the ordinariness of "pro-white activists," like her views on the importance of motherhood, furthers the goal of attempting to normalize the appearance of extreme white racism.

Racialized Reproduction

> Women are entrusted with bringing forth the next generation of White warriors.[25]

Turner and her followers have crafted a view of women and motherhood that places women at the center of the movement toward white dominance. As in virtually all white racist movements, white women's reproduction is understood to support racial purity. Women in the movement are considered first and foremost as the future mothers of the white race, who must be "entrusted with bringing forth the next generation of White warriors."[26] At bottom, women are viewed as "naturally" different from men:

> The female is endowed with psychological differences from the male, which are the outcome of physiological differences. The female has a specialized instinct arising out of the human need to protect the young. This is called the "mothering instinct," which is often exemplified by the tender loving care which a woman, especially the White female, bestows upon the young, the frail, the sick and even the ugly whatever species—animal or vegetable.[27]

Dominant ideologies of the naturalness of gender support WCOTC claims to further white purity.

Within the WCOTC, "good mothering" is tightly woven with what it means to be a good white woman. (Here again, as in dominant society, mothering and women are inextricably tied together in calling upon a norm of "essential motherhood" in which women's motherhood is constructed as natural and inevitable.[28]) Turner and other contributors to the WF object to the "feminist" criticism of traditional norms, claiming that far from a trap, motherhood is the essence of womanhood and the basis for securing the future for whites. She dismisses feminism as another "Jewish conspiracy" designed to destroy the white family:

> Now let's talk about what feminism is *not*. Feminism is not and never will be anything remotely connected with the World Church of the Creator or the Women's Frontier. . . . We believe that being a capable nurturing mother to White Children is the ultimate Holy "career" for any White woman and is the most natural role for a woman to fulfill, particularly as the White race faces extinction due to suicidally low birth rates.[29]

(Mothers are subordinated to the broader demands of the battle for white supremacy. This is illustrated when Turner congratulates "Sister Jessica" on "the birth of a new beautiful White baby."[30] In leaving out the word "your" in the announcement, Turner insinuates that "Sister Jessica's" role in furthering the white movement is more important than her role in the family. Reproduction is an obligation of women, according to WCOTC ideology, as it supports the white race.

White racism also helps to resolve for its followers potential paradoxes of reproductive and sexual politics that are currently circulating in our legal and social systems. Abortion politics are one target in which the current social crisis regarding gender and family is reduced to an issue of racial supremacy. The WF position is straightforward: abortion is legitimate and proper only for white women whose fetuses have been diagnosed with genetic malformation. Abortions are condoned only in the interests of creating a pure, healthy, white race:

> There are situations ... when abortion is necessary to insure and protect the health of our Race eugenically. . . . If an unborn White child has been diagnosed using technologies such as ultrasound or amniotic fluid testing to be suffering from a genetic condition, retardation or other serious medical disorder which will bring crippling dysfunction and burden to the child, to the suffering parties, and most important to the White society as a whole, it is far more humane to end such a life rather than permit it to continue. And really it is not a question of "humanity" but of racial purity and integrity.[31]

It is possible to see Turner's writing about abortion as forging alliances with the antiabortion movement. The rhetoric of the WCOTC potentially pulls in women who are otherwise attracted to antichoice politics because of reasons unrelated to race and racism.

> [T]he World Church of the Creator and the racial religion of Creativity is opposed to the murder of healthy White children through abortion, and ... the WCOTC has made a public commitment to speak out for White women on these issues.[32] Our stand is clear: the killing of a healthy White child through abortion is the ultimate sin against our Race and against Nature and any White woman who commits the crime of abortion is a race traitor of the highest order.[33]

In using abortion as a form of eugenics, leaders of WCOTC consciously use dominant medical technologies to serve white supremacist goals. "Never again will we raise a generation of Youth who think any form of 'life' is all that matters—but rather, RACE above all considerations."[34] Ironically, as we see below, leaders of the WCOTC reject the use of medical technologies, medication, and medical treatment in caring for children. This objection to medicalization, however, is suspended in the interests of culling out children with genetic defects, precisely because they represent a threat to the purity of the white race.

A related theme in reproductive politics is the so-called dangers of white women's interracial marriage and children. The focus on the dangers of "race-mixing" has been a recurrent theme in white-supremacist discourse, according to Ferber.[35]

> What must be made perfectly clear to all is that what we are fighting for and why we must fight with every fiber of our being is the simple Natural fact that WOMEN ARE THE VERY CORE OF OUR RACE. It is through women continually giving birth to new life [white Babies] that our future as a Race depends. The fight against contamination of the CORE [white Wombs] is by Nature one of the primary functions of the White Male. The stallions do not allow contamination of the herd by male jackasses. The core of our Race MUST be protected and nurtured at all costs. We have to establish once and for all times WHITE LIVING SPACE for our Women to give birth to White offspring and an environment in which healthy White families can flourish. Where are all the brave White warriors? RAHOWA.[36]

In a reference to the Holocaust, the WFN describes miscegenation as a threat to the future of the white race. Women of WCOTC must show their unity with white men in the movement by not seeking relationships outside their race.

> We have our own NEVER AGAIN will White Gentile women fall into the tragic trap of marrying or breeding with jew demons. That is because the Women's Frontier will never give up exposing them as the enemies of the White Race.[37]

> Women are constantly portrayed as being "race mixers" as well. . . . You have to remember that women not only are more trusting, but they also act and react on emotion.[38]

According to Ferber, it is through the construction of and maintenance of racial boundaries and the demarcation of "whiteness" as a racially pure identity that the white subject is constructed.[39] In believing that they are in a "racial holy war," WCOTC leaders perceive the female body as a site of contest:

> Jews have aimed the awesome and powerful force of their media weaponry squarely at our women like a loaded gun, playing their emotions like finely tuned instruments so that they are almost completely lost to our Race, committing race-mixing, abortion and feminism in massive numbers.[40]

The WF expresses the idea that white women have been trapped into interracial relationships and into mothering of biracial children because they have a "false compassion" for other races, and insinuates that women have been brainwashed by a "Jewish-controlled media" into believing in the importance and dignity of all races of people.

While the politics of reproduction in the WF are straightforward and clear-cut, it is also the case that this has opened up an area of conflict and tension within the movement. Blee's interviews with women in race-hate movements documents their reluctance to comply with norms of reproduction as they are espoused in movement rhetoric. She suggests that women's resistance, especially to high fecundity, may constitute an important contradiction in the long-term resilience and coherence of white-supremacist groups. Nonetheless, part of the continuing appeal of the ideology may be its basis in dominant ideologies of gender and motherhood. In particular, in drawing upon the dominant ideology of gender and motherhood, Turner and others connect white-supremacist activities with traditional and familiar gender norms.

Motherhood as Separatism

> As Proud, White Women, we shall create and build a world in which health, cleanliness, discipline, efficiency, and orderly life is restored and held in highest esteem.[41]

Women's contribution to white supremacy in WCOTC discourse is constructed entirely in gendered terms. It is through women's roles as caretakers of children and households that women are called upon to forge racial segregation. Indeed, women's key role is to maintain segregation between white and nonwhite society. Daily activities such as shopping, cooking, and schooling are interpreted as acts that either support or hinder racial pride. Women's caretaking and reproductive acts in the private sphere are the foundation for the transmission of white supremacy into the dominant culture.

As in the extremist movement in general, separatism is a key component of the racist discourse on motherhood. Indeed, motherhood is constructed as a set of practices that ideally forge symbolic and physical boundaries around households. "Race-mixing" of any kind is presented as a threat to the purity of the white household, and it is a mother's duty to make sure that her children have no contact with people from nonwhite races. It is the duty of "woman" as "mother" not only to procreate the next generation but to ensure that outside influences do not counteract the fundamentals they are teaching about race and society within their homes. In order to keep outside influences out of their homes, good mothers must maintain control within their homes. In doing so, good mothers perform all child care duties themselves and keep their children in the home through home schooling. Since women transmit culture through the informal education of children, the influence of the domestic sphere touches all parts of life, and white supremacy discourse has been brought into the homes, churches, and schools of many Americans.

While this research cannot document how women transmit these values in everyday practice or the extent to which children adopt these values, it can point to pressure points around which activist racist mothering is organized. We turn now to examine in more detail the ideals of white separatism that motherhood is supposed to exemplify.

Domestic Chores

Turner explains that "good mothers" should perform all their own domestic chores. White women should feel proud and confident in the realm of the domestic, especially in their roles as mothers. Women are responsible for cleaning, cooking, laundry, and other daily chores.[42] Turner writes extensively on the sense of accomplishment that women of the WCOTC should feel when doing household chores themselves:

> When we women take care of our household tasks, we must respect the intrinsic value of this work. It is not demeaning. Done properly, it results in a beautiful, clean, inviting, peaceful environment for our families, our husbands, and our children.... For women, this is an extremely important concept, because we must again celebrate there is nothing demeaning about domestic chores and domestic accord. We regard such work a noble pursuit.[43]

We view the value given domestic work in WF discourse as delineating a path for womanhood that is very much at issue in today's cultural politics regarding gender. By giving domestic chores intrinsic value, questions about the relative values of "work" versus "family" are resolved. At the same time, the discourse on the importance of motherhood curtails the social connections women can make; by placing overriding value on the cultural importance of mothers' practices, the mother becomes the gatekeeper between the purity of the family and the impurity of the external, racially mixed world.)

In this vein, Turner advises against the hiring of any domestic help, especially the hiring of racial minority women:

> Certainly our Holy commandments extend to the domestic sphere, which clearly prohibit, especially our womenfolk from hiring muds to clean our home or raise our children. Millions of lazy, traitor White women who continue to hire muds instead of doing as Nature intended: take care of their own domestic tasks and responsibilities, including the raising of their own precious White Children! The act of hiring someone else to "do your dirty work" makes you weak, it puts you at the mercy of their hidden resentments and boiling anger and thereby YOU become THEIR slave, not the other way around. I call on all White racially loyal women to publicly denounce all female White traitors who continue to hire labor in the domestic realm of life.... The White women who hire this muck feel no sense of altruism or responsibility toward their White Sisters who are raped are assaulted by their criminal "household staff." Such women are "me

first" all the way and to hell with anyone else. These women are prime examples of what the World Church of the Creator fights against everyday—those who behave like racial islands unto themselves and they think they can do whatever they want, with no consequence.[44]

[E]ven the hiring of White "au pair" girls from Europe should be discouraged among our women.... To separate oneself from the domestic chores of one's home is to distance oneself from the very substance of that home.[45]

Fathers are never mentioned in child care, and the hiring of nannies is highly discouraged. Outside influence is the threat when hiring outside help, and in allowing it these women would be contributing to the economic well-being of another race.

Feeding

Certain feeding and cooking practices are also markers of the good, white separatist mother. "Salubrious living" is a holistic lifestyle program developed by Ben Klassen. He espoused a recipe for creating a "sound body" which is in turn tied to maintaining a racially pure home. He advocates a lifestyle that promotes clean fresh air, clean water, sunshine, and outdoor activity. He also believes in the importance of "some form of strenuous physical exercise several times a week."[46] The salubrious living lifestyle includes eating only fresh raw fruits and vegetables. Klassen believes that medicine, vitamins, and processed food (including meat) create cancer inside the body and that the body can heal itself by eating the right foods: "This means eating fresh wholesome food in its natural state as Nature has given it to us. It must be uncooked, unprocessed, unpreserved and not tampered with in any other way. This further means it must be organically grown without the use of chemicals."[47]

What we find striking about Klassen's ideals of healthy living is that they parallel the movement of many middle-class Americans to "return to nature."[48] Indeed, many people in the United States and globally express similar ideals about food; concerns about health and nutrition are not the exclusive concern of white separatist groups. As in abortion politics and work/family conflict, the tensions surrounding healthy lifestyles is employed by racist leaders to promote racist practices:

Many people ask if being Salubrious and adhering to the raw food diet is a requirement for joining the WCOTC. No, it is not. We simply recommend it as the best way to stay healthy and eliminate the terrible and totally preventable diseases afflicting our people today such as cancer, heart disease, high blood pressure, arthritis and other maladies due to eating cooked, processed foods and the "junk" that passes for nutrition in the billion dollar jew food industry today. Our founder Ben Klassen knew that being a true White fighter is an overall way of life, and that includes our People's health and vitality. Salubrious living creates opportunities for creating purity inside the home.[49]

When women are free from the "drudgery of cooking" they will have more time to spend on activities that really matter, such as education on white separatist issues. Below is an example of how the WF "sells" the idea of eating a raw-food diet:

[W]e encourage our Folk to learn and understand Nature's way—raw food diet. . . . [A]nd since the raw food diet eliminates cooking, our women folk are truly "liberated" in the most positive sense of the word from being "chained to the stove" and can spend more time with their families, or working for our beloved pro-White Struggle, instead of spending countless hours in the kitchen.[50]

While women of the WCOTC are ideally freed from cooking, they are nonetheless responsible for feeding and other related duties associated with child care. On the WF Web site, Turner recommends an outside Web site concerning this issue:

[A]lso at the raw food web-site are several books written by women on topics including natural childbirth, natural conception, increased vitality for women, and personal testimony from women who are enthusiastic converts to the raw food diet. (Note: this is not a "political" website, it is strictly devoted to issues related to diet and health).[51]

In recommending the raw-food site, Turner is connecting white-supremacist women to an expanding movement toward organic production of foods and natural mothering. In suggesting this site, which is not connected to white-supremacist groups, Turner implicitly suggests to her readers that they may not be as radically far from others' views of mothering as they initially might have thought. Indeed, she attempts to build bridges among otherwise isolated mothers.

Home Schooling

The WF Web site and newsletter also advocate home-schooling children in the movement. The curriculum of home schooling is derived in opposition to the "liberal and multicultural" tendencies of contemporary schools. Turner references Klassen in her statement:

As Ben Klassen said, if all other White countries taught their children an excellent Latin from early childhood as a second language, then the White Man could have a universal language he could converse, no matter which country traveled.[52] Now-a-days many racialists are seeking alternative ways to educate their children. This underlying motivation is the conviction that the public schools have metamorphasized into liberal and multi-cultural cesspools of degeneracy. They are concerned for the racial training and character development as well as the physical and academic welfare of their children. It wasn't so long ago that one-room schoolhouses were the norm. Aside from protecting your children from the destructive influences being peddled in public schools, home-schooling provides the parents with quality time available to train and influence their child in areas they consider important.[53]

The goals of separatism animate the advocacy for home schooling; mothers must protect their children from the dangerous influences of the external world and must themselves be insulated from the destructive influences of alternative views. Indeed, the material presented through the WF is seen as material for the education of children:

The ideas expressed in this publication could very well be the first layer of groundwork for a future when White Parents will have all the tools to educate their children at home.... Therefore, we could cease dealings with the jews for these items.... If we had these items we wouldn't have to buy mainstream books, toys, cartoons, etc. from the jews.[54]

These advocates of racist home-schooling use a language of self-esteem and psychological health adapted from mainstream theories of childhood:

Do you want [children] to learn to become one of those self-hating whites? I certainly don't want my children learning these things.... We need them to know that slavery was one of the biggest mistakes the White Race ever made. If the slaves were never brought here we wouldn't have the problems we face today.[55]

Part of the task of being an acceptable mother is to identify and connect to other racially conscious women and organizations and to build networks in which information can be shared and exchanged:

We are pleased to announce that Sister Melody La Rue of our WCOTC Sisterhood Chapter is working with Sigrdrifa South to help sponsor an excellent on-line home-schooling e-zine, with contributions from other dedicated women in the racialist community. They recently put out their first issue which is filled with resources and information for partners and other who want to know more about home-schooling.[56]

Discussion: Normalizing Racism

We reached two main conclusions while examining the discourse of the WCOTC. First, we found that women in the movement are constructed wholly as mothers and that mothering practices are central components in the creation of white separatism and supremacy. Second, we have argued that racist rhetoric is normalized through its association with mothering. Through the discourse of motherhood—reproductive politics, care work, and educating the young—racism is contextualized as a feature of everyday mothering. In tapping into wider cultural anxieties and tensions around child rearing and motherhood, the WF provides simple but dangerous answers. Its rhetoric of the pure white home and pure white motherhood borrows many features of "intensive motherhood" that Hays has forcefully argued is the dominant model for mothering today.[57] We want to suggest that this normalization is what makes WCOTC rhetoric so dangerous: it builds on conventional and time-tested notions of "family" and "mother."

We also want to suggest that the danger lies in the very thin line that separates the ideology of white separatism from that of mainstream society. The racism embedded in the quotidian can be more influential and damaging than activities that we recognize as blatant discrimination and racism, such as parades, conventions, and protests.

Conclusion

When we began this research in 1999, finding information on or by white-supremacist women on the Web was almost impossible. The WF was one of three Web sites that existed on the subject; two of these three were designed and maintained by women of the WCOTC. There are now over twelve sites that are dedicated to white-supremacist or separatist women. Since this research began, the WF has disappeared, but in its place is a Web site called Women for Aryan Unity. Women for Aryan Unity is an organization run by Aryan women who have chosen to support the advancement of culture and the white race.[58] Women for Aryan Unity was founded more than twelve years ago and has chapters of sisters through out the world.[59] They are combination of Blood and Honour—The Hammerskin Nation and The World Church of the Creator.[60]

Although the Women's Frontier no longer exists, it could be argued that the revised Web site that the WCOTC is participating in is better suited to its goals. By forging alliances with other white separatist women, the WCOTC is combing economic resources and is creating cohesion among different white separatist groups. This collaboration can be seen as the formation of a united white separatist front. Is it true that women are the future of white-supremacist movements, as Turner argues? Does the development of women's Web sites and organizations indicate a new, more autonomous role for women in the movement? We believe that Blee is correct in asserting that the contradictions between women's race privilege and ambition and their secondary status in the movement potentially weakens women's long-term participation.

We have been interested in this paper in exploring how the ideology of white racism might appeal to women precisely because it taps into cultural contests about gender and family that are circulating in dominant culture. The place of feminism, the status of abortion, and the balance of career and domesticity are dominant social concerns that the WTOTC has used to construct a place for women in the movement. Since the September 11 attacks, we are even more concerned that a spirit of nationalism will further fuel white-extremist movements and that deep cultural crises of national identity will be resolved through a gendered sense of nationalist identity.

5

The White Separatist Movement: Worldviews on Gender, Feminism, Nature, and Change

BETTY A. DOBRATZ
STEPHANIE L. SHANKS-MEILE

In this chapter,[1] we focus on how white separatist movement participants view gender, feminism, nature, and the various social changes that challenge their arguments about race and gender. Indeed the various branches of white separatists are responding to societal changes promoting racial and gender equality that have especially occurred since the civil rights movement of the 1960s. Their desire for separatism grew out of their continuing frustrations with what they believe is growing discrimination against whites (e.g., reverse discrimination from affirmative action), increasing race-mixing that pollutes their racial heritage and identity, and growing threats to the family and to the masculinity of white men. This chapter provides a detailed, nuanced examination of white separatist views of gender, arguing that their views are complex and varied.

A key issue those who study gender consider is whether women and men are generally "alike and equal in all important respects" or whether they "are essentially unlike each other."[2] This debate often revolves around an essentialism versus social constructionist perspective on gender differences. Essentialism proposes that men and women are basically different, assuming fixed differences between them.[3] The social construction of gender refers to the processes by which the expectations associated with being male or female are passed on through society by ongoing interaction with others and meanings are formed through political, scientific, legal, and social practices.[4] Those in the white separatist movement typically strongly believe that men and women are basically different. Abby Ferber asserts: "While white supremacist discourse adamantly supports the notion that race is a biological and/or God-given essence . . . the discourse reveals the social construction of that essence."[5] She also recognizes that movement participants feel the white race is "under attack."[6] We feel it is important to link these two findings because, as Karen Rosenblum and Toni-Michelle Travis suggest: "It is understandable that those under attack would find essentialist orientations appealing."[7] Further, Margaret Andersen recognizes that "biological explanations of gender patterns in society have a deep hold in people's thinking," while for sociologists the process of social construction "pervades society."[8]

Diana Fuss argues that essentialism can be used effectively in either progressive or reactionary causes and claims "that constructionism (the position that differences are constructed, not innate) really operates as a more sophisticated form of essentialism."[9] Further "Constructionism may be more normative, and essentialism more variable" than often recognized.[10] Michael Messner studied various men's movements and for certain ones identified some differences in their "essentialist retreats." For example, mythopoetics espoused a "'loose' gender essentialism that has a belief in individual agency and flexibility in the shaping of gender" while Promise Keepers had more fixed and categorical views "on a leading edge of an antifeminist reassertion of essentialist views of male and female differences."[11] Catriona Sandilands, in her research on the rural lesbian-separatist communities, found that while lesbian separatism was rooted in essentialist constructions of nature and gender, not all the strategies used are essentialist. She argues that lesbian separatists deploy elements of essentialism in strategic and often uneven ways.[12] They also develop communities that enable them to withdraw from patriarchal influence of men and try to initiate an alternative transformative ecological and feminist culture. We argue that white separatists also draw upon essentialist arguments in similarly uneven ways and develop alternative realities as well.

Social scientists have at times oversimplified the ideology of those labeled as belonging to the right or the left and have failed to recognize adequately the tremendous variation among social movement activists. Drawing on Susan Marshall and Kathleen Blee, Verta Taylor, Nancy Whittier, and Cynthia Pelak suggest that the scholarly portrayal of antifeminist women as victims of false consciousness or as women who are passively expressing their husbands' interests may be overly simplistic interpretations.[13]

For example, Sally Gallagher and Christian Smith studied contemporary evangelical Christians and their perceptions of gender and family. Unlike fundamentalists, who favor separation from the modern world, evangelicals "advocate a greater connection to modernity while simultaneously maintaining a clear sense of religious identity."[14] The authors studied the changing meanings of "men's headship" in America, where society has been experiencing major economic and social changes. They examined the degree to which "feminist ideals and practices are broadly diffused throughout evangelicalism."[15] While symbolically men's headship, or leadership, was prominently recognized in discussions about decision-making, as was men's ultimate responsibility for the family in both material and spiritual senses (symbolic traditionalism), the actual practice of gender was much more egalitarian concerning women's employment, mutual respect, and joint decision-making (pragmatic egalitarianism). The large majority of the 265 evangelicals interviewed combined elements of both traditionalism and egalitarianism. Gallagher and Smith concluded that: "Rather than being profoundly influenced by feminism, the pragmatic egalitarianism of contemporary evangelicals appears to derive more from their own life experiences in a postindustrial economy."[16] We will examine how white separatists also utilize strategies of pragmatic egalitarianism.

Somewhat similarly, Judith Stacey studied two kin networks of working-class people in Silicon Valley, Santa Clara County, California in the postindustrial 1980s. She also found that the everyday life experiences of the individuals in these networks led to diverse forms of postfeminism being implemented, some of which were progressive, and some, reactionary. She described these versions as representative of "women's attempts to both retain and depoliticize the egalitarian family and work ideals of the second wave [of feminism]."[17]

Floyd Cochran and Loretta Ross found diverse images of women in the white-separatist movement, some of which challenge "the stereotypical image of wives in their husbands' arms." Many of the new recruits are "college educated, very sophisticated, and bring skills that only the most intellectual of the white supremacists previously displayed."[18] Ferber argued that the "central project of the contemporary white supremacist movement is the articulation of a white male identity."[19] Blee suggested that "the study of organized racism is deeply, but invisibly, gendered."[20] She argued that the lack of attention to women may distort our understanding of the movement. While women are seldom in positions of power in the movement, she recognized that some movement groups "espouse a more gender-inclusive organizational ideology" than others.[21]

Recent scholarship on feminist and antifeminist or conservative groups suggest that various belief systems about gender are socially constructed. Participants in such groups or movements use various gender strategies. For example, they make essentialist and traditionalist arguments, employ pragmatic egalitarian practices, and offer transformative alternatives that could radically change society and gendered relationships if they were implemented. Recent work on white separatist groups also suggest that the gendered relationships in the white separatist movement may be more nuanced than originally believed. We argue in this chapter that men and women in the white separatist movement draw upon a variety of essentialist and pragmatic egalitarian approaches and construct alternative visions of white separatist society. They are responding to a variety of social changes, many of which they see as detrimental to the family and the traditional system of gender relationships. Within the white separatist movement there are also significant differences among individuals and groups in how they respond to the challenges facing traditional notions of gender. At times they accommodate to the changes but more often they resist and offer their alternative patriarchal and racial realities for the future.

Methodology

Joel Charon points out that researchers need to understand "what the actors themselves believe about their world" and "try to reconstruct their reality."[22] Herbert Blumer makes clear the importance of doing this: "The contention that people act on the basis of the meaning of their objects has profound methodological implications. It signifies immediately that if the scholar wishes to understand the action of people, it is necessary to see their objects as they see them . . . not on the basis of the meaning that these things have for the outside scholar."[23]

In order to understand white separatist realities, we collected our own data as well as considered secondary source material. When we could not interview white separatists face-to-face, we conducted phone interviews or sent questionnaires. All instruments asked similar basic questions about a variety of aspects of the movement including gendered relationships, but interviews allowed for more probing of answers. Altogether 188 white separatists were interviewed or filled out questionnaires. Of these, 48 were female, 139 male, and one was anonymous, with no indication of his or her sex.[24]

Data Results

Respondents provided diverse answers when asked if the movement was sexist and to define the roles men and women played in the movement. Matt Hale, then the leader of the National Socialist White Americans Party and now the leader of the World Church of the Creator, stressed that women are part of the movement and not discriminated against. He argued that natural differences lead to some differentiation in roles:

> As far as sexist goes, we're certainly not sexist . . . we can testify to that in the fact that we have a number of female members and they are treated quite well. There is no chauvinism of any kind. We basically believe in nature and natural law and natural society. We don't believe that a man can make a better mother than a woman. And nor do we believe that a woman makes as good a breadwinner in many cases as a man. It's just simply the way that life is, but we're not against women by any means and nor would we discriminate against them.

Within the movement Matt Hale recognized natural differences in the roles of men and women, especially in identifying the females as mothers and males as breadwinners. Still, when discussing the breadwinner role, he adds the qualifier "in many cases." Hale also recognizes that bringing women into the movement is an excellent recruiting tool:

> The role of women in the movement is very similar to the role of the men in the movement—to propagate the white racial cause . . . having women in the movement makes it easier to actually bring men into the movement in a lot of ways because a lot of men will not do things that their wives or their spouses or whatever vehemently disagree with. So we try to get women in the movement, you know, and we try to bring their men in the movement.

David Dalby, a member of the Army of Israel, an Identity skinhead group, asked his girlfriend (later his wife) to comment about "sexism" in the movement. Amy wrote:

> I do not believe the movement is sexist. Women were blessed with the ability to have babies, and with the instincts to raise and nurture our children. Men have the instincts to protect their families. They make sure we have food on our tables and roofs over our heads. It is a shame that in today's society both parents have to work. As a result, our children are growing up with no family life and little moral structure.

For her, as for others in the movement, the socioeconomic system plays a part in shaping family relations, for when both parents have to work, children suffer. For both Matt Hale and Amy, the movement is not sexist because it is simply following natural gender roles.

John C. Sigler III, a.k.a. "Duck" of the Confederate Hammer Skinheads, recognized the childbearing function for women but also emphasized women's importance in sustaining the white man and keeping him sane:

> Women represent our future as well as the lighter side of life. Without women the race dies and man is in misery. Sexism be damned. . . . Women have proven themselves capable of playing any role in the movement they desire. However women preserve our continuity as well as the sentimental side of humanity

which can be easily overlooked once one joins a sacred crusade to preserve our genetic heritage. Women preserve our sanity while motivating us to continue our crusade.

For Sigler, appropriate white women fulfill their expressive, nurturing role in helping men stay sane and fulfill their role as mothers, thus saving the white race.

Thus far respondents stressed natural differences between men and women, women's expressive roles, and their roles in the family. Others, however, emphasized women's active role in the movement. Kim Alleyn Badynski, Regional Organizer of the Knights of the Ku Klux Klan (KKKK) and a "Seed Line" Christian Identity racial separatist, stressed how active women were in the KKKK:

> The Knights has included women in leadership roles, such as the office manager of our National Headquarters. I was even "Naturalized" (sworn in) by a female Klan leader. . . . The Knights of the Ku Klux Klan affords women the same potential for leadership as men have. Gone are the days of the Women's Auxiliary groups. Today women are active along with the men in meetings, in the Klan office and in public activities.

Badynski clearly recognizes that gender relationships are changing and he believes the KKKK are changing with the times because women are assuming more powerful roles in the Klan.

Generally, our respondents tend to believe that women are not discriminated against or treated unfairly, even though they often occupy different roles from men. In a much less typical response, Mary S. (Molly) Gill, who publishes a movement publication entitled *The Rational Feminist*, believes that the movement is sexist but finds this acceptable. However, like the previous respondent, she recognizes that ideas about gender in the broader culture have been changing, and she believes the movement is starting to reflect that. In her questionnaire she wrote:

> Yes [in response to sexist]; the Movement is dominated by men and should be. . . . Women do whatever needs to be done at any given time: support & nurturing; activism; fighting; running defense funds; family asst. projects; publishing. Cooking, serving, child care, teaching; leading, writing. . . . Women are assuming more exec. positions and being asked to. Aryan women are scarce and not answering men's pen friend ads because the men are abusive and too macho. In this world macho doesn't cut it, not to the extent they got away with it previously.

While women were not at the top of the power structure, women were certainly active in shaping their own lives and the movement. Matt V. belonged to no formal organization but found Odinism (a form of neopaganism) appealing and, like Gill, responded in an atypical manner. He did not see the movement in general as being sexist but did characterize the role of women in the movement as "somewhat subservient. They're not really equal partners yet. [In] The whole movement women play a very minute part." Both Matt's and Molly Gill's responses introduce issues that exist both in the movement and society in general.

Like Gallagher's and Smith's evangelicals, white separatists display signs of pragmatic egalitarianism, especially in their acceptance of women working in the paid labor force.[25] Economic hardships and the need for more than one family income have resulted in greater acceptance of women's employment. Another illustration of pragmatic egalitarianism is that movement leaders want to attract a strong base of supporters to save the white race, so they attempt to recruit vital, active women.

We will now explore in greater depth the experiences of four couples in the movement. These couples were selected because they are relatively well known in the movement and help to illustrate both the similarities and diversity within the white separatist movement.

Michael and Linda Storm

Along with Gerhard Lauck, Michael Storm plays an important role in the international National Socialist organization Nationalsozialistische Deutsche Arbeiterpartei Auslands- und Aufbauorganisation (NSDAP-AO). Michael Storm sees himself as an orthodox National Socialist, meaning that the core values of Hitler's National Socialism would be appropriate today, although not all the same policies and practices should be implemented.[26] He remembers being attracted to National Socialism early in life and putting swastikas on his tennis shoes at the age of twelve.

Michael Storm commented on the worldview of National Socialism and its primary ingredient of race: "a component part of National Socialism is that we view all of life, history, everything from a racial perspective. . . . That race is what made us what we are today. . . . Race is what makes the Jews what they are today and you cannot talk someone out of their genetic behavior." The slogan "For race, family, and nation" characterizes National Socialist ideology, suggesting that race and family are inextricably linked.

At the time of our first interview with Michael (1994), he pointed out that his wife was three quarters of the way to earning her Mother's Cross, an award given to women in Nazi Germany for having four children. She has now more than earned the Mother's Cross; the Storms have seven children. Linda Storm became involved in the movement through her marriage to Michael. Both of them are Christian.

Michael Storm believes the movement is racist and sexist, but he explains that women would be better off in a National Socialist society than they are in the United States. As Michael Storm constructs it, the National Socialist society is a healthy, natural society, where men and women know their roles:

> We believe that men and women have special sexual roles and that neither can substitute fully for the other. And through National Socialism, a woman's status is much more highly elevated than here in America where she is just an economic asset, a second income to the husband . . . raising children is the most natural function . . . of the family . . . all the drive in all species is to procreate [inaudible] and pass on. . . . And we believe that women, because of their unique role in creating and supporting the family, they have a status far superior to the nonsense of going out and getting a job and being an executive and having equality with men and making money. . . . I think that's far superior than being a mere income. I mean, that's a biological function for God's sake. But income? That's like getting a Social Security check and your pension check, you know? Big deal. . . . But women have been brainwashed in America that the ultimate goal in the society is to gain equality . . . the feminist movement which is all Jewish lesbians leading it—to get women to think that that's what they want . . . having to ship your children off and have strangers raise them is the most damaging and damning of all things that could happen in this country.

Michael believes in the biological basis of one's identity and is clearly upset by the changes in the family and gendered relations that are occurring as societal reforms press for greater equality. To him the feminist movement in particular has manipulated women to advocate for equality rather than respect natural gender differences and to have their children raised in day care centers that negatively affect their socialization. His view of the feminist movement as controlled by Jewish lesbians is consistent with statements from white separatist movement women.[27] Ferber argues that an "equality versus difference opposition . . . grounds white supremacist logic."[28] In other words, white separatists believe that men's and women's roles are different and rooted in nature, and those arguing for equality are pictured as trying to make women the same as men.

Linda Storm points out that National Socialism is about having a strong family, which she believes requires separate roles. She is critical of the socialization process and the mass media in capitalist American society for failing to reaffirm natural differences. In reaction to our query about whether the movement is sexist, she explained her view about distinct sex roles:

> You're taught that somehow that's wrong or that's bad. I think there's great security in that. I think it's important that everybody has their place. I think you're stronger that way. My husband can't bear children, but that doesn't make him any worse than me. We just have different roles to fulfill . . . the mainstream media again says that somehow that's horrible and wrong and bad. But I think that's actually a strength. When I'm not trying to fill his shoes and he's not trying

to fill mine, we're not fighting with each other. We're not having conflict with each other. We can support each other, and that makes a stronger bond and a stronger family.

For Linda Storm, the different gender roles provide various benefits. She finds security and strength in having well-defined gender roles and believes this results in much less conflict in the family and the development of stronger family solidarity. The Storms believe that the media and other institutions are trying to brainwash people to support equality and accept the same gender roles in society. They reject the feminist movement and the media's interpretations and believe Linda Storm should be home with the children, including home schooling them. She commented: "I think it's Mom's job to create a safe and pleasant environment for Dad to come home to. A safe place for kids to learn and be in and play in."

Linda also criticized the capitalist system that pressures women to work to provide family income and reiterated the importance of mothers caring for their children and fathers providing for the family. She argued that when the husband is the sole provider, this likely enhances his image:

> Children are a blessing from God. And I don't think they're something to be wasted and flushed down a sink. People have a tendency to think about what they can't do. . . . We can't have a baby now because we can't afford it. Can't have Mom home, because we can't afford it. It's too hard. I come up with all the excuses and while it's true—all those things are very hard to do—but when you make a decision . . . to do what's right by your family—then you find the ways to take care of those problems whatever they are. . . . We're there to support our husbands and I think the husband's role is to provide for the family. I think the Bible says that. And when the wife goes out to work, I think what she's really telling her husband is—I don't have the faith and belief in you to be able to provide for this family. And I think that takes away a lot from the men . . . where they [husbands and wives] have sacrificed . . . and made the cutbacks where they needed to—to have Mom with the kids and Dad's gone out there and done whatever he's had to do—two jobs, three jobs, whatever—to provide for the family. I think the family looks at him more highly. . . . I think that's when a man really finds out what it means to be a man too.

Linda Storm's comments may reflect a belief that contemporary changes in gender expectation are threatening men's masculinity. Family members and the man himself may believe that his being sole breadwinner and possibly working several jobs enhances his masculinity. For Linda Storm, properly filling gender roles is key to how both men and women see each other and perceive themselves as they live their lives. She also makes reference to God and the Bible to help support her views about different roles, especially that men are the providers.

Michael Storm commented further on what he saw in National Socialist Germany that would make it more likely to foster strong healthy societies and help solve economic stresses:

> National Socialism only had six years of peace ... to try and develop ... how that would have developed over time is totally open to speculation ... young people ... would be steered to and geared towards and educated ... to raise a happy, healthy family. ... In Nazi Germany a newly married family would get a loan to buy a house and furnish it and everything. Then they would pay back that loan, deducted from their wages like one percent interest—half percent interest—something like that—and then every child they bore would reduce the debt load, I believe, by somewhere between ten and twenty-five percent. ... The economics were therefore taken out. ... You started out right away with your home which reduced a lot of the stress so you could raise your kids without getting frustrated and upset about the money and the ... divorce rate goes down—the child abuse is going to go down—I mean, you could just see where it's going to end—where it would go. And for women, what I would see—because raising our children is a national asset, not a liability—that they should be compensated for that ... if you were a man and you had children, your wages were paid accordingly. You and I have the same job as men—it has to be as men—as head of our households—I've got six kids, you have none—I make a lot more money than you do because I've got six kids to support and that's what the money would go for.

Michael, too, is responding to contemporary social problems such as declining economic status, high costs of raising a family, high divorce rates, and abuse of children. The government's educational and financial policies facilitate the return to natural gender roles. The importance of Aryan children is emphasized, and even the number of children in a family is tied directly to the income of the breadwinner in Michael Storm's ideal society. Capitalism promoting select economic interests would be rejected. Michael maintained that the United States could adopt such a policy or practice to try to foster happy, healthy families, but he was not optimistic that the United States would change.

We also asked him whether women could be leaders under National Socialism. He used Germany again as his example:

> I don't see any reason why not. Hitler talks about how in the darkest days of the movement, it was the women who pulled it through and saved the movement. The men were scattered off. Most of them were in jail after the putsch. ... Now, in Germany of course at that time, they weren't allowed in political office ... yet Leni Riefenstahl had leadership when she did all the movies—you know—*Triumph of the Will*, and Hannah Reitsch was the world-famous test pilot. Now we had no one in America and we still don't to this day have anyone in America doing that and yet in male, sexist, Nazi Germany they had those women doing that.

Michael Storm also talked about the role of women in the movement. He noted that when he was a young storm trooper there were no women in the movement and most men would be around for a few weeks and then disappear for a few months. He felt that "if we had women involved, you'd see more consistency." He indicated that when women, young children, and families participate in the movement, it "gives tremendous stability." Women are thus viewed as more predictable and help bring balance and order to the family and to the movement. He continued describing his desire for "longevity" in the movement and how possible biological or genetic traits might distinguish men from women:

> Men come and go. They're short term. Women are long term. The woman stays. If she's in the movement, she's anchored in the movement. Her friends are in the movement. And the husband, he gets all hot and bothered about the movement for a while, gets excited and stuff, and then you know, wants [inaudible] to go fishing or watch the ball games or something. But the woman will stay. And then she'll be their reminder . . . and then he'll come back to the movement. . . . You can only do so much of something for a time. I just feel that women are . . . more suited; I guess it's biological, genetically—they're more suited for raising children than men are—in the direct care role. I play with my kids all the time. I love them. But they get on my nerves a lot faster than they get on my wife's nerves.

Michael believes that it is probably women's nature that makes them better equipped to socialize children and to facilitate continuity within the movement.

Linda Storm believes that filling her role as mother places her at the core of the family. It provides a test of her abilities, and when that role is properly filled, the family is much better off:

> I didn't have my kids to have the state raise them in a day care center or the public school system. My children are entrusted to me from God and it's my obligation to do right by them . . . when it comes time to meet your maker sort of thing and you're standing there and he says—OK, we're going to look back on your life now . . . what is it you're going to be proud of? Your job? Your career? I mean, I think there's a time for that. If your kids are grown and they're out of the house and then you want to go into other interests and things that you have gifts in—absolutely. But I think things have their time and their place. And I've seen too many kids that have been hurt . . . by not having Mom and Dad there. And it just pulls families apart and they ended up in the divorce rates and a whole multitude of problems. If Mom's home raising the kids and she's home supporting Dad—then Dad feels better about supporting them. They complement each other. . . . And there's no greater job than being a mom. Certainly has its frustrations. It also gives you a chance to find out what you're made of.

Again Linda Storm is emphasizing how complementary roles result in more harmony within the family. She also points out the importance of home schooling and that children are a gift from God.

The Storms repeatedly discuss different roles for men and women in the family that provide their ideal division of labor. When the Storms and others in the white separatist movement discuss the appropriate roles of husband and wife in the family, their underlying foundation is rooted in their perception of biological differences between males and females. God's word is also mentioned to justify separate gender roles and to stress the importance of children. However, they also recognize that the media, feminism, and the capitalist system all seem to challenge their ideal division of labor and promote a system where both parents work in the paid labor force. Under a National Socialist government though, natural gender roles would be encouraged. The Storms recognize how social and economic forces are threatening their beliefs, but they are unwilling to accept that those changes should strongly impact their everyday lives and how they raise their children. They believe that if mothers stay at home to raise their children, this would help solve many problems in the family and society.

David and Katja Lane

David Lane is regarded as a key intellectual voice of the movement and is renowned for his "14 Words": "We must secure the existence of our people and a future for White children." Although they no longer run 14 Word Press, the Lanes founded it more than seven years ago to, as David suggested, "focus our efforts on the preservation of our kind as stated in the 14 Words."[29] 14 Word Press espouses learning about one's heritage through Wotanism, a form of racial paganism. Since the mid-1980s, David has been serving 190 years in the U.S. federal penitentiary system for his part in the activities of the Silent Brotherhood.

According to Rosemary Guiley's The Encyclopedia of Witches and Witchcraft, neopaganism in general involves "a return to, or a reconstruction of pre-Christian Western nature religions."[30] While most pagans are generally liberal, Norse paganism is more conservative, with the religion being "heavily patriarchal," although "women in Norse Paganism find the Norse goddesses to be strong and assertive."[31] White separatist pagans tend to be viewed as being on the fringes of Norse paganism and may be attracted to this religion because of its "emphasis on blood ties and genetics, the warrior ethic and the Norse symbology."[32] Nicholas Goodrick-Clarke has described Lane's views as "deistic naturalism," maintaining that Lane now embraces a racialist pagan viewpoint that "sees the natural laws of the universe as divine."[33] For David Lane, religions like Christianity share their gods with other races, which destroys their uniqueness, but "Wotan [Will of the Aryan Nation] awakens our racial soul and genetic memory."[34]

David expressed his respect for Katja, describing her as follows:

> While incarcerated the Norns [the three goddesses representing the past, present, and future in Norse mythology] saw fit to send my treasure, Katja, back into my life along with five beautiful children. Blessed with many talents, including computer expertise and the ability to converse in numerous languages of our folk, makes Katja the focal point in spreading the 14 Words around the world. . . . Somehow she manages to support and home-school a houseful of children, run 14 Word Press, fight legal battles with ZOG [Zionist Occupied Government] and stay sane.[35]

Katja is a stabilizing force for the family and also provided the organizational tools to run an important international movement publication. She holds a bachelor's degree in Spanish and Portuguese literature and a master's in economics. When we first saw her, she was speaking fluent French to a skinhead couple from Canada. She is very articulate and certainly does not fit the stereotypical images of white separatist women.

In her preface to David's book *Deceived, Damned & Defiant,* she showed her respect for David's accomplishments, writing: "Always wanting to give my husband's essays the presentation they deserved, I was compelled to undertake the task myself. As a mother of five children, without my husband home to protect us and provide for us, life seemed quite uncertain. I needed David's courage to cope with my own trepidations."[36] In the face of uncertainties, David's bravery and toughness helped sustain Katja even though he was not physically present. She explained their shared purpose: "It has been our intent to lay foundations by which to guide future generations of Aryans and demonstrate the reality of our genetic uniqueness, our unrivalled and glorious legacy—fostering a will to survive!"[37] Their mutual respect for each other provided further support for the relevance of pragmatic egalitarianism.

When asked how he would describe the movement, David called it a white survival movement and stressed how important it was that "the beauty of our women shall not perish from the earth." To him, "a racist is one that is obedient to the first and highest law of nature—the preservation of his own kind." In order to save one's race, David demanded "exclusive White homelands"[38] in both Europe and North America. In our interview, Katja too pointed out the "need to find our own place on this planet . . . it's an absolute requirement if we're going to survive . . . our own nation, our own schools."

For David struggle characterizes the natural world. He identified one of the key issues facing the movement as a battle between the sexes that includes women's desire to feel valued:

> Existence, as we know it, requires polarity and by extrapolation the tension or struggle that results. . . . Be it war, a golf tournament or the Battle of the Sexes, the joy is in the struggle. On a false intellectual level we can speak of the

equilibrium of "peace," but it is sugar-coated deception, whether in the realms of religion, politics, sex or anything else. . . . In a primitive and natural society the strongest or otherwise most successful male captures the most females and the most desirable females. . . . Part of the Battle of the Sexes is a woman's need to be recognized as valuable. In the natural world, that means first of all sex appeal, especially for young women. A woman is in competition with other women. The book "Might is Right" proclaims that women dislike and distrust each other intensely. Women authors have written the same thing. Whether true or not, the competition is real. Men lust for women. Women in turn can meet the competition of other women by sharpening their "weapons of war" or by attempting to "tame" a man. The former is good, the latter she will inevitably try in this unnatural age, to her material benefit but sexual frustration.

A man cherishes what he desires and for which he has labored or struggled to attain. While there are exceptions to most rules, a man does not mistreat that which he cherishes. So a wise woman keeps herself desirable.[39]

For David, a key asset of women is their sexual attractiveness, and women compete with other women for the attention of men. Women, though, should never go against nature to try to control a man.

In his interview, David emphasized the differences between the sexes and how this impacts the movement. He felt many white women were abandoning their roles in promoting the survival of the white race:

I think one of the major problems that's going to have to be faced is this thing on the battle of the sexes. You go to a racist rally and there's fifty, a hundred, two hundred men and there's not—unattached—there's never a single, unattached female. Once in awhile there's a female that belongs to somebody. But it just demonstrates that there are profound differences between the sexes. . . . I've about reached a conclusion that since they're [women] all leaving, white men are just going to have to raise up an army, like it's going on for thousands of years, and take them back. . . . It's a sad commentary, and of course the modern, feminist movement is going to cut my head off for even insinuating that a woman shouldn't have an absolute free choice to leave her race and not have kids and all the different things—but the fact is—the life of the race is in the wombs of the women.

David complained that at rallies there were few single and available women for the men. He seems to view the women there as already possessions of men in the movement. He stresses the struggle and conflict between men and women and the importance of the reproductive role of white women. He disagrees with the feminist movement when he challenges women's freedom of choice and maintains that white men need to control women's bodies. David assumes that sexuality is a "natural drive" rather than one whose expression is shaped by one's culture. His image of natural sexuality is also heterosexual, and he rejects the idea that sex between the races is natural. Without white women giving birth to white children, David knows the race and movement are doomed.

David believes that contemporary white women are self-centered, rather than focusing on what is good for the race, and they fail to recognize the benefits they have accrued from living in a society dominated by whites:

> The modern, white woman simply has no conception—she lives in splendor undreamed by the Queen of England two hundred years ago due to white man's inventions—flush toilets, hot water heaters, central heating, cars, telephones, whatever—and she scoffs and spits in his face and calls him a racist and runs off with colored males.

Further, David Lane argues that white women need to be put in their proper roles, especially as bearers of children for the white race. This quite likely could involve men using force against women. In his novel *KD Rebel*, "many disenfranchised White males" in the United States gained tenuous control of parts of several Western states called the "Kinsland" and formed guerrilla forces called "Kinsland Defenders."[40] These men kidnapped desirable white women from the integrated society surrounding Kinsland and brought them back to be reeducated and become "mates" for the men and to produce white children. Control of women can clearly involve both physical and mental coercion.

According to David, various social forces, especially starting with Christianity, have greatly disrupted the biological harmony, and it will take a struggle to return to the natural world and natural roles for men and women:

> When women become competitors instead of cheerleaders, men cannot feel . . . a reason to provide. They can't feel a reason to protect. . . . When you take those certain natural instincts and you turn them upside down, ah, there's no answer. Boy, we live in a giant insane asylum. Our enemies just took everything—the whole natural world and it began with Christianity way back when—when they started with the sexes and the celibate nuns and priests and the whole idea that salvation is simply a few magic words instead of being earned. They turned us totally insane . . . we got to go back to a natural world somehow.

David sees Christianity as corrupting the "natural" expression of sexuality and lust and imposing its own morality on people. In the natural world men protect their women from harm.

Katja also perceives the importance of nature, natural laws, and Aryan man's natural dominance. In her preface to *Might is Right*, she writes:

> The fact that we might perceive the *ruthless cruelty* of Nature as *chaos* does not change our reality: Man and all his laws are subject to the mercilessly indomitable LAWS OF NATURE. Our racial survival depends on Aryan man rediscovering his Nature-ordained manhood. He must choose between cowardice and courage, between comfort and freedom, between extinction and a future for White children. There is no compromise.[41]

While being interviewed, she reinforced this view when discussing the struggle for survival: "The woman's role is to nurture and reproduce and the male's role is to secure a home and nation. Our role in the movement is dictated by nature." When asked about the importance of women in the movement, Katja replied: "Vitally important. It's as important as the movement itself. It's the wellspring of the passion of the movement. Sexual lust is the mother of battlelust. That the beauty of the White Aryan woman shall not perish from the face of this earth is the reason men are fighting this fight." Hence, while survival of the race may depend on the Aryan man, he is fighting for the Aryan woman, making her significant as well. While Katja's description of women's roles seems very conventional, her own role in the movement certainly has not been. Her work with 14 Word Press provided a significant contribution to the white separatist movement, and this illustrates how complex gender relations are within the movement. While the Lanes espoused essentialist views of gender, their lives also demonstrate pragmatic egalitarianism.

Katja's daughter, Kacy, is also critical of feminism because it has harmed the family. Mothers are no longer raising children properly:

> Back from the very beginning it's been a man's world and I think that one of the biggest problems is that women are trying to make it a woman's world . . . it's the whole women's liberation thing and it really has torn up the family. You know. The mothers . . . say—I'm going to do this and I'm going to do that and they're not rearing children correctly. They're off in day care centers.

Kacy also recognized how times have changed and argues that feminists have demonized natural sex roles and that this is destroying families. She sees her role and that of the women in the movement to "be a mother, a housewife . . . behind every great man is a strong woman. And I believe that when I have that opportunity, I will exploit that to the fullest. . . . I will bear many children for my husband. Be a good, proud, Aryan mother." Kacy also is reaffirming the reproductive role of women and recognizing that it is important for women to be strong and active because such activity facilitates the accomplishments of a noble Aryan man.

The Lanes see the white race as threatened by a variety of forces, including Christianity, government policies, and the women's movement. To preserve the race, they argue, whites should return to their ancestral roots and heritage, which include following distinct gender roles. They also believe that this will help white men to regain their masculinity and bring more women into the movement. While the Storms are Christian, the Lanes embrace Wotanism/Odinism as the best religion of the white race. For David, women should be coerced into fulfilling their roles with limited or perhaps no choice in their reproductive role if they are not acting to benefit the white race. In other words, David would deny women their sexual agency. Sexual lust and power are seen as natural and commonplace elements of a society experiencing great conflict. On the other hand, the Storms' image of women emphasizes complementary roles where women know their place and appreciate their role in both bearing and raising white children. The proper training of children is particularly important. The Storms' image is much more of a harmonious family working together while carrying out different but complementary roles. Kacy Lane's image of her role seems similar to the Storms' as she would willingly act to benefit her husband and the white race by having numerous children.

Pastor August and Karley Kreis

Pastor August B. Kreis III and his wife Karley are associated with Posse Comitatus and Racial Identity or Christian Identity.[42] Pastor Kreis has a long history with the movement, beginning with twelve or thirteen years in the Klan. He became involved with the Posse and Racial Identity in 1988. He currently leads one of the groups using the Aryan Nations title. Karley Kreis initially entered the movement through her skinhead associations. She defines her role in the movement as follows: "to educate our people. Have as many children as I can and raise them just like us. . . . I take care of my children and the house." She explained how busy she was filling these roles, especially since her two-and-a-half-year-old daughter at the time of the interview almost never took a nap and woke up very early in the mornings.

Pastor Kreis explains some of his Racial Identity beliefs:

> We are God's chosen people—the white, non-Jew race. I do believe that with all my heart. . . . We believe the North American continent was promised to us as a promised land to the sons and daughters of Abraham through Jacob Israel. So, I believe that this is our country. This is our land. And I believe that the coming together of all the tribes happened here—is happening here. But, right from the beginning we were not supposed to bring nonwhites here. And we were supposed to wipe out all the nonwhites—Native Americans.

Pastor Kreis stressed the importance of the survival of his or of Yahweh's (God's) race. We asked him whether the movement was sexist. Karley heard him comment "sexist?" and he continued:

> Are we sexist? My wife said—we better not be. She's my partner. You know. I mean, we both feel—the woman has less word—the man has the last word— that's what she's saying because we believe that man answers to God and woman answers to man—only if the man is answering to God though . . . that's not done to put the woman down or anything. . . . That doesn't mean that we don't sit down and discuss, you know, which way we should go and what we should do or anything—but the man has the last say—providing that he's godly.

In Karley's interview about a week later, she supported his position: "I was there when you asked this question [about sexism] too. No, I don't think it is. The men have the last say, but we're a family and we discuss things. . . . That's fine. That's the way it should be."

This exemplifies Gallagher's and Smith's previously mentioned idea of joint decision-making in the family that illustrates pragmatic egalitarianism. Such decision-making is not perceived as "being in conflict with the ideology of male headship and men's final authority."[43] Similar to the evangelical women of that study, Karley Kreis symbolically supports male leadership and in exchange receives practical reciprocity in the decision-making and mutual respect. Her deferring to her husband makes her worthy of his respect, and he assumes ultimate responsibility for the family, making him worthy of her respect.[44]

Like the other couples, the Kreises believe women in the movement should be supportive of their husbands. For Karley, men in the movement are "to be head of the household. To follow God. Support their family." While one might think this support means financially providing for the family, Pastor Kreis stated that he was not working in the paid labor force because no one would hire him because of his beliefs: "there's no possible way with as public as I have become to try to get a job." Instead, at the time of the interview, the Kreises were surviving because of food stamps, welfare, and child support he received from his former wife in a previous marriage. Although not employed, he maintained: "I'm going to take care of my family regardless."

Both the Kreises condemned racial intermarriage. Pastor Kreis noted that a typical question often asked him in interviews is what he would do if his daughter married a black. He asserted: "I said—don't even ask me that question. Because my daughter would never think of it. Because of the way I raised her. With the understanding she would never do anything like that." Karley Kreis, too, pointed out the desire for the separation of the races that she teaches their children: "I want all the races, you know, to be separate. I want the blacks back in Africa. I don't want to have to associate with them. . . . I don't want my daughters marrying them." She pointed out that it is important for women to "have their children and to raise them the proper way . . . bringing them up with morals and values." The Kreises have decided to send their five children to public school because they live in an all-white area and the school still seems to promote Christian values. If, however, the school were to teach "Melissa has two mommies, et cetera," they would then home-school them.[45] Both therefore socialize their children to preserve the white race.

Like David Lane, Pastor Kreis discussed the difficulties racialist men faced in finding women who understand the racial truth: we "are looking for good, strong women. Racially motivated women." For him, a strong woman is one who stands up for the white race even though she may be labeled as deviant or a bad mother for socializing her children to be racist and sexist. Women who are not strong engage in race-mixing: "Once a white woman has relations and has a baby with a black man or yellow man or whatever—outside of her own race and has a child—her blood is tainted forever. That's it. She is worthless to our race. She will never make a racially pure, white baby ever again." The value of a woman is therefore especially measured by her ability to bear white children.

Pastor Kreis could be described as a racial warrior proclaiming: "I'm not ashamed of what I believe in and I'm willing to die for my cause." He also discussed the 1992 Ruby Ridge, Idaho, incident where a U.S. marshal and the mother and only son in a white separatist family were killed: "If they ever killed anybody in my family, I would never walk out alive. . . . I have no respect for Randy Weaver that way. They killed his wife because she wore the pants in the family." Kreis was very negative about someone who would not die for the cause and whose wife was allegedly the leader of the family.

The Kreises rely on passages in the Bible such as I Corinthians 11:3 to explain the positions of husband and wife: "But I would have you know that the head of every man is Christ; and the head of the woman is the man; and the head of Christ is God."[46] Messner has pointed out that a group may turn to a "higher authority than the scientific method for its essentialist beliefs . . . to a *biblical essentialism*."[47] Such a view provides "respect" for women as long as they are in their proper places. Further, while biological essentialism can be scientifically questioned, biblical essentialism "is largely impervious to empirical refutation" because it is based on faith.[48] Like others who believe in Christian Identity, the Kreises draw on "biblical essentialism" to support their worldview.

While the Lanes are critical of any form of Christianity and advocate returning to one's ancestral European roots, the Kreises use Christian Identity as a basis for the white race being the chosen race and for men having the final decision-making authority. Linda Storm also made general references to the Bible and to God, using them to stress the importance of children and support the ideas of different yet complementary roles in the family. The couples all point out the importance of women bearing children, but David Lane and Pastor Kreis especially emphasize the reproductive role of women in the movement and are upset with white women who have a sexual relationship with someone of a different race. David particularly is willing to use force to make women bear children for the race. All three couples emphasize the cultural reproduction aspects of women's roles. For example, they are especially concerned that mothers properly educate and socialize their children, including home-schooling if necessary. The Storms especially stress that Linda provide a secure and healthy environment for all family members to thrive. The couples travel somewhat different paths as they build their arguments; some rely more on religion and others more on nature to justify their positions.

Pastor Thom and Muriel Robb

Pastor Thom Robb, a longtime racial activist, publishes *The Torch* newspaper, which contains "good, solid, Biblical Bible teaching, news and views for White Christians."[49] He was involved in the John Birch Society as a junior in high school. He joined the Knights of the Ku Klux Klan (KKKK) in 1979 and is now national director. His wife, Muriel, indicated that she had also been in the movement for a long time. The KKKK has typically been viewed as a rather moderate group within the movement, and some other movement groups have criticized it for trying to mainstream their ideas.[50] Some of the Robbs' views on gender seem less radical and/or perhaps more pragmatic than those of others in the movement.

Their daughter, Rachel Pendergraft, one of the Robbs' three adult children, has served on the Council of the KKKK. When we asked about the role of women in the organization, Pastor Robb pointed out that the Knights have "women Klan members" and "women recruiters. My daughter practically runs our national office. She knows more about what is going on in that office than I do." When we wondered about her chances of becoming imperial wizard, Pastor Robb responded: "She could, I'm going to be fully honest with you." He then drew an analogy to the forces of nature, pointing out one could pass a law forbidding hurricanes, but "that wouldn't change the laws of nature." He continued: "For the most part I believe most women would not want that responsibility. For the most part women don't seek that responsibility and for the most part men are not going to follow a woman in that position. Now you can say that's sexist, wrong, horrible all that stuff—I'm not going to . . . for the most, women prefer being mothers."

In a recent exchange of e-mails, Pastor Robb wanted to make sure that his intent was clear:

> I think what needs to be understood is that throughout society women do not usually take on leadership roles. However, when they do they have a harder time in earning respect than a man does. This is not only unfortunate, it is wrong. We see this in the corporate world by what is often referred to as the glass ceiling. This does not reflect upon a woman's ability, but rather upon society. I think that it has been proven far too many times than is necessary to even give an example that the capability of women is on par with men. I think that people in the Klan and perhaps other groups look upon feminists as whiny, wimpy women who continually see themselves as victims and thus fail to get the respect that men are willing to give to strong, assertive women who understand who they are, have the confidence to dream big dreams and are self-assured in their ability to accomplish such feats. This is precisely the reason the Klan was one of the first national organizations that endorsed women's suffrage.[51]

Pastor Robb's image of women suggests that most women embrace the mothering role while few want to be leaders. This doesn't mean they don't have the ability but, rather, certain societal factors including the feminist movement, which has pictured women as victims, have made it difficult for women to advance. At the same time, though, strong women can gain the respect of men and fill important leadership positions.

In our interview, Pastor Robb also discussed women working in the paid labor force, pointing out that his wife worked in a supervisory position: "So I have nothing against women having a profession." Indeed, he felt:

> Women make better workers. And I'm not just saying that. That is why the feminist movement took women out of the home, put them in the work force, because women make better workers. And I'll tell you why, because we exploit them, we trample over them, easier than men. . . . My wife sees young women come there who have been up all night long taking care of babies that are sick, you know. They got to take them to a baby sitter and the baby's crying when they gotta come there, worn out, exhausted and what happens? He gets mad at [inaudible] because they're five minutes late, you know, because they're worn out, and that's hard.

Pastor Robb blames the feminist movement for manipulating women to participate in the labor force, which results in women with children feeling stressed and needing child care. For Pastor Robb, the current economic system exploits women who "will stay there and will suffer abuse. They'll be trampled on, they'll accept low wages . . . because the women feel they— well what else can I do." Pastor Robb argues that women need to develop self-confidence and be assertive rather than be victims who complain and appear weak. He seems to suggest that individual women, feminism, and the structure may be responsible for there being few women in leadership roles.

Muriel Robb has worked numerous years in the paid labor force and noted the inequities in the workplace. She has experienced discrimination in the workforce.

> I had people for a time, fifteen years ago that were working for me and they were making more than I was, and I was the manager. . . . Or you would have somebody way up top in management and they would ask, "Now do you mind [a new employee] . . . working for a woman boss?" Now, they never asked me when I came: Do you mind working for a man? That's kind of prejudice. . . . I don't believe that you should go out and burn your bra, but it's been a hard fight.

While the Robbs recognize gender inequality, they do not believe feminism provides a viable solution. Pastor Robb commented: "I think the feminist movement has betrayed them because they've told women that being mothers is not good enough . . . you're not good enough unless you're like a man." Like the Storms, he condemns feminism for promulgating the idea that women and men need to be similar in order to be equal. As an alternative to feminism, Muriel Robb sees the Klan as giving opportunity to women as well as men:

> This is one reason I like our Klan. You don't find some of these little splintered Klans dealing with that. They tend to be more macho or more male oriented. And like Rachel . . . she was the first woman that's even been on the national board of a Klan. . . . Thom pushes and so does the whole national board, pushes for women to get into different positions . . . whether it's in the community or whether it's in the Klan or whatever, not because we're women or in spite of the fact that we're women but if you're capable, run for it, try it. A woman shouldn't be afraid of a leadership role, if she's got the ability and the training, and the knowledge. That's how I feel anyway and that's how the Knights feel. . . . Encourage women to take their rightful place.

The Klan, rather than the feminist movement, is seen as a major force in encouraging women to fill leadership roles.

Both Robbs recognize the importance of communication and support in their relationship. Muriel points out:

> I think as a whole we're pretty open minded, at least we'll communicate. . . . I was brought up that way and that's how Thom is and of course I wouldn't have been with him if he wasn't, and he's always encouraged me to be this way and it's just how I feel and I've raised my kids that way. If I hadn't, Rachel wouldn't be out doing what she's doing.

Pastor Robb has provided emotional support for his wife to engage in various activities just as she has for him and their children. She also has contributed support through her work in the paid labor force. Like the Lanes and Kreises, there is a kind of pragmatic egalitarianism in the decision-making process and a mutual respect. Muriel Robb takes pride in their children's decision-making abilities: "They're all independent. I mean they're not just little Thom Robbs or Muriel Robbs. They all have different agendas and different ways of looking at things and different personalities." Nathan Robb, their oldest son, did not see the KKKK or American society as sexist and also drew on his mother's and wife's experiences to support his view:

> I don't think, even in the movement, as far as our organization—definitely not [sexist]. In the movement, I don't think so. Even being conservative, I don't even think there's so much sexism. My mother's been a working woman all my life. My wife is a working woman—has a real good career. We have women in the Klan. Everyone has the same opportunities. . . . I don't think even the country is sexist because we got special rights for women. We can get women loans. If we were sexist, we'd say no.

Unlike the other three couples, Muriel has worked in the paid labor force for numerous years. The Robbs suggest that women who are employed ought to be treated more fairly and equitably in areas such as pay and work conditions. Blee has pointed out that various groups associated with Christian Identity may view women being employed outside the home as part of a Jewish plot,[52] but the Robb family has come to expect Muriel to work as part of their pragmatic egalitarianism. Of the couples and groups, the Robbs and the KKKK seem more moderate and accommodating to the changing times, while David Lane seems the most resistant to racial and gender changes.

Discussion

Typically social movements try to influence society in some way by bringing about social change. In doing so, they engage in the construction of meaning or what Benford and Snow call framing, which "denotes an active, processual phenomenon that implies agency and contention at the level of reality construction."[53] Two of the core framing tasks Benford and Snow identify are diagnostic framing (problem identification) and prognostic framing (solution oriented). We will first discuss how movement members especially blame the rise of feminism and the economic changes associated with capitalism and postindustrialization for the problems they see in gendered relationships. We will then examine how the women especially accept the patriarchal family structure. Both husbands and wives believe America should return to such a family structure to reduce their social problems. Finally, in the accommodation and resistance subsection, we look at pragmatic egalitarianism and consider how the various organizations and/or visions of a white separatist society provide some kind of potential alternative solutions to promote the survival of the white race.

Critique of Feminism and Postindustrialization

All four couples blame certain changing social forces, including the increasing influence of feminism and a declining economy, for the negative changes in gendered relationships. Our respondents especially criticized feminists for disrupting the natural order, promoting divorce, challenging the power of white men, and harming the family. David Lane used the term "programming" to help construct how girls or women end up following feminist expectations:

> From the time she was a toddler she had been programmed by teachers, preachers, TV, radio, magazines, movies, songs and every influence in her life that race-mixing was noble. . . . If young girls are taught that being cheerleaders, wives and mothers is a praise-worthy life, then this is what will make them happy and fulfilled. But if they are programmed to believe such lives are demeaning, and that careers as soldiers, construction workers, police, firemen, lawyers and the like are fulfilling, then they will demand and follow the Feminist agenda.[54]

The Storms also believed that feminists manipulated women to push for equality rather than engaging in complementary roles. Pastor Robb believed that the feminist movement created an image of whining women as victims but also that feminists devalued mothering and pushed many women into the paid labor force. In general white separatists criticize feminists for the decline of the family, the rising divorce rate, women needing to work in the paid labor force, and children being socialized in day-care centers rather than by their mothers.

Some interviewees also identified negative impacts of the changing economy on men and women. Michael and Linda Storm strongly advocated a National Socialist system over the current American capitalist one. The Robbs recognized the exploitation of women in the paid labor force, although one of their sons did not. David Lane expressed his concerns about modern industrialized society, which has promoted equality and racial homogenization, or white racial genocide: "Is the natural way and the upward path even possible in the modern, industrialized world? Self-evidently the natural way and the upward path are impossible within nation-states ruled by those dedicated to the mixing and extermination of the race that created so-called 'Western Civilization.'"[55] In general, white separatist movement members are critical of certain economic changes including the need for women to work, see the exploitative side of capitalism, and challenge the idea of equality (which typically means women being similar to men and doing the same things), vehemently reject that women should (or even could) be like men, and struggle against devaluing of motherhood.

Some feminists have also expressed similar concerns about how certain forms of feminism may have negatively influenced the status of certain women in postindustrial America. Sociologists Taylor, Whittier, and Pelak point out that:

> Liberal feminists ironically provided ideological support through the 1970s and 1980s for the massive transformation in work and family life that was occurring as the United States underwent the transition to a postindustrial order. Some writers even contend that by urging women to enter the workplace and adopt a male orientation, the equal opportunity approach to feminism unwittingly contributed to a host of problems that further disadvantaged women (especially working-class women and women of color), including the rise in divorce rates, the "feminization" of working-class occupations, and the devaluation of motherhood and traditionally female characteristics.[56]

On the other hand, Michael Kimmel has pointed out that feminism has "had enormous implications for American men, because feminism demanded that men change" and "it also empowered women to claim autonomy in their personal lives."[57] Messner, in his analysis of different men's movements, tended to agree; he pointed out: "Like it or not, men today must deal, on some level, with gender as a problematic construct rather than as a natural, taken-for-granted reality."[58] This certainly applies to white separatist men and also women. David Lane's characterizing the world as insane and worrying whether the society will return to nature is an excellent example of one man trying to deal with gender changes, but all the couples recognize certain social and cultural changes that they are not comfortable with. Messner also concluded that men in certain organizations blame or scapegoat women, especially feminists, for problems they experience. Our work illustrates that white separatist women also criticize feminists for changes in the family and workplace. Instead, both white separatist men and women typically devote themselves to a patriarchal family and generally advocate a return to a more patriarchal social structure.

Women and the Patriarchal Structure

Historically, many women have resisted various social changes that are intended to promote greater egalitarian gender relations. Seeking an explanation for such resistance, Lynn Davidman examined two Orthodox Jewish communities to understand why educated women would return to Orthodox Judaism that advocated traditional domestic roles for them. She argues that the women were actively and consciously making their decisions to follow this religious worldview. Those in the Lubavitch community especially resisted "the encroachment of modernity," and rabbis challenged pluralism and individualism.[59] Davidman argued that "joining a religious community in which women are placed squarely in the home is thus one way of avoiding the tensions and difficulties that face the women who challenge the system by attempting to have both successful careers and families."[60] Accepting patriarchal gender roles, especially those associated with Christian Identity or National Socialism, helps white separatist women deal with the uncertainties of changing gender relationships. Linda Storm, for example, found security in filling her roles.

To obtain an understanding of the complexities of gender in the movement, one must recognize that women are valued by the movement for a number of pragmatic reasons, including childbearing and the preservation of the white race. The four women discussed in detail have all fulfilled the reproductive role, with three of them having at least five children. They also provide various types of support for their families. All express agreement with their husbands' basic values and have accepted secondary roles. Linda Storm provides support by gladly carrying out her distinct roles in the family, giving Michael a pleasant family atmosphere, and praising him as the family breadwinner. Since David Lane is in prison, Katja supported the family in numerous ways, making sure they were fed, cared for, and home-schooled.

She provided David with key organizational support by developing a major outlet for his writings, thus promoting his views even though he has been imprisoned since the mid-1980s.

Karley Kreis has supported her husband by socializing their children to avoid any race-mixing. She gives her husband respect, recognizing his position as head of the family, but also participates in the family decision-making. She would question actions in the movement if she felt they were sexist and she will, if necessary, home-school her children. Muriel Robb works in the paid labor force, providing financial support for the family while Pastor Robb is doing movement work. Their daughter Rachel provides important organizational and leadership skills. Women are valued for their emotional support, caregiving, home-schooling, organizational skills, work in the paid labor force, recruiting members, and providing stability to the family and the movement. When women feel their contributions are valued, it validates their choices about filling gender roles and participating in the movement.

Even though the movement is patriarchal, "strong women" are recognized. For the Storms especially, strong women are ones who actively embrace their roles as wife and mother while the husband is the breadwinner. As Linda Storm put it, such women are tested and prove their capabilities by providing well-functioning homes and security for the family. Strong women, for the Kreises, are racially motivated women who bear white children and socialize them to avoid race-mixing, care for their homes, and participate in decision-making in the family but accept that they do not have the final say. The Robbs value strong, assertive women who can assume leadership positions and think independently. "Strong" thus means different things to each of the couples.

Accommodation and Resistance

Movement members are accommodating to some of the changes in society. Our discussion of pragmatic egalitarianism illustrates such accommodation. Movement members pragmatically understand that both white women and men need to be committed to the cause, so groups actively try to recruit both males and females and include women in some decision-making. Pastor Robb's KKKK has been especially active in incorporating women into various positions in the organization. His wife Muriel has worked in the paid labor force for numerous years, and not all movement women are stay-at-home mothers. The quotation early in this chapter from Amy, David Dalby's girlfriend, illustrates that perceptions of economic necessity influence women to participate in the labor force.

Resistance to change is another strategy of white separatists. It involves "establishing strong boundaries with the broader culture, resisting cultural encroachments as much as possible, and setting the groups up as a radical alternative."[61] Katja Lane and the Storms home-school their children rather than have their children exposed to the values of a multicultural society. If the values the school is teaching challenge the beliefs of the Kreises too much, Karley will then home-school their children.

White separatist movement organizations and members struggle with the social changes by proclaiming their arguments to be rooted in biological differences, rejecting equality, criticizing the social changes, and offering alternative organizations and/or worldviews. They actively construct or frame alternative prognostic visions of the ideal white separatist society. Such construction is a key form of resistance by movement members as their visions clearly distinguish the movement participants from the rest of society. Specifically, we see from the examples of the four couples that one has constructed the KKKK as a white-rights organization, "proclaiming a message of hope and deliverance for white Christian America"[62] and recognizing women's potential in Klan leadership positions and the community. The KKKK provides a fraternal organizational outlet with a long history of promoting the white race and patriarchy, yet now is seemingly adjusting its strategies to allow certain strong women to fill leadership roles. Another couple, the Storms, is working toward a National Socialist society where family, race, and community would be highly valued. National Socialists want to build on the reforms introduced during Hitler's regime in Germany in part because of the perceived emphasis on racial purity and the value placed on the family and the community (the folk). While constructing a group built on white rights and white Christian civilization builds boundaries against those advocating multiculturalism, National Socialists who display the swastika are even more strongly disconnected from the mainstream. As Charles Hall, one of our National Socialist interviewees, pointed out: "When you put . . . a swastika on your skin or you wear a shirt, you've separated yourself from ninety-nine point nine percent of the population."

The other two couples draw on certain religious beliefs considered marginal in American society to develop their sense of identity and community. The Kreises formulate and spread the message of Christian Identity that holds that whites are God's chosen people and men are the head of the family. Christian Identity has its theological roots in British Israelism, which argues that the lost tribes of Israel (the descendants of Jacob) ultimately became various Anglo-Saxon peoples who have a special racial destiny. Christian Identity leaders have modified British Israelism in the United States, including developing a more anti-Semitic tone.[63] Even before Kreises' involvement with Aryan Nations, their platform called for a nation state where only Aryans could be citizens and where Judaism and devil and heathen religions would be stopped.[64] Christian Identity provides a patriarchal alternative for those frustrated with the increasing acceptance of minorities in mainstream Christianity. On the other hand, for those who reject Christianity but want to retain a racial and patriarchal sense of heritage, racial paganism provides an important option. The Lanes founded 14 Word Press to promote racial paganism and instruct youth about their precious and unique racial heritage in order to further racial pride and collective identity. They both strongly believe that strictly white nations are necessary requirements for the race to survive. The publications of 14 Word Press actively framed what Wotanism/racial paganism means.

The examples of the four couples provide a microcosm of the patriarchal alternatives proffered by various segments of the movement. These alternatives mentioned should not be viewed as the only alternatives or as mutually exclusive options for movement members. For example, one may be a racial pagan and a National Socialist or a Klan member and Christian Identity and so on. Participants in the movement try to save the white race while resisting what they perceive as liberal and feminist values that are tearing America apart. In the face of various individual and societal uncertainties that they encounter related to feminism, changing gender roles, postindustrialization, secularization, and globalization, they develop a sense of collective identity with others who hold similar racial and patriarchal worldviews.[65] Collective identity sustains the movement in the face of it being labeled or recognized as a social problem that has attracted both popular and official opposition.

What movement men and women do in their everyday lives reinforces the dominant position of men in the movement. Movement members actively work toward promoting alternative visions of the ideal American family and society. They use arguments about natural differences between the sexes and biblical essentialism to explain their views. Such essentialist arguments are key ingredients of various strategies advanced by the movement. Arguing that something is fixed or inherent suggests an important justification for the differences that white separatists believe exist between the sexes and the races. Citing natural differences provides a defense for inequality and therefore for not implementing social policies to reduce the inequality. Biblical essentialism also adds a religious moral element that is based on faith rather than science.

While movement participants feel comfortable with arguments based on natural differences, they also recognize and experience social change, and it is important for them to feel they can respond to and possibly create their own social change. Therefore movement members actively construct their radical alternative visions, which modify National Socialism, promote racial and patriarchal aspects of paganism, advance Christian Identity, and adjust KKKK policy to allow more active participation of women. In other words, they use essentialist arguments and pragmatic egalitarianism to help them deal with the changes in society, *and* they construct alternatives to help frame movement strategies that challenge the existing culture and social structure, foster collective consciousness, and recruit new members to the movement. The white separatist movement thus uses a variety of different framings to promote the survival of the white race. We also argue that to understand gender in the movement, one must understand what people practice and do in their everyday lives and that those things are not mandated simply by one's biological sex.

Kimmel emphasized the differences in the social-constructionist versus the essentialist views when he argued that feminism is "an optimistic world-view that sees men as capable of change" while "right wing zealots ... believe that men cannot change their violent, abusive patterns and ... argue that women must remain subordinate."[66] We suggest that such dichotomizing oversimplifies white separatists' views and fails to recognize their pragmatic egalitarianism, accommodation, and resistance. Rather, social scientists need to recognize the multidimensionality of white-separatist worldviews and their strategies and try to modify or reframe the essentialist versus social-construction debate.

6
"White Men Are This Nation": Right-Wing Militias and the Restoration of Rural American Masculinity

ABBY L. FERBER
MICHAEL S. KIMMEL

In a 1987 illustration in *WAR* (see Fig. 6.1), the magazine of the White Aryan Resistance, a working-class white man, in hard hat and flak jacket, stands proudly before a suspension bridge while a jet plane soars overhead. "WHITE MEN Built This nation!!" reads the text, "WHITE MEN Are this nation!!!"

Most observers immediately see its racist intent. But rarely do we see the deeply gendered meaning of the statement. Here is a moment of fusion of racial and gendered discourses, when both race and gender are made visible. "This nation," we now understand, "is" neither white women, nor nonwhite men or women.

The White Aryan Resistance that produced this illustration is situated on a continuum of the far right that runs from older organizations, such as the John Birch Society, Ku Klux Klan, and the American Nazi Party, to Holocaust deniers, neo-Nazi or racist skinheads, white-power groups such as Posse Comitatus and White Aryan Resistance, and radical militias such as the Wisconsin Militia or the Militia of Montana. This last set of organizations,

Fig. 6.1 "White Men Built this nation!!" cartoon from *WAR* magazine, 1987.

the rural militias, appeared in the 1990s in the farm belt (and Rust Belt), and became especially visible in the aftermath of the standoff in Ruby Ridge, Idaho, and the bombing of the federal building in Oklahoma City.

In this chapter, we examine the ideology and organization of the rural militia movement, which reached its peak in the mid-1990s. First, we locate the emergence of this movement in the farm crisis of the 1980s. Next, we describe the movement's social composition, before turning to an exploration of its ideology. (We argue that the militias, like many of the groups on the far right, are both fiercely patriotic and simultaneously anticapitalist and anti–democratic government—or, more accurately, anti–corporate capitalist and anti–federal government.) To negotiate that apparent contradiction, the militias, like other groups, employ a gendered discourse about masculinity both to explain the baffling set of structural forces arrayed against them and to provide a set of "others" against which a unifying ideology can be projected.)

The Rural Context

(The economic restructuring of the global economy has had a dramatic effect on rural areas throughout the industrial world.[1] The Reagan Revolution in general meant corporate downsizing, declining real wages, changing technology, increasing the gap between the wealthy and everyone else, uncertainty in the stock market, new waves of Latino and Asian immigrants to the United States, and a steady decline in manufacturing jobs, which were replaced by lower-paying jobs in the service sector. Increased capital mobility and the elimination of tariff barriers have also weakened the bargaining power of labor and left the average American worker feeling vulnerable and betrayed.[2] Between 1980 and 1985 alone, 11 million American workers lost their jobs through plant closings and layoffs. Of those who found new jobs, over half experienced downward mobility.[3] For rural Americans, economic uncertainty was compounded by threats to traditional Western industries like logging, mining, ranching, and farming, where consolidation has also proceeded rapidly and markedly.[4] Squeezed between corporate capital (agribusiness) and the federal government (regulations, environmentalism, and the like), farmers felt themselves to be the "victim[s] of the global restructuring of the rural world."[5]

Since 1980, nearly three quarters of a million medium and small-sized family farms have been lost. During the 1980s farm crisis, "farmers faced the worst financial stress since the Great Depression."[6] For the affected farmers, it dashed the American Dream of upward mobility and replaced it with the stark reality of downward mobility. As Osha Davidson notes: "Many of the new rural poor had not only shared American cultural goals—they had achieved them for a time. They had been *in* the middle class, *of* the middle class. They had tasted the good life and then had fallen from it." Davidson also notes the irony—crucial to our analysis—that "the victims of this blight, the inhabitants of the new rural ghettos, have always been the most blindly patriotic of Americans, the keepers of the American dream."[7] The state of crisis continues today, as "family farms, which use little hired labor and whose households are sustained through farming alone, are being edged out."[8] Many are now speaking of a "new farm crisis," but it is more accurate to say that the crisis of the 1980s never truly ended.[9]

(Moreover, for many the continuing farm crisis is a gender crisis, a crisis of masculinity, as we argue below. Many white, rural, American men feel under siege and vulnerable, unsure of their manhood. They are furious and are looking for someone to blame.

Some direct their rage inwards, even to the point of suicidal thoughts and actions. Others direct this seething rage outwards. "Many debt ridden farm families will become more suspicious of government, as their self-worth, their sense of belonging, their hope for the future deteriorates," predicted Oklahoma psychologist Glen Wallace in 1989. "The farms are gone," writes Joel Dyer, "yet the farmers remain. They've been transformed into a wildfire of rage, fueled by the grief of their loss and blown by the winds of conspiracy and hate-filled rhetoric."[10]

It is not only many rural men that have faced wrenching economic transformations, however; many urban men, too, have tasted the good life and fallen from it. It is hardly surprising, then, that American men—lacking confidence in the government and the economy, troubled by the changing relations between the sexes, uncertain of their identity or their future—began to *dream*, to fantasize about the powers and features of another kind of man who could retake and reorder the world. And the hero of all these dreams was the paramilitary warrior."[11] The militia movement is one embodiment of these dreams, one that is strikingly rural both in the population it draws from and in the location of the majority of its activities.

The Militia Movement

The militia movement cannot be easily defined; there is no central organization or leadership. The movement is comprised of loosely connected paramilitary organizations who "perceive a global conspiracy in which key political and economic events are manipulated by a small group of elite insiders."[12] The movement consists of numerous unrelated groups who form private armies, share distrust in the government, and have armed themselves to fight back. According to the Militia Watchdog, an Internet organization that tracks the militia movement, the militias originated with the Posse Comitatus and the patriot movement from the 1970s and 1980s. (The Southern Poverty Law Center [SPLC], which tracks right-wing extremist groups, lists the militias as a subset of the patriot movement). Like their predecessors, militia members believe that the U.S. government has become totalitarian and seeks to disarm its citizenry and create a "One World Government."

Militia members believe that traditional political reform is useless and that they must resist our laws and attack the government. They believe that armed confrontation is inevitable. While not unified in any traditional sense, the movement is nonetheless tied together through the Internet, where groups and individuals share stories and tips. At places like survivalist expos and gun shows, they sell literature, recruit new members, and purchase arms and survivalist gear.[13] Some groups sell their wares via mail-order catalogs, and many meet on the weekends to train in guerilla-warfare tactics. Militia organizations frequent *Soldier of Fortune* conventions, subscribe to the magazine, and draw members from *Soldier of Fortune* enthusiasts. The Militia of Montana has had booths at *Soldier of Fortune* expositions, where they peddle T-shirts that read "Angry White Guy" and bumper stickers proclaiming "I Love My Country, but I Hate My Government."[14]

The Militia of Montana (with the deliciously unironically gendered acronym "MOM") may serve as the prototype American militia. Founded by former Aryan Nations member John Trochman with his brother and nephew in the aftermath of Ruby Ridge, MOM was the first significant militia organization and the largest national distributor of militia propaganda. At MOM meetings and through mail-order distribution, members sell their own manuals as well as a wide variety of books and videos including, *A Call to Arms, Battle Preparations Now, The Pestilence (AIDS), America in Crisis, The Illuminati Today, Booby Traps,* and *Big Sister Is Watching You* (discussed below). Numerous manuals encourage and train readers in kidnapping, murder, and explosives, urging acts of terrorism.[15]

Estimates of the militia movement's size and appeal vary. Since the first militias began appearing in the early 1990s, their numbers have expanded to include anywhere from 50,000 to 100,000 members in at least forty states.[16] In 1996, the number of militias and similar patriot groups hit an all-time high of 858, with militia units or organizers in every state.[17] That number declined to 435 in 1998, of which 171 were classified as militias, and in 2001, only 158 patriot groups remained active, with 73 classified as militias. This decline is attributable to a variety of factors. According to Mark Potok of the SPLC:

> They have gone home, disillusioned and tired of waiting for the revolution that never seems to come. They have been scared off, frightened by the arrests of thousands of comrades for engaging in illegal "common-law" court tactics, weapons violations and even terrorist plots. And they have, in great numbers, left the relatively non-racist Patriot world for the harder-line groups that now make up most of the radical right."[18]

In many respects the militia movement is dead, although a variety of militia and patriot groups still exists. It represented one brief, strong manifestation of the radical right, drawing from the organization and ideology of the white-supremacist movement in conjunction with other influences. Many who once participated in the movement have since moved into other radical-right organizations. There are few sharp lines dividing the various subgroups of the radical right. People flow between groups and have overlapping memberships and allegiances.[19] At its peak, one observer wrote, it was the "convergence of various streams of fanatical rightwing beliefs that seems to be sweeping the militia movement along. Overlapping right wing social movements with militant factions appear to be coalescing within the militias."[20] This demonstrates the important point that far-right groups are intricately interconnected and share a basic antigovernment, anti-Semitic, racist, and sexist/patriarchal ideology. Equally, the extent of involvement in the movement varies; some men simply correspond through e-mail and read militia literature; others attend training sessions, stockpile food supplies and weapons, and resist paying taxes. The most dangerous form small, secret cells of two to ten people who plan sabotage and terrorism. The cells have been linked to several terrorist acts, including the Oklahoma City bombing, the derailment of an Amtrak train in Arizona, and multiple bomb plots targeting "the Southern Poverty Law Center, offices of the Anti-Defamation League, federal buildings, abortion clinics and sites in the gay community."[21]

Militias provide training in weapons use, target practice, intelligence gathering, encryption and decryption, field radio operation, navigation, unarmed defense, the manufacture of explosives, and demolition, among other things.[22] Much of the instruction is provided by Vietnam veterans, Gulf War veterans, and active military and law enforcement officers.

Social Composition of the Militia

Who are the militia members? While no formal survey of the militias has been undertaken, several demographic characteristics can nonetheless be discerned. Numerous researchers have documented the rural nature of the militia movement; its roots are strongest in the intermountain Montana and Idaho panhandle.[23] Potok notes that the militia movement is "almost entirely rurally based."[24] Historian Carol McNichol Stock situates the militia movement within the historical tradition of rural radicalism on the left and right, rooted in the values of producerism and vigilantism. Stock explores what she labels the ideology of rural producer radicalism: "the desire to own small property, to produce crops and foodstuffs, to control local affairs, to be served but never coerced by a representative government, and to have traditional ways of life and labor respected . . . is the stuff of one of the oldest dreams in the United States."[25]

The militias are also Christian, and the movement is strongest in states with high concentrations of fundamentalist Christians. Many have embraced Christian Identity theology, which gained a foothold on the far right in the early 1980s. About half of the militia members in South Carolina, for example, are also followers of Christian Identity.[26] The Christian Identity focus on racism and anti-Semitism provides the theological underpinnings of the shift from a more "traditional agrarian protest" to the paramilitarism of the militias. While Christian Identity is surely a fringe movement, easily distinguished from mainline Protestantism, this move was nevertheless "encouraged by the evangelism—secular and sacred—of the New Right as well."[27] It is from the Christian Identity movement that the far right gets its theological claims that Adam is the ancestor of the Caucasian race, while nonwhites are pre-Adamic "mud people" without souls, and Jews are the children of Satan.[28] According to this doctrine, Jesus was not Jewish but northern European; his Second Coming, heralded by the Apocalypse, is at hand, and followers can bring the Apocalypse closer. It is the birthright of Anglo-Saxons to establish God's Kingdom on earth; America and Britain's "birthright is to be the wealthiest, most powerful nations on earth . . . able, by divine right, to dominate and colonize the world."[29]

That militia members are white and male is also evident but equally analytically significant. According to several researchers, militia members tend to be middle-aged, in their late thirties to fifties, while the active terrorists tend to be somewhat younger—in their twenties.[30] Many hate crimes are committed by teenagers; in their early twenties, they "graduate" to militias and other radical-right organizations.[31] Like other groups of ethnic nationalists, the militias and their followers consist of two generations of dispossessed and displaced lower-middle-class men—small farmers, shopkeepers, craftsmen, skilled workers. Some are men who have worked all their adult lives, hoping to pass on the family farm to their sons and retire comfortably. They believed that if they worked hard, their legacy would be assured, but they leave their sons little but a legacy of foreclosures, economic insecurity, and debt. Tom Metzger, head of White Aryan Resistance (WAR), estimates that while 10 percent of his followers are skinheads, most are "businessmen and artisans."[32] The sons of these farmers and shopkeepers expected to—and felt entitled to—inherit their fathers' legacy.[33] As Tim McVeigh, from Lockport, New York, wrote in a letter to the editor in his hometown paper just a few years before he blew up the federal building in Oklahoma City, "the American dream of the middle class has all but disappeared, substituted with people struggling just to buy next week's groceries."[34] And when it became evident that they would not inherit that legacy, some of them became murderously angry—at a system that had emasculated their fathers and threatened their manhood.

Of course, the militias are not composed entirely of men. Lori Linzer, a militia researcher at the Anti-Defamation League, found that while there are small numbers of women involved in the movement, they are most likely to become involved with Internet discussions and Web sites and less likely to be active in paramilitary training and other militia activities. Though many women have played active roles in the movement, it remains "vastly, mainly, white Christian men."[35]

Many militia and white-supremacist groups have sought to establish refuge in rural communities, where they could practice military tactics, stockpile food and weapons, hone their survivalist skills, and become self-sufficient in preparation for Armageddon, the final race war, or whatever cataclysm they envision. For example, while preparing for the year 2000 (Y2K), some groups set up "covenant communities." These were self-sufficient and heavily armed rural settlements of white people, who feared that "when the computers crash, government checks to minorities in the inner cities will stop. Then starving Hispanics and blacks will flood into the rural parts of America, armed to the teeth and willing to stop at nothing in order to wrench food from the tables of white Christians."[36]

In addition, rural areas are seen by far-right extremist leaders as a strong base for possible recruiting. Accurately reading the signs of rural decline and downward mobility, these leaders "see an opportunity to increase their political base by recruiting economically troubled farmers into their ranks."[37] While "the spread of far-right groups over the last decade has not been limited to rural areas alone," writes Davidson, "the social and economic unraveling of rural communities—especially in the midwest—has provided far-right groups with new audiences for their messages of hate."[38] For many farmers facing foreclosures, far-right promises to help them save their land have been appealing, offering farmers various schemes and legal maneuvers to help prevent foreclosures, blaming the farmers' troubles on Jewish bankers and the One World Government. In stark contrast to the government indifference encountered by rural Americans, a range of far-right groups, most recently the militias, have seemingly provided support, community, and answers.

In that sense, the militias are simply following in the footsteps of the Ku Klux Klan, the Posse Comitatus, and other far-right patriot groups that recruited members in rural America throughout the 1980s. In fact, rural America has an especially entrenched history of racism and an equally long tradition of collective local action and vigilante justice. There remains a widespread notion "that Jews, African-Americans, and other minority-group members 'do not entirely belong,'" which may, in part, "be responsible for rural people's easy acceptance of the far right's agenda of hate."[39] "The far right didn't create bigotry in the Midwest; it didn't need to," Davidson concludes. "It merely had to tap into the existing undercurrent of prejudice once this had been inflamed by widespread economic failure and social discontent."[40]

Many militia members are also military veterans. Several leaders served in Vietnam and were shocked at the national disgust that greeted them as they returned home after that debacle.[41] Some veterans believed they were sold out by the government caving in to effeminate cowardly protesters; they can no longer trust the government to fight for what is right. Louis

Beam, for example, served eighteen months in Vietnam before returning to start his own paramilitary organization, which was broken up in the 1980s by lawsuits. He now advocates "leaderless resistance," the formation of underground terrorist cells.

Bo Gritz, a former Green Beret in Vietnam, returned to Southeast Asia several times in clandestine missions to search for prisoners of war (POWs) and was the real-life basis for the film *Rambo*. He used his military heroism to increase his credibility among potential recruits; one brochure described him as "this country's most decorated Vietnam veteran" who "killed some 400 Communists in his illustrious military career."[42] In 1993, Gritz began a traveling training program, Specially Prepared Individuals for Key Events (SPIKE), a rigorous survival course in paramilitary techniques. Gritz and a colleague, Jack McLamb, a retired police officer, created their own community, Almost Heaven, in Idaho. Gritz captures the military element of the militias. They believed they were entitled to be hailed as heroes, as had earlier generations of American veterans, not to be scorned as outcasts. Now he symbolizes "true" warrior-style masculinity, the reward for men who join the militia.

What characterizes these scions of small-town rural America—both the fathers and the sons—is not only their ideological vision of producerism threatened by economic transformation, their sense of small-town democratic community, an inclusive community that was based on the exclusion of broad segments of the population; it is also their sense of entitlement to economic, social, political, and even military power. To cast the middle-class, straight, white man as the hegemonic holder of power in America would be to miss fully the daily experience of these straight white men. They believe themselves to be *entitled* to power—by a combination of historical legacy, religious fiat, biological destiny, and moral legitimacy. But they believe they do not have power. That power, in their view, has been both surrendered by white men—their fathers—and stolen from them by a federal government controlled and staffed by legions of the newly enfranchised minorities, women, and immigrants, all in service to the omnipotent Jews who control international economic and political life. "Heaven help the God-fearing, law-abiding Caucasian middle class," explained Charlton Heston to a recent Christian Coalition convention, especially:

> Protestant or even worse evangelical Christian, Midwest or Southern or even worse rural, apparently straight or even worse admittedly [heterosexual], gun-owning or even worse NRA card–carrying average working stiff, or even worst of all, male working stiff. Because not only don't you count, you're a downright obstacle to social progress.[43]

Downwardly mobile rural white men—those who lost the family farms and those who expected to take them over—are squeezed between the omnivorous jaws of capital concentration and a federal bureaucracy which is at best indifferent to their plight and at worst facilitates their further demise.

Militia Ideology

Militia ideology reflects this squeeze yet cannot fully confront its causes. Rooted in heartland conservatism, the militias have no difficulty blaming the federal government for their ills but are loathe to blame capitalism. After all, they are strong defenders in capitalist economics of the self-made man, and many have served in the armed forces defending the capitalist system that ensures individual freedom.[44] As a result, a certain rhetorical maneuvering must displace the analysis of capitalism onto another force that distorts and disfigures the pure capitalist impulse. This rhetorical maneuvering is the deployment of racism, sexism, homophobia, and anti-Semitism into a rhetoric of emasculating "others" against whom the militias' fantasies of the restoration of American masculinity are played out.

Central to the militia ideology is its antistatist position. It is big government, not big capital, that is eroding Americans' constitutional rights. International economic arrangements such as NAFTA or GATT are understood as politically disenfranchising white American workers. Recent governmental initiatives such as the Brady Bill, which requires a waiting period before the purchase of handguns and that ban certain assault rifles are seen as compromising the Constitutional right to bear arms and are perceived as a threat to white men's ability to protect and defend their families. Gun control is seen as a further attempt by the government to emasculate white men. The 1993 FBI/ATF assault on the Branch Davidian compound in Waco, Texas, and the 1992 standoff and shootout with white separatist Randy Weaver at Ruby Ridge, Idaho, which resulted in the death of Weaver's wife and son, have further exacerbated their distrust in the federal government.[45] Restrictions on the right to bear arms are perceived as just further steps in the government's attempt to disarm and eventually control all citizens, leading inevitably to a UN invasion and the New World Order.

Militia publications are replete with stories of government conspiracies, and many believe the U.S. government is working with international forces to control U.S. citizens. For example, some argue that black helicopters are spying on citizens, monitoring devices are being implanted in newborns, Hong Kong police forces are being trained in Montana to disarm U.S. citizens, and markings on the back of road signs are secret codes to direct invading UN forces.[46] In response, militias have established "common law courts"—self-appointed groups that usurp the authority of the law, staging their own trials and issuing their own legal documents.

In many respects, the militias' ideology reflects the ideologies of other fringe groups on the far right, from whom they typically recruit and with which they overlap.) While the militias may not be as overtly racist and anti-Semitic as some other white-supremacist groups, many researchers have documented the extensive links between the two.[47] For example, from white-supremacist groups they embrace the theory of the international Jewish conspiracy for world control. From Christian Identity groups they take their idiosyncratic reading of the Bible, which holds that Jews are descendants of Satan (through Cain), that people of color are "pre-Adamic mud people," and that Aryans are the true people of God. Militia member Rodney Skurdal used Christian Identity theology to justify his refusal to pay taxes, arguing that "[if] we the white race are God's chosen people . . . and our Lord God stated that 'the earth is mine,' why are we paying taxes on 'His land'?"[48]

And from all sides the militias take racism, homophobia, nativism, sexism, and anti-Semitism. Like antistatism, these discourses provide an explanation for the feelings of entitlement thwarted, fixing the blame squarely on "others" whom the state must now serve at the expense of white men. What is central to our analysis here is that the unifying theme of all these discourses, which have traditionally formed the rhetorical package Richard Hofstadter has labeled "paranoid politics," is *gender*. Specifically, it is by framing state policies as emasculating and problematizing the masculinity of these various "others" that rural white militia members seek to restore their own masculinity.

In this way, militias can claim a long historical lineage. Since the early nineteenth century, American manhood has pivoted around the status of breadwinner—the independent, self-made man who supports his family by his own labor. The breadwinner was economically independent, king of his own castle, embedded in a political community of like-minded and equally free men. When this self-made masculinity has been threatened, one of American men's responses has been to exclude others from staking their claim to manhood. Like the Sons of Liberty who threw off the British yoke of tyranny in 1776, these contemporary Sons of Liberty see "R-2," the Second American Revolution, as restorative—to retrieve and refound traditional masculinity on the exclusion of others. The entire rhetorical apparatus that serves this purpose is saturated with gendered readings—of the problematized masculinity of the "others," of the emasculating policies of the state, and of the rightful masculine entitlement of white men.)

That such ardent patriots as militia members are so passionately antigovernment might strike the observer as contradictory. After all, are these not the same men who served their country in Vietnam or in the Gulf War? Are these not the same men who believe so passionately in the American Dream? Were they not the backbone of the Reagan Revolution? Indeed they are and were. Militia members face the difficult theoretical task of maintaining their faith in America and capitalism and simultaneously providing an analysis of an indifferent state, at best, or an actively interventionist one, at worst, coupled with a contemporary articulation of corporate capitalist logic that leaves them, often literally, out in the cold.)

It is through a decidedly gendered and sexualized rhetoric of masculinity that this contradiction between loving America and hating its government, loving capitalism and hating its corporate iterations, is resolved. First, like others on the far right, militia members believe that the state has been captured by evil, even Satanic forces; the original virtue of the American political regime has been deeply and irretrievably corrupted. Environmental regulations, state policies dictated by urban and Northern interests, the Internal Revenue Service—in their view, these are the outcomes of a state now utterly controlled by feminists, environmentalists, blacks, and Jews.[49]

According to this logic, the welfare state has been captured by feminists, so that now, like all feminists and feminist institutions, it serves to emasculate white manhood. Several call for the invalidation of the thirteenth and fourteenth Amendments, which eliminated slavery and provided equal protection.[50] One leader, John Trochman, argues that women must relinquish the right to vote and to own property.[51] One book sold by MOM well illustrates these themes. In *Big Sister Is Watching You: Hillary Clinton and the White House Feminists Who Now Control America—And Tell the President What to Do,* Texe Marrs argues that Hillary Clinton and her feminist coconspirators were controlling the country and threatening American's rights and our national sovereignty. Marrs describes "Hillary's Hellcats" and "Gore's Whores"—a "motley collection [including] lesbians, sex perverts, child molester advocates, Christian haters, and the most doctrinaire of communists."[52] These women—such as Jocelyn Elders, Janet Reno, Maya Angelou, Donna Shalala, Laura D'Andrea Tyson, Roberta Actenberg, and Ruth Bader Ginsburg—are said to be members of the "conspiratorial Council on Foreign Relations and the elitist Trilateral Commission [, they] attend the annual conclave of the notorious Bilderbergers [and are] hirelings of the left-wing, radical foundations designed to promote the New World Order."[53] These "feminist vultures . . . the most militant of the militant . . . femiNazis . . . control a heartless police establishment more efficient than Stalin's."

Marrs claims that "Big Sister" intends nothing short of a New World Order, to be accomplished through a "10 Part Plan" which includes:

> the replacement of Christianity with feminist, new-age spirituality. . . . History will be rewritten, discarding our True heroes. . . . Homosexuality will be made noble, and the male-female relationship undesirable. . . . Patriotism will be smashed, while multiculturalism shall be exalted, and the masses will come to despise white, male dominated society as a throwback to the failed age of militarism and conflict. The masses shall be taught to revile nationalism, patriotism, and

family... abortion and infanticide... encouraged.... Women will dominate in all walks of life—in law, medicine, literature, religion, economics, entertainment, education, and especially in politics.[54]

In this vision, feminism, multiculturalism, homosexuality, and Christian-bashing are all tied together, part and parcel of the New World Order. On the other hand, Christianity, traditional history, heterosexuality, male dom-ination, white racial superiority and power, individualism, meritocracy, and the value of individual hard work describe the True, Right America which is at risk and must be protected. These facets are all intertwined, so that multicultural textbooks, women in government, and legalized abortion can individually be taken as signs of the impending New World Order.

Marrs's book displays tremendous anxiety over changing gender roles. Working within the difference-versus-equality framework, race and gender equality are unthinkable and necessarily a threat to white men. Increased opportunities for women can only lead to the oppression of men. Marrs pro-claims: "In the New Order, woman is finally on top. She is not a mere equal. *She is Goddess.*"[55] Hillary, he writes, "represents the ascendance and preem-inence of Woman... *Woman in Control.*"[56] However, real power is never truly granted women, who must continue to be thought of as passive and incapable of possessing real power. Marrs argues: "Hillary Rodham Clinton is Big Brother in drag. She is in effect, a politically correct, transvestite Big Brother."[57] Not really a woman after all, she comes to represent the confu-sion of gender boundaries and the demasculinization of men, symbolizing a future where men are not allowed to be real men.

This text suggests several themes of interest to us here. The notion that the state has been taken over means that it no longer acts in the interests of "true" American men. The state is an engine of gender inversion, feminizing men, while feminism masculinizes women. Feminist women, it turns out, are more masculine than men are. Not only does this call the masculinity of white men into question, but it uses gender as the rhetorical vehicle for criticizing "other" men. Typically, problematizing the masculinity of these others takes two forms simultaneously: other men are both "too masculine" and "not masculine enough." We call this the "Goldilocks Paradox," after the fairy-tale heroine who found chairs too big or too small, porridge too hot or too cold, never "just right." So, too, the "others" are seen as too masculine—violent rapacious beasts with no self-control—or not masculine enough—weak, helpless, effete, incapable of supporting a family.

Hence, in the logic of militias and other white-supremacist organiza-tions, gay men are both promiscuously carnal and sexually voracious, and effete fops who do to men what men should only have done to them by women. Black men are both violent hypersexual beasts, possessed of an

.sible sexuality," seeking white women to rape, and less than fully ∕weak, stupid, lazy."[58] In *The Turner Diaries*, the apocalyptic novel that served as the blueprint for the Oklahoma City bombing and is widely read and peddled by militias, author William Pierce depicts a nightmarish world where white women and girls are constantly threatened and raped by "gangs of Black thugs."[59] Blacks are primal nature—untamed, cannibalistic, uncontrolled, but also stupid and lazy—and whites are the driving force of civilization. "America and all civilized society are the exclusive products of White man's mind and muscle," is how *The Thunderbolt* put it.[60] Whites are the "instruments of God," proclaims *The Turner Diaries*. "[T]he White race is the Master race of the earth ... the Master Builders, the Master Minds, and the Master warriors of civilization." What can a black man do but "clumsily shuffle off, scratching his wooley head, to search for shoebrush and mop."[61]

Most interesting is the portrait of the Jew. One the one hand, the Jew is a greedy, cunning, conniving, omnivorous predator; on the other, the Jew is small, beady-eyed, and incapable of masculine virtue. By asserting the hypermasculine power of the Jew, the far right can support capitalism as a system while decrying the actions of capitalists and their corporations. According to militia logic, it is not the capitalist corporations that have turned the government against them, but the international cartel of Jewish bankers and financiers, media moguls, and intellectuals who have already taken over the U.S. state and turned it into ZOG (Zionist Occupied Government). The United States is called the "Jewnited States," and Jews are blamed for orchestrating the demise of the once-proud Aryan man.

In white-supremacist ideology, the Jew is the archetype villain, both hypermasculine—greedy, omnivorous, sexually predatory, capable of the destruction of the Aryan way of life—and hypomasculine, small, effete, homosexual, pernicious, weasely. A cartoon in *Racial Loyalty* from 1991 illustrates this simultaneous position (see Fig. 6.2).

In their anti-Semitism, the militias join a long lineage of American paranoia. Recall that in *The International Jew*, Henry Ford accused Jews of promoting a decay of morality, loss of family values, intrusive central government, monopolies, and corrupt banks. A 1986 Harris poll found that 27 percent of Nebraska and Iowa residents believed that "farmers have always been exploited by international Jewish bankers who are behind those who overcharge them for farm equipment or jack up the interest on their loans."[62] Wisconsin Militia's pamphlet, "American Farmer: 20th Century Slave" explains how banks were foreclosing on farms because Jews, incapable of farming themselves, had to control the world's monetary system in order to control the global food supply. "Is this what you work your fingers to the bone for—to pay usury to a private group of bankers who make up the Fed?" a militia publication entitled *Why a Bankrupt America?* asks.[63]

THE EVIL JEW

"WE WANT TO DESTROY THE WHITE RACE AND TAKE EVERYTHING YOU OWN."

Fig. 6.2 "The Evil Jew" cartoon from *Racial Loyalty,* 1991.

Eustace Mullins, a popular speaker on the militia circuit and author of the anti-Semitic *Secrets of the Federal Reserve,* argues that militias are "the only organized threat to the Zionists' absolute control of the U.S."[64]

In the militia cosmology, Jews are both hypermasculine and effeminate. Hypermasculinity is expressed in the Jewish domination of the world's media and financial institutions, and especially Hollywood. They're sexually omnivorous, but calling them "rabid, sex-perverted" is not a compliment. The *Thunderbolt** claims that 90 percent of pornographers are Jewish. At the same time, Jewish men are seen as wimpish, small, nerdy, and utterly unmasculine—likely, in fact, to be homosexual. It is Jewish *women* who are seen as "real men"—strong, large, and hairy. In lieu of their brawn power, Jewish men have harnessed their brain power in their quest for world domination. Jews are seen as the masterminds behind the other social groups

*The *Thunderbolt* no. 301, p. 6.

who are seen as dispossessing rural American men of their birthright. And toward that end, they have co-opted blacks, women, gays, and brainwashed and cowardly white men to do their bidding. In a remarkable passage, white supremacists cast the economic plight of white workers as being squeezed between nonwhite workers and Jewish owners:

> It is our RACE we must preserve, not just one class... White Power means a permanent end to unemployment because with the non-Whites gone, the labor market will no longer be over-crowded with unproductive niggers, spics and other racial low-life. It means an end to inflation eating up a man's paycheck faster than he can raise it because OUR economy will not be run by a criminal pack of international Jewish bankers, bent on using the White worker's tax money in selfish and even destructive schemes."[65]

Since Jews are incapable of acting like real men—strong, hardy, virtuous manual workers and farmers—a central axiom of the international Jewish conspiracy for world domination is their plan to "feminize White men and to masculinize White women."[66] *The Turner Diaries* describes the "Jewish-liberal-democratic-equalitarian" perspective as "an essentially feminine, submissive worldview."[67] WAR echoes this theme: "One of the characteristics of nations which are controlled by the Jews is the gradual eradication of masculine influence and power and the transfer of influence into feminine forms."[68]

Embedded in this anti-Semitic slander is a critique of white American manhood as soft, feminized, weakened—indeed, emasculated. Article after article decries "the whimpering collapse of the blond male," as if White men have surrendered to the plot.[69] According to *The Turner Diaries*, American men have lost the right to be free; slavery "is the just and proper state for a people who have grown soft."[70] Yet it is here that the militias simultaneously offer White men an analysis of their present situation and a political strategy for retrieving their manhood. As *National Vanguard* puts it:

> As Northern males have continued to become more wimpish, the result of the media-created image of the "new male"—more pacifist, less authoritarian, more "sensitive," less competitive, more androgynous, less possessive—the controlled media, the homosexual lobby and the feminist movement have cheered ... the number of effeminate males has increased greatly ... legions of sissies and weaklings, of flabby, limp-wristed, non-aggressive, non-physical, indecisive, slack-jawed, fearful males who, while still heterosexual in theory and practice, have not even a vestige of the old macho spirit, so deprecated today, left in them.[71]

It is through the militias that American manhood can be restored and revived—a manhood in which individual white men control the fruits of their own labor and are not subject to the emasculation of Jewish-owned finance capital, a black-and feminist-controlled welfare state. It is a militarized

Fig. 6.3 "The Aryan that made a Man out of 'Mac'" cartoon from *WAR* magazine.

manhood of the heroic John Rambo—a manhood that celebrates their God-sanctioned right to band together in armed militias if any one—or any governmental agency—tries to take it away from them. If the state and capital emasculate them, and if the masculinity of the "others" is problematic, then only real White men can rescue this American Eden from a feminized, multicultural, androgynous melting pot. "The world is in trouble now only because the White man is divided, confused, and misled," we read in *New Order.* "Once he is united, inspired by a great ideal and led by real men, his world will again become livable, safe, and happy."[72] The militias seek to reclaim their manhood gloriously, violently. On the recorded message of the Militia of Michigan, one could hear the following telling narrative:

> Once they were praised. Once they were toasted. But that was over two hundred years ago. Today the Militia Men are a threat. Our new King has told us so. "Begone with your pride and away with your honor! Who cares about what has been? Down with the old! It's a new world order—there's no place for you Militia Men. Give up your guns, you have no right. Just who do you think you are? Your God is dead and so is your dream." Stand firm, stand strong, Militia Men! America has much need of you today. Be vigilant now, as never before. Evil is trying to steal our country away. Perhaps tomorrow or in a thousand years you will receive the rewards you are due. Our flag will fly, our spirit will soar, and it will happen because of you. History will record many of your names, stories will tell of where you've been.[73]

As these first brave white men reclaimed their nation, "millions of soft, city-bred, brainwashed Whites" gradually began to regain their manhood, recalls the narrator of *The Turner Diaries*. And the rest of us? "The rest died."[74]

We conclude this article as we began it, with a cartoon (Fig. 6.3) from *WAR*, the magazine of the White Aryan Resistance. In this deliberate parody of countless Charles Atlas advertisements, the timid, white, ninety-seven-pound weakling finds his power, his strength as a man, through racial hatred. In the ideology of the white-supremacist movement and their organized militia allies, it is racism that will again enable white men to reclaim their manhood. The amorphous groups of white supremacists, skinheads, and neo-Nazis may be the symbolic shock troops of this movement, but the rural militias are their well-organized and highly regimented infantry.

7
"Getting It": The Role of Women in Male Desistance from Hate Groups

RANDY BLAZAK

Introduction: Trajectories of Desisters

The hate movement has been described as "hypermasculine." While Kathleen Blee, Betty Dobratz and Stephanie Shanks-Meile, and others have looked at the increasing recruitment of women into hate groups, the general hate agenda is still dominated by traditional gendered ideas about social power, sexuality, family, and war.[1] Abby Ferber and Michael Kimmel write: "The white supremacist project is primarily concerned with reaffirming white men's masculinity. The white supremacist movement offers itself as a solution—white men may regain their rightful position as patriarchs by joining the movement."[2] The research discussed in this chapter emerges out of ethnographic studies of male skinheads and racist groups as sexist groups. It is argued here that female intimates play a significant role in both convincing male hate-group members that hate groups do not satisfy their psychological-strain and sociological-anomie concerns and that those concerns should change, helping them to exit the group.

It is not always easy for a young man to leave a racist subculture. The sanctions against it are very strong. Leavers have at worst been murdered and at best become members of the most despised group among racists, the "race-traitor." Much has been written about "aging out" of crime through maturation and the development of social bonds, but little has been written about exiting hate groups. Leaving hate subcultures such as the skinheads or the Aryan Brotherhood is similar to leaving gangs. Leavers are often shunned, verbally or physically attacked, and occasionally killed.

The classic case of Greg Withrow demonstrates the dangers of leaving. In 1986, twenty-five-year-old Withrow was a rising star in the White Aryan Resistance, giving fiery speeches at the Aryan Nations compound in Idaho. In 1987 he fell in love with a young woman whose family had been persecuted by the Nazis in the 1930s. In the film *Blink,* Withrow says:

> It just never occurred [to me] that anybody would ever like me. I had accepted the fact that nobody ever will. I said to myself, I just want to live a normal life. I realized that none of these people [other white supremacists] had ever really cared anything about me, and I really never cared anything about them. It was like opening up a hallway that I couldn't begin to describe. It was scary. To leave the racist movement was a frightening thing.[3]

Shortly after his exit, Withrow was attacked by his former skinhead colleagues with baseball bats. His hands were allegedly nailed to a board in a mock crucifixion and he was left for dead.

Criminologists who research desistance from criminal behavior often talk about changes in the "life cycle" associated with aging. For example, as youth age they are more able to resist the need for immediate gratification that drives much impulsive crime.[4] James Wilson and Richard Herrnstein found that establishing long-term relationships and starting a family often ends criminal careers.[5] Erich Labouvie's research on drug use reports that those who maintain healthy marriages are more likely to desist from crime than those who do not.[6] But scholarship on desistance says little about the gendered nature of those bonding experiences.

More common than research on desistance is work on what attracts people to hate groups.[7] Research on racism shows that people are drawn into hate groups for microlevel psychological and macrolevel sociological reasons. Both levels can manifest as forms of strain. Robert Agnew and Niko Passas make the case that strain theory, also referred to as anomie theory, descends from the writings of Durkheim and Merton as a personal and societal response.[8] First is the strain that comes from the disjunction between goals and means and the resultant pressure for deviance. An example would be an individual who feels strained because he or she cannot afford a car, so the decision is made to steal a car. Second, the theorists refer to the inability of society effectively to regulate conduct as the source of anomie, or "normlessness."[9] This anomie is evident in Blee's research on women in the hate movement who see their "conversion" to organized racism as creating a "sense of ultimate grounding" in a well-regulated subculture.[10]

On the micropsychological level, the factors are more similar to the strain arising from blocked opportunities and negative experiences described in Agnew's General Strain Theory, which broadened the theory beyond Merton's focus on economic goals.[11] The macrosociological-level sources of strain are similar to Albert Cohen's and Blazak's discussion of the experience of anomie leading to subcultural solutions (gangs for Cohen, skinheads for Blazak).[12] Therefore microlevel strain arises from an inability to achieve a specific outcome, while macrolevel anomie arises from seeing societal conditions blocking culturally valued goals.

The different types of strain offer individuals different trajectories into hate groups. The experience of strain as an emotional or psychological phenomenon is addressed by hate groups. Based on the ethnographic research discussed here, five microstrain patterns emerged. Each is illustrated here with a comment from a racist skinhead from this research:

1. A complex worldview based on moral relativism and negotiating shades of gray causes strain. Hate groups provide a simplistic world view of good and evil that is "morally grounded." ("Either you are on the side of white people or you are on the side of the Jews.")
2. The inability to express aggression in a culture that decries violence causes strain. Hate groups provide an outlet for aggression and sociopathic behavior. ("I love kickin' ass. That's why I'm a skinhead.")
3. A fear of changing physical and social environments causes strain. Hate groups explain that change and seek to reverse it. ("Everything is different from when my grandfather was my age.")
4. The inability to attain specific goals causes strain. Hate groups provide a sense of personal efficacy through a utilitarian focus. ("We get results. People look at us and say, 'At least they're doing something about it.'")
5. Feeling blocked from social interaction creates strain. Hate groups provide a structured in-group membership that facilitates high-level social interaction. ("These guys are my family. It's about love, not hate.")

Hate groups also work to reduce the macrolevel anomie experienced from the normlessness of society. Like Durkheim's discussion of the rule-bound Catholic Church creating a barrier against suicide (compared to the anomic Protestants), hate groups offer a structured subcultural world "that reveals the essential difference between clarity and confusion."[13] In this research on skinheads, three macroanomie patterns emerged:

1. Increasing change in constructions of masculinity and femininity creates anomie. Hate groups reinforce the need for men to perform hegemonic masculinity and women to perform "natural" female roles. ("White men are being beaten down in every corner of society. By Jewish dykes and feminists. It's time to be a man.")

2. Loss of socially defined status because of a movement to reevaluate heterosexual, white, male power creates anomie. Hate groups desire to reclaim or defend social status. ("Where else can we go? What else can we give up? It's time to fight back.")

3. Lack of mainstream advocacy groups and movements for the "victims" of social change creates anomie. Hate groups cater to the desire to be a part of a social movement. ("It's exciting, man. We're the heroes of the white race. We're making history.")

Members may employ multiple reasons for moving toward a racist subculture, for example a need for efficacy and a desire to be a part of a social movement, but each will look to the group to meet its specific strain reducing needs.

Membership in hate groups can be relatively short-lived. Sustaining members will have their needs met, and continued involvement will seem like a rational choice, the rewards of staying outweighing the costs of leaving.[14] But, as with cults and gangs, there is much drifting in and out.[15] Membership is rarely permanent. Those who leave either will not have had their needs met or their needs will change. The question then emerges: How is that leaving facilitated? While youth-gang workers have strategies to help gang youth deal with both emotional issues and larger worldviews, hate-group members receive little outreach from the nonracist community.

Women and Hate Groups

The gender focus of understanding hate has concentrated primarily on organized racism as an expression of masculinity and on female participation in hate groups.[16] Recent research on women in the hate movement has explored the contradictory roles of females in a subculture that is seen as sexist as well as racist. Female participation has been a factor in extremist groups since the early twentieth century. Women led popular "women's auxiliaries" of the Ku Klux Klan in the 1920s. Linda Thompson claimed to be the leader of the patriot militia movement in the early 1990s. In the 2000s, groups such as Women for Aryan Unity appeal to white women to take on their racial role. The following example from the Stormfront Web site illustrates the gendered nature of hate:

> Other areas of interest that women should be getting involved in are the following: self-defense; midwifery; survival cooking and once our goals have been achieved, education! These and previous items discussed will be some of the topics discussed in a magazine put out by Aryan women. This magazine should prove very interesting for both men and women, although it is geared mainly towards women's roles in our upcoming battles.[17]

Despite claims that women make up nearly half of the members in some hate groups, the reality of the racist movement is that it is biased against women.[18] Jessie Daniels' and Ferber's work on modern racist groups demonstrates the patriarchal foundation of white-supremacist ideology.[19] White maleness is the standard. White women must be defended from black rapists and Jewish feminists and lesbians. While there are fluctuating numbers of women in hate groups (including some leadership roles) their position is still often limited to two roles: the breeding mother or the prized sex object. Jessie Daniels' analysis of white-supremacist propaganda found five dominant portrayals of white women:

1. women as glorious mothers, naturally maternal;
2. women as objects of sexual desire (the "good whore"), proof of white supremacy;
3. women in need of protection from black rapists, Jewish feminists, and others;
4. women as racial traitors (the "bad whore"), weak toward black men, feminism, and homosexuality; and, least commonly;
5. women as racial warriors, supporting their men.[20]

Abby Ferber's research on hate-group writings leads her to conclude "that white supremacist discourse is about redefining masculinity."[21] The white woman's body represents the white race at risk. Mixed-race children destroy the dichotomous racial-category system (white and nonwhite); therefore white women's sexuality must be controlled by white men. This is evident in the antiabortion rhetoric in hate groups. Abortionists are often portrayed as Jewish doctors aborting white babies while encouraging high minority birthrates. Ferber argues that women's participation is largely due to recruiting efforts targeting women and families in order to stabilize the membership and retain men in the movement, but the movement remains highly gendered.

More recently, Kathleen Blee published her analysis of interviews with thirty-four women from various racist and anti-Semitic groups.[22] The women in the study broke many of the commonly held misconceptions about female hate-group members. For example, they were not more likely to be from abusive families. Only seven of the thirty-four had husbands or boyfriends who had encouraged them to join. Still, the desire to be "a part of something" seems to outweigh their commitment to the racist ideology (many maintained friendships with minorities and homosexuals). The women have difficulty reconciling the lofty "Aryan" ideals with their actual experiences in the group. Blee connects this resignation to the male politics to their perceived victimization by black rapists: "Women's talk of bodily harm underscores the sense of vulnerability that justifies their entrance into organized racism, while the desire to safeguard their children from a life in organized racism highlights their sense of dissatisfaction with the life they have found there."[23]

Dobratz and Shanks-Meile discuss in this book how supremacists feel about the idea that their movement is sexist. The majority of their 101 survey respondents answered that they were racist (82 percent) and also not sexist (77 percent). But the interviews with supremacists do not reveal a feminist-racist nexus. Instead, women are promoted in their gendered roles. World Church of the Creator leader Matt Hale says: "We basically believe in nature and natural law and natural society." Women perform supportive roles like office managers and, of course, mothers (there is little discussion of men's fathering roles). While the subjects of their interviews were critical of feminism, Dobratz and Shanks-Meile point out that the multidimensionality of their views on women's roles shares some of the tenets of ecofeminism. Racist women see their importance in their connection to nature and reproduction.

While the participation of women in hate crimes is limited, participation in hate groups is less so. Some groups, such as the Klan or Canada's Sigrdrifa, will recruit women to reinforce traditional female roles. Street-level skinhead groups may be more likely to recruit women as girlfriends or sexual objects. But other racist groups, such as the Odinists, may present themselves as nonsexist. Volksfront, an Oregon skinhead group that has evolved into an Odinist "cultural heritage organization," has distanced itself from its street-fighting past. The leader of Volksfront responded to the following questions on the discussion page of the Web site of Oregon Spotlight, a group that monitors hate activity:

1. How are women viewed by Volksfront?
   For years the Christian Identity movement made statements that it was a disgrace for women to pick up the fight for men or in place of men. We view them as a critical part of our organization. We are not a Christian Identity group. In defense of the home women should and do take up arms.

2. Has the role of women changed over the last several years? Only in your movement, this local area or is it a movement wide phenomena?
   I don't give a shit about the rest of the movement, to quote Tom Metzger it is a "bowel movement." In our local movement women have come into their own and are a respected and important part of it.

3. What influences led to your current view of women in the movement? Has Asatru had an effect?
   I was raised to respect women.[24]

The dominant role for women is centered on her reproductive role. The white mother does her racial duty by helping to counter the tide of the nonwhite population. She is a breeder who plays her racial role by birthing as many white children as possible. Motherhood is defined as a glorious racial calling. The sex object performs the job of recruiting. She is the prize for young men who enlist in the cause. She is not smart or family-oriented, just available and dispensable. It cannot be overstated that the dominant racist groups in America are also sexist groups. More violent groups, such as Nazi skinheads, further exclude women with their hypermasculine solutions to the race problem. Militaristic fantasies of a coming "racial holy war" appeal to boys who grew up playing army and developed macho desires to "kick some ass." Hate violence, devoid of compassion, is not the domain of mothers.

Women as Categorical Targets

The problem of defining what constitutes a "hate crime" is a starting point in understanding how men and women might see hate-motivated criminality differently. The concept was not defined federally until the signing of the Hate Crime Statistics Act in 1990, and the subsequent Hate Crime Prevention Act stalled in Congress in 2002 largely due to its broad definition of what constitutes a hate crime. Currently, only forty-five states have hate crime laws. Of those, only twenty-nine include sexual orientation as a protected status, and even fewer have managed to make the case that crimes against women constitute hate crimes. In their book *Hate Crimes: New Social Movements and the Politics of Violence,* Jenness and Broad argue that the gay rights movement, the women's movement, and the victims' rights movement have built on the lessons of the civil rights movement and have "expanded the domain" of bias-motivated violence to include more than racial minorities.[25] The current debate over "protected status" involves what domains to include in hate crime laws: race, ethnicity, sexual orientation, gender, disability, and so on.

It has been argued by Blazak and Kathy Farr that this expansion of domains, as well as their own experiences as potential or actual victims of gender-motivated violence, provides women with an appreciation of the random, albeit categorical, nature of hate crimes.[26] Women's symbolic position as potential targets of sex-related crimes contributes to their understanding of the symbolic status of random targets of other bias-motivated acts.

In spite of the decline in violent crime in the 1990s, the FBI's *Uniform Crime Report* (UCR) recorded 90,186 rapes in 2000, or 32 per 100,000 people.[27] Because of the high rate of nonreporting of rape by women for various reasons (many of them similar to the nonreporting of hate crimes), self-report studies put the incidence of rape at as much as ten times the official rate.[28] The National Crime Victimization Survey (NCVS), which does not include figures on victims aged twelve or younger, reported 261,000 rapes, attempted rapes, and sexual assaults in 2000.[29] Many studies find that that one in four women will be raped in her lifetime, making crime victimization a reality all women are aware of. The figures from the UCR and NCVS may not begin to approach the scope of rape. Research from the National Women's Study found 683,000 rapes in 1992, four times the rate in the NCVS. A 1987 survey of college women found that 27.7 percent had experienced a sexual experience since the age of fourteen that met the legal definition of rape or attempted rape.[30] As feminist Susan Griffin wrote in 1971, "rape and the fear of rape are a daily part of every woman's consciousness."[31]

Research on the fear of crime has reinforced the gender differences due to rape victimization. Gender is the greatest predictor of crime, although Dana Haynie found the gender gap decreasing slightly as men become more fearful.[32] K. F. Ferraro found that sexual assault serves as a "master offense" for women, influencing their fear of other crimes.[33] Pamela Rountree explored the multidimensional nature of crime by examining victimization surveys, official crime reports, and census data.[34] She found that age had a negative effect on fear, but sex fitted the expected model. Men were 53 percent less fearful of violent crime than women, while women were less fearful of property crime. In Mark Warr's mail survey of Seattle residents, rape was feared by women under the age of thirty-six more than any other offense.[35] Fifty-two percent of the women in the survey and 67 percent of young women reported being fearful of rape. Warr linked the high rate of rape fear to both the crime's seriousness as well as its likeliness.[36] The risk affected women's behavior, with 42 percent reporting that the fear of crime caused them to avoid going out alone (compared to 8 percent of men).

There is a consensus in the research that women's fear of crime is greater than men's even though their actual risk of victimization is less. This is likely due to the nature of sexual victimization. First, stranger-rapes are relatively random. Any woman could be selected for victimization. Second, the crime is inherently intimate, involving risks of pregnancy, sexually transmitted disease, and internal injury. Finally, rape victims can be highly stigmatized, both by the community and the criminal justice system, in labeling victims as somehow unclean or at fault.

Cultural representations of women as potential victims of male crimes of violence (slasher films, books, etc.) may lead individual women to internalize a perception of self as a categorical other at risk of victimization and hence in much the same position as others who are randomly selected victims of bias-motivated offenses. The role of gender in the process of defining general hate crimes remains unexplored. My earlier research with Farr is an initial attempt to explain how women's broader domains allow them to conceptualize ambiguous hate crime scenarios more broadly than men.[37]

The Blazak and Farr research surveyed 325 university students regarding their definitions of bias-related incidents. Students were asked whether they thought fourteen particular scenarios did or did not constitute a hate crime (see Appendix A). The subjects were not given a formal definition of hate crime to use but instead relied on their common understanding of the term. The finding that women were more likely than men to define relatively ambiguous scenarios as hate crimes is consistent with this gender argument. It also suggests that Jenness's and Broad's argument that domains of bias-related crime have been expanded may apply differentially to understandings of particular categories of people. In this research, almost all respondents— female and male—agreed that two of the fourteen incidents were hate crimes. These two scenarios read:

> A group of Asian teens are out looking for a "white devil" to kill. They see some white teens hanging out on a high school field and shoot into the crowd, killing one.

> A group of suburban youths ride into Portland to do some "queer bashing" and beat a man they think is a homosexual. He's not.

These two scenarios constituted for our respondents the clearest cases of the category "hate crimes." In each situation, there was intent to do bias-motivated physical harm to a representative victim, and actual bias-motivated physical harm was done to such a victim. Indeed, these two characteristics—stated intent and actual harm—appear to have been most important to our respondents in defining a particular incident as a hate crime. The particular victim categories reflect expanded domains, but in different ways: in the first, while the category is race, the categorical victim is of the dominant race; in the second, the intended victim was a gay man, however the actual victim was not. The facts that the victim was a member of the "dominant" race in the first case and that the victim in the second scenario was mistaken for but not actually a representative of the target category did not sway respondents from overwhelming agreement that these were a hate crime.

About 98 percent of the total sample agreed that each of these scenarios constituted a hate crime; gender differences were negligible. There was also substantial agreement among both women and men, 92 percent and 80 percent respectively, that the very brief scenario "Abortion clinic bombed" constituted a hate crime. Here, however, a moderate gender gap appeared. It does seem likely that women's "expanded domain" applies in this case, as females in later discussions saw abortion clinic bombings as crimes designed to terrorize women. For the majority, hate-motivated intent, although not stated, was clearly present in this situation, as was potential if not actual physical harm to the target victims.

Of the fourteen scenarios, the following were the least likely (in order of least likelihood) to be defined as hate crimes:

> A man is battered by his gay partner.

> A husband kills his wife in an argument.

Although women were almost twice as likely as men to define these scenarios as hate crimes, less than a quarter of the women saw these individual acts against an intimate other as examples of bias-motivated violence. The percentage-point gender gaps were greatest for those scenarios that were arguably the most ambiguous. The largest gaps in order of magnitude, with women more likely than men to define the situation as a hate crime, were for the following:

> A group of illegal migrant workers beaten by police when they won't leave a public park (gap of 24.6 percent points).

> A woman is raped by a stranger (gap of 22.8 percent points).

> Someone spray-paints their "tag" on a synagogue (gap of 20 percent points).

> A gang of black youth decides to go rob some rich white folk (gap of 19.7 percent points).

These scenarios are ambiguous in several ways. In none but the last is there any direct indication of intent to do bias-motivated harm. Even in the last, where the victim-to-be is of the dominant race and class, there is no direct statement of hate-motivated intent. Over twice as many women (40.7 percent) as men (17.9 percent) saw the stranger-rape as a hate crime; certainly the case could be made here that women's potential position as the victims of this violent crime makes them more sensitive to it. Moreover, it is quite possible that the movements identified by Jenness and Broad have provided the expanded framework necessary for defining stranger-rape as a hate crime.

The research discussed above demonstrates that women have a much wider domain of hate crime categories. All women are potential victims of bias-motivated criminality as women. The specter of stranger-rape and other violence surrounds women constantly. Violence against women is portrayed in movies, music, even fashion advertisements (as "rape chic"), reminding them of their vulnerability.

The ability of women to see crimes against women as a form of hate crime gives them the ability to develop compassion for other potential victims of hate crimes. June Stephenson has argued that compassion is viewed primarily as a female emotion in American culture and that men are socialized to be hard and "guiltless."[38] A woman who can see the terror of the randomness of bias-motivated violence against women can also understand, on some level, the terror of violence against ethnic and racial minorities, sexual and religious minorities, and other targets of hate. A woman who must fear walking alone to her car at night shares much in common with a gay man who must walk alone to his car at night. Both live without the security associated with the position of privilege.

Methodology

This research is based on recording "life histories" of former racist skinheads. The method of using life histories has been useful for understanding the experiences and decisions that lead individuals into criminal lifestyles.[39] I have been interviewing racist skinheads, antiracist skinheads, and former skinheads since 1986, inductively developing a theory about motivations for joining the subculture. In the process, I have heard repeated stories of those who had successfully exited the racist movement. Some former skinheads were not subjects but colleagues, friends, or men with whom I appeared on television programs. As I listened to them speak about their lives, one pattern began to emerge as a primary route out of the life of hate. Often there was a woman who had an impact on their need to be in the subculture and questioned the legitimacy of the subculture itself. These women were teachers, wives, girlfriends, mothers of their children, their own mothers, and foster mothers. Somehow these women helped these young men to "see the light."

There is no significant sociological research on leaving the white supremacist movement. The goal of inductive ethnographic research is not to test theories but to raise theoretical questions to be tested in future research. In this paper, the life histories of five ex-skinheads are discussed that are representative of many cases I have seen in my research. They all live in Oregon and were interviewed in various settings. My research from 1986 to 1995 was conducted as an unknown investigator. Now, as a known "hate-crimes expert," youth outreach volunteer, and civil rights activist, my interviews take place in schools, clandestine cafés, and juvenile detention facilities. Interviews were generally conducted with notes and transcribed later. For the purpose of this project, interview data was coded that related to the impact of females and "psychological" (strain) and "sociological" (anomie) factors to explain their exiting trajectories.

Findings

Each of the five former skinheads were interviewed after they had left the movement. They lead dramatically different lives from each other now, but each is candid about how much their lives have changed since leaving the subculture of hate. The names of the subjects have been changed.

Stan

Stan is a thirty-two-year-old antiracist activist. He works as a security guard and tries to use his experience to help other young skinheads leave the movement. When Stan was a teenager, he ran with a group of violent skinheads for a few years in Seattle. They regularly beat up and robbed gay prostitutes and black drug dealers under the guise of "cleaning up the streets." He spent most of his youth in group homes for wards of the state after his mother shot him when he was eleven. In one of those homes he regularly terrorized a Jewish boy, his hulking size making it relatively easy to strike fear into the hearts of his targets.

With a great amount of clarity, Stan tells the story of the event that changed his life. At the age of seventeen he was moved into a foster home with a foster mother who did not judge Stan for his past. She had a dramatic impact on his psychological and sociological need to be a skinhead:

> It was easy. She gave me unconditional love. I had never experienced that before. Before that I was always angry and looking for someone to blame, someone to beat. Being a skin gave me an outlet. She loved the hate right out of me. All of a sudden, being a skinhead didn't make any sense. If this woman doesn't hate anybody, why should I? I had to reevaluate myself and my whole way of looking at the world. I couldn't rationalize beating people up anymore. I couldn't rationalize racism. It was a dead end street. So I just got out of it. I grew up.
>
> I got a better idea of how to be a man instead of a victim from a woman.

Stan's foster mother dealt with the strain from his anger and his picture of society in which minorities blocked his mobility ("being a skin gave me an outlet") as a well as the anomie associated with his ideas about masculinity and social status ("my whole way of looking at the world"). Stan ended up leaving the Nazi skinhead world behind and creating an advocacy group that helps young people leave hate groups.

Ken

Ken is a twenty-six-year-old electrician. He was a notorious member of a Portland skinhead group that was responsible for killing an Ethiopian man in 1989. He was active until the "skinhead wars" between racists and antiracists in the early 1990s. He now lives a life far away from the skinhead culture while being wary of their hatred for "turncoats." He credits his exit to his wife and the birth of his daughter:

> When we were first dating, she put up with the Nazi shit for a while. I think she thought it was all a big joke. But then she realized how into it I was, we had a big fight. She was like, "It's just a bunch of macho guys getting drunk and shouting,

'white power!' What's the difference between you guys going out and beating up a black guy and me getting raped by a bunch of frat boys?" We broke up after that. But then I thought about it and realized she was right. Besides, I'd rather be with her than them any day.... Then when my daughter was born, I really got it. Like, do I want her to be a breeder to some dumb bonehead or do I want her to have her own life? I really started feeling guilty for all the negative shit I'd put out in the world. Some of that is going to come back on her.

Ken's wife helped him with the strain associated his anomic picture of the world ("I'd rather be with her than them") as well as the scapegoating done by neo-Nazis. She also addressed the anomie associated with macrolevel views of masculinity and white victimization ("I really started feeling guilty for all the negative shit I'd put out in the world"), with guilt facilitating compassion.

Jay

Jay is a fifteen-year-old high school student. He had been drawn into the skinhead movement at school a year earlier. His absent father and a mother he perceived to be domineering propelled him to find an alternative family and a clearer model of masculinity. Jay was enlisted as a "fresh-cut" recruit in a growing suburban skinhead gang. He was becoming increasingly violent and hateful, including making class presentations on the merits of Nazism. It was a student teacher who appealed to both his psychological and sociological reasons for membership.

She was amazing. Just really straightened my head out. I was all like, "the Jews are behind everything!" She explained how that way of looking at the world was too easy. It's too easy to just blame someone instead of looking at yourself. The conspiracy was like a drug. The hate definitely was a drug. It just kept building and building, and she was the first person to say, "look in the mirror at what you're doing to yourself...." I was really angry about my dad and society. I felt like everything was being taken away from me. She was cool. She was like, "look Jay, your life is just starting. Why should you get a free ride? Do you think I get a free ride being a woman? Create your own future." She's really bad-ass and made me feel more bad-ass for walking away from the skinheads and doing it on my own.

Jay's teacher addressed the strain from a need for a simple worldview ("The conspiracy was like a drug") as well as the anomie associated with a lack of identity for ethnic whites ("Create your own future"). Afterwards he contacted a group to help him leave the skinhead world and has maintained an independent identity.

Don

Don is a seventeen-year-old inmate at a juvenile correctional facility. He ran with a skinhead gang from fifteen to seventeen. At seventeen he left the skinheads and joined a drug gang, and was arrested for robbery. He credits his mother for straightening him out on his racism issues. But her appeal addressed only his psychological rationalizations, and he joined a minority gang to address his need for social status:

> I don't know how into the whole skinhead thing I was. It was just fun going around shouting Nazi stuff out and being mean. I was having trouble with the Hispanics at school and when I became a skin, they left me alone. My mom found a bunch of racist shit in my bedroom and sat me down. She's always been straight with me, and I figured I should listen. We talked for hours about what was going on in the world. She's an old hippie, so you can imagine her views. But it just started to make sense to me. So things are changing, they're always changing. I mean, why shouldn't I be friends with the Mexicans? So I said, screw it and just started hanging out with them. I should have just hung out with myself, I guess. Everyone's fucked.

Don's mother confronted his strain based on his fear of a changing world ("So things are changing, they're always changing") but not the anomie from his lack of status in that changing world. The result was that Don left the skinheads for another utilitarian subculture.

Josh

Josh is a twenty-five-year-old antiracist skinhead (a SHARP, or Skinhead Against Racial Prejudice). He spent his early twenties as a racist skinhead, even attending rallies at the Aryan Nations compound in Idaho. He describes himself as having been "hard-core" in the racist movement until he began dating an Asian woman in the punk-rock scene. It is clear that she had an impact on his psychological motivations but not his sociological ones:

> Yeah, she kicked my ass. She was like, "this shit is so bullshit!" I got the whole story about how she has to deal with racism and sexism every single day. All kinds of little things I never even thought about. I thought whites had it so rough, but I had no idea. It's like I couldn't even see what is so obvious. . . . I became a SHARP because I wanted to be a part of something important. The Nazis have stolen the identity of skinhead, and we're going to take it back. And I also want to undo all the bullshit that I did, so if I can do that and beat some bonehead into the ground at the same time, well then right on!

While Josh's girlfriend dealt with the strain from his inability to reach personal goals ("I thought whites had it so rough, but I had no idea"), she did not deal with the anomie that comes with not being part of a social movement. So Dan moved from the racist skinhead subculture to the antiracist subculture.

Discussion

Don's mother and Josh's girlfriend managed to convince Don and Josh of the psychological fallacy of racism by linking it to sexism. As women they faced discrimination and victimization similar to the objects of skinhead hatred. They helped replace the negative stimuli of being a "white victim" with the positive stimuli of friendship and romance with previously off-limit people, but the strain of status frustration was not removed. Even though they left their hate groups, they sought out status in other dangerous subcultures—a drug gang and the SHARPs. On the other hand, Stan's fostermother, Ken's wife, and Jay's teacher helped both with the individual-level strain as well as the macrolevel anomie of living in an ambiguous society that has unclear rules. They no longer needed a subcultural scene to find status in. They found status in their own work as activists, family members, or students.

What the five stories have in common is the ability of the female intimates to impress upon these young men compassion for the victims of hate. Their potential victimhood as women helped them "wake up" the skinheads—not victimization by black rapists but male rapists or the general victimization of sexism. The five subjects of this analysis may not be representative of the typical hate-group leaver. Surely other factors are a part of the decision to leave the movement. Beside the general reasons young men "age out" of crime (increased social bonds, decreased peer pressure, etc.), hate-group members may grow to fear violence from other racists or the more extreme elements of the antiracist community. They may also see hate-group membership itself as blocking their personal goals of upward mobility, making some desired employment or personal relationships more difficult. Of course, many "get it" on their own, realizing the fallacy of racism without the help of women. But as the Blazak and Farr research shows, women's broader definition of "hate crime" points to a greater empathy with victims that may be appealing to young men.[40]

The women in these young men's life had close emotional connections to the skinheads: foster mother, wife, student teacher, mother, and girlfriend. The men cared about what the women thought. The women were able to use the ideas of both love and victimization to impress upon the subjects the value of compassion over reactionary masculinity.

In 1999, I was on an episode of *The Sally Jesse Raphael Show* as a "hate-group expert." The show's theme was children being raised as racists. Among the Klansmen and skinheads was a young man who was claiming to raise his baby with "white pride." Throughout the interview he seemed to be trying to convince the baby's mother more than the audience. It was not her ideology, and one got the sense that she would be the voice of reason in this family. The five subjects here all found women who provided that reason. These stories are not uncommon. Greg Withrow, the White Aryan Resistance recruiter, is now married to a Hispanic woman who helps him deal with the rage he learned from his father. "We've been angry and even fought but I have no right to lay my burden on her. She's been through enough on her own," he says of her.[41]

Young men are attracted to the world of racist skinheads on two levels. Personally, the skinheads resolve issues of strain. Racism is a simple worldview of evil conspiracies and macho heroes. Aggression against enemies is rewarded. It seeks to stop or reverse social change that is blamed for lack of status. The skinhead world is utilitarian, working toward specific goals. Also, it provides a social environment that supplies friends, mates, and father figures. The subculture also confronts the anomie of a normless world. It constructs a hegemonic masculinity and a subordinate femininity. Hate groups explain the loss of economic and social status of whites with a specific ideology. Finally, the subculture forms a normative social movement where change can be affected on a local as a well as global level.

Conclusion

While this piece is an exploratory examination of previously collected data, it presents some theoretical questions for future research on leaving hate groups. The first possibility is that the data may simply represent further evidence of the contention by social-control theory that increased social bonds give deviants a "stake in conformity" and ease them out of criminal lifestyles. In Robert Sampson's and John Laub's revaluation of Glueck's famous study of criminal life histories, this idea was supported.[42] The major events that led to adult desistance from crime were good marriages and stable employment. Perhaps the skinheads here are experiencing their first significant attachments to nondeviant individuals who just happen to be female. The second theoretical possibility emerges from both liberal and radical feminist perspectives. It is that women, through the expression of their experience *as* women, can affect men's own construction of masculinity, encouraging men to move away from the value of random violence and anger. The third perspective, made here, is the value of strain theory. The nature of the impact these various women had on the skinheads was to reduce the anomie of a changing world and alleviate (for some) the various forms of goal blockage. Future research could look at larger samples to explore the relevance of strain/anomie variables to crime desistance.

The important theme here is gender, and it may hold clues to why women themselves join hate groups. Men are attracted to the white-supremacist culture because masculinity is in crisis. Ferber links the contemporary hate movement to a backlash against the feminist, the gay rights, and the civil rights movements.[43] Based on Susan Faludi's concept of backlash, the growing power of women and sexual minorities is seen as a zero-sum game for men. The only recourse to positions of power is to reestablish a role for "real men" by attacking those who are perceived as threatening the status quo. Similarly, Blazak found that racist skinhead men were "doing gender" by celebrating working-class identities (i.e., masculine manufacturing jobs), homophobia, and sexism and targeting anyone who was thought to undermine the status of white men (black criminals, Jewish liberals, etc.).[44] Both Ferber and Blazak find a cartoonish construction of masculinity as virile Aryan warriors, battling against Zionist forces to save their families and their race. They construct an unambiguous world that can be attractive to women as well.

This research provides a hopeful insight into the power of women to negate violent racism, to replace hate with love. Despite the oddities of racist women or female hate-group members (who are often reluctantly brought in by men), my research suggests that women also provide an avenue out of hate. We also get a more subtle interpretation of the changing nature of masculinity associated with maturation and desistance from criminal behavior. It is a masculinity that moves from power, anger, and blame to compassion.

Appendix A

Hate Crimes Survey

What is your gender?   ____Female   ____Male

What is your age?   _____

What is your ethnicity?   _____

Which of the following scenarios would you define as a hate crime?

1. A group of suburban youths ride into Portland to do some "queer bashing" and beat a man who they think is a homosexual. He's not.
   ____Hate crime
   ____Not a hate crime
2. A black male and a white male get into a fight. They know each other and are fighting over money. As the white man is punching the black man, he is shouting, "Give me the money, nigger!"
   ____Hate crime
   ____Not a hate crime

3. A group of Asian teens are out looking for a "white devil" to kill. They see some white teens hanging out on a high school field and shoot into the crowd, killing one.

____Hate crime

____Not a hate crime

4. A husband kills his wife in an argument.

____Hate crime

____Not a hate crime

5. A man is battered by his gay partner.

____Hate crime

____Not a hate crime

6. An abortion clinic is bombed.

____Hate crime

____Not a hate crime

7. A group of Democrats vandalize a Republican candidate's campaign headquarters.

____Hate crime

____Not a hate crime

8. Someone spray-paints their "tag" on a synagogue.

____Hate crime

____Not a hate crime

9. A gang of black ghetto youths decide to go rob some rich white people.

____Hate crime

____Not a hate crime

10. A group of illegal migrant farm workers are beaten by police when they won't leave a public park.

____Hate crime

____Not a hate crime

11. A woman is raped by a stranger.

____Hate crime

____Not a hate crime

12. A Nazi skinhead hands out flyers that say all Jews should be killed.

____Hate crime

____Not a hate crime

13. Poor people are exposed to toxic chemicals when a company purposely dumps illegal waste in their neighborhood.

    _____Hate crime

    _____Not a hate crime

14. A white teenager phones in a fake anthrax threat to a predominately black high school.

    _____Hate crime

    _____Not a hate crime

15. All crimes are "hate" crimes.

    _____Agree

    _____Disagree

8

The Dilemma of Difference: Gender and Hate Crime Policy

VALERIE JENNESS

Nearly six years after two women were bound and gagged and had their throats slit while camping and hiking in the Shenandoah National Park, U.S. Attorney General John D. Ashcroft held an historic nationally televised press conference on April 11, 2001, to announce that the U.S. Justice Department had invoked the federal hate crimes statute for the first time to charge the alleged murderer with hate crime. In announcing the indictment, Ashcroft spoke at length about his meeting with the parents of the victims and about the lives and character of the young women: two Midwesterners who migrated to New England, met and became lovers, and shared a love of science and the outdoors. Justifying the invocation of federal hate crime law, which carries with it enhanced penalties, Ashcroft said: "criminal acts of hate run counter to what is best in America, our belief in equality and freedom. The Department of Justice will aggressively investigate, prosecute, and punish criminal acts of violence and vigilantism motivated by hate and intolerance." Moreover, he said, "we will pursue, prosecute, and punish those who attack law-abiding Americans out of hatred for who they are," and "hatred is the enemy of justice, regardless of its source."[1]

In this case, evidence suggests that the "source of hatred" was twofold: sexuality and gender. According to prosecutors, Darrell David Rice, a computer programmer from Columbia, Maryland, is, by his own account, a man who hates lesbians and enjoys intimidating and assaulting women. According to

181

law enforcement, sometime after being arrested, Rice told law-enforcement officials that he intentionally selected women to assault "because they are more vulnerable than men," that he "hates gays," and that the victims in this case "deserved to die because they were lesbian whores."[2] Accordingly, lead Assistant U.S. Attorney Tom Bondurant, Jr., plans to argue that Rice chose to slit the throats of the two young women because of their gender and because of their "actual or perceived sexual orientation."[3] According to court documents, Bondurant will introduce evidence of the defendant's numerous physical and verbal assaults upon randomly selected women, including acts of road rage, physical assaults, demeaning sexual comments, and threats of injury or death. The assistant U.S. Attorney plans to argue in court "that the defendant's killing of the two women was part of an ongoing plan, scheme, or modus operandi to assault, intimidate, and injure and kill women because of their gender."[4]

As the first federal prosecution of a hate crime based on gender, this case raises a plethora of questions about the status, meaning, and workings of gender in hate crime policy in the United States. Although there is a growing body of literature on the ways in which public policy associated with crime control is gendered, the literature is surprisingly silent when it comes to understanding the ways in which gender—as a central axis of differentiation around which violence and discrimination manifest—has been constructed, positioned, and reacted to via the emergence, content, and evolution of public policy on bias-motivated violence, especially legal reform and law.[5] Most notably, an examination of gender as a feature of policy connected to hate crime has been notably absent in recent journal publications devoted specifically to the study of hate crime in the United States and abroad. For example, neither the recent special issue of the *American Behavioral Scientist* devoted to "Hate Crimes and Ethnic Conflict: A Comparative Perspective" nor the recent special issue of *Law and Critique* on "Hate Crime: Critical Reflections" contains an article that focuses specifically on gender and hate crime policy, including law.[6]

To fill this gap, this chapter provides an overview of the status of gender in hate crime policy in the United States. To do so, it first introduces the concept of "hate crime" as a politically determined and legislatively defined subset of criminal behavior. This section treats "hate crime" as a recently developed term that is now commonly used to signify age-old forms of conduct. With this in mind, it then inventories the ways in which gender has—and more notably, has not—loomed large in state and federal lawmakers' most institutionalized response to bias-motivated violence in the United States (i.e., the law). This section reveals that gender is best envisioned as a "second-class citizen" in social, political, and legal discourse in the United States that speaks directly to the larger problem of violence motivated by bigotry and manifest as discrimination (i.e., bias-motivated violence). Thereafter, this chapter offers a discussion of what feminist legal scholars refer to as "the dilemma of difference" inherent in hate crime policy in the United States.[7] Here the focus is on how the dilemma of difference has been attended to in the formulation of hate crime policy in the United States, which recognizes the ways in which gender is both distinct from and similar to other status provisions that anchor hate crime law in the United States (i.e., race, religion, ethnicity, sexual orientation, disabilities, etc.).

Hate Crime (Loosely Construed) in the United States

In the latter part of the twentieth century, the term "hate crime" and the legal logic it implies diffused across the globe as civil rights groups and criminal justice systems responded to an age-old form of violence—that which is organized around axes of social differentiation and targets minorities—in newfound ways. Hence it is appropriate to conceptualize hate crime as part of a larger complex process of legal and cultural regulation of violence directed toward minorities in the United States and, recently, across the globe.[8]

The Emergence of Hate Crime in the United States

The concept "hate crime" first emerged in the United States in the late 1970s and has since been institutionalized in social, political, and legislative discourse in the United States and abroad.[9] Although it remains an empirical question whether the United States and other countries that use the term to reference a subset of crime are experiencing greater levels of hate- or bias-motivated violence than in the past, it is beyond dispute that the term "hate crime" has found a home in various spheres of social and institutional life.[10] From the introduction and politicization of the term in the late 1970s to the continued enforcement of hate crime law at the beginning of the twenty-first century, modern civil rights movements have constructed the problem of bias-motivated violence in ways that distinguish it from other forms of violent crime; state and federal politicians have made legislation that defines the parameters of hate crime in ways that distinguish it from other types of violent crime; judicial decision-makers have elaborated upon and enriched the meaning of hate crime as they determined the constitutionality of "hate crime" as a legal concept that distinguishes types of violence based on the motivation of the perpetrator; and law-enforcement officials have continued to investigate and prosecute bias-motivated incidents as a special type of crime that warrants enhanced penalties.[11]

As a result of these changes, violence born of bigotry and manifest as discrimination has been resignified and reacted to in ways that result in the reconfiguration of violence directed toward minorities.[12] The result is twofold. First, in the United States it is increasingly understood that criminal conduct takes on a new meaning when it involves an act motivated by bigotry. Second, people of color, Jews, immigrants, and gays and lesbians are routinely recognized as victims of hate crime, while other vulnerable victims—for example, union members, octogenarians, the elderly, children, and police officers—are not. As this chapter will reveal, girls and women fall somewhere in between. This classification reflects the unique politics of hate crime in the United States.[13]

In the United States the use of the term "hate crime" is now commonplace in settings as diverse as prime-time television, the evening news, academic conferences, presidential proclamations, and all levels of lawmaking. In the last decade alone, a steady stream of seemingly disparate incidents have been presented to the public as hate crime, including repeated attacks on African Americans who moved into a predominately white neighborhood in Philadelphia; attacks by neighborhood youths on families of Cambodian refugees who fled to Brooklyn; the beating to death of a Chinese American because he was presumed to be Japanese; the harassment of Laotian fishermen in Texas; the brutal attack on two men in Manhattan by a group of knife- and bat-wielding teenage boys shouting "homos!" and "fags!"; the assault on three women in Portland, Maine, after their assailant yelled antilesbian epithets at them; the gang rape with bottles, lighted matches, and other implements of a gay man who was repeatedly told "what faggots deserve"; the stabbing to death of a heterosexual man in San Francisco because he was presumed to be gay; and the gang rapes of a female jogger in Central Park and a mentally handicapped teenager in Glen Ridge, New Jersey.[14]

Considering Three High Profile Cases

In the latter part of the 1990s, three highly publicized cases of homicide occurred in which the victims were chosen because of a social characteristic. The first was the murder of James Byrd in Jasper, Texas, in June of 1998. This event, covered extensively in the national media, presented the murder as a "hate crime" after it was revealed that Byrd, a forty-nine-year-old black man, had been beaten and then dragged to his death behind a truck by three white men known to be affiliated with a white-supremacist group.[15] Shortly thereafter, the murder of Matthew Shepard, a young gay man who was pistol-whipped, tied to a fence, and left to die, was treated as a hate crime by the national news media.[16] In contrast to these two incidents, the murder of four young girls in a Jonesboro, Arkansas schoolyard in March of 1998 has generally not been viewed as a hate crime, despite the revelation that the young boys in custody for the killings sought to shoot girls because it was girls that angered them. That is, they selected their victims on the basis of gender. Nonetheless, *Time* referred to it as a "youth crime" and *Newsweek* called it "schoolyard crime."[17] Because of this framing, the incident triggered a different set of legal and policy discussions, most often discussed in terms of school violence and the debate over gun control.

Despite the empirical dissimilarities in the details of these three high-profile cases, they nonetheless share an underlying parameter: in all of these cases the victims were apparently chosen by the perpetrators not because of *who* they were but because of *what* they were. The fact that the events in Jasper, Texas, and Laramie, Wyoming, were interpreted as hate crimes and the event in Jonesboro, Arkansas, was not reveals a key aspect of the contested terrain of hate crime: who and what is included is a matter of interpretation, legal and otherwise. Clearly, then, if one were to rely upon media portrayals, gender would not be constitutive of "the hate crime problem in the United States"; that is, it does not loom large in the most highly visible and widely discussed events that fall under the rubric of hate crime. However, it is important to note that the media does not define *crime*, at least not in a technical sense. It is the state that defines crime through the passage of law. Therefore, as most criminologists would agree, it is appropriate to define crime, including *hate* crime, with reference to statutes. Accordingly, the next section examines the standing of "gender" in both state and federal hate crime law in the United States.

The Engendering of Hate Crime (Legally Defined) in the United States

As others have documented, in the latter part of the twentieth century the law became the primary institution charged with defining and curbing hate- or bias-motivated violence.[18] During a congressional debate on hate crime, U.S. Representative Mario Biaggi said it most succinctly when he argued: "the obvious point is that we are dealing with a national problem and we must look to our laws for remedies."[19] Concurring, U.S. Representative John Conyers, Jr., the ranking member of the Judiciary Committee, explained that the enactment of hate crime legislation: "will carry to offenders, to victims, and to society at large an important message, that the Nation is committed to battling the violent manifestations of bigotry."[20] Consistent with these views, in the late 1970s and early 1980s, lawmakers throughout the United States began to respond to what they perceived to be an escalation of violence directed at minorities with a novel legal strategy: the criminalization of discriminatory violence, now commonly referred to as "hate crime." As result, by the turn of the century, "in seemingly no time at all, a 'hate crimes jurisprudence' had sprung up."[21]

Defining the Parameters of Hate Crime Law

With considerable variation in wording and content, (criminal hate crime statutes are laws that criminalize or further criminalize activities motivated by bias toward individuals or groups because of their real or imagined characteristics) Drawing from Ryken Grattet, Valerie Jenness, and Theodore Curry, this definition consists of three elements.[22] (First, the law provides a new state policy action, by creating a new criminal category, altering an existing law, or enhancing penalties for select extant crimes when they are committed for bias reasons. Second, hate crime laws contain an intent standard.[23] In other words, statutes contain wording that refers to the subjective intention of the perpetrator rather than relying solely on the basis of objective behavior. Finally, hate crime laws specify a list of protected social statuses, such as race, religion, ethnicity, sexual orientation, gender, disabilities, and so on.[24] These elements of the definition of hate crime law capture the spirit and essence of hate crime legislation designed to punish bias-motivated *conduct.*

The Content of State Hate Crime Law

At the state level, in the last two decades almost every state in the United States has adopted at least one hate crime statute that simultaneously recognizes, defines, and responds to discriminatory violence. (Hate crime statutes have taken many forms throughout the United States, including statutes proscribing criminal penalties for civil rights violations; specific "ethnic intimidation" and "malicious harassment" statutes; and provisions in previously enacted statutes for enhanced penalties if an extant crime is committed for bias or prejudicial reasons) These laws specify provisions for race, religion, color, ethnicity, ancestry, national origin, sexual orientation, gender, age, disability, creed, marital status, political affiliation, age, marital status, involvement in civil or human rights, and armed service personnel. In addition, a few states have adopted statutes that require authorities to collect data on hate- or bias-motivated crimes; mandate law-enforcement training; prohibit the undertaking of paramilitary training; specify parental liability; and provide for victim compensation. Finally, many states have statutes that prohibit institutional vandalism and the desecration or defacement of religious objects, the interference with or disturbance of religious worship, cross-burning, the wearing of hoods or masks, the formation of secret societies, and the distribution of publications and advertisements designed to harass select groups of individuals. This last group of laws reference a previous generation of what, in retrospect, could be termed "hate crime" law.[25]

(More important, hate crime statutes vary in terms of the specific-status provisions recognized by law. Status provisions such as race, religion, ethnicity, ancestry, sexual orientation, gender, disability, and so on implicitly reference what Soule and Earl refer to as "target groups";[26] that is, race is a proxy for nonwhites, religion is a proxy for non-Christians, sexual orientation is a proxy for gays and lesbians, gender is a proxy for girls and women, and so on. Given this, status provisions clearly single out some axes of oppression and minorities as worthy of legislative attention and attendant legal intervention while rendering invisible other axes of oppression around which violence is organized with attendant vulnerable victims.)

In other words, status provisions contained in hate crime law define who does and does not count as a hate crime victim; likewise, status provisions in hate crime law delineate who does and does not qualify as a hate crime perpetrator. This determination and attendant differentiation are important insofar as they affect the kinds of people protected by hate crime law as well as the kinds of perpetrators prosecutors can pursue using hate crime law. For example, if gender is included in a hate crime law, a person victimized because of her gender qualifies as a victim of hate crime; if, on the other hand, gender is not included in a hate crime law, the crime is not charged as a hate crime.

As lawmakers drafted, revised, and adopted hate crime law, especially early on in the process of thinking about the parameters of hate crime in the United States, which types of distinctions should be written into law was an open-ended question. Activists and policy-makers alike had to ponder a series of related questions such as: Who should be represented in hate crime law? Why? On what grounds? To emphasize the political rather than legal nature of this question, Laurence Tribe, Professor of Constitutional Law at Harvard University, informed lawmakers that the question of which status provisions to include in hate crime law presents no Constitutional problem. As he explained in U.S. Congressional hearings on hate crime: "Nothing in the U.S. Constitution prevents the Government from penalizing with added severity those crimes directed against people or their property because of their race, color, religion, national origin, ethnicity, gender or sexual orientation, and nothing in the Constitution requires that this list be infinitely expanded.[27] If, as Tribe suggests, legislators had considerable latitude, how did they proceed to demarcate status provisions in hate crime law? In particular, how did gender fare in the process, both in absolute terms and in comparative terms?

Some state lawmakers and attendant legislatures have ensured that "gender" found a home state hate crime law. When it appears in hate crime law, the status provision for gender is articulated in different ways. First, it often is coded as "sex" in the legal definition of a hate crime. For example, in 1999

North Dakota passed a law that says:

> A person is guilty of a class B misdemeanor if, whether acting under the color of law, he by force, or threat of force or by economic coercion, intentionally: 1) Injures, intimidates, or interferes with another because of his sex, race, color, religion, or national origin and because he is or has been exercising or attempting to exercise his right to full and equal enjoyment of any facility open to the public. 2) Injures, intimidates, or interferes with another because of his sex, race, color, religion, or national origin in order to intimidate him or any other person from exercising or attempting to exercise his right to full and equal enjoyment of any facility open to the public.[28]

Similarly, West Virginia hate crime law declares the following:

> All persons within the boundaries of the state of West Virginia have the right to be free from any violence, or intimidation by threat of violence, committed against their persons or property because of their race, color, religion, ancestry, national origin, political affiliation, or sex. If any person does by force or threat of force, willfully injure, intimidate or interfere with, or attempt to interfere with, or oppress or threaten any other person in the free exercise or enjoyment of any right or privilege secured to him or her by the Constitution or laws of the state of West Virginia or by the Constitution or laws of the United States, because of such other person's race, color, religion, ancestry, national origin, political affiliation, or sex, he or she shall be guilty of a felony, and, upon conviction, shall be fined not more than five thousand dollars or imprisoned not more than ten years, or both.[29]

Second, consistent with the example in the introduction to this chapter, gender often appears alongside sexual orientation. For example, in 1991 Illinois passed a law that included both gender and sexual orientation as factors that shall be accorded weight as reasons to impose a more severe sanction (i.e., enhanced penalty). This law defines a hate crime as a crime in which: "[T]he defendant committed the offense against a person or person's property because of such person's race, color, creed, religion, ancestry, gender, sexual orientation, physical or mental disability, or national origin. For the purposes of this section, 'sexual orientation means heterosexuality, homosexuality, or bisexuality.'"[30]

Similarly, Rhode Island's Hate Crime Sentencing Act specifies the following:

> [I]f any person has been convicted of a crime charged by complaint, information, or indictment, in which he or she intentionally selected the person against whom the offense is committed or selected that property that is damaged or otherwise affected by the offense because of the actor's hatred or animus toward the actual or perceived disability, religion, color, race, national origin or ancestry, sexual orientation, or gender of that person or the owner or occupant of that property, he or she shall be subject to the [enhanced] penalties provided in this section.[31]

Finally, in some cases the status provision for gender has been included in hate crime law as an amendment to a previously articulated hate crime law. For example, in 1987 California adopted an Interference with Exercise of Civil Rights Law. It stated that:

> No person, whether or not acting under color of law, shall by force or threat of force, willfully injure, intimidate, interfere with, oppress, or threaten any other person in the free exercise or enjoyment of any right or privilege secured to him or her by the Constitution or laws of this state or by the Constitution or the laws of the United States because of the other person's race, color, religion, ancestry, national origin, or sexual orientation.[32]

Thereafter, the California state legislature amended the law in two ways. First, in 1991 it amended the law to include "disability" and "gender." Then, in 1994, it amended the law to include "or because he or she perceives that the person has one or more of those characteristics." The law now reads:

> No person, whether or not acting under color of law, shall by force or threat of force, willfully injure, intimidate, interfere with, oppress, or threaten any other person in the free exercise or enjoyment of any right or privilege secured to him or her by the Constitution or laws of this state or by the Constitution or the laws of the United States because of the other person's race, color, religion, ancestry, national origin, disability, gender, or sexual orientation or because he or she perceives that the other person has one or more of these characteristics.[33]

Clearly, then, "gender" has been recognized as a source of bias-motivated violence by some legislators and legislatures. Nonetheless, it is fair to ask: How *much* as it been recognized as part and parcel of a larger hate crime problem in the United States? How does it compare to other axes of inequality and attendant discriminatory violence?

Figure 8.1 presents the total number of status provisions, by type, in the United States. The most common status provisions are for race, religion, color, and national origin. These status provisions are associated with the most visible, recognizable, and stereotypical kinds of discriminatory behavior in U.S. history and in the current era.[34] For example, in the United States the stereotypical hate crime involves violence toward or harassment of blacks, immigrants, and Jews. Accordingly, these status provisions can be referred to as "core" hate crime provisions in state hate crime law. In terms of frequency counts, a second tier of provisions includes sexual orientation, disability, ancestry, gender, creed, and ethnicity. Given that legislators, like the population at large, tend to conflate ancestry, creed, and ethnicity with race, religion, color, and national origins, at least at the level of terminology and attendant identity politics, these status provisions can also arguably be classified as core provisions. As a result, sexual orientation, disability, and gender stand alone as "second-tier" provisions insofar as they appear

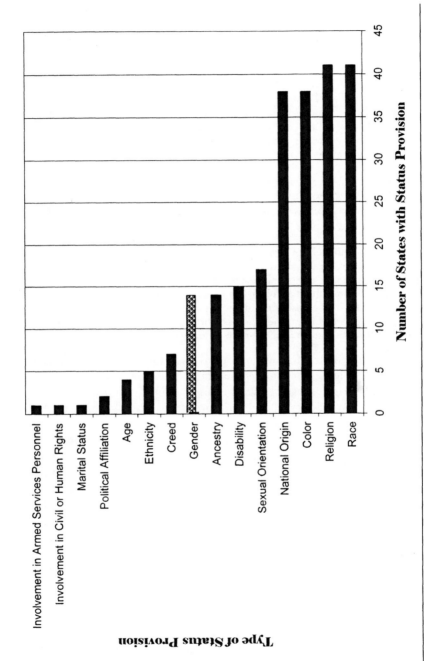

Fig. 8.1 Frequency of Status Provisions in State Hate Crime Law in the United States, 2001

with comparable frequency—and less frequently than core provisions. Finally, there are some comparatively anomalous status provisions, including age, political affiliation, marital status, involvement in civil or human rights, and involvement in armed services personnel. These status provisions can be classified as anomalous insofar as they appear in state hate crime law with comparable frequency. When compared with core and second-tier status provisions, as described above, these anomalous status provisions appear in state hate crime law infrequently (i.e., only a few states have included them in hate crime law). Indeed, they have failed to gain a foothold as a key component of hate crime law.[35]

Figure 8.2 reveals the *cumulative* frequency of the status provisions included in state hate crime laws from 1978, the year the first state hate crime law was passed, until 2001, the last year for which systematic data on hate crime law are available. The respective unfolding of these clusters of status provisions—the core, the second tier, and the anomalous provisions—reveals that although the idea of including gender in hate crime policy was introduced very early on in the process of making hate crime policy, it did not find a secure home in hate crime law until about halfway through a larger process of legal reform designed to curb bias-motivated violence.[36] Moreover, once it gained legitimacy and subsequent inclusion in law, gender nonetheless remained a less accepted provision in hate crime policy than those identified as core provisions.

The ways in which gender has been demoted in the politics of hate crime lawmaking are revealed in Jenness's work on the politics of hate crime.[37] Namely, early on in federal lawmaking, the Coalition on Hate Crime, the primary group responsible for defining the parameters of proposed hate crime legislation, contemplated recommending including gender as a protected status in legislation, but eventually decided against it for a variety of reasons.[38] First, some members of the coalition believed that the inclusion of gender would delay, if not completely impede, the timely passage of the law. Second, some members of the coalition argued that including gender would open the door to age, disability, position in a labor dispute, party affiliation, and/or membership in the armed forces provisions. At the time this was seen as an undesirable outcome. Third, some believed that including gender would make enactment of the law too cumbersome, if not entirely impossible, since violent crimes against women are so pervasive and, arguably, caused by factors other than bigotry or discrimination. Fourth, and related, others argued that not all acts of violence against women fit (what was then) the working definition of a hate crime. Fifth, some members of the coalition argued that expanding the categories of officially recognized hate crimes to include gender would not improve upon current efforts to collect official data on rape and domestic violence, two categories of gender-based violence

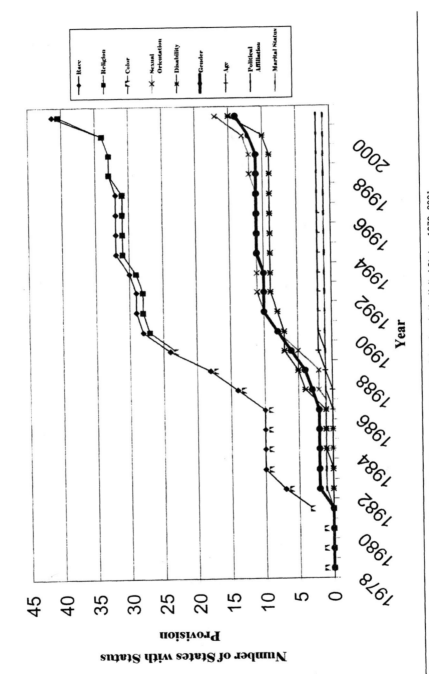

Fig. 8.2 Cumulative Frequency of Selected Status Provisons in State Hate Crime Law in the United States, 1978–2001

deemed most worthy of special concern.)Focusing on feasibility, opponents feared that adding gender as a provision would simply overwhelm the data-collection efforts of law enforcement agencies and human-rights organizations that track hate crimes. In addition, the large number of crimes against women would overshadow statistics on hate crimes against members of other groups.[39])

The patterns revealed in Figures 8.1 and 8.2 are consistent with the history of various post-1960s civil rights movements in the United States.[40] Race, religion, color, national origin, ancestry, creed, and ethnicity reflect the early legal contestation of minorities' status and rights. Hence there is a developed history of invoking and then deploying the law, especially civil rights law, to protect and enhance the status of blacks, Jews, and immigrants. In contrast, the gay/lesbian movement, the women's movement, and the disability movement reflect a "second wave" of civil rights activism and "identity politics" in the United States.[41] Accordingly, sexual orientation, gender, and disability have been only recently recognized as status provisions in hate crime law in the United States. As Jenness has shown in her work on the U.S. congressional hearings on hate crime, these are also more heavily contested protected statuses than the "first wave" (i.e., core) categories.[42] Not surprisingly, they remain less embedded in hate crime law. Finally, marital status, creed, age, membership in the armed service personnel, and political affiliation are not visibly connected to issues of discrimination and victimization by any particular mass movement, and they are fairly anomalous status provisions in hate crime law in the United States.

The Content of Federal Hate Crime Law

(Following the states' lead, the U.S. Congress has passed three laws specifically designed to address bias-motivated violence, only two of which reference gender as an element of hate crime.)In 1990(President Bush signed the Hate Crimes Statistics Act, which requires the U.S. Attorney General to collect statistical data on "crimes that manifest evidence of prejudice based on race, religion, sexual orientation, or ethnicity, including where appropriate the crimes of murder, non-negligent manslaughter; forcible rape; aggravated assault, simple assault, intimidation; arson; and destruction, damage or vandalism of property."[43])As a data-collection law, the Hate Crimes Statistics Act merely requires the Attorney General to gather and make available to the public data on bias-motivated crime, which has been accomplished every year since 1991. (It does not in any way stipulate new penalties for bias-motivated crimes nor does it provide legal recourse for victims of bias-motivated crime. Most important, it does not include a provision for "gender," hence gender-based bias-motivated crime is not visible in official hate crime statistics in the United States produced by the Uniform Crime Report on Hate Crime in the United States.)

In 1994, Congress passed two more hate crime laws. The Violence Against Women Act specifies that "all persons within the United States shall have the right to be free from crimes of violence motivated by gender."[44] The Violence Against Women Act allocated over $1.6 billion for education, rape crisis hot lines, training of justice personnel, victim services (especially shelters for victims of battery), and special units of police and prosecutors to deal with crimes against women. The heart of the legislation, Title III, provides a civil remedy for "gender crimes." The justification for such a remedy is as follows:

> Congress finds that (1) crimes motivated by the victim's gender constitute bias crimes in violation of the victim's right to be free from discrimination on the basis of gender; (2) current law provides a civil remedy for crimes committed in the workplace, but not for gender crimes committed on the street and in the home; and (3) State and Federal laws do not adequately protect against the bias element of gender crimes, which separates these crimes from acts of random violence, no do they adequately provide victims the opportunity to vindicate their interests.[45]

In essence, Title III entitles victims to compensatory and punitive damages through the federal courts for a crime of violence if it is motivated, at least in part, by animus toward the victim's gender. This allowance implicitly acknowledges that some, if not most, violence against women is not gender-neutral; instead, it establishes the possibility that violence motivated by gender animus is a proper subject for civil rights action. In so doing, it affixed the term "hate crime" to "a crime of violence committed because of gender or on the basis of gender, and due, at least in part, to animus based on the victim's gender."[46] Although this law was recently ruled unconstitutional, it was predicated upon and promoted the inclusion of gender in the concept of a hate crime.[47]

Also in 1994, Congress passed the Hate Crimes Sentencing Enhancement Act. This law identifies eight predicate crimes—murder; nonnegligent manslaughter; forcible rape; aggravated assault; simple assault; intimidation; arson; and destruction, damage, or vandalism of property—for which judges are allowed to enhance penalties by "not less than three offense levels for offenses that finder of fact at trial determines beyond a reasonable doubt are hate crimes."[48] For the purposes of this law, hate crime is defined as criminal conduct wherein "the defendant intentionally selected any victim or property as the object of the offense because of the actual or perceived race, color, religion, national origin, ethnicity, gender, disability, or sexual orientation of any person."[49] Although broad in form, this law addresses only those hate crimes that take place on federal lands and properties. This is this law that U.S. Attorney General Ashcroft invoked in the case described in the opening paragraphs of this chapter.)

Enforcement of Gender Provisions in Hate Crime Law

The state and federal laws described above suggest that in the contemporary era, many lawmakers and other policy-makers share a commitment to using the law, law enforcement, and the criminal justice system as a vehicle to enhance the status and welfare of minority constituencies deemed differentially vulnerable to violence motivated by bigotry. However, the place of gender in this commitment is distinct in empirically identifiable ways. First, gender is present in hate crime law but only a second-class citizen in larger legal efforts to respond to bias-motivated violence. As described above and summarized in Figures 8.1 and 8.2, the distribution of provisions for gender in state and federal hate crime law reveals that gender has found a home in legal discourse on hate crime legislation, but it remains in the guest room of that home.

Second, connected to the location of gender in hate crime law, both federal and state efforts to collect data on bias crimes directed at people because of their gender have lagged behind efforts to collect data on the other types of bias crimes. For example, the Hate Crime Statistics Act does not mandate the Federal Bureau of Investigation (FBI) to collect data on bias crimes based on gender as part of the Uniform Crime Report (UCR), hence gender-based violence is not referenced in official statistics on hate crime in the United States. Similarly, at the state level, efforts to gather reports on gender-based hate crime have been delayed. For example, California, one of the largest and most heterogeneous states in the United States, reports very few hate crimes based on gender. In 2001 California's Attorney General's Civil Rights Commission on Hate Crime published a report on the Attorney General's Web site which stated that "hate crimes based on gender are not reported generally." Accordingly, the report "recommended that the California Commission on Peace Officer Standards and Training (POST) revise its training and guidelines to provide special emphasis on gender-based crimes."[50]

Third, consistent with reporting practices, police training publications and curricula at federal, state, and local levels tend to discuss gender-based hate crime only infrequently, if at all. For example, the word "gender" does not appear in the major national bias-crime training manual for law enforcement and victim-assistance professionals, the *Training Guide for Hate Crime Data Collection,* published by the U.S. Department of Justice.[51] Moreover, gender often does not appear in law enforcement hate crime policies. For example, as Figure 8.3 reveals, in a large, heterogeneous, and progressive state like California, which has had a gender provision in its state hate crime law since 1991, gender appears in law enforcement hate crime policies less

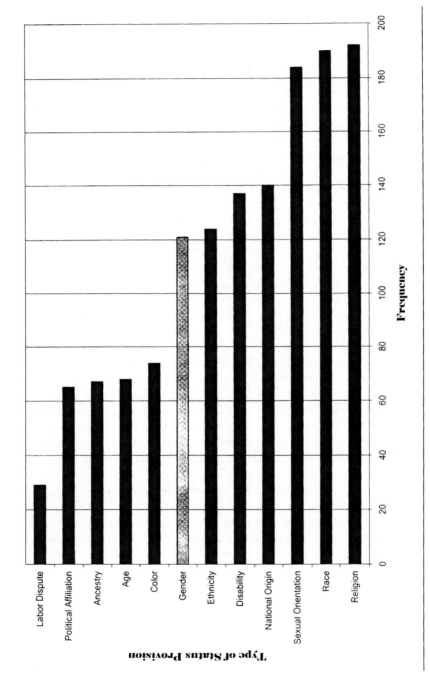

Fig. 8.3 Status Provisions in Police and Sheriff Departments' Hate Crime Policies in California, 2001

than one third of the time. Specifically, only 121 law enforcement agencies out of a total of 397 direct their officers to attend to gender-based hate crime. As a result, gender-based hate crime remains largely invisible to frontline law enforcers, who tend to focus mostly on race, religion, sexual orientation, and nationality. A lack of emphasis on gender in law-enforcement curricula and policies leads to a lack of recognition within law enforcement, which in turn results in an underreporting of bias-motivated crimes based on gender.

Fourth and finally, when law-enforcement personnel attempt to enforce gender provisions in hate crime law, they do so with added complications. For example, in Massachusetts the Attorney General has instituted a policy whereby gender-based hate crimes require at least two previous restraining orders issued to protect two different domestic partners. Over the past ten years there have been fewer than ten cases in which these criteria have been met.[52] Restrictive policies such as these ensure that hate crimes based on gender are extremely difficult to prosecute.

Moving beyond the question of enforceability, as with any policy reform that directs attention to any minority constituency, the inclusion/exclusion of gender in hate crime law raises the larger question of how best to resolve the dilemma of difference in policy- and lawmaking. This question is addressed in the next section.

Gender, Hate Crime, and the Dilemma of Difference

For legal scholars, the "dilemma of difference" can best be stated as a question: Should those interested in enhancing the status and welfare of minority groups pursue policies that provide "special" treatment for minorities, including women? Or alternatively, should they pursue policies that ignore the unique social location, special qualities, and socially structured obstacles faced by minorities, including women, and work solely towards improving "equality" for all members of society? With regard to crime control policies in particular, should the law recognize the "special" needs of minorities, including women, or should the same social and legal resources be made available to all victims of crime, regardless of their social characteristics or group membership? Stated more succinctly, should all victims of crime be treated the same, or should some victims of crime, namely "vulnerable victims" and people who face unique barriers when accessing the criminal justice system and pursuing justice, be distinguished and treated differently?

Historically and in the current era, advocates for minorities, feminist and other critical legal scholars, and policy-makers of all stripes have had to respond to these questions. This section addresses this familiar yet pressing concern by examining the contours of and justifications for status provisions, especially "gender," in American hate crime law. In so doing, this section concludes this chapter by arguing that the inclusion of gender in hate crime policy allows the "sameness/difference" debate to be solved in a way that both (1) treats girls and women as a special category of crime victim and, at the same time, the same as other hate crime victims; and (2) treats perpetrators of gender-based crime as a special category of offender and, at the same time, the same as other types of bias-motivated offenders. How does it do this?

Gender and the Dilemma of Difference Historically

In the latter part of the twentieth century, feminist legal scholars debated how best to invoke and position gender when using the law to advocate on behalf of girls and women in the pursuit of their full participation in U.S. society. Early on, scholars split over the following seemingly simple question: How should the law attend to institutionalized gender inequality? The so-called "equal treatment" advocates argue that gender equality requires identical treatment of the sexes, without regard to pregnancy, differential vulnerability to crime, under representation in the workplace, and so on.[53] As Williams argued in her often cited article, "Equality's Riddle: Pregnancy and the Equal Treatment/Special Treatment Debate": "an anti-discrimination provision is a device for telling legislators, governments and designated others what they may not do, thus setting parameters with which they must operate. It does not, and cannot, do the basic work of readjusting the social order."[54]

In contrast, the so-called "special treatment" camp rejects the equal treatment model in favor of an equal-opportunity model, often labeled a "special treatment" or a "positive action" approach.[55] Here the idea is that the law must treat classes of persons, for example girls and women, differently insofar as they are differently situated in society.

Still others advanced an approach that tried to "split the difference," as it were, between the poles represented by the "sameness/difference" positions. For example, in her classic work on "Equality and Difference: The Case of Pregnancy," Herma Hill Kay put forth an "episodic analysis" for dealing with pregnancy (or any other gender-related difference). Kay argued that the law should treat biologically derived sex differences as legally significant *only* when they are being utilized for reproductive purpose—that is, only when the differences matter in the context under legal scrutiny.[56]

More recently, the choice between whether or not to emphasize and delineate social difference(s) in social policy, especially law, has been astutely characterized by Harvard Law Professor Martha Minow as the "dilemma of difference." As Minow details in her book *Making All the Difference: Inclusion, Exclusion, and American Law,* the dilemma of difference is a philosophical, legal, and strategic issue that has implications for an array of social issues ranging from affirmative action to maternal leave policies to gay marriage to discrimination in the workplace against persons with disabilities. Minow writes:

> The stigma of difference may be recreated both by ignoring and by focusing on it. Decisions about education, employment, benefits, and other opportunities in society should not turn on an individual's ethnicity, disability, race, gender, religion, or membership in any other group about which some have deprecating or hostile attitudes. Yet refusing to acknowledge these differences may make them continue to matter in a world constructed with some groups, but not others, in mind. These problems of inequality can be exacerbated both by treating members of minority groups the same as members of the majority and by treating the two groups differently.[57]

Often summarized as a tension between "same" versus "different" treatment policies, "the dilemma of difference may be posed as a choice between integration and separation, as a choice between similar treatment and special treatment, or as a choice between neutrality and accommodation."[58] As such, it obviously evokes questions about how to treat social differences, such as those loosely referenced under the rubric of "gender," in public policy, especially lawmaking, as there are costs and benefits associated with both choices to policy-making.

Policies that emphasize gender as a significant axis of social differentiation by focusing on the "special" needs of women, such as pregnancy leave and affirmative-action policies, risk reinforcing cultural distinctions between women and men. Such policies can construct women as different from men, underscore their "incapacities" and special needs as the defining feature of their social identities, and ultimately place them in subordinate positions within both public and privates spheres of social life. Arguably, one of the unintended consequences of social policies that single out women for "special" protections and treatment is the reinforcement of the idea that women are more vulnerable members of society and less capable of responding to real and perceived vulnerabilities.[59] And so it is with the *presence* of gender in hate crime law, which clearly treats girls and women as "target groups" in need of special treatment.[60]

In contrast, policies that ignore differences between types of victims risk being insensitive to the increasingly well-documented institutional, organizational, and interactional disadvantages faced by women, including those who find themselves confronting a criminal justice system with ideologies and structures that were enacted with men in mind.[61] Treating women the same as other crime victims does little to challenge the biases and stereotypes with which criminal justice officials often operate. A sizeable body of evidence suggests that ignoring social difference is seldom enough to produce equality, especially in the criminal justice system. Indeed, failing to acknowledge the differences around which systematic injustices revolve allows state officials to continue to do business as usual and does little to remedy systematic inequality. And so it is with the *absence* of gender in hate crime law, which clearly ignores girls and women as "target groups" in need of special treatment.[62]

Resolving the Dilemma of Difference

As described in the previous section, the presence *and* absence of gender are evident in the introduction, adoption, and enforcement of a body of law properly called "hate crime law." This situation speaks to both the positive and the negative consequences of including gender in hate crime law. On the negative side, the inclusion of gender in hate crime law is often perceived to be creating "special" treatment where such treatment directly or indirectly reproduces stereotypes about women as vulnerable victims in need of state protection. On the positive side, the inclusion of gender in hate crime law serves to acknowledge the drawbacks of ignoring girls' and women's differential vulnerability to violence. Clearly, at this point in history, both the negative side and the positive side of the dilemma of difference remain evident in the inclusion and exclusion of provisions for gender in hate crime law.

To the degree that gender has been recognized as a component of hate crime in the United States, violence directed at girls and women because they are girls and women is segregated from other types of violence, and perpetrators of gender-based violence are deemed different from other types of perpetrators. Consistent with the spirit of hate crime law, when a crime involves a "gender bias" it receives different treatment and evokes segregated practices.[63] Such is the case with the high-profile crime introduced at the beginning of this chapter. In this case, U.S. Attorney General Ashcroft did something historic: he called the double murder a hate crime, invoked the relevant law to legitimate this definition, and treated the double murder as a "special" case of murder—one that deserves enhanced penalties. In this somewhat unique case, this criminal category hate crime evokes special prosecutorial concerns and harsher penalties, as well as immense media coverage of heretofore unheard of state action. This is no small result of decades of legal reform around bias-motivated violence.

Paradoxically, the same legal reform that resulted in the U.S. Attorney General distinguishing the murder described in the opening paragraph of this chapter as a hate crime also embraced the "norm of sameness." As a basic assumption of American law and hence of lawmaking, the "norm of sameness" is best expressed in the equal protection clause of the U.S. Constitution and is echoed in innumerable other locations. Simply put, the ("norm of sameness" stipulates that laws must apply equally to all groups and individuals in society) As a journalist recently observed and questioned with regard to the proliferation of hate crime law: "a large stone in the foundation of the American dream is the idea that every person is equal in citizenship and that every life should be equally valued and protected. No one should accept less, but is anyone entitled to more."[64] For the most part, "equal treatment" has historically meant "sameness." That is, a law must not give one group benefits or protections that it does not extend to others; all groups must be treated the same.[65])

Applying the "Norm of Sameness"

In the case of hate crime law the norm of sameness is evident in two outcomes: ("across-category sameness" and "within-category sameness" (see Figure 8.4). With regard to the former, violence against girls and women is rendered equivalent to other types of "crimes against minorities." The institutionalization of gender provisions in hate crime law serves to include girls and women into the coalition of status groups already covered under the law, ensuring that there is nothing "special" nor "different" about girls and women when compared to blacks, Jews, persons with disabilities, immigrants, and so on. That is, "girls and women" are extended the "same" treatment accorded to other similarly situated (minority) groups deemed "vulnerable victims," in this case other "target groups" recognized in hate crime law. As a result, hate crimes against women are rendered equivalent to hate crimes against immigrants, just as hate crimes against persons with disabilities are rendered equivalent to hate crimes against Muslims.[66]

The second way in which the "norm of sameness" has been manifest in legal reform related to hate crime is through what might best be called "within-category sameness." Although the spirit of hate crime law is to protect minorities, each side of the minority/majority dualism is—technically speaking—equally protected by law. Like the other antidiscrimination laws that preceded them, hate crime laws are written in a way that elides the historical basis and meaning of specific forms of bias-motivated violence by translating specific categories of persons (e.g., blacks, Jews, gays and lesbians, Mexicans, etc.) into all-encompassing and seemingly neutral categories (e.g., race, religion, sexual orientation, national origin). In doing so, the laws do not offer any remedies or protections to members of minority groups that are not simultaneously available to all other races, religions, genders, sexual orientations, nationalities, and so on. Minorities are treated the same as their counterparts. With regard to gender provisions in particular, violence against girls and women is rendered equivalent to violence against boys and men when the violence occurs because of gender.)

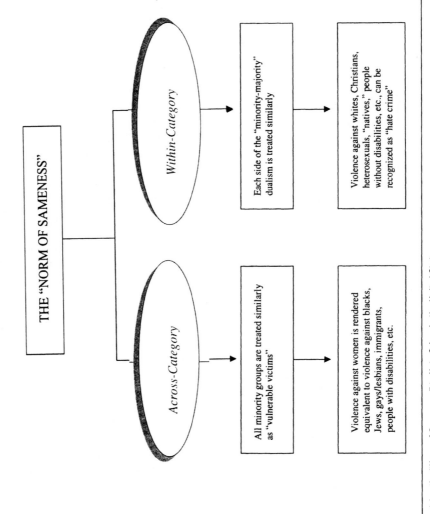

Fig. 8.4 Applying the "Norm of Sameness" to Hate Crime in the United States

THE "NORM OF SAMENESS"

Across-Category

All minority groups are treated similarly as "vulnerable victims"

Violence against women is rendered equivalent to violence against blacks, Jews, gays/lesbians, immigrants, people with disabilities, etc.

Within-Category

Each side of the "minority-majority" dualism is treated similarly

Violence against whites, Christians, heterosexuals, "natives," people without disabilities, etc., can be recognized as "hate crime"

Conclusion

At the end of the day, members *within* and *across* socially recognized minority and majority groups have equal standing before the law. Although hate crime law can, at a glance, appear to identify, demarcate, and promote attentiveness to social differences and the social disadvantages that accrue around them, the way it is written and enforced promotes sameness overriding differences. Hence, in the case of gender, hate crime law, and the dilemma of difference, it is possible that state and federal hate crime law manages to increase the public awareness of criminal victimization of women as gendered beings without defining them as "different" from other minorities—or men, for that matter! As a result, in the case described in the opening paragraph of this chapter, the U.S. Attorney General, a Republican appointee, is able to treat the murder of Julianne Marie Williams and Laura Winans, two women who happen to be lesbians, as simultaneously significantly *different* from most murders that occurred in the United States in 1996 and basically the *same* as other hate crimes perpetrated against other minorities in the United States. That is no small feat. It is as much an historic moment as it is a paradoxical expression.

9
Green or Brown? White Nativist Environmental Movements

RAJANI BHATIA

Popular misconceptions of "environmentalism" as something politically neutral and for the common good have masked recent right-wing environmental mobilizations in the United States. Many people fail to recognize that organizing on environmental themes has always spanned a broad political spectrum. The general lack of analysis of the politics of environmental movements has itself abetted right-wing advances.

The central motivations and ideology of right-wing environmentalism stem from a tradition of reactionary ecology and the politics of population control yet have significant overlap with organized white supremacy in the United States. Referred to variously as the greening of hate, green nativism, anti-immigrant or population environmentalism, the right-wing environmental movement uses language that conceals an agenda essentially about asserting a white American nativist cultural identity in the United States. They exploit a construct promoted by mainstream population and environmental organizations, that population size and growth are a primary cause of environmental degradation, to scapegoat immigrants and people of color for environmental problems.

Intertwined with right-wing environmental preoccupation with population growth, land and resource scarcity, urban sprawl, and degradation of "pristine open spaces" of the "American landscape" is a preoccupation with the disappearance of white America in the face of rising numbers

205

of nonwhites.[1] This is an identical concern of the contemporary white-supremacist movement. White "American" culture is treated as an endangered species in need of protection. In the name of the environment, this right-wing lobby openly rejects values of multiculturalism, diversity, and bilingualism, instead advocating restrictions on immigration and immigrant rights. Environmental arguments against immigration particularly view the presence of immigrant women as taxing scarce natural resources and government services because of women's role in the reproduction and settlement of their communities in the United States. Alarmism around waves of immigration and higher fertility rates among immigrant women of color elicit panic about the future of (white) Americans. This, like other agendas of preserving white America, represents fundamentally an assertion of race and gender hierarchy via intensive immigration and reproductive and other social controls.

The right-wing environment lobby is comprised of a complex network of organizations, key individuals, and foundations that articulate opposition to immigration in the context of a broader set of conservative goals. Focusing on overlap with organized white supremacism in the United States, this essay begins by situating green nativist thought in the United States within a right-wing framework, followed by an examination of the movement's network, ideology, agenda, and far-reaching impact.

Situating the Movement: Environmentalism on the Right

Right-wing mobilizing on the environment is not new. An examination into the way population environmentalists and white supremacists conceptualize population and environment reveals ideological underpinnings that resonate with Nazi discourse on these concepts. Nazi ideas and policy on population and the environment underscore not only the possibility but also a tradition of fascist interpretation and application of these concepts in socially regressive ways. Current right-wing trends on population and the environment in the United States exhibit these very racist and nativist impulses.

It is significant that the "green wing" of the National Socialist Party in Germany elicited some policies familiarly environmental. Especially during the early years after their rise to power, the Nazis institutionalized and spread methods of organic farming, established the first ecological preservation sites in Europe, and implemented programs of reforestation and animal and plant species protection. They also promoted ecologically responsible industrial development and technology. The 1935 *Reichsnaturschutzgesetz* (Nature Protection Law), an accomplishment of Nazi ecologists, established rules of special protection for flora, fauna, and undeveloped lands.[2] While the Nazi record on the environment may at first appear redeeming, it is crucial to understand that this program was intimately linked in ideology and practice to some of the worst crimes against humanity. Protecting German national ethos was the primary project of national-socialist environmentalism.

The Nazis understood population in the context of a social-Darwinist struggle between races for survival and power. They viewed population as an aggressive force, a means by which races compete against each other to occupy and control space and land. They depicted population "pressures" from Eastern Europe as a threat to German *Lebensraum* or living space.[3] Current right-wing discourse on environment in the United States portrays the presence of immigrants as a threat to "American" culture. In this conception, "culture" or "ethnic group" replaces "race" as the primary category of division among peoples, but the idea of population as a hostile force by which one group generatively competes against another remains the same.

The Nazi conception of the environment, through the notion of intimately bound "blood and soil," projected the German people as part of the environment or landscape. Nazi ideologues posited an exclusive, even mystical connection of the German people to the land, or environment. Not only were Germans thought to have a higher propensity than others to care for the environment, but the mere presence of the "superior" race enhanced rather than degraded it. Similarly, the anti-immigrant, radical-right interpretation of the environment in the United States is not a study of the way humans interact with the nonhuman environment. It views "American" culture as an integral part of an environment enclosed by the U.S. borders. In this conception, environment is not treated as global in scope. Protecting the environment translates foremost into protecting white, American culture, or the "European-derived" peoples.

Thrown into the current rise of right-wing interpretations of population and environment is the connection established between the two concepts three decades ago. As the presumed threat of "overpopulation" to the world's food supply became increasingly discredited, environmental degradation emerged as a legitimization for global population control.[4] In the late 1960s and 1970s, mainstream organizations concerned with population first promoted the idea that "overpopulation" threatens the environment, which soon gained a foothold in mainstream environmental organizations such as the Sierra Club and the National Audubon Society.[5]

During the 1980s and increasingly in the 1990s, the new right-wing environmental lobby focusing on the United States emerged, producing a particularly reactionary take on the population and environment connection.[6] The assertion "population growth is a primary cause of environmental degradation" unleashed nativist impulses in defense of "American" culture and heritage against increases in non-"American" population.

(Increasingly detached from international development discourse, this interpretation of population encompasses a worldview in which people, divided primarily along race and ethnic lines, compete with each other for power and survival. In this struggle, immigration and fertility can be used as demographic ammunition to encroach upon a "host" society. "Host" or "native" societies refer to white people from the North, while population itself is personified by the "overbreeding" poor and people of color from the South.)

This current right-wing conception of population borrows much from the mainstream projection of an absolute "overpopulation" in the global South. During the last half a century, international population control policies stemming from the United States and other countries in the global North have sought to control the fertility rates in the so-called Third World, primarily through the scientific development and administration of birth control. The global "overpopulation crisis," as projected by the mainstream, produced images of illiterate, poor, dark-skinned masses breeding indiscriminately to the point where they would spill beyond their country's borders.

(Since white people from the North are not perceived as part of the population problem, the notion of population itself does not connotatively encompass them. The people who make up population, therefore, are "foreign," "alien," teeming masses of poor people of color from the South.)The political ramifications of the by-now well-established construct, "population growth degrades the environment," become clearer, especially when population growth is understood mainly as rising rates of "foreign" immigration and fertility.)In this way, right-wing environmentalists contrast depleting environmental "purity" and whiteness with growing pollution and communities of color. Moreover, "Americans" are absolved of responsibility for environmental problems. Conceived as an integral part of the environment, they cannot contribute to the population-environment tension that results in environmental degradation.

Green Nativist Network

Prominent individuals in the right-wing environment network include John H. Tanton, Garrett Hardin, Virginia Abernethy, Kevin MacDonald, J. Philippe Rushton, and Richard Lynn. Many of them contribute to the journal *Population and Environment* or engage in network organizations, including Carrying Capacity Network (CCN), Californians for Population Stabilization (CAPS), Population Environment Balance (PEB), Federation for American Immigration Reform (FAIR), ProjectUSA, California Coalition for Immigration Reform (CCIR), and Negative Population Growth (NPG). Some of the network's funders include the Weeden, S. H. Cowell, McConnel, and Scaife family foundations and the Pioneer Fund.

(The role of John H. Tanton, described as the "the founding father of America's modern anti-immigration movement" by the Southern Poverty Law Center (SPLC), sheds light on the motivations of the lobby and its intersections with other nativist impulses, such as the "English Only" movement. An ophthamologist from Michigan, Tanton founded, funded, or otherwise aided in establishing thirteen anti-immigrant organizations. These range from organizations whose statement of purpose is mainly on population and environment issues (e.g., CAPS and PEB), to "immigration reform" organizations that use environmental arguments (e.g., FAIR and ProjectUSA), to those designated as hate groups by the SPLC, (e.g., American Immigration Control Foundation). Tanton also founded and funded the "English Only" organizations, U.S. English and Pro English.[7]

As a key figure within this network, Tanton's conversion to right-wing environmental thought is telling. According to the SPLC's *Intelligence Report*:

> It was an odd turn of events for an erstwhile liberal activist who loved beekeeping and the rural life.... Tanton started out as a passionate environmentalist. In the 1960s and early 1970s, he was a leader in the National Audubon Society, and the Sierra Club and other mainstream environmental groups. But Tanton soon became fixated on population control, seeing environmental degradation as the inevitable result of overpopulation. When the indigenous birth rate fell below replacement level in the United States, his preoccupation turned to immigration. And this soon led him to race.[8]

Whether the evolution in Tanton's position as depicted here from mainstream to extreme is typical of the movement is unclear. But as white-collar professionals, many of them professors in universities, all of the network leaders leverage some degree of academic legitimacy within mainstream circles.)

The WITAN (short for the Old English term "witenangemot," meaning "council of wise men") memos, written by Tanton in the mid-1980s for anti-immigrant colleagues who met at retreats, mapped out congressional, grassroots, media, and a variety of other strategies for the movement.* In a section on conservation and demography from a memo dated October 10, 1986, Tanton exclaims: "On the demographic point: perhaps this is the first instance in which those with their pants up are going to get caught by those with their pants down!" Full of disparaging comments directed at new immigrants, especially Latinos, the memos suggest that they will not hold the same high environmental values and conservation ethic of white Anglo-Americans.[9]

Garrett Hardin, professor of human ecology at University of California, Santa Barbara, and Virginia Abernethy, professor emeritus of psychiatry at Vanderbilt University School of Medicine are two other leading advocates

*(SPLC, 2002).

of the anti-immigrant environmental movement. They steer a host of organizations that embrace right-wing environmentalist thought and promote anti-immigrant racism. These include FAIR, CCN, PEB, CAPS, CCIR, and NPG. Abernethy sits on the board of directors for both CCN and PEB, while Hardin presides in various steering and advisory roles for CAPS, PEB (as honorary chairman and advisory board member), and FAIR.[10]

The Weeden and S. H. Cowell foundations, which fund NPG, FAIR, CCN, PEB, and CAPS, also fund the "English Only" movement. Other prominent funders of the movement include the Scaife family foundations, the McConnel Foundation, and the Pioneer Fund, which has a long history of supporting eugenics research.[11] In fact, the first president of the Pioneer Fund, Harry Laughlin, wrote the Model Eugenic Sterilization Law in the 1920s, which was enacted by twenty-seven states in various versions and resulted in the forced sterilization of over 60,000 people.[12] The fund supported South Africa's system of apartheid and opposed desegregation in the United States.

More recently, the Pioneer Fund has financed the research of Garret Hardin, J. Philippe Rushton, and Richard Lynn. Rushton's and Lynn's writings also figure prominently in current right-wing conceptualizations linking population and the environment. A notorious eugenicist, Rushton teaches psychology at the University of Western Ontario and is known for his theory on racial differences, which he bases on an inverse relationship between sex organ and brain size.[13] His writings are frequently cited in contemporary white-supremacist publications. Richard Lynn is a psychology professor at the University of Ulster in Northern Ireland. Lynn advocates eugenics, classifying the poor and sick as "weak specimens whose proliferation needs to be discouraged in the interests of the improvement of the genetic quality of the group, and ultimately of group survival."[14]

Relatively new on the scene is Kevin MacDonald, professor of psychology at California State University at Long Beach. Recently he testified on behalf of David Irving, who denies the existence of gas chambers at Auschwitz and disputes the number of Jewish victims of the Holocaust. Irving accused Deborah Lipstadt of libeling him in her 1993 book, *Denying the Holocaust: The Growing Assault on Truth and Memory.*

MacDonald is currently the editor of *Population and Environment*, a peer-reviewed journal published by Kluwer Academic/Human Sciences Press. Virginia Abernethy edited the journal prior to MacDonald for eleven years until July 1999. She continues to sit on the journal's advisory board alongside Garrett Hardin and J. Philippe Rushton. *Population and Environment* exemplifies one vehicle by which the movement infuses its ideology into the mainstream. Respected environmentalists like Vaclav Smil also sit on the journal's board, and moderate articles intermix with the anti-immigrant and eugenic ones.[15]

According to the SPLC, since 1998 there has been increasing overlap between key individuals in the anti-immigrant environmentalist network and white-supremacist organizations. In 2001, for example, Abernethy joined the editorial board of the *Citizen's Informer,* a publication of the white-supremacist Council of Conservative Citizens (CCC). Like former Senate majority leader, Trent Lott, who praised the CCC for its "right principles and right philosophy," Abernethy also supports the CCC. "My view of the Council of Conservative Citizens is that they support traditional values and the freedom of people to associate with people that they want to associate with." The SPLC has traced the recent contributions of several anti-immigrant professionals to white-supremacist extremism as speakers at CCC conferences, contributors to the *Citizen's Informer,* or even by joining CCC organized protests (such as the 1998 Cullman, Alabama, protest against rising numbers of Mexican workers).[16] However, it is not clear whether these connections actually cost the movement legitimacy in mainstream circles. As Betsy Hartmann points out:

> Increasingly tied to the racist right on one side, the anti-immigrant movement is also tied to mainstream government, media and academic circles on the other. It provides a practical and ideological conduit for racist ideas and interests to influence politics as usual. In this sense it is a mistake to view it as just about immigration; it is about protecting and reinforcing white power in the U.S.[17]

Indeed, the network has increased lobbying influence on the hill post-9/11 and continues to spread racist messages couched in academic language in educational settings, journals, and the media. The far-right hate movement utilizes these to enhance their legitimacy and authority within the mainstream.

Ideology

Abby Ferber's work exposes how contemporary white supremacism is primarily preoccupied with the construction of white racial identity via reassertion of white masculinity (i.e., through the possession and control of white women).[18] Likewise, anti-immigrant environmentalism is mainly concerned with the construction of a white American nativist identity. Both discourses employ metaphors of purity in reference to the larger U.S. territory/environment and white folk or national body. Both construct a threat to white identity by using metaphors of contamination via immigration of nonwhite folk. Yet white supremacists additionally obsess over purity of the female body and its contamination through interracial sexuality.[19])

Right-wing population and environment discourse is preoccupied with repossession and control of U.S. nationhood and territory for white

Anglo-Americans. "The construction of racial identities," Ferber explains, "requires a policing of the borders, a maintenance of the boundaries between 'one's own kind' and others."[20] Ferber further draws attention to the multiple levels of these identity politics:

> The bodily boundaries of the white female body are at risk of penetration by nonwhite, especially black male bodies, and this is simultaneously the penetration of the white race; white racial identity is threatened and mingled with the blood and genes of the black race, leading to the mongrelization and genocide of the white race. At yet another level, the boundaries of the white nation are threatened with infiltration by nonwhite immigration, which again is depicted as leading to the penetration of white bodies and the genocide of the white race. Clear boundaries are essential to the preservation of whiteness.[21]

Echoing salient ideas of contemporary white-supremacist discourse, anti-immigrant environmentalism constructs a white identity under threat and inherent biological differences between races/cultures. It projects alarmism about impending culture wars and employs a theory of Jewish conspiracy.

Population, Environment, and the Construction of a White Identity under Threat

For this anti-immigration contingency, "culture," or ethnicity, has replaced "race" as the primary category of division between peoples. Janet Biehl observes this phenomenon in her account of ecofascism in today's Germany, where ideas about the organic connections between German *Volk* (people), *Heimat* (homeland), and *Lebensraum* (living space) have begun to reassert themselves not only in neofascist organizations and parties, but in green and New Age circles.[22] "Most often, the far right claims to be defending cultures rather than races; if the Nazis persecuted those who practiced '*race* mixing' and sought to preserve '*racial* purity,' today's fascists say they oppose *cultural* mixing and seek to preserve their *culture*."[23] Indeed, European and Anglo-American "culture" is treated as an imperiled species, ever threatened by an "onslaught" of immigrants and "overpopulation." John Tanton, in one WITAN memo, hints at the lobby's strategic use of language:

> Novak's term "unmeltable ethnics" is probably better than some of the others that have been suggested. Similarly, ethnicity is a more acceptable term than race. It should also be noted that 50% of all Hispanic surname people on the census forms designate themselves as White. So perhaps we should speak of Hispanic Whites and non-Hispanic Whites, to further diffuse the issue. Is Anglo a better term than White? LANGUAGE IS VERY important here.[24]

Ecofascist trends on both sides of the Atlantic refer to their primary culture of concern as part of the environment, part of that which needs protection. Other non-"native" cultures, on the other hand, belong to the degrading elements, those that destroy the environment. For example, according to Herbert Gruhl, a founder of the right-wing Ecological Democratic Party in Germany, European culture will "perish not because of the degeneration of its own people, as previous high civilizations have, but because of physical laws: the constantly overflowing mass of humanity on an earth's surface that remains constant."[25]

Similarly, in the United States, white-supremacist discourse touches on environmental themes in order to compare white "American" culture to an endangered habitat or a species on the verge of extinction. For example, Tom Metzger, who founded White Aryan Resistance (WAR), notes, "it seems to me that as we are becoming more aware of our precarious state, the white man, the white woman's state in the world, being only about 10 percent of the population, we begin to sympathize, empathize more, with the wolves and other animals."[26] Both Gruhl and Metzger describe their cultures as "perishing" or in a "precarious state." A photo of a blonde white girl holding a chick under the caption "Endangered Species" in *White Power* echoes this theme.[27] It is the more explicit white-supremacist manifestation on which the far-right environmental protection impulse is based.

The messages put forth by the anti-immigrant environmentalists focus more strictly on producing alarm about population size, nonwhite fertility rates, and immigration numbers spiraling out of control. This lends their argument a seemingly scientific basis and logic. They single out population size as a primary cause of sprawl and congestion, leaving out any analysis of a consumer culture based on strip malls and SUVs. A billboard put up by ProjectUSA, for example, reads: "Immigration will double U.S. Population in Your Child's Lifetime. AmericaIsFull.com. Talk About It." Another reads: "Tired of sitting in traffic? Every day, another 6000 immigrants arrive. Every day!!"[28]

Nature Given Difference: Views on Reproduction and Fertility

Unlike mainstream organizations concerned with "overpopulation," the population-environment right prioritizes anti-immigration stances over fertility reduction schemes involving the development and dissemination of birth control. The right-wing views individuals as prone to fertility behavior genetically determined by their race or ethnicity. Garrett Hardin, for example, rejects contraception as a primary means for reducing population: "Better technology is always welcome, of course, but improvements in reproductive control will not, by themselves, keep the human race from 'trashing' the environment that supports it."[29] Similarly, John Tanton writes: "Can *homo contraceptivus* compete with *homo progenitiva* if borders aren't controlled? Or is advice to limit ones family simply advice to move over and let someone else with greater reproductive powers occupy the space?"[30] For the anti-immigrant population-environment lobby, birth control can only marginally affect population growth rates. Therefore its main response to population and environmental problems is to prevent "the highly fertile" from entering United States borders.)

A closer look at some of their views on fertility, reproduction, sexuality, and parenting reveal another overlap with the white-supremacist belief system, that is,(naturalizing race/culture difference and hierarchy.)According to Adam Miller, author of "Professors of Hate," J. Philippe Rushton:

> [C]laims that less evolved organisms—such as blacks—fight for survival by coupling promiscuously, flooding the environment with offspring for whom they provide little care and many of whom die. He says more evolved forms—such as Asians—wage their battle through monogamous relationships, producing few children upon whom they lavish care and many of whom survive.[31]

Rushton believes that races have evolved distinct reproductive strategies. Similar to Rushton, Kevin MacDonald depicts two fundamentally different kinds of human fertility behavior: "K-selected species," those adults who have few but well-cared-for children, and "r-selected species," those who have many but poorly cared-for children.[32]

These differences evolved in response to ancestral environments, MacDonald argues, expressing in evolutionary terms a particular (one would infer superior or inferior) level of "biological fitness." Simply by virtue of their genes, for example, "K-selected species" are friendlier to the environment, because, "while r-selected species tend to overshoot their resource base, adversity selected and K-selected species remain within the carrying capacity of the environment."[33] MacDonald writes of the presence of both "genetic proclivities" as developed over time and "environmental triggers" which can induce a particular style of parenting. He claims that variables such as age of the onset of puberty, age of first sexual intercourse, and especially intelligence determine the outcome of fertility behavior and are heritable.

With regard to the political and social movements of the 1960s and that decade's effect on reproductive behavior and fertility, MacDonald suggests that the years prior to 1965 were characterized by low levels of "illegitimacy" and single parenting maintained through "powerful social controls embedded in the religious and legal framework of Western societies."[34] He contends that the cultural changes of the 1960s, which challenged and removed these social controls, resulted in increased rates of single parenting, teenage sexual activity, pregnancy, and out-of-wedlock births. This led to "irresponsible" sexuality, childbearing, and higher rates of fertility, but not across the board for all races and ethnicities. Based on evidence from *The Bell Curve*, MacDonald attests that these rates remained relatively unchanged for white women with high IQs, and therefore, he concludes, "the erosion of traditional Western controls on sexuality have had far more effect on those who are genetically inclined toward precocious sexuality."[35]

MacDonald compares the birth rates in the United States in 1995 among women aged fifteen to forty-four by race/ethnicity (white, black, and Hispanic), and contends that differences in fertility rates exist, "even in response to the same environmental context." Yet his assumption of "same environmental context" blatantly disregards the historical and current realities of race, gender, and class exploitation and oppression. He invokes race and ethnicity only to define members of racial and ethnic minorities as having low intelligence, being lazy, irresponsible, overly fertile, and oversexed. In a reference to the work of eugenicist Richard Lynn, MacDonald writes:

> [L]ow-IQ individuals who engage in low-investment parenting under contemporary conditions may be low on the personality trait of Conscientiousness and therefore less able to defer gratification, engage in sustained work, use birth control consistently, persevere in long term goals, etc.[36]

Impending Race or Culture War

(The anti-immigrant population-environment lobby displays a particular contempt for multiculturalism and diversity, which, it says, will ultimately lead to balkanization and "race or culture wars."]For example, Hardin notes that "the blessings of 'diversity' evaporate when we try to meld many cultures into one. Recurrent violence in the Balkans and in the Near East indicates that the most dependable outcome of 'multiculturalism' is the violence of civic disorder."[37] This theme is further developed by Kevin MacDonald, who assumes that ethnic conflict is something natural, having "deep biological roots."[38] He relies on theories that describe ethnicity and ethnic conflict as either a product of human biological predisposition or "evolved psychological adaptation." According to MacDonald, these theories establish the primacy of ethnicity or culture over class-based divisions in society. Outward signs of ethnic group membership, including "physical features, religion, and, not uncommonly, clothing or other obvious markers of group membership," he claims, ultimately begin in the genes.[39] MacDonald posits that ethnic groups, when not involved in violent conflict, engage in ethnic competition via migration and fertility:)

> Immigration policy and group differences in fertility influence political power within and between societies, often with explosive results. Demographic expansion has often been an instrument of ethnic competition and is an important source of conflict in the contemporary world.[40]

(MacDonald contends that this type of demographic encroachment sets off the "social identity mechanisms" of the "host" society, which in the extreme can lead to various forms of ethnic cleansing.)

(Not surprisingly, MacDonald interprets both immigration and fertility as forms of aggression on "European-derived" peoples.) According to MacDonald, the net effect of immigration of ethnic groups with high fertility is to further suppress the already low fertility of the native population. This represents "natural selection against the genes of the native population. . . . Given that 90 percent of recent immigrants to the United States are non-European, this implies selection differentials against European peoples."[41] He estimates that "US women are foregoing over one million births per year as a result of immigration,"[42] and suggests that this supports the predictions of early twentieth-century eugenicist and immigration restrictionist Madison Grant, who authored *The Passing of the Great Race* in 1916.[43]

(MacDonald predicts ethnic warfare in the United States, because multiculturalism for him is really a code word for ethnic separatism, which has led to balkanization and ethnic cleansing most recently in Yugoslavia and Rwanda. MacDonald foresees a United States "heading down a volatile path—a path that leads to ethnic warfare and to the development of collectivist, authoritarian, and racialist enclaves."[44]) He warns: "It is noteworthy that minority groups, especially African-American and Latino groups, have already developed strong ethnic identities in the United States. These movements often have militant, racialist overtones. . . . Latino ethnic activists have a clearly articulated policy of 'reconquering' parts of the United States via immigration and high birth rates."[45] Similarly, Virginia Abernethy suggests that a secessionist conflict will arise in the United States, due to high immigration and fertility of Latinos. Mexicans, in particular, she claims, are planning an irredentist movement, called Aztlan, to reconquer the states of California, Arizona, New Mexico, Texas, and southern Colorado.

(Both Abernethy and MacDonald attribute the cause of recent ethnic conflicts in other parts of the world to demographic and population "pressures.") In an editorial in *Population and Environment*, Abernethy writes: "The root causes [of the Kosovo conflict] are the combination of immigration and the much higher fertility rate of Albanians, who are mostly Muslim."[46] Likewise, MacDonald analyzes conflict in Yugoslavia thus:

> Demography may be destiny, but from an evolutionary perspective it is not surprising that the destiny of groups with a high reproductive rate to rule the areas where their numbers come to eclipse other groups may be hotly contested by the groups being eclipsed. In theoretical terms this may often be a conflict between r-strategists, relatively speaking, and K-strategists. By definition, r-strategists in

this case the Albanians, out-reproduce K-strategists, but K-strategists may use other means of competition, including warfare, "ethnic cleansing" via expulsion, and genocide.[47]

MacDonald casually invokes the most violent crimes against humanity, genocide and ethnic cleansing, and does not seem to acknowledge them as crimes at all. Indeed, MacDonald has depicted ethnic cleansing as "a rather clear rationale," adding in an academic afterthought, "obviously in the perceived ethnic interests of the group doing the cleansing."[48] He views these forms of violence as simply another means of ethnic competition, a legitimate evolutionary psychological reaction of one group whose presence and power is ostensibly threatened by the demographic expansion of another. Since he presupposes the inevitability of ethnic conflict, he suggests that the most horrific means by which ethnic groups compete might always come into play.

MacDonald naturalizes "ethnic cleansing" and "genocide" as legitimate behavior in a world he characterizes by power and survival struggles between ethnic groups and cultural areas. Furthermore, MacDonald uses a sophisticated form of scapegoating to implicate Jews for his prediction of impending cultural warfare.

Jewish Conspiracy

Kevin MacDonald's views on immigration and fertility are linked to his primary work on Judaism, stemming from a three-volume work: *A People that Shall Dwell Alone: Judaism as a Group Evolutionary Strategy* (Praeger, 1994); *Separation and Discontents: Toward an Evolutionary Theory of Anti-Semitism* (Praeger, 1998); and *The Culture of Critique: An Evolutionary Analysis of Jewish Involvement in Twentieth-Century Intellectual and Political Movements* (Praeger, 1998).[49] In this trilogy, Kevin MacDonald depicts Judaism as a "group evolutionary strategy," a genetic blueprint of behavior, which predicts that individual Jews across the Diaspora will engage in positive eugenics and form cohesive and exclusive groups in order to ensure their primacy in a social-Darwinian struggle for power and survival. MacDonald claims that Jews had an ulterior motive in initiating and carrying out prominent intellectual and political movements of the past century. In his view, these movements, which include the Boasian school of anthropology, psychoanalysis, and leftist ideology and activism, primarily serve Jewish interests, or "evolutionary group strategy."

MacDonald views United States immigration and fertility rates among ethnic minorities within this overall framework of a larger conspiracy by Jewish communities around the world to protect themselves and their interests. Population problems manifest in immigration levels and fertility rates, he claims, have somehow benefited Jewish ethnic interests at the expense of non-Jewish "natives." MacDonald's analysis resonates with contemporary white-supremacist thought, which imagines a Jewish world conspiracy behind all social and economic problems.[50]

In his essay, "Jewish Involvement in Shaping American Immigration Policy, 1881–1965: A Historical Review," Kevin MacDonald claims that Jews plotted to liberalize restrictionist immigration legislation from the 1920s and succeeded with the Immigration Act of 1965. Jewish organizations, determined to break the homogeneity and hegemony of white Protestant culture, advocated not only for liberal immigration policy but also for the secularization of United States society and a foreign policy based on internationalism. Motivated by a leftist ideology and his strong identification as a Jew, according to MacDonald, Franz Boas pioneered a whole new school of anthropology to replace biological explanations of race and human behavior differences with cultural or environmental explanations.

This "ideology of racial equality," as MacDonald refers to the Boasian view, was "an important weapon" in Jewish efforts to break down immigration restrictions. In this discussion, MacDonald repeatedly invokes differences between ethnicities and races as inherent: "In the real world, ethnic groups differ in their talents and abilities; they differ in their numbers, fertility, and the extent to which they encourage parenting practices conducive to resource acquisition; and they differ in the resources held at any point in time and in their political power."[51] MacDonald regrets what he sees as the dominance of "Boasian cultural determination" over "biologism" in the human sciences.

In addition to instigating a revolution in academia, MacDonald further claims that Jews led a highly organized effort to turn the United States into a multicultural society. So as not to reveal the Jewish interest in their endeavor, Jews developed proimmigration arguments "couched in terms of universalist humanitarian ideals" and recruited non-Jews to serve as "window dressing" for their battles.[52]

Jews even employ the memory of the Holocaust. Although MacDonald's testimony in the Irving case did not touch on his own view of the Holocaust, he has described it as: "an instrument of Jewish ethnic interests not only as a symbol intended to create moral revulsion to violence directed at minority ethnic groups... but also as an instrument to silence opponents of high levels of multi-ethnic immigration into Western societies."[53]

According to MacDonald, Jewish interests in liberalizing immigration laws were threefold. Apart from securing the entry of Jews themselves into the United States, open immigration would lead to a pluralistic society, which, MacDonald asserts, safeguards Jewish cohesive cultural characteristics against pressure to integrate into the mainstream and decreases the chance that Jews will be singled out as scapegoats by a hostile majority. In pluralism, Jews would be just one among many minority groups. "Indeed," MacDonald writes in his conclusion, "lowering the political and demographic power of the European-derived peoples of the United States has clearly been the aim of the Jewish political and intellectual activities discussed here."[54]

What is the consequence of this Jewish plot to subvert the power of the "European-derived" peoples through liberal immigration policy? Ultimately, the "morality," "altruism," and "self-sacrifice," of the "host" white Protestant culture will run low. "I rather doubt such altruism will continue to occur if there are obvious signs that the status and political power of the European-derived group is decreasing while the power of other groups increases as a result of immigration and other social policies."[55]

Less forthrightly than in his discussions on immigration, MacDonald implicates Jews for fertility problems he perceives stemming from the 1960s social movements. He suggests that Jews started the "sexual revolution" that led to irresponsible sexuality and reproductive behavior:

> My personal experience at Wisconsin during the 1960s was that the student protest movement was originated and dominated by Jews and that a great many of them were "red diaper babies" whose parents had been radicals.... These students had very positive attitudes toward Judaism as well as negative attitudes toward Christianity, but perhaps surprisingly, the most salient contrast between Judaism and Christianity in their minds was in attitudes toward sexuality. In line with the very large Freudian influence of the period, the general tendency was to contrast a putative sexual permissiveness of Judaism with the sexual repression and prudery of Christianity, and this contrast was then linked with psychoanalytic analyses that attributed various forms of psychopathology and even capitalism, racism, and other forms of political oppression to Christian sexual attitudes.[56]

MacDonald utilizes complex but classic techniques of scapegoating. His perspectives on U.S. immigration policy and fertility lend an ever more explicit, neofascist interpretation to population-environmentalism.

Agenda and Impact

The population and environment extreme shares with contemporary white supremacism the overall goal of preserving a white America and a preoccupation with immigration, population numbers, reproduction, and the social control of nonwhites. Though specific programs differ, common campaigns of population-environmentalists include calling for immigration moratoria and opposing multiculturalism, bilingual education, affirmative action, dual citizenship, citizenship rights of children born to immigrant parents, and health, education, and welfare rights for the undocumented or elderly and disabled immigrants.[57]

Broad-based, mainstream discourse on population and the environment has largely served to mask the radical-right orientation of this movement. Advancing under its neutral, depoliticized pretense, the consequences of this agenda, in terms of its impact on both women and society more generally are particularly far-reaching.

Impacting Moderate Environmental Organizations

Writing in a 1986 WITAN memo, John Tanton exclaims: "The Sierra Club may not want to touch the immigration issue, but the immigration issue is going to touch the Sierrra Club!"[58] Just over a decade later, in a highly organized effort, PEB, FAIR, and the Sierrans for US Population Stabilization (SUSPS) came close to successfully lobbying Sierra Club members to vote for a call for net reductions in immigration as part of a "comprehensive population policy for the United States" known as Alternative A.[59] Sixty percent of the club membership voted instead for Alternative B, which not only affirmed the club's neutral policy on immigration but also called instead for women's empowerment, human rights, and environmentally responsible consumption to address the root causes of migration and global population problems. Disturbingly, only a few months after the vote, proponents of Alternative B were taken off the club's National Population Committee, and the Sierra Club Board of Directors changed club policy to advocate for population reductions in the United States and the world. In her analysis of these changes, Betsy Hartmann writes: "the recent policy shift from population stabilization to population reductions reflects the disenfranchisement of those who supported the Alternative B approach to population issues as well as the growing power of anti-immigrant opponents."[60]

E Magazine has recently featured articles replete with alarmist rhetoric on population and the environment. In an article on U.S. population, the magazine's editor, Jim Motavalli, gives ample voice to Abernethy, PEB, NPG and others, as he argues that U.S. population growth, primarily fueled by immigration, will devastate the environment, and ends by asking: "If there's one thing that Americans can agree on, it's that we need to hold onto our dwindling natural heritage. And what chance is there of doing that if, as predicted, the US population doubles to 500 million by 2100?" Motavalli's use of "Americans" and "heritage" appeals unambiguously to a sense of nativism.[61]

In her exploration of recent anti-immigration environmental trends, Syd Lindsley draws attention to the number of mainstream environmental organizations signing onto ASAP (Alliance for Stabilizing America's Population), a PEB initiative begun in 1997. ASAP calls on the president and Congress to institute immigration moratoriums, do away with amnesty programs, step up deportation of undocumented immigrants, and even repeal citizenship rights to their children.

About half of ASAP's signatories are groups working primarily on land and wildlife protection and restoration issues, including Earth First! (LA), the Gaia Institute, the Inland Empire Public Lands Council, the International Society for the Preservation of the Tropical Rainforest, Northwest Environmental Advocates, and many more.[62] On the question of why ASAP appeals to well-intentioned environmental advocates, Lindsley contends that a "lack of social analysis leaves such organizations open and vulnerable to racist scapegoating messages cloaked in the language of sustainability."[63]

Immigration Control and the Social Control of Nonwhites

Perhaps more disturbing than inroads made into moderate environmental circles is the influence on the popular imagination of anti-immigrant messages central to green nativist thought. The scapegoating of immigrants peaked around the time when Californians voted to pass Proposition 187 in 1994, which would have denied undocumented immigrants access to public social services, education, welfare, and nonemergency health care.[64] Although declared unconstitutional by a federal judge in 1998, denial of immigrant access to public services for both the documented and undocumented made its way into the 1996 federal welfare "reform" law, or Federal Personal Responsibility and Work Opportunity Reconciliation Act (PRWORA).[65] Following on PRWORA's heels, the 1996 federal immigration "reform" act stepped up border control and policing and detention of immigrants.

A general atmosphere of fear and suspicion of immigrants, which we thought had culminated during the last decade, has reached heretofore unimaginable heights post-9/11. Anti-immigrant sentiment has fueled a host of official immigration control measures and anti-immigrant racist acts that impact the undocumented, documented, noncitizens, and citizens alike. The expansion of the law-enforcement apparatus through the new Department of Homeland Security has also reached unprecedented levels. In this new era of "American" patriotism and xenophobia, even segments of the more liberal mainstream have come to believe that compromising protection of civil liberties may be necessary if national security interests are prioritized. Chillingly, racial profiling and "guilty until proven innocent" posturing have won acceptability at large. As a result, immigrant communities in their homes and workplaces face more violence, more containment, and more surveillance. Against an aggressive law-enforcement apparatus, increased deportations, detentions, and barriers to accessing public services, immigrant women struggle to sustain themselves, their families and communities.[66]

In her gender analysis on anti-immigrant assaults, Syd Lindsley describes how immigrant women and their children represent a particular menace to the environmental argument against immigration because of their role in reproduction and family settlement:

> Immigrant women of color and their children are targeted because of white anxieties about a racially pluralized society. Whereas Mexican immigrant men have been perceived as temporary laborers, the presence of Mexican women and children suggests permanence, and the full integration of Mexican-American communities into society. Mexican immigrant women, both by their activities in consolidating settlement and by their linkage to raising and reproducing children, are key to their families' process of integration with US society. Therefore, the mythologized foundations of the American (white) national identity are profoundly shaken by the presence of Mexican and other non-white immigrant women.[67]

Whereas national security arguments against immigration tend to project images of immigrant men as violent terrorists, green nativism rather views immigrant women and their "too many" children as the enemy, taxing the public service system and depleting scarce space and natural resources.[68] Similarly, contemporary white-supremacist discourse shares this obsession with nonwhite "over"-consumption of scarce resources. Denials of immigrant access to public services such as health, education, and welfare are primary assaults on women's roles in having and raising children and maintaining communities. Former California governor Pete Wilson's ban on undocumented women's access to prenatal care immediately after the passage of the federal welfare "reform" act in 1996 is a primary example. It represents a particularly caustic attack on immigrant women's reproductive rights. Lindsley further points out how other key aspects of the anti-immigrant environmental agenda, such as advocating to repeal citizenship rights to an immigrant woman's offspring, fundamentally devalues her reproduction.[69]

Reproductive and Sexual Control

"What is remarkable about the [white-supremacist] politics of reproduction is the extent to which it reflects the mainstream," sums up Barbara Perry in this volume.[70] She points out the leading tenets of the white-supremacist agenda on reproduction: pronatalism among whites, antinatalism among nonwhites, and compulsory hetero- and same-race sexuality. In general, the right-wing environment agenda focuses more on immigration than reproduction, but it contributes to the white-supremacist agenda by fueling alarmism on nonwhite fertility rates. Yet, rather than explicitly advocate a pronatalist program among white women, right-wing environmentalists view lower fertility among white women as a sign of advanced reproductive behavior that reflects white folk's harmony with nature. Antinatalism among nonwhites, on the other hand, is reflected in the agendas of a broad political spectrum, ranging from racist hate groups to liberal population experts and environmentalists. As a result, women of color in the United States have long faced a de facto mainstream agenda of population control. Women of color who are reproductive rights activists raise the issues of sterilization abuse, coercive contraceptive practices, and disproportionate promotion of riskier, long-term, provider-controlled contraceptives such as Depo-Provera and Norplant in their communities.

Implications of 9/11

Since 9/11, conservative, probusiness interests have stepped up attacks on left-wing environmentalists for activity they label antinationalist and "ecoterrorist."[71] This may have the inadvertent effect of bolstering the position of green nativism within an increasingly rightward-leaning society. Calling on the FBI to investigate environmental organizations, this lobby has published opinion pieces in newspapers across the country and promoted "ecoharassment" bills in state legislatures. The antienvironmental watchdog group, CLEAR, claims that this lobby defines "ecoterrorist" activity to include such "civil disobedience as tree sitting, blocking roads, targeting corporations with boycotts, and even advocating that the U.S. ratify the Kyoto global warming treaty."[72] In June 2002, Dan Borne, president of the Louisiana Chemical Association, wrote in the [New Orleans] *Times-Picayune:*

> Greenpeace . . . owes its allegiance to no nation. It has put its own agenda ahead of America's well-being, answering only to its left-wing ideology and to unnamed fellow travelers who pump millions into its coffers. Federal investigators and enterprising journalists should ask whether its funding is influenced by donors who do not have America's security interests at heart.[73]

As a result of these efforts, radical to moderate left environmentalists may be under pressure to demonstrate patriotic missions. In the clear, right-wing environmentalism can and does take advantage of natural security concerns to gain mainstream support for its anti-immigrant position.

While national security arguments against immigrants easily trump environmental ones in the post-9/11 era, right-wing environmentalists take advantage of concerns for national security to suggest "mass immigration" as a primary cause of terrorism and advance a racialized understanding of "American" that implies that "immigrant" equates with "un-American."[74]

NumbersUSA, another organization in John Tanton's network, claims that U.S. "overpopulation" represents a threat to "environment, farmland, community quality of life, schools, wage fairness and freedom."[75] It has fostered strong ties to conservative congressmen such as Tom Tancredo of Colorado and Lamar Smith of Texas.[76] Tancredo chairs the Congressional Immigration Reform Caucus, whose Web site carries links to several organizations in the anti-immigrant population and environment network and even to the racist hate group, American Patrol. Cordelia Strom, previously FAIR's legal director, became counsel to the director and coordinator of congressional affairs for the Immigration and Naturalization Service (whose functions were recently subsumed within the new Department of Homeland Security on March 1, 2003).[77] Arriving at positions of power and influence, the lobby continues unabashedly to foster ties with organized white-supremacist groups such as the 15,000-member Council of Conservative Citizens.[78]

Conclusion

Population environmentalism, like contemporary white supremacism, is a white chauvinist movement with an agenda that evokes gender hate and hierarchy and calls for policies of control over women's bodies and women's practices. Some of the leading opposition to the rightward lean of the environment movement has come from feminists with a strong commitment to social justice and international perspectives. The international women's health movement has long critiqued the dangerously narrow worldview of population-control thinking intrinsic to right-wing environmental thought. Among the first to initiate campaigns to educate environmentalists on racist and anti-immigrant agendas, the Committee on Women, Population and the Environment[79] has monitored right-wing environmental activism and networking for over a decade.

The legacies of population control and eugenics, manifested in green nativism, stem from a particular tradition of liberal thought that explicitly lacks a social analysis condemning sexism and racism. Herein lies substantial opportunity for convergence with the politics of organized white supremacism.

In fact, there is considerable overlap between the two movements, whose goals, ideological concerns, and agenda, if not language, are nearly identical. White-supremacist groups draw from the writings of anti-immigrant environmentalists, who impart a mask of legitimacy and authority to the mission. The analysis of population environmentalism appears in mainstream media and academic publications and meetings but is also featured in the publications, Web sites, and conferences of white-supremacist organizations. Additionally, there is evidence of interconnections between some key individuals in the green nativist network and those in white-supremacist groups. Albeit less overtly, it is clear that green nativism operates on the same continuum as contemporary white supremacism to promote politics of white power and hate.

Given the far-reaching impact of green nativist thought, it is essential to reexamine the predominant, popular notions of population and environment and how these mask racist and dangerous ideology and politics. Actions and campaigns mobilized in the name of population and environment stem from all points along the political spectrum. It is important to identify the ideological underpinnings of these movements, so that they can be situated within a broader political framework and evaluated for socially regressive content. In a very powerful argument, Peter Staudenmaier refers to the dangers of denying a political orientation to environmental movements:

> Environmental themes can be mobilized from the left or from the right, indeed they require an explicit social context if they are to have any political valence whatsoever. "Ecology" alone does not prescribe a politics; it must be interpreted, mediated through some theory of society in order to acquire political meaning. Failure to heed this mediated interrelationship between the social and ecological is the hallmark of reactionary ecology.[80]

Therefore, to dismiss ecofascism as feigned environmentalism ignores the ideological traditions of an ecology movement from the far right. The link between population and environment can lend itself to a particularly reactionary "blood and soil" interpretation, which leads to politics of fear and scapegoating. Yet these politics remain masked by depoliticized and liberalized notions of population and environment.

Afterword: The Growing Influence of Right-Wing Thought

PEGGY McINTOSH

I feel that the contributors to this volume have done a major service by identifying differences and distinctions between right-wing groups. With such help, we who are not aligned with the right may do our work or make our decisions more wisely and effectively. I also admire the ways in which these authors exercise the discipline that Peter Elbow named "the believing game": immersing in others' points of view in order to understand more fully their assumptions and visions. The analysis and research reported in this volume correct a liberal temptation to dismiss familiar right-wing themes or else to hear only their many iterations, that is, to "lump" rather than to "split." I have found it useful to learn about distinctions between hate groups and am grateful to the volume's authors for their care and discipline in documenting attitudes that may be anathema to them. In this day and age, it is imperative that U.S. citizens be aware that their nation may be wrested from them by ideologues of the far right.

The book helps also in identifying simple dualisms that can be seen in all sectors of the right regarding gender, race, religion, nation, and sexual orientation. Though each sector of the right does its work differently, there are many similarities across groups, which can be seen in the shared dependence on either/or and superior/inferior distinctions. There is a generalized race- and gender-supremacist vision set against whatever is seen as inferior to the supremacist norm. The authors identify many ways in which gender hierarchy informs right-wing thought and action. As Ferber and Kimmel see it, one aim of the right is to reclaim male control over women within white heteropatriarchy. Women's development of self-understanding and agency is at odds with this political, economic, social, intellectual, and spiritual agenda of the right. The white men of the right described in this volume implicitly and explicitly frame everything hierarchically: sexes, races, ethnic groups, religions, nations. Women's permitted roles are subordinated to men's decision-making. To track this kind of knowledge requires careful reading of right-wing materials; those who have most power get most attention and validation, so male privilege keeps the subjects of gender relations and women's experience out of most of the discourses of the right. The nearly hidden pictures of misogyny and fear of women need attention as matters of growing concern for citizens in an avowed democracy.

Reading these chapters has drawn my attention to the growing U.S. presence of supremacist and hate-filled speech in sectors that used to be considered moderate or centrist. I hear hate messages coming out of the present U.S. administration and members of Congress. The conceptualizations of the hard right described in this volume may have been conceptions of fringe groups at the time the research was done. Now many are in the mainstream of U.S. government policy and action.

Before September 11, 2001, I could have made this argument, but would have had to document it with footnotes to events, actions, and analyses which were not widely known. Now, citizens of the United States both know about and have taken part in the marked shift to the right. I use my contribution to this book to express my own "shock and awe" at the extent to which the accepted policies of the U.S. government now exhibit hard-right ideologies as described in the chapters of this book.

For example, in response to September 11, 2001, the U.S. government exhibited to a heightened degree, with public support from huge numbers of U.S. citizens, all four of the "overarching styles and master frames," which Berlet identifies as "important in U.S. right-wing movements." These include dualism, an apocalyptic style, populist rhetoric, and authoritarian assertions of dominance. Dualism has been reflected in the government's "either you're with us or you're against us" assertion, in the presentation of the Iraq War as a good-versus-evil struggle, and in the identification of the "Axis of Evil," consisting of three nonwhite nations. Apocalyptic style was evident in President Bush's insistence that Saddam Hussein's weapons of mass destruction (not ours) endangered the world. Populist rhetoric framed President Bush's policy speeches, which associated the war with the hearts and minds of the American people. Authoritarian assertion of dominance was made clear in the U.S. government's decision to bypass the UN, disrupt and bypass NATO, and go to war unilaterally, with or without a "coalition of the willing." With these actions and with the passage of the controlling Patriot Act as well, the U.S. government turned farther to the right than it was before 9/11 and appeared to use 9/11 to do what some sectors of the hard right probably wanted to do all along.

Many domestic developments in U.S. policy and budget decisions, which appear to be widely accepted, fit with eight of the agendas that Berlet identifies with the dissident right. Current Republican policies or legislative moves are anti-affirmative action, anti-immigrant, anti-welfare, anti-tax, pro-United States, pro-business, pro-economic liberty, and pro-Christian. The escalation into worldwide authoritarianism by the United States is now an openly discussed aim of the administration: military and space domination under the ideology of the New American Century. This set of agendas of world domination matches the aspirations of only the most extreme of the right-wing groups discussed in this volume.

Each platform of the administrative agenda listed above rests on economic and social hierarchies, winners and losers, and assumed superiority and inferiority. Poor people, non-Christians, women and men of color, and white women are the losers; white "Christian" men are the primary beneficiaries of these agendas. The caretaking roles projected onto and expected of people who by sex, class, religion, or race are "lower-caste" are roles that are disregarded, disparaged, or taken for granted in this agenda. This kind of inequity is not new, but the escalation of intended disenfranchisement and takeover is striking. Most current White House behaviors, attitudes, presumption, assumptions, and actions are either right in line with what Berlet describes as the dissident right or go still further, to a plan for global empire. But in one striking respect the Bush government abstains from one of the hatreds in some right-wing groups: virulent anti-Semitism is not to be seen in the Bush agenda, and in fact a number of its architects are Jewish men valued by the administration.

In other respects, I see many connections between the organized Christian Right and the dualistic construction of reality that the president of the United States and his administration put on the Afghan and Iraq wars. There is no doubt that Osama bin Laden was a vicious leader and Saddam Hussein was an evil despot. Therefore, the 2003 Iraq War could be presented to the U.S. populace as a holy war, a war of good versus evil.

The president and his advisors probably differ as individuals with regard to whether the good/evil rhetoric is truth or "spin." Their actual political and economic aims may have little to do with a vision of good and evil, but it was hard for the electorate to read their psychological and strategic aims. I felt that at a deep level, the Iraq War they were bent on fighting was not only a war against Saddam Hussein but also a religious war against Islam, a gendered war ignoring and injuring all who bear and care for the vulnerable, a race war against darker-skinned people, and a class war over access to oil.

Perhaps it was also a war to put white males "back in the saddle" after their perceived losses as described by Kimmel and Ferber. The energizing effects of flags, combat, patriotism, and conquest may have been a tonic in times of doubt and malaise for white males. Suddenly, white males had a lot to talk about. Though opinion polls cannot be fully trusted, they indicated that most white males identified with the nation itself, and the acts of its leaders, under the flag. It was those who did not so readily identify—men and women of color and white women—who were the most resistent to the idea of military retaliation against the attacks of 9/11. Those who felt least respected and included by the white, Right, male government of the United States were the least supportive of its determination to go to war. For this population, government policies have not been felt as such a blessing or protection at home. In any case, the government has now begun to talk about another war, against Iran, also a race and gender matter, with a white and chiefly male military taking on another nonwhite member of the "axis of evil."

But can the right wing claim to be located on an axis of good? Many U.S. citizens feel that indeed it is. This is understandable, even if for no other reason than we want to love our country. It may be hard at any time to look at one's country, and its leadership, through a lens that may reveal some aspects of it that one would rather not see. Now we are in a time when the right wing is in control of the leadership of the country. In this world of complex information overload, conflicting opinion, and feelings of threat, it can be a comfort to simply cut through, or avoid, complexities, and rest on what feel like truths. Many people feel that it is a truth that the United States is on an axis of good. It has played a very important and often positive role in the history and development of the world.

There is, however, a high price to be paid for choosing only comfort and refusing to think complexly about powerful authorities and their uses of their power. Now that right-wing habits of mind have been given so much support by the population as a whole, right-wing habits of mind in our government's leaders have been allowed to tip over into their extreme forms. Consistency has tipped over into rigidity, conviction into fundamentalism, discipline into coercion, intentionality into authoritarianism, dogmatism into hatred, certainty into violence. All of the relational values projected onto and expected of women get erased when such extremes develop, and women's plural capacity to care about the health, education, and welfare of all can be construed as not central to the national interest.

Most women in the United States today tend to go along, as we have been taught to go along, with male public authority. It is not only right-wing women who are identified with the authority of the apparent protector. On the left and in the middle, however, more women speak up for the values of caretaking, thinking globally, and feeling in plural, complex ways.

Beyond the fears and actions of groups of women, I wondered how gender roles play out in President Bush's combative statement after 9/11, "Either you're with us or you're against us." Who is "us"? The "us" was the tiny group that makes policy for the U.S. government, extrapolated to represent the entire population, as if we were all in agreement about who we are as members of a U.S. democracy and where our diverse interests lie. As I thought about "either you're with us or you're against us," I saw that women's assigned plural, mediating functions have no place in this either/or formulation. War, like right-wing thinking in general, depends on and valorizes either/or thinking. Plural thinking, or bonding, is legitimate only with the approved allies. Psychologically, the self must be arrayed against the rest of the world in a stance which is competitive and aggressive or else shelter-seeking under the wing of the protectors. Dichotomous thinking is essential to fundamentalism and militarism. That women in the armed services are now trained for and valorized for us-versus-them behavior does not mean that the military or gender roles have changed significantly. Rather, women's bodies got assimilated into the world of men's uniforms and military values.

Looking at the projection of "evil" onto Iraq, more than half of whose actual population is children, called to my attention the extent to which the administration, like the Christian Right, can construe whole nations as adult males and thinks of men when referring to nations. What was the role of children and women in the vision of "Iraq" as evil? Invisibility or anomaly—they did not fit the picture of our troops' toppling and emasculating the evil nation. Damage done to most of the people, that is, to the women and children and the old men, was denied or ignored by the press at the request of the U.S. government. Men of military age were the Iraqis whom the government featured in the image of Iraq as "evil." Their suffering relatives were simply unlucky enough to be born to the "evil" people.

I notice that the relational, pluralistic, familial mode of dealing with human needs that has been assigned to women is almost entirely lacking from the administration's repertoire of ways of dealing with people in the rest of the world. Some ally-relationality may be sought and developed, as with England's Tony Blair, for the sake of "winning." But in a win/lose, good/evil framework of feeling, there is no place for the human mutuality or relationality that allows development of parallel noncompeting interests by two or more entities at once. Within hierarchy, two cannot thrive equally; one must be superior, as men are in the ideologies of the right. The caring mode is at odds with the dominance mode.

Treaties and coalitions potentially have mutuality at their heart, in the sense of mutual interests. But in the mode of the United States at present, our ascendancy is presented as the overriding good. The sense of being God's favorite has led to U.S. willingness, perhaps eagerness, to weaken or break NATO and weaken or break the UN. Perhaps the mandate of the UN is too global, too lateral, too inclusive, even too *maternal* to be of any consequence to what this administration sees as its place in the world.

In the wake of the attacks on the United States on 9/11, our national image, as seen from the perspective of many other nations, has become that of a white, male, Judeo-Christian crusader, more imperious than before, acting unilaterally among nations, and claiming it is sanctioned by a higher power to fight whatever it names as evil. Kimmel and Ferber discuss this image of the white supremacist warrior in personal and U.S. contexts.

The intentions of the U.S. government after 2003 are not known by the public or by the rest of the world at this time. But after President Bush declared that Iraq is one of three nations constituting the Axis of Evil, his high-level advisors became increasingly willing to speak of world domination as the legitimate aim of the United States. One administration advisor said impatiently: "What's wrong with world domination if the cause is just?" The United States cast itself as God's chosen crusader against not just one but several "evil" nations. On TV, on the radio, and in writing, the leaders of the war invoked the name of the highest moral authority only on behalf of the United States. "God Bless America" was not expanded even to "God Bless the Coalition," let alone "God Bless Those Who Suffer in War," "God Bless the World," or "God Bless Us Every One."

Of course, the Bush administration was not the first male Anglo-European body on these shores to promulgate the conviction that God is in our corner. The habit goes back to the founding of the Colonies, seen as His political and spiritual favorites, while He is imagined to have nothing to do with the indigenous peoples already on the land or with the societies in the rest of the created world. I think that just as Christ is seen by the Christian Right as the personal Savior of individuals, God is seen as the national equivalent: the supreme Savior of the Chosen Nation. I hear the theme of "Onward Christian Soldiers" behind the white male march toward world domination.

In daily life, survival, growth, and development are key needs of all beings. All humans rely on the caretaking and practical work done by women toward our collective survival. But this cannot easily be acknowledged in the framework of good-versus-evil thinking about people. Domestic life must be kept below the polarizing pictures of good versus evil people, since in fact "their" women, as best they can, fulfill the same domestic functions as "our" women do. Providing food, water, clothing, and shelter are things women everywhere do. In this area, the good/evil, superior/inferior distinctions falter. Discourse must remain on the male functions in which the success in winning can be spotlighted to justify struggle. For war-makers, prevailing over the Other is important, as is History. People making and mending the fabrics of the society are not important and are not History. Getting ahead is important and is History. Trying to survive is not. Winning matters; working for the decent survival of all does not. Lateral work is not seen as nation-defining; violence is. So women's work everywhere is rendered invisible in male-fostered narratives of opposite sides and dualistic struggles within hierarchical situations.

The right is strong now because of its well-organized resistance to the growth and development of alternative egalitarian efforts that have come especially from men of color and women of all colors over the last seventy years. The spread of inclusive values and policies has accelerated especially over the last forty years, both in the United States and elsewhere in the world. The response of the right has been to attack the changes.

As a person working in education, I have noticed a great uniformity of tone and content in articles by the right about this field. I do not find reflection, curiosity, speculation, empathy, attention, or constructive conversation. I find the same attacks, the same vocabulary, and the same misrepresentation of the varieties of liberal thought repeated endlessly. The Christian Right acts like a dictator, aggressive, fearful, powerful, ruthless, and holding onto its conviction of the need for men to profess heterosexuality and to control women. I feel the Christian Right is doing terrible things in the name of Christ.

But for women as individuals under the wing of the Christian Right, the right wing sense of protection and salvation that provides resolution for all of life's complex problems takes on a spiritual dimension, and provides spiritual respite and security, within a paradoxical mix of feelings of dependency and claims to superiority. The chapter by Dobratz and Shanks-Meile suggests this relief from worry that the right can bring to its followers.

In this administration and in the last two decades, we see the growing influence of the right wing in campaigns against birth control, abortion, the Equal Rights Amendment, women's studies, affirmative action, sex education, justice for victims of rape, welfare for poor families, gun control, liberal media, progressive education, higher education, and democratic dissent. All of these relate intimately to the social role assignments given to women in the expectation that we will preserve life, health, and growth. The campaigns of the right undermine our capacity to work for the commonweal which has been our charge.

In 2002, members of the Christian Right protested vehemently when the University of North Carolina assigned a book about the Koran as summer reading for incoming students. I think that for the far right learning is understood to consist in mastering doctrine and ideology. It is not about the liberal arts values of reflection, self-knowledge, critical thinking, and empathetic awareness of others' cultural ways. When a *New York Times* reporter went to Chapel Hill to interview University of North Carolina students on the book about the Koran, they said they did not understand what the fuss was about. It was just a book! The liberal arts ideal had penetrated students' awareness to that extent: assigned books are not doctrine and ideology; they are part of a selection of readings for comparison, contrast, and deepened understanding.

There are crucial years ahead in which the United States' intentions toward the rest of the world will determine whether it becomes more feared, hated, and formidable, or whether the U.S. electorate will decide it should be less violent and more consultative in world affairs. In a worst-case scenario, several branches of the right will have their day in producing a white male, facist ruling group that will invoke their God to justify their persecution of all at home and elsewhere who challenge them. I feel we have seen signs of this antidemocratic control in the silence of most members of Congress, in the Patriot Act, in the rise of right-wing pundits on radio and TV, and in the inability of the press to go beyond simple dualisms in coverage of political and cultural life.

Would women resist the worst-case scenario I have sketched? I feel most women will not forsake the conscious and unconscious dreams of protection by men which we have and which the right fosters. It is hard to learn to see systemically if one has not been taught to do so and has been rewarded for *not* doing so, not getting "strident," not getting independent as a woman. It is hard to recognize internalized oppression and realize that one was taught not to work for one's own interests. I feel most women will continue not to recognize the system of male control called patriarchy and not to recognize the ways in which the Christian Right intends to push them further under the system of heterosexual male control. Women have been taught not to recognize the shaping forces and negative effects of patriarchy on our well-being. Indeed, most women do not even know the "P" word.

The essays in this book show us how supremacist race/gender/religious ideology gives right-wing people permission to impose supremacist actions at home and in the world. The permission to hate, the permission to be violent, the permission to persecute, harass, and lead killing crusades: these threaten the bodies, souls, minds, and emotions not only of U.S. individuals and U.S. civil society, but also of other people and nations who suffer at our hands from the supremacist behaviors of our leaders and our largely complicit population. At risk are the qualities of making and mending the cultural, relational, ecological, connective fabrics that human beings (half of us as women) have woven in the past. I hope that United States people have the resources of courage, humility, and intelligence to organize and to model effective alternatives to right-wing extremes.

Notes

Foreword

1. Dyer, 1997: 63.
2. Yardley, 2001.
3. Ronson, 2002: 188.
4. Suhayda, 2001.

Introduction

1. White Power 101: 3.
2. Southern Poverty Law Center, April 28, 2003.
3. Aho, 1990; Ferber, 1998a.
4. Southern Poverty Law Center, April 28, 2003.
5. Feagin, 2000; Feagin, Vera, and Batur, 2001; Ferber, 1998a.
6. Einwohner, Hollander, and Olson, 2000: 679.
7. Einwohner et al., 2000; Taylor, 1999; Ferree and Merrill, 2000.
8. Kuumba, 2001: 2.
9. Swidler, 1986; Williams, 1995.
10. Ferber, 1998a.
11. www.resist.com/positions/women.html.
12. Einwohner et al., 2000: 688.
13. Ibid., 690.
14. Ibid., 691.
15. Ferree and Merrill, 2000: 457.
16. Collins, 1991; hooks, 1984; Spelman, 1988; Anzaldua and Keating, 2002.
17. Ferber, 1998a.
18. Kuumba, 2001: 15.
19. Ibid.

Chapter 1

1. My research in this area would not have been possible without the support and assistance of my colleagues over the years at Political Research Associates, especially Jean Hardisty, Margaret Quigley, Surina Khan, Mitra Rastegar, Nikhil Aziz, Palak Shah, and Toby Beauchamp. In addition, I have benefited from conversations over many years with Matthew N. Lyons, Sara Diamond, Fred Clarkson, Russ Bellant, Suzanne Pharr, Loretta Ross, and Paul de Armond. More formal interviews with Kathleen Blee, Mark Pitcavage, and John C. Green provided much useful information. Thanks to Betty Dobratz, Stephanie Shanks-Meile, Martin Durham, Jerome Himmelstein, Michael Barkun, Lisa K. Waldner, and Timothy Buzzell for their work and encouragement. Special thanks are due to Abby Ferber and Myra Marx Ferree for their helpful comments. All mistakes of fact and interpretation, alas, are mine alone.
2. Guillaumin, 1995; Goldman, 1996; Pharr, 1996a; Fraser, 1997; Wing, 2000; Rothenberg, 2001.
3. Young-Bruehl, 1996: 23, 460.
4. Buechler, 2000: 105–107.
5. Felice, 1996: 1–4.
6. Omi and Winant, 1994: 72. They point out that some racial projects are racial supremacist but not all—for example, "an association . . . of black accountants," 71.
7. Omi and Winant, 1994: 74–75.
8. Here we are focusing on broad societal oppression and not narrower interpersonal forms.
9. Along the way I criticize some of my earlier work.
10. Diamond, 1989, 1995, Aho, 1990; Corcoran, [1990] 1997; Barkun, [1994] 1997; Hamm, 1994, 1997, 1998; Ezekiel, 1995; Lamy, 1996; Dobratz and Shanks-Miehle, 1997; Ferber, 1998a; Hardisty, 1999; Berlet & Lyons, 2000; Blee, 2002.
11. Durham, 2000: 181–182.
12. Betz, 1994; Betz and Immerfall, 1998; Mudde, 2000. Usually the middle sector is called the "radical right," but here I will use the term dissident right. Not all dissident-right groups are populist, but in the United States even elitist groups will sometimes use populist rhetoric. The Christian Right and the patriot movement both use populist rhetoric extensively.
13. Barron, 1992; Clarkson, 1997; Berlet and Lyons, 2000: 248–250.
14. Berlet and Lyons, 2000: 16.
15. Allport, 1954: 363–366.
16. Himmelstein, 1998: 7.
17. On framing in social movements, see Goffman, 1959, 1974; Gamson, [1975] 1990; Snow, et al., [1986] 1997; Snow and Benford, 1988, Johnston 1995; Zald 1996; Klandermans, 1997. On the construction of overarching master frames, see Snow and Benford, 1992. On framing in right-wing movements, see Dobratz and Shanks-Meile, 1996, 1997; Berlet, 2001.
18. Allport, 1954: 243–260; Fenster, 1999; Berlet and Lyons, 2000; Goldberg, 2001.
19. Roediger, 1991: 58; Hobgood, 2000: 46–49.
20. Boyer, 1992; O'Leary, 1994; Kovel, 1994; Strozier, 1994; Fuller, 1995; Lamy, 1996; Barkun, 1997. Scholars debate distinctions among apocalyptic, millennialist, and millenarian social movements, but they share enough similarity for this discussion to lump them together.
21. Goldberg, 2001: 1.
22. Berlet and Lyons, 2000: 9.
23. Hofstadter, 1965; D. Thompson, [1996] 1998: 307.
24. Fenster, 1999.
25. Curry and Brown, 1972; Cumings, 1990: 767.
26. Davis, 1971: 361; Donner, 1980: 11.
27. Canovan, 1981: 3–16, 46–51, 289–301; Brinkley, 1982: 165–168; Berlet and Lyons, 2000, 4–6.
28. Betz, 1994; Kazin, 1995; Junas, 1995; Berlet and Lyons, 2000.
29. Laclau, 1977; Berlet and Lyons, 2000.
30. Canovan, 1981, 54–55; Kazin, 1995: 35–36, 52–54, 143–144; Stock, 1996: 15–86; Berlet and Lyons, 2000: 4–6.
31. Kantrowitz, 2000: 4–6, 109–114, 153.
32. Payne, 1995: 52–53; Postone, 1986.

33. Marsden, 1991; Junas, 1995b.
34. Quinby, 1994: 78.
35. Kintz, 1997: 257.
36. Omi and Winant, 1994: 121–122; Herman, 1997; Kintz, 1997; Quinby, 1997; Ferber, 1998a; Faludi, 1999; Hardisty, 1999: 9–36.
37. Klatch, 1987; Blee, 1991, 2002; Brasher, 1998.
38. Durham, on the other hand, argues that the situation is far more complex than can be explained just by blaming angry white men (2000: 24–42).
39. Oberschall, 1973: 119; Tilly, 1978: 143–151, 279.
40. Durham, 2000: 168–183. See also Ferber, 1998a; 2000.
41. Berlet and Lyons, 2000.
42. Tolchin, 1996.
43. Ehrenreich, 1989: 144–195.
44. Shanks-Meile and Dobratz, "Linkages of Hatred," n.d.
45. Bobbio, 1996: 27–28.
46. Kittrie, 1995, 2000.
47. Della Porta, 1992; Kittrie, 1995; 2000.
48. Gamson, 1995: 174–175; Oberschall, 1973: 325.
49. Kittrie, 2000: 341–350.
50. Scher, 2001; Dempsey and Cole, 2002; Chang, 2002.
51. Dobratz and Shanks-Meile, 1997.
52. Hixson, 1992; Dobratz and Shanks-Meile, 1997; Durham, 2000; Berlet and Lyons, 2000; Dobratz, Walder, and Buzzell, 2001; Blee, 2002.
53. Mehler, 1989, 1994, 1999.
54. Grant, [1916] 1923: xx–xxii.
55. Berlet and Lyons, 2000: 335–336.
56. Ibid., 336.
57. Barkun, [1994] 1997: 103, 107.
58. Anti-Defamation League, 1999b; Hoskins, 1985.
59. Hoskins, [1958] 1996: 5.
60. Ibid., Foreword.
61. Ibid., 27.
62. Ibid., 38.
63. Ibid., 39.
64. Perry, 2000.
65. Beam, 1983.
66. Beck, 2000.
67. Dobratz and Shanks-Meile, 1997.
68. Burghart, 1996; Burris, Smith, and Strahm, 2000; Schroer, 2001.
69. Allport, 1954.
70. Aho, 1990.
71. Blee, 2002: 9.
72. Ferber, 1998a; Kimmel and Ferber, 2000; Ferber and Kimmel, 2000.
73. I hesitate to claim that no such group exists, although this may be a form of apocalyptic cynicism.
74. This is based on reading issues of the *WAR* newspaper for ten years.
75. Stern, 1996a: 137–162; Davidian, 1996: 18; Gibson, 1997; Lamy, 1996: 153–191; Berlet and Lyons, 2000: 287–304.
76. Davidson, 1996; Dyer, 1998; Neiwert, 1999.
77. Roches, 1985.
78. Levitas, 2002.
79. Durham, 2000: 146, citing Barkun, [1994] 1997: 217–222.
80. Hamm, 1997.
81. Southern Poverty Law Center, 2001a: 8.
82. Stern, 1996a: 109; Halpern and Levin, 1996; Hamm, 1997.
83. Mahan, 1997: 186.
84. Stock, 1996; Berlet and Lyons, 2000; Freilich, Peinick, and Howard, 2001; Freilich, 2003; Crothers, forthcoming.

85. Akins, 1998: 144–145.
86. Berlet and Lyons, 2000: 287–293; see especially the list on p. 288.
87. Aho, 2001; Blee, 2002.
88. Kraft, 1992; McEvoy, 1969; Grupp, 1969.
89. Van Dyke and Soule, 2000; D. Kaplan, 1998; Mele, 1995.
90. Freilich, 2003.
91. Gallaher, 2003.
92. Betz, 1994: 106–108, 174.
93. Kimmel and Ferber, 2000.
94. Ibid., 584.
95. Junas, 1995b: 21.
96. Arrington, quoted in Ladd and Swofford, 1995, on-line archive.
97. Ehrenreich, 1997.
98. Gibson, 1994.
99. Gibson, 2001.
100. Lembcke, 1998, and forthcoming.
101. Franklin, 1992.
102. Gibson, 1994: 9–10, 161–165, 298–309; Lamy, 1996: 85–89.
103. Militia of Montana, 2000.
104. Enloe, 2000: 1.
105. Ibid., 2.
106. In studying the militias, distinctions among masculinism, sexism, antifeminism, patriarchy, misogyny, and heterosexism are sometimes lost. A few analysts simply omit from their discussion the fact that Linda Thompson, a libertarian described by friends as a feminist, was an early key leader of the armed citizens' militias. Women can lead antifeminist organizations or use masculinist narratives and styles, but they do not generally lead misogynist organizations.
107. Katz and Bailey, 2000: 139.
108. Kimmel and Ferber, 2000: 587.
109. Stern, 1996a; Crawford and Burghart, 1997; Zeskind, 1999; Levitas, 2002.
110. I confess, at the outset, so did I.
111. I demure, at the outset, I did not.
112. Pitcavage, interviewed in Berlet, 2002. Mark Pitcavage is national fact-finding director for the Anti-Defamation League.
113. Pitcavage, interviewed in Berlet, 2002.
114. Southern Poverty Law Center, 2001b: 9.
115. Pitcavage, interviewed in Berlet, 2002.
116. Stern, 1996a: 61–63.
117. A. Thompson, 1995.
118. Berlet and Lyons, 2000: 287–304.
119. Berlet, 2002: 10–11.
120. Durham, 2000: 138.
121. Green, interviewed in Berlet, 2002. John C. Green is director of the Ray Bliss Center at the Institute of Applied Politics of the University of Akron in Ohio.
122. Stern, 1996a: 36.
123. Ibid., 37.
124. Pitcavage, interviewed in Berlet, 2002.
125. Stern, 1996a: 12, 36, 67–74.
126. Pitcavage, interviewed in Berlet, 2002.
127. Ibid. Peters is an extreme-right Christian Identity leader from Colorado.
128. Pitcavage, interviewed in Berlet, 2002.
129. Kimmel and Ferber, 2000: 594 (citing Crawford and Burghart, 1997: 190), 602.
130. Ibid., 2000: 582.
131. Katz and Bailey, 2000: 139.
132. Carter, 1995: 379.
133. J. Kaplan, 1997a: 127–163.
134. J. Kaplan, 1997a: 170. J. Kaplan's arguments raised a flurry of comments: Robbins, 1997; J. Kaplan, 1997b; Wright, 1999. The debate centers on whether or not federal agencies and

watchdog groups sometimes exaggerate the threat of hard-right groups; see also Chermak, 2002.
135. Rupert, 1997: 96.
136. Berlet and Lyons, 2000: 303.
137. Levitas, 2002.
138. Pitcavage, interviewed in Berlet, 2002.
139. Perry, 2000: 123.
140. Wallace, 1956; Tuveson, 1968.
141. Marsden, 1991; Martin, 1996.
142. Green, Guth, and Hill, 1993: 80–91; C. Smith, et al., 1998: 75–84; Morin and Wilson, 1997.
143. Burris, 2001.
144. Herman, 1997; Quinby, 1997, 1999; Diamond, 1998; Berlet and Lyons, 2000; Durham, 2000.
145. Kintz, 1997; Newton, 1999; Kimmel, 1999; Ferber and Kimmel, 2000.
146. Berlet and Lyons, 2000: 228.
147. Stern, 1996b; Durham, 2000; Blee and Green, interviewed in Berlet, 2002.
148. Donner, 1980; Kovel, 1994.
149. Marsden, 1991.
150. Diamond, 1989; Marsden, 1991; Martin, 1996; D. Thompson, [1996] 1998.
151. Diamond, 1995, 1996, 1998; Clarkson, 1997.
152. Clarkson, 2001, 9.
153. Kaminer, 2001.
154. Kintz, 1997: 6–9, 257.
155. Gardner, 1996: 4.
156. Johnson, 1995; Bellant, 1995; Ross and Cokorinos, 1996; Conason, Ross, and Cokorinos, 1996; Novosad, 1996, 2000; Berkowitz, 1996; Neiberger, 1996.
157. Berlet and Lyons, 2000: 328.
158. Ryle, quoted in Bellant, 1995: 83.
159. Bellant, 1995: 82.
160. Ross and Cokorinos, 1996.
161. Newton, 1998: 597, n. 40.
162. Williams and Blackburn, 1996.
163. Newton, 1998: 597, n. 40.
164. Ibid., citing Colburn and Rogers, 1995.
165. The author has attended meetings of both the Christian Coalition and the Promise Keepers.
166. Minkowitz, 1995, 1998.
167. Schindler, 1998: 25.
168. C. Anderson, 1997.
169. Jaffe, 1999: 139–141.
170. Cable News Network 1997: 9.
171. Ibid. I assisted the early national leadership of Equal Partners in Faith.
172. Brasher, 1998.
173. C. Smith, 2000: 60–191. This section of C. Smith's book was written with Melinda Lundquist.
174. Diamond, 1998; Kimmel, 1999: 114.
175. Heath, forthcoming.
176. L. Williams, 1997.
177. Brickner, 1999: 4–6.
178. Schindler, 1998:1.
179. Khan, 1998.
180. Quinby, 1997: 154–156.
181. Diamond, 1995: 166.
182. Edsall and Edsall, 1991: 131–134; W. Martin, 1996: 77–80, 168–171.
183. Berlet and Quigley, 1995; Berlet and Lyons, 2000.
184. Kintz, 1997; Diamond, 1998; Burlein, 2002; Mason, 2002.
185. Heath, forthcoming.
186. Some activists organizing against the Christian Right use the phrase "religious political extremist" to create a frame where the Christian Right and the extreme right are portrayed

as somehow connected. This is objectionable due to dubious accuracy and doubtful ethics. See discussion in Diamond, 1996: 92, 209; Himmelstein, 1998.

187. Monroe, 1997; Diamond, 1998.
188. See, for example, *New Man,* January-February, 1998; March-April, 1998; March-April 1999; September-October, 1999.
189. L. Williams, 1997; Equal Partners in Faith, 1997; A. Smith, 2002.
190. A. Smith, 2002.
191. Toler, 1995.
192. Berlet and Quigley, 1995; Berlet, 1998; Hardisty, 1999; Fredrickson, 2000; Berlet and Lyons, 2000; Bonilla-Silva, 2001.
193. This does not represent the main current of modern denominational Protestant Calvinism.
194. Kintz, 1997: 136–139.
195. Gardiner, 1998.
196. R. Williams, 2001: 2.
197. Newton, 1999: 41.
198. Ibid.
199. A. Smith, 2002.
200. Pharr, 1996b; Minkowitz, 1995, 1998.
201. Feagin, 2001: 139–140. See also Feagin and Vera, 1995.
202. Guillaumin, 1995: 56–57.
203. Ibid., 179.
204. Ibid., 272.
205. Ibid.
206. Blee, 2001: 179.

Chapter 2

1. Feminist scholars have argued that a number of social movements organize women on the basis of a "female consciousness" grounded not in feminism but in the commonality of women's tasks. See T. Kaplan 1982; Cott, 1989.
2. Robert Miles is quoted in *Spokane Spokesman Review,* 1986.
3. Berezin, 1997.
4. Conflicting stances toward families and family life have also characterized extremist right-wing movements of the past, which sought at once to appropriate families and to reshape them. For example, the propaganda (though not the practice) of the 1920s Ku Klux Klan strongly emphasized the need to transform white Christian family life along racist lines, particularly by punishing philandering husbands. The modern racist movement shows little interest in such reshaping of personal or family life despite some pressure from racist activist women to do so.
5. NSDAP-AIO, *The New Order,* September-October 1994: 2.
6. From testimony of Robert E. Miles given in the 1988 Ft. Smith, Arkansas, trial of white supremacists for sedition; in "Extremist" file, Anti-Defamation League of B'nai B'rith, New York.
7. *Viking Viewpoint: Truth and Honor,* 1993.
8. Hamm, 1994: 180.
9. Quoted in New York *Daily News,* July 27, 1993; clipping in Anti-Defamation League files.
10. Ibid.
11. "Klan Kid Korp," in *Prescript of the Order of the * of the ***, distributed by Knights of the Ku Klux Klan, ca. 1997, 15.
12. "Special information for Homeschoolers," distributed by Scriptures for America, ca. 1996.
13. *WAR,* 1989: 6.
14. *White Sisters,* 1992: 11.
15. Researchers generally assume that political socialization takes place largely within families. See Johnston, 1994; Golden, 1988; Robb, 1954.

16. See also Hamm, 1994: 8.
17. Blee, 1985; Frank, 1994.
18. For example, "Kosher Racket Revealed: Secret Jewish Tax on Gentiles," pamphlet distributed by an anonymous racist group, ca. 1991.
19. Advertisement for Debbie's Crafts in *Race and Reason*, ca. 1994; see also "Aryan Women's League: Crafts, Products, and Informational Services," flyer distributed by the Aryan Women's League, ca. 1994.
20. See the "Aryan Women's League" file, clippings ca. 1993, Anti-Defamation League.
21. *Valkyrie Voice*, 1997.
22. On the importance of social ties in organizing and maintaining social movements, see, for example, Della Porta, 1995; Fielding, 1981; Crenshaw, 1988; Harris, 1988; Staggenborg, 1998; Chelser and Schmuch, 1963; Buhmann, 1992; Campbell, 1987; McRobbie and Garber, 1976; C. Taylor, 1990.
23. Mueller, 1994.
24. See Johnston, Laraña, and Gusfield, 1994; Crenshaw, 1988; Kelly and Breinlinger, 1996.
25. *Chicago Tribune*, 1985.
26. *Aryan Research Fellowship Newsletter*, 1990: 8–12.
27. Self-sufficiency is not a new idea within organized racism. The Aryan Knights of the Ku Klux Klan of Pennsylvania in the early 1970s claimed to offer its members benefits that ranged from "places to stay as you travel" to "mechanics, blood banks, and...AAA benefits." Bill Sickles, letter of April 8, 1972, in "Aryan Knights, Export PA" file, Special Collections, Howard-Tilton Memorial Library, Tulane University.
28. Aryan Women flyer, 1992.
29. Cochran, 1993.
30. See Back, Keith, and Solomos, 1998: 73–101.
31. *Aryan Research Fellowship Newsletter*, 1990.
32. Benfer, 1999.
33. *Aryan Research Fellowship Newsletter*, 1990.
34. "Aryan Update" phone line, May 25, 1993.
35. Robnett, 1997. On ties between members of organized social movements and those in their larger environment, see Lo, 1992: 229.
36. *National Socialist Vanguard Report*, 1987.
37. White Aryan Resistance, hate line transcription, October 10, 1989; see also *WAR*, 1989: 8.
38. *WAR*, 1989: 8.
39. *Aryan Research Fellowship Newsletter*, 1990.
40. Preston, 1999.
41. For example, Jessie Daniels overlooks the informal leadership of women when she asserts that "white women are primarily valuable to the movement for two qualities: their reproductive abilities and sexual attractiveness"; see Daniels, 1997: 57.
42. Brodkin Sacks, 1998: 85–95. See also Rose, 1987: 245–258. On the development of collective identity, see Johnston, Laraña, and Gusfield, 1994; Johnston and Klandermans, 1995: 3–24. On mediation as leadership, see Passerini, 1987: 139.
43. For example, see Ezekiel, 1995: 61–148.
44. Anthony and Robbins, 1996: 10–50.
45. See *The Record—North Jersey's Intelligence Report*, August 26, 1993; and "Loveland Man Heads Nazi Group," *Greeley Tribune*, February 15, 1993; both clippings in the collection of the Anti-Defamation League.
46. Fangen, 1998: 201–230.
47. Klanwatch *Intelligence Report*, 1991. There is little literature on women as terrorists. Two important studies are Braungart and Braungart, 1992: 45–78; Zwerman, 1994: 33–56. A more superficial account is Georges-Abeyie, 1983: 71–84.
48. Despite such violent activities, the stereotype of racist women as merely the sexual chattel of men persists. In their introduction to *Racist Violence in Europe*, the collection of essays they edited, Tore Bjørgo and Rob White insist that "female activists in racist and other right-wing groups tend to be assigned to non-fighting and subordinate roles"; 1993: 11. Women in gangs are similarly either ignored or sexualized in research and journalism, though feminist

studies find that gang girls, while still quite dependent on boys, have been steadily gaining independence. See Joe and Chesney-Lind, 1995: 412; Chesney-Lind, Shelden, and Joe, 1996: 185–204.

49. Chideya, 1994: 134–137, 186.
50. Benfer, 1999.
51. "Bounties Bestowing . . . Blessings Bequeathed," ca. 1996, n.p.
52. Ibid.; see also "The Jubilee's 'Captive Christian Penfriends Correspondence List,'" December 1994, n.p.
53. Lisa Turner of Church of the Creator, quoted in Anti-Defamation League, 1999: 48.
54. Passerini, 1992: 193.
55. Excellent discussions of fraternalism as a ideological motif are found in Mosse, 1985; B. Anderson, 1991; Clawson, 1989. Clawson's account is particularly insightful about the connections between fraternalism and masculinity.
56. See, for example, interviewees quoted in Dobie, 1997: 257.
57. *Aryan Action Line*, 1992.
58. For example, see Leaman, 1992, 1994 (publications of the Aryan Nations). See also the discussion of the Women's Frontier of the World Church of the Creator in a special report published by the Chicago-based Center for New Community, 2000.
59. *Aryan Nations*, 1992.
60. S. Mason, 1993. Though most racist leaders and literature strongly criticize feminism, some use feminist rhetoric to present racism as guaranteeing the rights of Aryan women. These white women, they insist, will gain as racist movements eradicate those religions and cultures that racists regard as oppressive to women—Muslim, Jewish, Mexican American, African American, and so on. Italian fascists also argued for a "feminism" untainted by concerns for equality but based on race, family, and tradition; see De Grazia, 1992: 236.
61. Kerr, 1983: 4.
62. Hammerbringer Baxter the Pagan, 1989.
63. See Dobie, 1992: 22–32; *Aryan Action Line*, 1992: 2. Local skingirl groups are covered in *The Monitor*, the newsletter of the Center for Democratic Renewal, which is based in Atlanta.
64. See Blazak, 1995; Dobie, 1992, 1997.
65. *The Code of the Skinhead*, 1993; anonymous skinhead 'zine, n.p., 1994.
66. Skorzeny, 1993.
67. "Women Skinheads," episode of *Geraldo*, ca. 1991, transcription in the files of the Anti-Defamation League.
68. White Aryan Resistance, hate-line transcription, August 16, 1993; in the files of the Anti-Defamation League.
69. *Sigrdrifa*, 1997a.
70. Hamm, 1994: 75–76.
71. "Women Skinheads," *Geraldo*, ca. 1991.
72. *Sigrdrifa*, 1997b.
73. Male Klan leader, quoted in Ezekiel, 1995: 110.
74. Female racist, quoted in the New York *Daily News*, July 17, 1993, clipping in the files of the Anti-Defamation League.
75. "WAR" file, 1993, Anti-Defamation League, 1999.
76. *WAR*, 1992; *White Sisters*, October 1992; and *Race and Reality* 2, 1994. In response to male complaints about their difficulty in finding "suitably racially aware" Aryan women as wives and girlfriends, one woman suggested that they should recruit female partners from women's prisons, arguing that the numbers of women from racial minorities in prisons "should do wonders for a lady's racial perspective." See NSWPP, 1994: 9.
77. See B. Anderson, 1991: 143; Della Porta, 1995: 281; Jacobs, 1984: 155–171; and Richardson, van der Lans, and Derks, 1986: 97–126.
78. Eighteen-year-old woman, quoted in "Second Wife Is Disillusioned," Associated Press article, January 26, 1994, in the files of the Anti-Defamation League.
79. Conflict over gender roles and women's place in racist movements also exists elsewhere in the world—for example, in Great Britain's National Front, in which women have been active participants. See Durham, 1995: 280, 285.

Chapter 3

1.   People's Resistance Movement, at www.resist.com.
2.   Cited in Anti-Defamation League, 1996a: 178.
3.   See Anti-Defamation League, 1996a, 1996b; Aho, 1994; Dobratz and Shanks-Meile, 1997; MacLean, 1994; Ridgeway, 1995.
4.   Ferber, 1998b: 51.
5.   Web sites sponsored by hate groups move around quite regularly. Approximately one quarter of the sites listed on the Hate Directory had been closed or moved and could not be found. Moreover, since the time when my observations were first made, many of the sites have either moved or closed. (Hatedirectory.com)
6.   See Perry, 1999.
7.   McAdam, 1982.
8.   Dobratz and Shanks-Meile, 1997.
9.   See Klanwatch, 1998; Dobratz and Shanks-Meile, 1997; Ferber, 1998b.
10. Dobratz and Shanks-Meile, 1997: 279.
11. Cited in Kleg, 1993: 216.
12. Cited in Anti-Defamation League, 1996a: 36.
13. Cited in Ridgeway, 1995: 38.
14. Blee, this volume, 1991, 1996.
15. Blee, 1996: 682.
16. Ibid., 697–698.
17. Dees, 1996.
18. Center for Democratic Renewal, n.d.
19. Center for Democratic Renewal, 1995: 4.
20. McAdam, 1982.
21. Anti-Defamation League, 1996a.
22. D. Goldberg, 1990: 297.
23. National Alliance, at www.natall.com.
24. Omi and Winant, 1994: 60.
25. Weis, Proweller, and Centri, 1997: 214.
26. Fine, 1997: 58.
27. Weis, Proweller, and Centri, 1997: 214.
28. Frankenberg, 1993: 236.
29. Sapp, Holder, and Wiggins, 1993: 127.
30. Center for Democratic Renewal, n.d.
31. Pierce, at www.natvan.com.
32. Karst, 1993: 54.
33. Strom, at www.freespeech.com.
34. Pierce, at www.natvan.com.
35. Ibid.
36. Kimmel and Ferber, this volume.
37. Pierce, at www.natvan.com.
38. Ferber and Kimmel, this volume.
39. www.resist.com.
40. www.tommetzger.net.
41. Ibid.
42. www.resist.com.
43. www.tommetzger.net.
44. Strom, at www.freespeech.com.
45. Ferber and Kimmel, this volume.
46. www.kkkk.net/ikuk.
47. Daniels, 1997; Ferber, 1998b.
48. National Alliance, at www.natall.com.
49. Ibid.
50. Cited in Sapp, Holden, and Wiggins, 1993: 123–124.
51. Roots, at home1gte.net/nri.html.

52. Cited in Roots, at home1gte.net/nri.html.
53. Ezekiel, 1995: 10.
54. Strom, at www.freespeech.com.
55. Ibid.
56. National Alliance, at www.natall.com/free-speech.
57. Roots, at home1gte.net/nri.html.
58. www.nationalist.org.
59. Yggdrasil, at www.netcom.com.
60. Confederate White Pride, at www.whitepower.com.
61. Strom, at www.freespeech.com.
62. Ferber and Kimmel, this volume.
63. Frankenberg, 1993: 75.
64. Messerschmidt, 1997: 23.
65. Ibid., 36.
66. West, 1993: 119.
67. Cited in Weigman, 1993: 237–238.
68. www.14words.com.
69. Ferber and Kimmel, this volume.
70. www.natvan.com.
71. Daniels, 1997: 112.
72. Strom, at www.freespeech.com.
73. Creator's Rights Party, at 209.41.174.82/artsfag.htm.
74. www.NatSoc.com.
75. Rev. White's Christian Politics, at www.wcp.com.
76. American Christian Nationalist CyberMinistries, at www.cyberministry.com.
77. Knights of the Ku Klux Klan, at www.kkkk.net.
78. Strom, at www.freespeech.com.
79. Ferber, 1998b: 22.
80. Feagin and Vera, 1995.
81. McAdam, 1982.
82. Ferber and Kimmel, this volume.
83. Young, 1990.
84. Minow, 1990: 377.

Chapter 4

1. *Women's Frontier,* August 26AC: 5
    Matt Hale has created a unique numbering system by which to document time. Matt Hale has also decreed that the members of the WCOTC will no longer use the Christian calender system. The WCOTC calendar begins in 1973, the year the COTC was founded. He calls the years before Creativity, "Prius Creativitat," and the years following, "Incepto de Creativitat." So the old year "1997" will now become 24 A.C. or the 24th year of Creativity.
 2. Bobel, 2002; Schor, 1998.
 3. *The Creator Manual,* 2000.
 4. Dobratz and Shanks-Meile, 1997.
 5. Anti-Defamation League, 2000.
 6. Hatewatch 1999; Anti-Defamation League, 2000.
 7. Klassen, 1981.
 8. Anti-Defamation League, http://www.adl.org/learn/ext_us/hale.asp, retrieved 11/17/2002.
 9. Hale, 1999.
10. Southern Poverty Law Center, 1999.
11. Anti-Defamation League, 1999.
12. The Women's Frontier is the Web page or the chapter of the women's organization; the *Women's Frontier* or WFN is the newsletter. Some of the Web site addresses have changed since the original printing dates. Moreover, as is common practice in extreme racist groups with a Web presence, much of the Web material has been removed since this research was first conducted in 1999.

13. Anderson, 1991.
14. Hale, 1999.
15. *Women's Frontier,* August 26AC: 3.
16. Sister Lisa Turner. *Women's Frontier* 1, April 26AC: 3.
17. Blee, this volume.
18. See also Ferber, 1998a; Kimmel and Ferber, 2000.
19. Blee, Kathleen M. *Women of the Klan: Racism and Gender in the 1920s,* University of California Press, 1991.
20. Blee, 2001.
21. Women's Frontier, http://216.221.171.242/wcotcwf/oregon.html. Web site no longer available.
22. Turner, 1999.
23. Turner, 1999.
24. Women's Frontier, http://216.221.171.242/wcotcwf/oregon.html.
25. *Women's Frontier,* August 26AC: 5.
26. Ibid., April 26AC: 3.
27. Ibid., August 26AC: 7.
28. Diquinzio, 1999.
29. *Women's Frontier,* August 26AC.
30. Ibid., 14.
31. Women's Frontier, http://www.front14.org/wfrontier/abortion.html.
32. *Women's Frontier,* April 26AC: 3.
33. Ibid.
34. Ibid.
35. Ferber, 1998.
36. *Women's Frontier,* December 26AC.
37. Ibid., April 26AC.
38. Ibid.
39. Ferber, 1997.
40. *Women's Frontier,* August 26AC.
41. Ibid., January 26AC.
42. Joe, "Letters to the Editor" *Womens Frontier* 1, December 26AC: 15.
43. *Women's Frontier,* September 26AC: 3.
44. Ibid., 2–4.
45. Ibid., 4.
46. Klassen, 1981: 36.
47. Ibid., 30.
48. Bobel, 2002.
49. *Women's Frontier,* October 26AC. 11.
50. Ibid.
51. Ibid.
52. Nature's Eternal Religion pg. 470–471. Reprinted in the *Women's Frontier, January* Source Benklassen (original) from 26AC: 13.
53. *Women's Frontier,* January 26AC: 13.
54. Issue One, August 26AC. Http://www.front14.org/Sisterhood/whs1.html-home schooling zine, 1 of 9.
55. Sister Melody La Rue, Http://www.front14.org/Sisterhood/whs1.html-home schooling zine, 2 of 9. Retrieved November 20, 2000. The zine is called White Home Schoolers or WHS. It was a web site dedicated for the parents of white children who are interested in or are home-schooling their children. The site lists pros and cons of home schooling plus lists appropriate textbooks and materials.
56. *Women's Frontier,* October 26AC: 9.
57. Hays, 1996.
58. Women for Aryan Unity, http://www.wcotc.com/womenforunity, retrieved December 7, 2002. No longer available.
59. Ibid.
60. Ibid.

Chapter 5

1. This paper is a revised version of a manuscript prepared for the session on "Analyzing Gender in the White Supremacist Movement" for the 2001 American Sociological Association (ASA) meetings, Anaheim, CA, August 21, 2001, and also presented at the Iowa State University Women's Studies Research Seminars 2002 (April 17, 2002). We would like to thank Sine Anahita, Iowa State University, Tanice G. Foltz, Indiana University Northwest, Wendy Griffin, California State University at Long Beach, and Mary Thimmesch, Iowa State University for their helpful suggestions. Betty also thanks the Women's Studies Program and the Sociology Department at Iowa State University for travel support to the 2001 ASA meetings.
2. Wood, 2001: 64.
3. Andersen, 2000: 302.
4. Ibid., 391–392, Rosenblum and Travis, 2000: 1.
5. Ferber, 1998a: 70.
6. Ibid., 4.
7. Rosenblum and Travis, 2000: 5.
8. Andersen, 2000: 25, 19.
9. Fuss, 1989: xii.
10. Ibid., 119.
11. Messner, 1997: 27.
12. Sandilands, 2002: 159.
13. Marshall, 1997; Blee, 1991; Taylor, Whittier, and Pelak, 2001: 570.
14. Gallagher and Smith, 1999: 213.
15. Ibid., 215.
16. Ibid., 227.
17. Stacey, 1987: 24.
18. Cochran and Ross, 1993: 1.
19. Ferber, 1998a: 4.
20. Blee, 1996: 680.
21. Ibid., 682.
22. Charon, 2001: 206.
23. Blumer, 1969: 50–51.
24. For a more detailed discussion of our interviews, see Dobratz and Shanks-Meile, 1997.
25. Gallagher and Smith, 1999.
26. Phone conversation between Dobratz and Michael Storm, July 25, 2001.
27. Blee, 2002: 445.
28. Ferber, 1998a: 69.
29. D. Lane, 1999: 285.
30. Guiley, 1989: 241.
31. Ibid., 246.
32. Ibid.
33. Goodrick-Clark, 2002: 271.
34. D. Lane, 1999: 8.
35. Ibid., 287–288.
36. K. Lane, 1999a: xxv.
37. Ibid., xxvi.
38. D. Lane, 1999: 6.
39. Ibid., 321–324.
40. Lane, 2001: 3.
41. K. Lane, 1999b: xi.
42. Barkun (1997a: x–xi) identified three core beliefs of much of Christian Identity: (1) white "Aryans" are the offspring of the tribes of Israel, according to the Bible; (2) Jews are the children of the devil, a relationship that is traced back to the sexual relationship between Satan and Eve in the Garden of Eden; and (3) the world is rapidly approaching a final apocalyptic struggle between good and evil, with Aryans battling a Jewish conspiracy to try to save the world. See also Dobratz and Shanks-Meile, 1997: chap. 3: and Dobratz, 2001.
43. Gallagher and Smith, 1999: 225.

44. Ibid., 223.
45. E-mail between Dobratz and Pastor August Kreis and family, July 21, 2001.
46. Hallimore, n.d.: 13.
47. Messner, 1997: 30.
48. Ibid.
49. The *Torch* Announcement, *The White Patriot*, 128: 4.
50. Dobratz and Shanks-Meile, 1995.
51. E-mail between Pastor Robb and Dobratz, July 30, 2001.
52. Blee, 2002: 145.
53. Benford and Snow, 2000: 614.
54. D. Lane, 1999: 320.
55. Ibid., 319.
56. Taylor, Whittier, and Pelak, 2001: 563; Mitchell, 1986; Stacey, 1987; Gordon, 1991.
57. Kimmel, 1996: 273.
58. Messner, 1997: 2.
59. Davidman, 1991: 197.
60. Ibid., 59.
61. Ibid., 32.
62. See the KKK Web site, especially www.kkk.com/new_page_4.htm, retrieved on June 24, 2003.
63. Dobratz and Shanks-Meile, 1997.
64. Ibid., 102.
65. Dobratz, 2001.
66. Kimmel, 1996: 365.

Chapter 6

1. Bonanno et al., 1994; Jobes, 1997: 331.
2. Gouveia and Rousseau, 1995.
3. See Weis, 1993.
4. Jobes, 1997.
5. Dyer, 1997: 61.
6. Lobao and Meyer, 1995: 6.
7. Davidson, 1996: 118, 9.
8. Labao and Meyer, 1995: 61; see also Hanson, 1996.
9. Bell, 1999.
10. Dyer, 1997.
11. Gibson, 1994: 11.
12. Junas, 1995a: 227.
13. Rand, 1996.
14. Lamy, 1996: 26.
15. Stern, 1996a: 78.
16. Potok, interview, July 21, 1999.
17. Southern Poverty Law Center, 1999.
18. Potok, interview, December 23, 2002.
19. Berlet and Lyons, 1995.
20. Ibid., 24.
21. Coalition for Human Dignity, 1995; Southern Poverty Law Center, 1999: 23.
22. Southern Poverty Law Center, 1999: 20.
23. Corcoran, 1997; Dyer, 1997; Stern, 1996a; Stock, 1996.
24. Potok, interview, July 21, 1999.
25. Stock, 1996: 16.
26. Potok, interview, July 21, 1999.
27. Stock, 1996: 173.
28. Aho, 1990; Anti-Defamation League, 1988; Barkun, 1997.
29. Zeskind, 1999: 19.
30. See Aho, 1990; Linzer, 1999.

31. See O'Matz, 1996.
32. Serrano, 1990.
33. Junas, 1995a.
34. In Dyer, 1997: 63.
35. Potok, interview, July 21, 1999.
36. Southern Poverty Law Center, 1999, 13.
37. Young, 1990: 15.
38. Davidson, 1996: 109.
39. See Snipp, 1996: 127, 122.
40. Davidson, 1996: 120.
41. Gibson, 1994: 10.
42. Mozzochi and Rhinegaard, 1991: 4.
43. Citizens Project, 1998/1999: 3.
44. See Kimmel, 1996.
45. Dees, 1996; Southern Poverty Law Center, 1997; Stern, 1996a.
46. Southern Poverty Law Center, 1997.
47. Crawford and Burghart, 1997: 190.
48. Stern, 1996a: 89.
49. See Dyer, 1997.
50. Stern, 1996a: 82.
51. Crawford and Burghart, 1997; Stern, 1996a: 69.
52. Marrs, 1993: 11.
53. Ibid., 13.
54. Ibid., 22–23.
55. Ibid., 28.
56. Ibid., 31.
57. Ibid., 28.
58. NS Mobilizer, cited in Ferber, 1998a: 81.
59. Pierce, 1978: 58.
60. Cited in Ferber, 1998: 76.
61. Pierce, 1978: 71; in *New Order*, cited in Ferber, 1998a: 91.
62. In Ferber, 1998a: 149.
63. See Stern, 1996a: 120.
64. Anti-Defamation League 1997, 28.
65. Cited in Ferber, 1998a: 140.
66. *Racial Loyalty*, 72, 1991: 3.
67. Pierce, 1978: 42.
68. Cited in Ferber, 1998a: 125–126.
69. In Ferber, 1998a: 127.
70. Pierce, 1978: 33.
71. Cited in Ferber, 1998a: 136.
72. In Ferber, 1998a: 139.
73. Cited in "Special Investigative Report" *Metrotimes*, 1995: 46.
74. Pierce, 1978: 207.

Chapter 7

1. Blee, 2002; Dobratz and Shanks-Meile, this volume.
2. Ferber and Kimmel, 2000.
3. *Blink*, 2001.
4. Mulvey and LaRosa, 1986.
5. Wilson and Herrnstein, 1985.
6. Labouvie, 1996.
7. On what attracts people to hate groups, see, for example, Hamm, 1993; Blazak, 1998; Blee, 2002.
8. Agnew and Passas, 1997.
9. Ibid., 10.

10. Blee, 2002.
11. Agnew, 1992.
12. A. Cohen, 1955.
13. Blee, 2002.
14. Blazak, 1998.
15. Matza, 1964.
16. Ferber, 1998; Blee, 1991, 2002.
17. Stormfront, 2002.
18. Blee, 2002.
19. Daniels, 1996; Ferber, 1998a.
20. Daniels, 1996.
21. Ferber, 1998a.
22. Blee, 2002.
23. Ibid., 53.
24. Oregon Spotlight, 2002.
25. Jenness and Broad, 1997.
26. Blazak and Farr, 1999.
27. Federal Bureau of Investigation, 2002.
28. Robertson, 1987.
29. Rape Abuse Incest National Network, 2002.
30. Centers for Disease Control, 2002.
31. Griffin, 1971.
32. Haynie, 1998.
33. Ferraro, 1996.
34. Rountree, 1998.
35. Warr, 1985.
36. Ibid., 243.
37. Blazak and Farr, 1999.
38. Stephenson, 1991.
39. Messerschmidt, 1999.
40. Blazak and Farr, 1999.
41. *Blink*, 2001.
42. Sampson and Laub, 1993.
43. Ferber, 1998a.
44. Blazak, 1998.

Chapter 8

* Also forthcoming in the *Journal of Hate Studies*. I would like to thank Ryken Grattet for contributions to the development of ideas contained in this chapter and Kimberley Richman for assistance with legal research required to write this chapter.
1. U.S. Department of Justice, 2001.
2. Ibid.
3. Ibid.
4. Associated Press, 2002.
5. See, for example, Farr, 1995; Gomez, 1997.
6. 2001, vols. 45 and 12. The one article that does directly address gender as a key component of hate crime, "Renaming Violence," by Debra Renee Kaufman, examines the "ways in which gender forces us to revisit the meaning of violence through the sins of omission as well as commission, through a deepening of the understanding of public and private spheres of life, and to expand what we mean by victims, survivors, and resisters"; Kaufman, 2001: 654.
7. Minow, 1990.
8. Jacobs and Potter, 1998; Jenness, in press; Jenness and Grattet, 2001; Moran, 2001.
9. Jenness and Grattet, 2001; Jenness, in press.
10. Jacobs and Potter, 1998; Levin and McDevitt, 2002.
11. Broad and Jenness, 1996; Jenness and Broad, 1997; Jenness, 1999; Jenness and Grattet, 1996;

Grattet, Jenness, and Curry, 1998; Jenness and Grattet, 2001; Phillips and Grattet, 2000; Boyd, Berk, and Hamner, 1996; Martin, 1995, 1996; Wexler and Marx, 1986.

12. Jenness and Grattet, 2001; Moran, 2001; Perry, 2001.
13. For a complete review of the emergence and evolution of the concept in the United States, see Jenness and Grattet, 2001; Jenness, 2001. More recently, the U.S.- born concept of hate crime has diffused across international borders, as various Western countries, especially those sharing a predominantly English-speaking culture, appropriate and deploy the concept to reference bias-motivated conduct in their respective legal and cultural milieu (Jenness, in press). Australia, for example, has outlawed at the federal, state, and territorial level words and images that incite hatred towards particular groups of people. Relying on discrimination law, Australian legislators have outlawed conduct that constitutes "vilification" or "racial hatred." Britain and Canada have also passed a series of laws designed to curb racial-ethnic violence. Finally, Germany has passed laws that forbid "public incitement" and "instigation of racial hatred," including the distribution of Nazi propaganda or literature liable to corrupt the youth. Unlike the United States, other countries have adopted a fairly limited view of hate crime, focusing primarily on racial, ethnic, and religious violence, and still other countries— mostly in the non-Western world—have not adopted the term to reference racial, ethnic, religious, and other forms of intergroup conflict.
14. Sheffield, 1992.
15. Despite this media portrayal of the incident, the case was not prosecuted under the Texas hate-crime law. While publicly understood as a hate crime, in legal terms the incident was defined as aggravated homicide. The maximum penalty for the murder could not have been enhanced because aggravated homicide is a capital crime.
16. Like the Byrd case, this case was not prosecuted as a hate crime.
17. Labi, 1998; McCormick, 1998.
18. Jacobs and Potter, 1998; Jenness and Grattet, 2001; Lawrence, 1999; Levin, 2001; Perry, 2001.
19. *Congressional Record* 1985: 19844.
20. U.S. Congress, 1985.
21. Maroney, 1998: 567–568.
22. 1997.
23. Grattet and Jenness, 2001; Lawrence, 1999.
24. Jenness, 1999.
25. These laws appeared as early as the late 1800s in response to perceived escalation of Klan activity. They are distinct from the contemporary hate-crime laws insofar as they are considerably older, do not contain a bias "intent standard," do not specify protected statuses, and, most notably, were not introduced under the rubric of "hate-crimes legislation."
26. Soule and Earl, 1999.
27. U.S. Congress, 1992: 7.
28. N.D. Cent Code §12.1-14-04 (1999).
29. W.V. ST §61-6-21 (1982).
30. 730 ILCS §5/5-5-3.2.
31. R.I. Gen. Laws §12-19-38 (1998).
32. California Penal Code §422.7.
33. California Penal Code §422.7.
34. Levin and McDevitt, 2002; Perry, 2001.
35. Anomalous status provisions continue to be introduced in states. For example, in 2001 a bill was introduced in Portland, Oregon, that calls for an additional five years in prison for an offender whose crime is motivated by "a hatred of people who subscribe to a set of political beliefs that support capitalism and the needs of people with respect to their balance with nature"; *Oregonian,* 2001: D01. According to the local press, if passed, this legislation would "expand the definition of hate crimes in a novel direction: to include the actions of eco-terrorists and critics of capitalism"; *Oregonian,* 2001: D01. Interpreted by the national press, this bill would "make it a hate crime to smash a Starbucks window or sabotage a timber company"; Associated Press, 2001.
36. See Broad and Jenness, 1996, for a larger discussion along these lines.
37. Jenness, 1999; Jenness and Broad, 1994, 1997.

38. The Coalition on Hate Crimes was comprised of civil rights, religious, ethnic, and law-enforcement groups, as well as a diverse array of professional organizations, including: the ADL, the American Bar Association, thirty Attorneys General, the National Institute Against Prejudice and Violence, the National Gay and Lesbian Task Force, the American Psychological Association, the American Psychiatric Association, the Center for Democratic Renewal, the American Civil Liberties Union, the American Jewish Congress, People for the American Way, the National Organization of Black Law Enforcement Executives, the U.S. Civil Rights Commission, the Police Executives Research Forum, the Criminal Justice Statistics Administration, the International Association of Police Chiefs, the National Council of Churches, the National Coalition of American Nuns, and the American Arab Anti-Discrimination Committee.
39. For a more detailed discussion of the debates around whether or not to include gender in hate-crime law, see Jenness's and Broad's (1997; 1994) work on the topic.
40. R. Goldberg, 1991; Jenness and Broad, 1997.
41. Adam, 1987; Vaid, 1995; Ferree and Hess, 1985; Scotch, 1984; Shapiro, 1993; R. Goldberg, 1991.
42. Jenness, 1999.
43. Pub. L. §101-275 (1990).
44. Pub. L. §103-322 (1994).
45. U.S. Congress, 1990: 23.
46. Pub. L. §103-322 (1994).
47. United States v. Antonio J. Morrison, et al.; and Christy Brzonkala v. Antonio J. Morrison, et al. 529 U.S. 598; 120 S. Ct. 1740; 146 L. Ed. 2d 658; 2000 U.S. LEXIS 4322; 68 U.S.L.W 4351; 82 Fair Empl. Prac. Cas (BNA) 1313; 77 Empl. Prac. Dec. (CCH) P46,376; 2000 Cal. Daily Op. Services 3788; 2000 Daily Journal DAR 5061; 2000 Colo. J. C.A.R. 2583; 13 Fla. L. Weekly Fed. S 287.
48. Pub. L. §103-322 (1994).
49. Ibid.
50. Lockyer, 2001: 3–4.
51. U.S. Department of Justice, 1996.
52. Cited in Levin and McDevitt, 2002: 21.
53. Weisberg, 1993.
54. Williams, cited in Weisburg, 1993: 151.
55. Krieger and Cooney, 1983.
56. Kay, 1985.
57. Minow, 1991: 20.
58. Ibid., 20–21.
59. Ibid.; Olsen, 1995; Weisberg, 1993.
60. Soule and Earl, 1999; Bufkin, 1999.
61. Minow, 1991; Olsen, 1995; Weisberg, 1993.
62. Soule and Earle, 1999; Bufkin, 1999.
63. Jenness and Broad, 1997; Jenness, 2001.
64. Dickey, 2000: 29.
65. Minow, 1991.
66. It is important to emphasize, of course, that the history and content of violence organized around gender is not equivalent to other forms of discriminatory violence, such as those organized around race, religion, nationality, disabilities, sexual orientation, political affiliation, and so on. Each axis of social differentiation carries with it a different context for bias-motivated violence, as well as different causes, manifestations, and consequences of bias-motivated violence.

Chapter 9

1. http://www.npg.org/public_awareness/assorted_ads.html. These phrases stem from an advertisement used in Iowa as part of a public awareness campaign conducted by Negative Population Growth.
2. Staudenmaier, 1995: 19–23.

3. Heim and Schaz, 1996: 53, 63.
4. Dyson, 1996.
5. Hartmann, 1995b: 141.
6. Lindsley, 2001: 15; Hartmann, 1994: 5; Hartmann 1995a: 4–5.
7. Lindsley, 2000: 69; Southern Poverty Law Center, 2002; Lindsley, 2002b.
8. Southern Poverty Law Center, 2002.
9. Tanton, 1986.
10. Lindsley, 2000: 69.
11. Lindsley, 2000; Southern Poverty Law Center, 2002.
12. Ollove, 2001.
13. Miller, 1994: 109.
14. Quoted in Ortega, 2000a.
15. Hartmann, 2002.
16. Southern Poverty Law Center, 2002.
17. Hartmann, 2002.
18. Ferber, 1995.
19. Ferber, 1998a.
20. Ferber, 1995: 8.
21. Kimmel and Ferber, 2000b: 205.
22. Biehl, 1995: 53.
23. Ibid., 59.
24. Tanton, 1986.
25. Quoted in Biehl, 1995: 63.
26. Ibid., 64–65.
27. Kimmel and Ferber, 2000b: 203.
28. ProjectUSA. projectusa.org/pics.html.
29. Hardin, 1993: ix.
30. Tanton, 1986.
31. Miller, 1994: 109.
32. MacDonald, 1999: 225.
33. Ibid.
34. Ibid., 233.
35. Ibid., 234.
36. Ibid., 235.
37. Hardin, 1993: xi.
38. MacDonald, 2000: 421.
39. Ibid.
40. MacDonald, 1999: 223.
41. Ibid., 237.
42. Ibid.
43. Ibid.
44. Quoted in Ortega, 2000b.
45. MacDonald, 1999: 423.
46. Abernethy, 1999: 394.
47. MacDonald, 1999: 238.
48. MacDonald, 2000: 415.
49. Shulevitz, 2000; Ortega, 2000a.
50. Ferber, 1998a.
51. MacDonald, 1998a: 348.
52. Ibid., 311.
53. MacDonald, 2000: 420.
54. MacDonald, 1998a: 348.
55. Ibid., 350.
56. MacDonald, 1998c.
57. Lindsley, 2000.
58. Tanton, 1986.
59. Brotsky, 1998: 1.

60. Hartmann, 1999/2000: 18.
61. Motavalli, 2000: 33.
62. Lindsley, 2001: 19.
63. Ibid.
64. Lindsley, 2002: 184.
65. Ibid., 185.
66. Bhattacharjee, 2002.
67. Lindsley, 2002: 190.
68. Cho, 2002.
69. Lindsley, 2002b.
70. Perry, in this volume.
71. Berkowitz, 2002.
72. Quoted in Berkowitz, 2002.
73. Ibid.
74. Shariatmadar, 2002.
75. Numbers USA, http://www.numbersusa.com/index.
76. Hartmann, 2002.
77. Southern Poverty Law Center, 2002.
78. Ibid.
79. The Committee on Women, Population, and the Environment (CWPE) is an alliance of feminist scholars, activists, and health practitioners that since 1991 has produced feminist analysis on population, environment, and development issues.
80. Staudenmaier, 1995: 25.

References

Abernethy, Virginia. 1999. "Secession, Good for the Goose but Not for the Gander?" *Population and Environment: A Journal of Interdisciplinary Studies* 20:5 (393–399).
———. 1998. "Moishe's Friend." *Population and Environment: A Journal of Interdisciplinary Studies* 19:4 (293–294).
———. 1993. *Population Politics: The Choices That Shape Our Future.* New York: Plenum Press.
Adam, Barry. 1987. *The Rise of a Gay and Lesbian Movement.* Boston: Twayne Publishers.
Agnew, Robert. 1992. "Foundations for a General Strain Theory of Crime and Delinquency." *Criminology* 30 (47–87).
———, and Niko Passas. 1997. *The Future of Anomie Theory.* Boston: Northeastern University Press.
Aho, James A. 2001. "Sociology and the Mobilization of Marquette Park." *Research in Political Sociology* 9: *The Politics of Social Inequality,* ed. Betty A. Dobratz, Lisa K. Waldner, and Timothy Buzzell. Amsterdam: JAI/Elsevier.
———. 1994. *This Thing of Darkness: A Sociology of the Enemy.* Seattle: University of Washington Press.
———. 1990. *The Politics of Righteousness: Idaho Christian Patriotism.* Seattle: University of Washington Press.
Akins, John Keith. 1998. "God, Guns, and Guts: Religion and Violence in Florida Militias." Ph.D. dissertation, University of Florida.
Allport, Gordon W. 1954. *The Nature of Prejudice.* Cambridge, MA: Addison-Wesley.
American Behavioral Scientist. 2002. Special Issue on "Hate Crimes and Ethnic Conflict: A Comparative Perspective," 45.
Andersen, Margaret. 2000. *Thinking About Women,* 5th ed. Needham Heights, MA: Allyn and Bacon.
Anderson, Benedict. 1991. *Imagined Communities: Reflections on the Origin and Spread of Nationalism.* Revised edition. London and New York: Verso.
Anderson, Connie. 1997. "Visions of Involved Fatherhood: Pro-Feminists and 'Promise Keepers.'" Paper presented at the annual meeting of the American Sociological Association, Toronto.
Anthony, Dick, and Thomas Robbins. 1996. "Religious Totalism, Violence and Exemplary Dualism: Beyond the Extrinsic Model." *Millennialism and Violence,* ed. Michael Barkun. London: Frank Cass & Co.
Anti-Defamation League. 2000. *A Brief Guide to Cyberspace Bigotry: World Church of the Creator.* Available at www.adl.org/special_reports/hate_on_www/www_wcotc.html.
———. 1999a. *Poisoning the Web: Hatred Online.* New York: ADL.
———. 1999b. *Backgrounder: The Order and Phineas Priesthood.* New York: ADL.

————. 1988. *Hate Groups in America: A Record of Bigotry and Violence.* New York: ADL.

————. 1998b. *Explosion of Hate: The Growing Danger of the National Alliance.* New York: ADL.

————. 1997. *Vigilante Justice.* New York: ADL.

————. 1996a. *Hate Groups in America.* New York: ADL.

————. 1996b. *Danger: Extremism, the Major Vehicles and Voices on America's Far-Right Fringe.* New York: ADL.

Anti-Defamation League of B'nai B'rith. 1986. *The American Farmer and the Extremists.* New York: ADL.

Anzaldua, Gloria E., and Analouise Keating, eds. 2002. *This Bridge We Call Home: Radical Visions for Transformation.* New York: Routledge.

Associated Press. 2001. "Legislator Seeks to Expand Hate Crime Laws, Sort Of," February 20.

————. 2002. "Man Indicted in 1996 Slayings of Two Female Hikers in Virginia," April 11.

Back, Les, Michael Keith, and John Solomos. 1998. "Racism on the Internet: Mapping Neo-Fascist Subcultures in Cyberspace." *Nation and Race: The Developing Euro-American Racist Subculture,* eds. Jeffrey Kaplan and Tore Bjørgo. Boston: Northeastern University Press.

Barkun, Michael. [1994] 1997. *Religion and the Racist Right: The Origins of the Christian Identity Movement.* Chapel Hill: University of North Carolina Press.

————. 1997. "Racist Apocalypse: Millennialism on the Far Right." *The Year 2000: Essays on the End,* ed. Charles B. Strozier and Michael Flynn. New York: New York University Press.

Barrett, Michelle. 1980. *Women's Oppression Today.* London: Verso.

Barron, Bruce. 1992. *Heaven on Earth? The Social and Political Agendas of Dominion Theology.* Grand Rapids, MI: Zondervan.

Baxter the Pagan, Hammerbringer. 1989. "From a Man's Point of View," *WAR* 8.4.

Beam, Louis. 1983. "Leaderless Resistance." *Inter-Klan Newsletter & Survival Alert.* Undated, circa May, pages not numbered, on file at Political Research Associates.

Beck, E. M. 2000. "Guess Who's Coming to Town." *Sociological Focus* 33:2 (153–174).

Bell, M. M. 1999. "The Social Construction of Farm Crises." Presented at the Annual meetings of the Rural Sociological Society, Aug. 5, Chicago.

Bellant, Russ. 1995. "Promise Keepers: Christian Soldiers for Theocracy." *Eyes Right: Challenging the Right Wing Backlash,* ed. Chip Berlet. Boston: South End Press.

Benfer, Amy. 1999. "Salon Mothers Who Think: Nazi Family Values." *Salon,* July 15. Available at www.archive.salon.com/mwt/hot/1999/07/15/aryan-compound/.

Benford, Robert D., and David A. Snow. 2000. "Framing Processes and Social Movements: An Overview and Assessment." *Annual Review of Sociology* 26: 611–39.

Berezin, Mabel. 1997. *Making the Fascist Self: The Political Culture of Interwar Italy.* Ithaca: Cornell University Press.

Berkowitz, Bill. 2002. "'The Green al-Qaeda?'" August 27. Available at http://www.workingforchange.com/article.cfm?ItemID=13742.

————. 1996. "Promise Keepers: Brotherhood and Backlash." *Culture Watch,* September (1, 4).

Berlet, Chip. 2002. "Hard Times on the Hard Right: Why Progressives Must Remain Vigilant." *Public Eye* 16:1, Spring (1–22).

————. 2001. "Hate Groups, Racial Tension and Ethnoviolence in an Integrating Chicago Neighborhood 1976–1988." *Research in Political Sociology* 9: *The Politics of Social Inequality,* ed. Betty A. Dobratz, Lisa K. Waldner, and Timothy Buzzell. Amsterdam: JAI/Elsevier.

————, and Matthew N. Lyons. 2000. *Right-Wing Populism in America: Too Close for Comfort.* New York: Guilford Press.

————. 1998. "Following the Threads." *Unraveling the Right: The New Conservatism in American Thought and Politics,* ed. Amy E. Ansell. Boulder, CO: Westview.

————, and Margaret Quigley. 1995. "Theocracy and White Supremacy: Behind the Culture War to Restore Traditional Values." *Eyes Right! Challenging the Right Wing Backlash,* ed. Chip Berlet. Boston: South End Press.

————, and Matthew Lyons. 1995. "Militia Nation." *The Progressive,* June (22–25).

Betz, Hans-Georg. 1994. *Radical Right-Wing Populism in Western Europe.* New York: St. Martin's Press.

————, and Stefan Immerfall, eds. 1998. *The New Politics of the Right: Neo-Populist Parties and Movements in Established Democracies.* New York: St. Martin's Press.

Bhattacharjee, Anannya. 2002. "Private Fists and Public Force: Race, Gender and Surveillance." *Policing the National Body: Race, Gender and Criminalization,* eds. Jael Silliman and Anannya Bhattacharjee. Massachusetts: South End Press.

Biehl, Janet. 1995. "'Ecology' and the Modernization of Fascism in the German Ultra-Right." *Ecofascism: Lessons from the German Experience,* eds. Janet Biehl and Peter Staudenmaier. San Francisco: AK Press.

Bjørgo, Tore. 1998. "Entry, Bridge-Building, and Exit Options: What Happens to Young People Who Join Racist Groups—and Want to Leave?" *Nation and Race: The Developing Euro-American Racist Subculture,* eds. Jeffrey Kaplan and Tore Bjørgo. Boston: Northeastern University Press.

———. 1993. "Role of the Media in Racist Violence." *Racist Violence in Europe,* eds. Tore Bjørgo and Rob White. New York: St. Martin's Press.

Blazak, Randy. 1998. "Hate in the Suburbs: The Rise of the Skinhead Counterculture." *The Practical Skeptic: Readings in Sociology,* ed. Lisa J. McIntyre. Boston: McGraw Hill.

———. 1995. "The Suburbanization of Hate: An Ethnographic Study of the Skinhead Culture." Ph.D. dissertation, Emory University.

———, and Kathy Farr. 1999. "The Role of Gender in Defining Hate Crimes: Women as Categorical Targets." Paper presented at the annual meeting of the American Society of Criminology, Toronto, Canada, November 17–20.

Blee, Kathleen. "Women and Organized Racism." In this volume.

———. 2002. *Inside Organized Racism: Women in the Hate Movement.* Berkeley: University of California Press.

———. 2001. "What Else We Need to Know: An Agenda for Studying the Racist Movement." *Research in Political Sociology* 9: *The Politics of Social Inequality,* ed. Betty A. Dobratz, Lisa K. Waldner, and Timothy Buzzell. Amsterdam: JAI/Elsevier.

———. 1996. "Becoming a Racist: Women in Contemporary Ku Klux Klan and Neo-Nazi Groups." *Gender and Society* 10: 6 (680–702).

———. 1991. *Women of the Klan: Racism and Gender in the 1920s.* Berkeley: University of California Press.

———. 1985. "Family Patterns and the Politicization of Consumption Relations." *Sociological Spectrum* 5 (295–316).

Blink. 2001. Available at www.itvs.org/blink/racism1.html.

Blumer, Herbert. 1969. *Symbolic Interactionism.* Englewood Cliffs, NJ: Prentice Hall.

Bobbio, Norberto. 1996. *Left and Right: The Significance of Political Distinction.* Chicago: University of Chicago Press.

Bobel, Chris. 2002. *The Paradox of Natural Mothering.* Philadelphia: Temple University Press.

Bonanno, A., L. Busch, W. Friedland, L. Gouveia, and E. Mingione, eds. 1994. *From Columbus to Conagra: The Globalization of Agriculture and Food.* Lawrence, KS: University Press of Kansas.

Bonilla-Silva, Eduardo. 2001. *White Supremacy and Racism in the Post-Civil Right Era.* Boulder, CO: Lynne Rienner.

Boyd, Elizabeth, Richard Berk, and Karl Hamner. 1996. "Motivated by Hatred or Prejudice: Categorization of Hate-Motivated Crimes in Two Police Divisions." *Law & Society Review* 30 (819–850).

Boyer, Paul. 1992. *When Time Shall Be No More: Prophecy Belief in Modern American Culture.* Cambridge, MA: Belknap/Harvard University Press.

Brasher, Brenda E. 1998. *Godly Women: Fundamentalism and Female Power.* New Brunswick, NJ: Rutgers University Press.

Braungart, Richard G., and Margaret M. Braungart. 1992. "From Protest to Terrorism: The Case of SDS and the Weathermen." *International Social Movement Research,* vol. 4: *Social Movements and Violence: Participation in Underground Organizations,* ed. Donatella della Porta. London: JAI Press.

Brickner, Bryan W. 1999. *The Promise Keepers: Politics and Promises.* Lanham, MD: Lexington Books.

Brinkley, Alan. 1982. *Voices of Protest: Huey Long, Father Coughlin, and the Great Depression.* New York: Alfred A. Knopf.

Broad, Kendal, and Valerie Jenness. 1996. "The Institutionalizing Work of Contemporary Anti-Violence against Women Campaigns in the U.S.: Mesolevel Social Movement Activism and the Production of Cultural Forms." *Research in Social Movements, Conflicts and Change* 19 (75–123).

Brodkin Sacks, Karen. 1998. *How Jews Became White Folks and What That Says about Race in America.* New Brunswick, NJ: Rutgers University Press.

Brotsky, China. 1998. "A Defeat for the Greening of Hate." *Political Environments: A Publication of the Committee on Women, Population and the Environment* 6 (1, 3).

Bufkin, Jana L. 1999. "Bias Crime as Gendered Behavior." *Social Justice* 26:1 (155–176).

Buechler, Steven M. 2000. *Social Movements in Advanced Capitalism: The Political Economy and Cultural Construction of Social Activism.* New York: Oxford University Press.

Buhmann, Elizabeth T. 1992. "Rethinking the Problem of Girls in Gangs." Austin, TX: Office of the Attorney General.

Burghart, Devin. 1996. "Cyberh@te: A Reappraisal." *The Dignity Report.* Coalition for Human Dignity Fall (12–16). An adaptation of this article is available at www.newcomm.org/cyberhate_text.htm. October 24, 2002.

Burlein, Ann. 2002. *Lift High the Cross: Where White Supremacy and the Christian Right Converge.* Durham, NC: Duke University Press.

Burris, Val. 2001. "Small Business, Status Politics, and the Social Base of New Christian Right Activism." *Critical Sociology* 27:1 (29–55).

———, Emery Smith, and Ann Strahm. 2000. "White Supremacist Networks on the Internet." *Sociological Focus* 33:2 (215–235).

Cable News Network (CNN). 1997. *Late Edition.* Television program transcript (including interviews with Randy Phillips and Meg Riley), October 5.

Callender, Harold. 1933. "Europe's Population Trends: A Cause of Great Uneasiness." *New York Times,* June 11 (XX3).

Campbell, Anne. 1987. "Self-Definition by Rejection: The Case of Gang Girls." *Social Problems* 34 (451–466).

Canovan, Margaret. 1981. *Populism.* New York: Harcourt Brace Jovanovich.

Carter, Dan T. 1995. *The Politics of Rage: George Wallace, the Origins of the New Conservatism, and the Transformation of American Politics.* New York: Simon and Schuster.

Center for Democratic Renewal. 1995. *1994: A Year of Intolerance.* Atlanta: CDR.

———. n.d. *Militias: Exploding into the Mainstream.* Atlanta: CDR.

Center for New Community. 2000. "World Church of the Creator: One Year Later," 6.

Centers for Disease Control. 2002. "Rape Fact Sheet." Available at www.cdc.gov/ncipc/factsheets/rape.htm.

Chang, Nancy. 2002. *Silencing Political Dissent: How Post–September 11 Anti-Terrorism Measures Threaten Our Civil Liberties.* New York: Seven Stories.

Charon, Joel M. 2001. *Symbolic Interactionism.* Upper Saddle River, NJ: Prentice Hall.

Chermak, Steven M. 2002. *Searching for a Demon: The Media Construction of the Militia Movement.* Boston: Northeastern University Press.

Chesler, Mark, and Richard Schmuch. 1963. "Participant Observation in a Super-Patriot Discussion Group." *Journal of Social Issues* 19 (18–30).

Chesney-Lind, Meda, Randall G. Shelden, and Karen A. Joe. 1996. "Girls, Delinquency, and Gang Membership." *Gangs in America,* 2nd ed., ed. C. Ronald Huff. Thousand Oaks, CA: Sage.

Chicago Tribune. 1985. "Preaching a Gospel of Hate," May 23.

Chideya, Farai. 1994. "Women Who Love to Hate." *Mademoiselle,* August (134–137, 186).

Cho, Eunice. 2002. "The Greening of Hate." Presentation at Annual meeting of the Committee on Women, Population and the Environment. University of Illinois, Chicago, June 20–23, 2002.

Citizens Project. 1998/1999. *Freedom Watch.* Colorado Springs. December/January.

Clarkson, Frederick. 2001. "The Culture Wars Are Not Over: The Institutionalization of the Christian Right." *Public Eye* 15:1 Spring (1–18).

———. 1997. *Eternal Hostility: The Struggle between Theocracy and Democracy.* Monroe, ME: Common Courage.

Clawson, Mary Ann. 1989. *Constructing Brotherhood: Class, Gender, and Fraternalism.* Princeton, NJ: Princeton University Press.

Cochran, Floyd. 1993. "Sisterhood of Hate." Privately published.

———, and Loretta J. Ross. 1993. *Procreating White Supremacy.* Atlanta: Center for Democratic Renewal.

Cohen, Albert. 1955. *Delinquent Boys.* New York: Free Press.

Cohen, Roger. 2000. "Odd Couple of German Politics: Left-Right Alliance." *New York Times,* September 8.

Colburn, Bruce, and Joel Rogers. 1995. "What's Next? Beyond the Election," *Nation,* November 18 (11–16).

Collins, Patricia Hill. 1991. *Black Feminist Thought: Knowledge, Consciousness, and the Politics of Empowerment.* New York: Routledge.

Conason, Joe, Alfred Ross, and Lee Cokorinos. 1996. "The Promise Keepers Are Coming: The Third Wave of the Religious Right." *Nation,* October 7 (1–19).

Congressional Record. 1985. 131 Cong. Rec. H 5988, vol. 131, no. 98. Hate Crimes Statistics Act. 99th Congress, 1st session, July 22.

Corcoran, James. [1990] 1997. *Bitter Harvest: The Birth of Paramilitary Terrorism in the Heartland.* New York: Penguin Books.

Cott, Nancy F. 1989. "What's in a Name? The Limits of 'Social Feminism'; or, Expanding the Vocabulary of Women's History." *Journal of American History* 76 (809–829).

Crawford, Robert, and Devin Burghart. 1997. "Guns and Gavels: Common Law Courts, Militias and White Supremacy." *The Second Revolution: States Rights, Sovereignty, and Power of the County,* ed. Eric Ward. Seattle: Peanut Butter Publishing.

Crenshaw, Martha. 1988. "Theories of Terrorism: Instrumental and Organizational Approaches." *Inside Terrorist Organizations,* ed. David C. Rapoport. New York: Columbia University Press.

Crothers, Lane. 2003. *Rage on the Right: The American Militia Movement from Ruby Ridge to Home-land Security.* Lanham, MD: Rowman & Littlefield.

Cumings, Bruce. 1990. *The Roaring of the Cataract, 1947–1950: The Origins of the Korean War,* vol. 2. Princeton, NJ: Princeton University Press.

Curry, Richard O., and Thomas M. Brown. 1972. "Introduction." *Conspiracy: The Fear of Subversion in American History,* ed. Richard O. Curry and Thomas M. Brown. New York: Holt, Rinehart and Winston.

Dally, Ann. 1982. *Inventing Motherhood: The Consequences of an Ideal.* New York: Routledge.

Daniels, Jessie. 1997. *White Lies: Race, Class, Gender and Sexuality in White Supremacist Discourse.* New York: Routledge.

Davidian, Blanche. 1996. "The Performance of Patriotism: Infiltration and Identity at the End of the World." *Theatre* 27:1 (7–28).

Davidman, Lynn. 1991. *Tradition in a Rootless World.* Berkeley: University of California Press.

Davidson, Osha Gray. 1996. *Broken Heartland: The Rise of America's Rural Ghetto.* Iowa City: University of Iowa Press.

Davis, David Brion, ed. 1971. *The Fear of Conspiracy: Images of Un-American Subversion from the Revolution to the Present.* Ithaca, NY: Cornell University Press.

Dees, Morris. 1996. *Gathering Storm: America's Militia Threat.* New York: Harper Perennial.

DeGrazia, Victoria. 1992. *How Fascism Ruled Women: Italy, 1922–1945.* Berkeley: University of California Press.

Della Porta, Donnatella. 1995. *Social Movements, Political Violence and the State: A Comparative Analysis of Italy and Germany.* Cambridge, UK: Cambridge University Press.

———. 1992. "Political Socialization in Left-Wing Underground Organizations: Biographies of Italian and German Militants." In *International Social Movement Research,* vol. 4: *Social Movements and Violence: Participation in Underground Organizations,* ed. Donatella della Porta. London: JAI Press.

Dempsey, James X., and David Cole. 2002. *Terrorism and the Constitution: Sacrificing Civil Liberties in the Name of National Security,* 2nd ed. Los Angeles: First Amendment Foundation.

Diamond, Sara. 1998. *Not by Politics Alone: The Enduring Influence of the Christian Right.* New York: Guilford Press.

———. 1996. *Facing the Wrath: Confronting the Right in Dangerous Times.* Monroe, ME: Common Courage Press.

———. 1995. *Roads to Dominion: Right-Wing Movements and Political Power in the United States.* New York: Guilford Press.

———. 1989. *Spiritual Warfare: The Politics of the Christian Right.* Boston: South End Press.

Dickey, Fred. 2000. "Of Course Hate Crimes Are Wrong: But So Are the Laws against Them." *Los Angeles Times Magazine,* October 22 (10–29).

Diquinzio, Patrice. 1999. *The Impossibility of Motherhood: Feminism, Individualism, and the Problem of Mothering.* New York: Routledge.

Dobie, Kathy. 1997. "Skingirl Mothers: From Thelma and Louise to Ozzie and Harriet." *The Politics of Motherhood: Activist Voices from Left to Right,* eds. Alexis Jetter, Annelise Orleck, and Diana Taylor. Hanover, NH: University Press of New England.

———. 1992. "Long Day's Journey into White." *Village Voice,* April 28 (22–32).

Dobratz, Betty A. 2001. "The Role of Religion in the Collective Identity of the White Racialist Movement." *Journal for the Scientific Study of Religion* 40 (287–301).

————, and Shanks-Meile, Stephanie. 2003. "The White Separatist Movement: Worldviews on Gender, Nature and Change." In this volume.

————. 1997. *"White Power, White Pride!" The White Separatist Movement in the United States.* New York: Twayne Publishers.

————. 1996. "Ideology and the Framing Process in the White Separatist/Supremacist Movement in the United States." *Quarterly Journal of Ideology* 19:1–2 (3–29).

————. 1995. "Conflict in the White Supremacist/Racialist Movement in the U.S." *International Journal of Group Tensions* 25 (57–75).

————, Lisa K. Waldner, and Timothy Buzzell, eds. 2001. *Research in Political Sociology 9: The Politics of Social Inequality.* Amsterdam: JAI/Elsevier.

Donner, Frank. 1980. *The Age of Surveillance: The Aims and Methods of America's Political Intelligence System.* New York: Alfred Knopf.

Durham, Martin. 2000. *The Christian Right, the Far Right and the Boundaries of American Conservatism.* Manchester, UK: Manchester University Press.

————. 1995. "Women and the British Extreme Right." *The Far Right in Western and Eastern Europe,* 2nd ed., eds. Luciano Cheles, Ronnie Ferguson, and Michalina Vaughan. New York: Longman.

Dyer, Joel. [1997] 1998. *Harvest of Rage: Why Oklahoma City Is only the Beginning.* Boulder: Westview Press.

Dyson, Tim. 1996. *Population and Food: Global Trends and Future Prospects.* London: Routledge.

Edsall, Thomas Byrne, and Mary D. Edsall. 1991. *Chain Reaction: The Impact of Race, Rights, and Taxes on American Politics.* New York: Norton.

Ehrenreich, Barbara. 1997. *Blood Rites: Origins and History of the Passions of War.* New York: Henry Holt.

————. 1989. *Fear of Falling: The Inner Life of the Middle Class* New York: Harper Perennial.

Einwohner, Rachel L., Jocelyn A. Hollander, and Toska Olson. 2000. "Engendering Social Movements: Cultural Images and Movement Dynamics." *Gender and Society* 14:5 (679–699).

Enloe, Cynthia. 2000. "Masculinity as Foreign Policy Issue." *Foreign Policy in Focus* 5:36 October (1–3).

Equal Partners in Faith. 1997. "Promise Keepers and 'Racial Reconciliation.'" Fact Sheet. On file at Political Research Associates.

Ezekiel, Raphael S. 1995. *The Racist Mind: Portraits of American Neo-Nazis and Klansmen.* New York: Viking.

Faludi, Susan. 1999. *Stiffed: The Betrayal of the American Man.* New York: William Morrow.

Fangen, Katrine. 1998. "Living out Our Ethnic Instincts: Ideological Beliefs among Right-Wing Activists in Norway." *Nation and Race: The Developing Euro-American Racist Subculture,* eds. Jeffrey Kaplan and Tore Bjørgo. Boston: Northeastern University Press.

Farr, Kathryn. 1995. "Fetal Abuse and Criminalization of Behavior During Pregnancy." *Crime and Delinquency* 41 (235–245).

Feagin, Joe R. 2001. *Racist America: Roots, Current Realities, and Future Reparations.* New York: Routledge.

————. 2000. *Racist America.* New York: Routledge.

————, Hernán Vera, and Pinar Batur. 2001. *White Racism,* 2nd ed. New York: Routledge.

————, and Hernán Vera. 1995. *White Racism: The Basics.* New York: Routledge.

Federal Bureau of Investigation. 2002. *Uniform Crime Report, 2000.* Available at www.fbi.gov/ucr.

Felice, William F. 1996. *Taking Suffering Seriously: The Importance of Collective Human Rights.* Albany, NY: State University of New York Press.

Fenster, Mark. 1999. *Conspiracy Theories: Secrecy and Power in American Culture.* Minneapolis: University of Minnesota Press.

Ferber, Abby L. 2000. "Racial Warriors and Weekend Warriors: The Construction of Masculinity in Mythopoetic and White Supremacist Discourse." *Men and Masculinities* 3:1.

————. 1998a. *White Man Falling: Race, Gender and White Supremacy.* Lanham, MD: Rowman and Littlefield.

————. 1998b. "Constructing Whiteness: The Intersections of Race and Gender in U.S. White Supremacist Discourse." *Ethnic and Racial Studies* 21:1 (48–63).

————. 1997. "Of Mongrels and Jews: The Deconstruction of Radicalized Identities in White Supremacist Discourse." *Social Identities* 13:2 (193–208).

————. 1995. "'Shame of White Men': Interracial Sexuality and the Construction of White Masculinity in Contemporary White Supremacist Discourse." *Masculinities* 3:2 (1–24).

————, Ryken Grattet, and Valerie Jenness. 2000. *Hate Crime in America: What Do We Know?* Washington, DC: American Sociological Association.

————, and Michael Kimmel 2000. "Reading Right: The Western Tradition in White Supremacist Discourse." *Sociological Focus* 33:2 (193–213).

Ferraro, K. F. 1996. "Women's Fear of Victimization: Shadow of Sexual Assault?" *Social Forces* 75:2 (667–690).

Ferree, Myra Marx, and Beth B. Hess. 1985. *Controversy and Coalition: The New Feminist Movement.* Boston: Twayne Publishers.

————, and David A. Merrill. 2000. "Hot Movements, Cold Cognition: Thinking about Social Movements in Gendered Frames." *Contemporary Sociology* 29:3 (454–462).

Fielding, Nigel G. 1981. *The National Front.* London: Routledge and Kegan Paul.

Fine, Michelle. 1997. "Witnessing Whiteness." *Off White: Readings on Race, Power and Society,* eds. Michelle Fine, Lois Weis, Linda Powell, and L. Mun Wong. New York: Routledge.

Frank, Dana. 1994. *Purchasing Power: Consumer Organizing, Gender, and the Seattle Labor Movement, 1919–1929.* New York: Cambridge University Press.

Frankenberg, Ruth. 1993. *White Women, Race Matters: The Social Construction of Whiteness.* Minneapolis: University of Minnesota Press.

Franklin, H. Bruce. 1992. *M.I.A. or Mythmaking in America.* Brooklyn, NY: Lawrence Hill Books.

Fraser, Nancy. 1997. *Justice Interruptus: Critical Reflections on the "Postsocialist" Condition.* New York: Routledge.

Fredrickson, George M. 2000. *The Comparative Imagination on the History of Racism, Nationalism and Social Movements.* Berkeley: University of California.

Freilich, Joshua D. 2003. *American Militias: State Level Variations in Militia Activities.* New York: LFB Scholarly Publishing.

————, Jeremy A. Peinick, and Gregory J. Howard. 2001. "Toward Comparative Studies of the U.S. Militia Movement." *International Journal of Comparative Sociology* 42:1–2 (163–210).

Fuller, Robert C. 1995. *Naming the Antichrist: The History of an American Obsession.* New York: Oxford University Press.

Fuss, Diana. 1989. *Essentially Speaking.* New York: Routledge.

Gallagher, Sally K., and Christian Smith. 1999. "Symbolic Traditionalism and Pragmatic Egalitarianism." *Gender and Society* 13 (211–233).

Gallaher, Carolyn. 2003. *On the Fault Line: Race, Class, and the American Patriot Movement.* Lanham, MD: Rowman and Littlefield.

Gallup. 1993. "Racial Overtones Evident in Americans: Attitudes about Crime." *Gallup Poll Monthly* December (37–42).

Galton, Francis. 1870. *Hereditary Genius: An Inquiry into Its Laws and Consequences.* New York: D. Appleton & Co.

Gamson, William. A. 1995. "Constructing Social Protest." *Social Movements and Culture,* ed. Hank Johnston and Bert Klandermans. Minneapolis, MN: University of Minnesota Press.

————. [1975] 1990. *The Strategy of Social Protest,* 2nd ed. Belmont, CA: Wadsworth Publishing.

Gardiner, Steven. 1998. "Through the Looking Glass and What the Christian Right Found There." *Culture, Media, and the Religious Right,* ed. Linda Kintz and Julia Lesage. Minneapolis: University of Minnesota Press.

Gardner, S. L. 1996. "Promises to Keep: the Christian Right Men's Movement." *Dignity Report* 3:4 Fall:1 (4–9).

Georges-Abeyie, Daniel E. 1983. "Women as Terrorists." *Perspectives on Terrorism,* eds. L. Z. Freeman and Y. Alexander. Wilmington, DE: Scholarly Resources.

Gibson, James William. 2001. "The Blast that Finished off Militia Culture." *Los Angeles Times,* May 13. http://www.latimes.com/.

————. 1997. "Is the Apocalypse Coming? Paramilitary Culture after the Cold War." *The Year 2000: Essays on the End,* ed. Charles B. Strozier and Michael Flynn. New York: New York University Press.

————. 1994. *Warrior Dreams: Violence and Manhood in Post-Vietnam America.* New York: Hill and Wang.

Gobineau, Arthur (Count Joseph Arthur de Gobineau), and Adrian Collins. [1853–1855] 1983. *The Inequality of Human Races*, 2nd ed., repr. Torrance, CA: Noontide Press.

Goffman, Erving. 1974. *Frame Analysis: An Essay on the Organization of Experience.* Cambridge: Harvard University Press.

———. 1959. *The Presentation of Self in Everyday Life.* Garden City, NY: Anchor Doubleday.

Goldberg, David Theo. 1990. "The Social Formation of Racist Discourse." *Anatomy of Racism,* ed. David T. Goldberg. Minneapolis: University of Minnesota Press.

Goldberg, Robert A. 2001. *Enemies Within: The Culture of Conspiracy in Modern America.* New Haven, CT: Yale University Press.

———. 1991. *Grassroots Resistance: Social Movements in the Twentieth Century.* Belmont, CA: Wadsworth Publishing.

Golden, Miriam A. 1988. "Historical Memory and Ideological Orientations in the Italian Workers' Movement." *Politics and Society* 16 (1–34).

Goldman, Ruth. 1996. "Who Is That *Queer* Queer? Exploring Norms around Sexuality, Race, and Class in Queer Theory." *Queer Studies: A Lesbian, Gay, Bisexual, & Transgender Anthology,* ed. Brett Beemyn and Mickey Eliason. New York: New York University Press.

Gomez, Laura. 1997. *Misconceiving Mothers: Legislators, Prosecutors, and the Politics of Prenatal Drug Exposure.* Philadelphia: Temple University Press.

Goodrick-Clarke, N. 2002. *Black Sun.* New York: New York University Press.

Gordon, Suzanne. 1991. *Prisoners of Men's Dreams.* New York: Little, Brown.

Gouveia, Lourdes, and Mark O. Rousseau. 1995. "Talk is Cheap: The Value of Language in the World Economy—Illustrations from the United States and Quebec." *Sociological Inquiry* 65:2 (156–180).

Grant, Madison. [1916] 1923. *The Passing of the Great Race: or The Racial Basis of European History,* 4th ed., revised, with a documentary supplement, and with prefaces by Henry Fairfield Osborn. New York: Charles Scribner's Sons.

Grattet, Ryken, Valerie Jenness, and Theodore Curry. 1998. "The Homogenization and Differentiation of Hate Crime Law in the United States, 1978–1995: Innovation and Diffusion in the Criminalization of Bigotry." *American Sociological Review* 63 (286–307).

Green, John C., James L. Guth, and Kevin Hill. 1993. "Faith and Election: The Christian Right in Congressional Campaigns 1978–1988." *Journal of Politics* 55:1 February (80–91).

Griffin, Susan. 1971. "Rape: The All-American Crime." *Ramparts* 10 (26–36).

Grupp, Fred W., Jr. 1969. "The Political Perspectives of Birch Society Members." *The American Right Wing: Readings in Political Behavior,* ed. Robert A. Schoenberger. New York: Holt, Rinehart & Winston.

Guiley, Rosemary Ellen. 1989. *The Encyclopedia of Witches and Witchcraft.* New York: Facts on File.

Guillaumin, Colette. 1995. *Racism, Sexism, Power and Ideology.* London: Routledge.

Guttenplan, D. D. February 2000. "The Holocaust on Trial." *Atlantic Monthly* (45–66).

Hallimore, M. K. n.d. *God's Answer to Women's Lib.* Harrison, AR: Kingdom Identity Ministries.

Halpern, Thomas and Brian Levin. 1996. *The Limits of Dissent: The Constitutional Status of Armed Civilian Militias.* Amherst, MA: Aletheia Press.

Hamm, Mark S. 1997. *Apocalypse in Oklahoma: Waco and Ruby Ridge Revenged.* Boston: Northeastern University Press.

———. 1994. *American Skinheads: The Criminology and Control of Hate Crimes.* Westport, CT: Praeger.

Hanson, Victor D. 1996. *Fields without Dreams: Defending the Agrarian Idea.* New York: Free Press.

Hardin, Garrett. 1993. "Foreword." *Population Politics: The Choices that Shape our Future,* ed. Virginia Abernethy. New York: Plenum Press.

Hardisty, Jean V. 1999. *Mobilizing Resentment: Conservative Resurgence from the John Birch Society to the Promise Keepers.* Boston: Beacon Press.

Harris, Mary G. 1988. *Cholas: Latino Girls and Gangs.* New York: AMS Press.

Hartmann, Betsy. 2002. "White Supremacy and the Anti-Immigrant Movement." *ZNet Commentary.* December 23. Available at www.zmag.org/sustainers/content/2002–12/21hartmann.cfm.

———. 1999/2000. "What's in a Word? The Sierra Club Moves Right and away from Democracy." *Political Environments: A Publication of the Committee on Women, Population and the Environment* 7 (17–18).

———. 1995a. "Dangerous Intersections." *Political Environments: A Publication of the Committee on Women, Population and the Environment* 2 (1, 3–7).

———. 1995b. *Reproductive Rights and Wrongs: the Global Politics of Population Control.* Boston: MA: South End Press.

———. 1994. "To Vanquish the Hydra." *Political Environments: A Publication of the Committee on Women, Population and the Environment* 1 (1, 3–7).

Hatewatch. 2001. Available at www.hatewatch.org.

Haynie, Dana L. 1998. "The Gender Gap in Fear of Crime, 1973–1994: A Methodological Approach." *Criminal Justice Review* 23:1 (29–50).

Hays, Sharon. 1996. *The Cultural Contradictions of Motherhood.* New Haven, CT: Yale University.

Heath, Melanie. 2003. "Soft-Boiled Masculinity: Renegotiating Gender and Racial Ideologies in the Promise Keepers Movement." *Gender and Society* 17 (423–444).

Heim, Susanne, and Ulrike Schaz. 1996. *Berechnung und Beschwörung: Überbevölkerung Kritik einer Debatte.* Berlin: Schwarze Risse Rote Strasse.

———. 1993. *Population Explosion: The Making of a Vision,* Hamburg: FINRRAGE.

Herman, Didi. 1997. *The Antigay Agenda: Orthodox Vision and the Christian Right.* Chicago: University of Chicago Press.

Himmelstein, Jerome L. 1998. "All but Sleeping with the Enemy: Studying the Radical Right up Close." Paper presented at the annual meeting of the American Sociological Association, San Francisco.

Hixson, William B., Jr., 1992. *Search for the American Right Wing: An Analysis of the Social Science Record, 1955–1987.* Princeton, NJ: Princeton University Press.

Hobgood, Mary Elizabeth. 2000. *Dismantling Privilege: An Ethics of Accountability.* Cleveland: Pilgrim Press.

Hofstadter, Richard. 1965. *The Paranoid Style in American Politics, and Other Essays.* New York: Knopf.

hooks, bell. 1984. *Feminist Theory from Margin to Center.* Boston: South End Press.

Hoskins, Richard Kelly. [1958] 1996. *Our Nordic Race.* Pamphlet. Republished. Reedy, WV: Liberty Bell.

———. 1985. *War Cycles, Peace Cycles.* Lynchburg, VA: Virginia Publishing Company.

Jacobs, James, and Kimberly Potter. 1998. *Hate Crimes: Criminal Law and Identity Politics.* New York: Oxford University Press.

Jacobs, Jane. 1984. "The Economy of Love in Religious Commitment: The Deconversion of Women from Nontraditional Religious Movements." *Journal for the Scientific Study of Religion* 23 (155–171).

Jaffe, Clella Iles. 1999. "Promise Keepers Welcomed Home by Wives." *Standing on the Promises: The Promise Keepers and the Revival of Manhood,* ed. Dane S. Claussen. Cleveland: Pilgrim Press.

Jellison, Katherine. 1993. *Entitled to Power: Farm Women and Technology, 1913–1963.* Chapel Hill: University of North Carolina Press.

Jenness, Valerie. In Press. "Hate Crime in the U.S. and Abroad." In *The Encyclopedia Britannica.* Chicago: Encyclopedia Britannica, Inc.

———. 2001. "The Hate Crime Cannon and Beyond: A Critical Assessment." *Law and Critique* 12 (279–308).

———. 1999. "Managing Differences and Making Legislation: Social Movements and the Racialization, Sexualization, and Gendering of Federal Hate Crime Law in the U.S., 1985–1998." *Social Problems* 46 (548–571).

———, and Kendal Broad. 1997. *Hate Crimes: New Social Movements and the Politics of Violence.* Hawthorne, NY: Aldine deGruyter.

———, and Kendal Broad. 1994. "Anti-Violence Activism and the (In)Visibility of Gender in the Gay/Lesbian Movement and the Women's Movement." *Gender and Society* 8 (402–423).

———, and Ryken Grattet. 2001. *Making Hate a Crime: From Social Movement to Law Enforcement.* New York: Russell Sage Publications.

———, and Ryken Grattet. 1996. "The Criminalization of Hate: A Comparison of Structural and Polity Influences on the Passage of 'Bias-Crime' Legislation in the United States." *Sociological Perspectives* 39 (129–154).

Jobes, Patrick C. 1997. "Gender Competition and the Preservation of Community in the Allocation of Administrative Positions in Small Rural Towns in Montana: A Research Note." *Rural Sociology* 62:3 (315–334).

Joe, Karen A., and Meda Chesney-Lind. 1995. "'Just Every Mother's Angel': An Analysis of Gender and Ethnic Variations in Youth Gang Membership." *Gender and Society* 9 (408–431).

Johnson, Hans. 1995. "Broken Promise?" *Church and State,* May (9–12).

Johnston, Hank. 1995. "A Methodology for Frame Analysis: From Discourse to Cognitive Schemata." *Social Movements and Culture,* ed. Hank Johnston and Bert Klandermans. Minneapolis: University of Minnesota Press.

———. 1994. "New Social Movements and Old Regional Nationalisms." *New Social Movements: From Ideology to Identity,* eds. Enrique Laraña, Hank Johnston, and Joseph R. Gusfield. Philadelphia: Temple University Press.

———, Enrique Laraña, and Joseph R. Gusfield. 1994. "Identities, Grievances, and New Social Movements." In *New Social Movements: From Ideology to Identity,* ed. Enrique Laraña, Hank Johnston, and Joseph Gusfield. Philadelphia: Temple University Press.

———, and Bert Klandermans. 1995. "The Cultural Analysis of Social Movements." *Social Movements and Culture,* eds. Hank Johnston and Bert Klandermans. Minneapolis: University of Minnesota Press.

Junas, Daniel. 1995a. "The Rise of Citizen Militias: Angry White Guys with Guns." *Eyes Right: Challenging the Right Wing Backlash,* ed. C. Berlet. Boston: South End Press.

———. 1995b. "The Rise of Citizen Militias: Angry White Guys with Guns." *CovertAction Quarterly* 52 Spring (20–25).

Kaminer, Wendy. 2001. "Law and Marriage." *American Prospect,* July 2, 12:12.

Kantrowitz, Stephen. 2000. *Ben Tillman and the Reconstruction of White Supremacy.* Chapel Hill: University of North Carolina.

Kaplan, Deborah. 1998. "Republic of Rage: A Look inside the Patriot Movement." Paper presented at the annual meeting of the American Sociological Association, San Francisco.

Kaplan, Jeffrey. 1997a. *Radical Religion in America: Millenarian Movements from the Far Right to the Children of Noah.* Syracuse, NY: Syracuse University Press.

———. 1997b. "Interpreting the Interpretive Approach: A Friendly Reply to Thomas Robbins." *Nova Religio,* 1:1 (30–49).

Kaplan, Temma. 1982. "Female Consciousness and Collective Action: The Case of Barcelona, 1910–1918." *Signs: Journal of Women in Culture and Society* 7 (545–566).

Karst, Kenneth. 1993. *Law's Promise, Law's Expression.* New Haven, CT: Yale University Press.

Katz, Rebecca S., and Joey Bailey. 2000. "The Militia, a Legal and Social Movement Analysis: Will the Real Militia Please Stand Up? Militia Hate Group or the Constitutional Militia?" *Sociological Focus* 33:2 (133–151).

Kaufman, Debra. 2001. "Renaming Violence." *American Behavioral Scientist* 45:4 (654–667).

Kay, Herma Hill. 1985. "Equality and Difference: The Case of Pregnancy." *Berkeley Women's Law Journal* 1 (1–38).

Kazin, Michael. 1995. *The Populist Persuasion: An American History.* New York: Basic Books.

Kelly, Caroline, and Sara Breinlinger. 1996. *The Social Psychology of Collective Action: Identity, Injustice and Gender.* London: Taylor & Francis.

Kerr, Martin. 1983. "On Women's Rights and White Rights." *White Power: The Revolutionary Voice of National Socialism* 105 (4).

Khan, Surina. 1998. *Calculated Compassion: How the Ex-Gay Movement Serves the Right's Attack on Democracy.* Somerville, MA: Political Research Associates.

Kimmel, Michael S. 1999. "Patriarchy's Second Coming as Masculine Renewal." *Standing on the Promises: The Promise Keepers and the Revival of Manhood,* ed. Dane S. Claussen. Cleveland: Pilgrim Press.

———. 1996. *Manhood in America: A Cultural History.* New York: The Free Press.

———, and Abby Ferber. 2000. "White Men Are This Nation: Right Wing Militias and the Restoration of Rural American Masculinity." *Rural Sociology* 65:4 (582–604).

Kintz, Linda. 1997. *Between Jesus and the Market: The Emotions that Matter in Right-Wing America.* Durham, NC: Duke University Press.

Kittrie, Nicholas N. 2000. *Rebels with a Cause: The Minds and Morality of Political Offenders.* Boulder, CO: Westview Press.

———. 1995. *The War against Authority: From the Crisis of Legitimacy to a New Social Contract.* Baltimore: Johns Hopkins University Press.

Klandermans, Bert. 1997. *The Social Psychology of Protest*. Oxford: Blackwell Publishers.

Klanwatch. 1998. *Intelligence Report*. Montgomery, AL: Southern Poverty Law Center.

———. 1991. "Cookbooks and Combat Boots." *Intelligence Report*. Montgomery, AL: Southern Poverty Law Center.

Klassen, Ben. 1981. *The White Man's Bible*. Milwaukee: Milwaukee Church of the Creator.

Klatch, Rebecca E. 1987. *Women of the New Right*. Philadelphia: Temple University Press.

Kleg, Milton. 1993. *Hate Prejudice and Racism*. Albany, NY: SUNY Press.

Kovel, Joel. 1994. *Red Hunting in the Promised Land: Anticommunism and the Making of America*. New York: Basic Books.

Kraft, Charles Jeffrey. 1992. *A Preliminary Socio-Economic and State Demographic Profile of the John Birch Society*, monograph. Cambridge, MA: Political Research Associates.

Krieger, Linda J., and Patricia N. Cooney. 1983. "The Miller-Wohl Controversy: Equal Treatment, Positive Action and the Meaning of Women's Equality." *Golden Gate University Law Review* 13 (513).

Kuumba, M. Bahati. 2001. *Gender and Social Movements*. Walnut Creek: Altamira Press.

Labi, Nadyi. 1998. "The Hunter and the Choirboy." *Time*, April 6 (28–39).

Labouvie. Erich. 1996. "Maturing out of Substance Use: Selection and Self-Correction." *Journal of Drug Issues* 26 (457–474).

Laclau, Ernesto. 1977. *Politics and Ideology in Marxist Theory: Capitalism, Fascism, Populism*. London: NLB/Atlantic Highlands Humanities Press.

Ladd, Susan, and Stan Swofford. 1995. "Patriot Aims/The Militias." *News & Record*, Greensboro, NC, June 25–27.

Lamy, Philip. 1996. *Millennium Rage: White Supremacists, and the Doomsday Prophecy*. New York: Plenum Press.

Lane, David. 2001. *KD Rebel*. No publisher listed.

———. 1999. *Deceived, Damned & Defiant*. St. Maries, ID: 14 Word Press.

Lane, Katja. 1999a. "Preface." *Deceived, Damned & Defiant*, David Lane. St. Maries, ID: 14 Word Press.

———. 1999b. "Editor's Note, Preface." *Might Is Right*, Ragnar Redbeard (reprint of 1910 edition, London), Millennial Wotansvolk edition.

Law and Critique. 2001. Special Issue on "Hate Crime," 12.

Lawrence, Frederick M. 1999. *Punishing Hate: Bias Crimes under American Law*. Cambridge, MA: Harvard University Press.

Lembcke, Jerry. 2003. *CNN's Tailwind Tale: Inside Vietnam's Last Great Myth*. Lanham, MD: Rowman & Littlefield.

———. 1998. *The Spitting Image: Myth, Memory, and the Legacy of Vietnam*. New York: New York University Press.

Levin, Brian. 2001. "The Vindication of Hate Violence Victims via Criminal and Civil Adjudications." *Journal of Hate Studies* 1 (133–165).

Levin, Jack, and Jack McDevitt. 2002. *Hate Crimes Revisited: America's War on Those Who Are Different*. Boulder, CO: Westview Press.

Levitas, Daniel. 2002. *The Terrorist Next Door: The Militia Movement and the Radical Right*. New York: St. Martin's Press.

Lindsley, Syd. 2002a. "The Gendered Assaults on Immigrants." *Policing the National Body: Race, Gender and Criminalization*, eds. Jael Silliman and Anannya Bhattacharjee. Boston: South End Press.

———. 2002b. "The Greening of Hate." Presentation at annual meeting of the Committee on Women, Population and the Environment. Chicago: University of Illinois. June 20–23, 2002.

———. 2001. "The Greening of Hate Continues." *Political Environments: A Publication of the Committee on Women, Population and the Environment* 8 (15–22).

———. 2000. *Discourses of Blame: Race and Reproduction in the 1990s Anti-Immigrant Agenda in California*. Amherst, MA: Hampshire College, Division III.

Linzer, Lori. 1999. Anti-Defamation League researcher. Telephone interview, July 16.

Litt, Jacquelyn S. 2000. *Medicalized Motherhood: Perspectives from the Lives of African-American and Jewish Women*. NJ: Routledge.

Lo, Clarence. 1992. "Communities of Challengers in Social Movement Theory." In *Frontiers in Social Movement Theory*, eds. Aldon D. Morris and Carol M. Mueller. New Haven, CT: Yale University Press.

Lobao, Linda, and Katherine Meyer. 1995. "Restructuring the Rural Farm Economy: Midwestern Women's and Men's Work Roles during the Farm Crisis Period." *Economic Development Quarterly* 9:1 (60–73).

Lockyer, Bill. 2001. *Reporting Hate Crimes.* Sacramento, CA: Attorney General's Office.

Lyall, Sarah. 2000. "Critic of a Holocaust Denier Is Cleared in British Libel Suit." *New York Times* April 12, (A1, A6).

MacDonald, Kevin. "Professional Résumé." Available at http://www.csulb.edu/~kmacd/vitae.htm.

———. "Books on Religion and Ethnic Relations from an Evolutionary Perspective." Available at http://www.csulb.edu/~kmacd/books.htm.

———. 2000. "The Numbers Game: Ethnic Conflict in the Contemporary World." *Population and Environment: A Journal of Interdisciplinary Studies* 21:4 (413–425).

———. 1999. "An Evolutionary Perspective on Human Fertility." *Population and Environment: A Journal of Interdisciplinary Studies* 21:2 (223–246).

———. 1998a. "Jewish Involvement in Shaping American Immigration Policy, 1881–1965: A Historical Review." *Population and the Environment: A Journal of Interdisciplinary Studies* 19:4 (295–356).

———. 1998b. *Separation and Its Discontents: Toward an Evolutionary Theory of Anti-Semitism.* Westport, CT: Praeger.

———. 1998c. *The Culture of Critique: An Evolutionary Analysis of Jewish Involvement in Twentieth-Century Intellectual and Political Movements.* Westport, CT: Praeger.

———. 1994. *A People That Shall Dwell Alone: Judaism as a Group Evolutionary Strategy.* Westport, CT: Praeger.

MacLean, Nancy. 1994. *Behind the Mask of Chivalry.* New York: Oxford.

Mahan, Sarah Elizabeth. 1997. *A Dramatistic Analysis of the Video Rhetoric of the Militia of Montana.* Ph.D. dissertation, Ohio University.

Maroney, Terry A. 1998. "The Struggle against Hate Crime: Movement at a Crossroads." *New York University Law Review* 73 (564–620).

Marrs, Texe. 1993. *Big Sister Is Watching You: Hillary Clinton and the White House Feminists Who now Control America—And Tell the President What to Do.* Austin, TX: Living Truth Publishers.

Marsden, George M. 1991. *Understanding Fundamentalism and Evangelicalism.* Grand Rapids, MI: William B. Eerdmans Publishing Co.

Marshall, Susan E. 1997. *Splintered Sisterhood.* Madison: University of Wisconsin Press.

Martin, Susan. 1996. "Investigating Hate Crimes: Case Characteristics and Law Enforcement Responses." *Justice Quarterly* 13:3 (455–480).

———. 1995. "A Cross-Burning Is Not just an Arson: Police Social Construction of Hate in Baltimore Country." *Criminology* 33 (303–326).

Martin, William. 1996. *With God on Our Side: The Rise of the Religious Right in America.* New York: Broadway Books.

Mason, Carol. 2002. *Killing for Life: The Apocalyptic Narrative of Pro-Life Politics.* Ithaca, NY: Cornell University Press.

Mason, Shane. 1993. "Working Mothers." *Calling Our Nation* 71 (32).

Matza, David. 1964. *Delinquency and Drift.* New York: John Wiley and Sons.

McAdam, Doug. 1982. *Political Process and the Development of Black Insurgency, 1930–1970.* Chicago: University of Chicago Press.

McCarthy, John, and Mark Wolfson. 1992. "Consensus Movements, Conflict Movements, and the Cooptation of Civic and State Infrastructures." *Frontiers in Social Movement Theory,* eds. Aldon Morris and Carol McClurg Mueller. New Haven, CT: Yale University Press.

McCormick, John. 1998. "The Schoolyard Killers." *Newsweek* April 6 (21–27).

McEvoy, James, III. 1969. "Conservatism or Extremism: Goldwater Supporters in the 1964 Presidential Election." *The American Right Wing: Readings in Political Behavior,* ed. Robert A. Schoenberger. New York: Holt, Rinehart & Winston.

McRobbie, Angela, and Jenny Garber. 1976. "Girls and Subcultures." *Resistance through Rituals: Youth Subcultures in Post-War Britain,* eds. Stuart Hall and Tony Jefferson. New York: Holmes and Meier.

Mehler, Barry. 1999. "Race and 'Reason': Academic Ideas a Pillar of Racist Thought." *Intelligence Report.* Southern Poverty Law Center Winter (27–32).

———. 1994. "In Genes We Trust: When Science Bows to Racism." *Reform Judaism* 23 (10–13, 77–79).

————. 1989. "Foundation for Fascism: The New Eugenics Movement in the United States." *Patterns of Prejudice* 23:4 (17–25).

Mele, Christopher. 1995. "The Militias Stand Up." *Sunday Record*. Middletown, NY, February 12 (1, 3, 26).

Messerschmidt, James W. 1999. "Making Bodies Matter: Adolescent Masculinities, the Body, and Varieties of Violence." *Theoretical Criminology* 3:2 (197–220).

————. 1997. *Crime as Structured Action*. Thousand Oaks, CA: Sage.

Messner, Michael. 1997. *Politics of Masculinities*. Thousand Oaks, CA: Sage.

Militia of Montana. 2000. "One Bullet at a Time: That's How You'll Get Our Guns." *Taking Aim: The Militiaman's Newsletter* 6:10 April. Available at http://www.militiaofmontana.com/reports.htm. July 4, 2001.

Miller, Adam. 1994. "Professors of Hate." *Rolling Stone* 693, October 20 (106–112).

Minkowitz, Donna. 1998. *Ferocious Romance: What My Encounters with the Right Taught Me about Sex, God, and Fury*. New York: Free Press.

————. 1995. "In the Name of the Father." *Ms. Magazine*. December (64–71).

Minow, Martha. 1990. *Making All the Difference: Inclusion, Exclusion and American Law*. Ithaca, NY: Cornell University Press.

Mitchell, Juliet. 1986. "Reflections on Twenty Years of Feminism." *What Is Feminism?* ed. Juliet Mitchell and Ann Oakley. Oxford: Basil Blackwell.

Monroe, Ann. 1997. "Race to the Right." *Mother Jones* May/June (34–39).

Moran, Leslie. 2001. "Affairs of the Heart: Hate Crimes and the Politics of Crime Control." *Law and Critique* 12:3 (331–344).

Morin, Richard, and Scott Wilson. 1997. "Men Were Driven to 'Confess Their Sins': In Survey, Attendees Say They also Are Concerned about Women, Politics." *Washington Post*, October 5 (1).

Mosse, George L. 1985. *Nationalism and Sexuality: Middle-Class Morality and Sexual Norms in Modern Europe*. Madison: University of Wisconsin Press.

Motavalli, Jim. 2000. "Balancing Act: Can America Sustain a Population of 500 Million—or even a Billion—by 2100?" *E Magazine*, November–December (33).

Mozzochi, Jonathan, and L. Events Rhinegard. 1991. "Rambo, Gnomes and the New World Order: The Emerging Politics of 'Populism.'" Portland, OR: Coalition for Human Dignity.

Mudde, Cas. 2000. *The Ideology of the Extreme Right*. Manchester, UK: Manchester University Press.

Mueller, Carol McClurg. 1994. "Conflict Networks and the Origins of Women's Liberation." *New Social Movements: From Ideology to Identity*, eds. Enrique Laraña, Hank Johnston, and Joseph R. Gusfield. Philadelphia: Temple University Press.

Mulvey, Edward, and John LaRosa. 1986. "Delinquency Cessation and Adolescent Development: Preliminary Data." *American Journal of Orthopsychiatry* 56 (212–224).

Negative Population Growth. Public Awareness Advertising. www.npg.org/public.awarenes/assorted_ads.html.

Neiberger, Ami. 1996. "Promise Keepers: Seven Reasons You Should Watch Out." *Freedom Writer Magazine*, September (3–10).

Neiwert, David A. 1999. *In God's Country: The Patriot Movement and the Pacific Northwest*. Pullman, WA: Washington State University Press.

Newton, Judith L. 1999. "A Reaction to Declining Market and Religious Influence." *Standing on the Promises: The Promise Keepers and the Revival of Manhood*, ed. Dane S. Claussen. Cleveland: Pilgrim Press.

————. 1998. "White Guys." Review essay. *Feminist Studies* 24:3 Fall (572–598).

Novick, Michael. 1995. *White Lies White Power*. Monroe, ME: Courage Press.

Novosad, Nancy. 2000. *Promise Keepers: Playing God*. Amherst, NY: Prometheus Books.

————. 1996. "God Squad: The Promise Keepers Fight for a Man's World." *Progressive*, August (25–27).

Nyquist, J. R. 2000. "Merchants of Hate." *World Net Daily*, September 3. Available at www.worldnetdaily.com.

Oberschall, Anthony. 1973. *Social Conflict and Social Movements*. Englewood Cliffs, NJ: Prentice-Hall.

O'Leary, Stephen D. 1994. *Arguing the Apocalypse: A Theory of Millennial Rhetoric*. New York: Oxford University Press.

Ollove, Michael. 2001. "The Lessons of Lynchburg." *Baltimore Sun*, May 6 (6F).

Olsen, Frances E., ed. 1995. *Feminist Legal Theory*, vol. I: *Foundations and Outlooks*. New York: New York University Press.

O'Matz, Megan. 1996. "More Hate Crimes Blamed on Juveniles." *Morning Call*, October 23.

Omi, Michael, and Howard Winant. 1994. *Racial Formation in the United States: From the 1960s to the 1990s*. New York: Routledge.

Oregon Spotlight. 2002. Available at www.oregonspotlight.org. Aug. 30.

Oregonian. 2001. "Senator Questions Laws against Hate Crimes." February 10 (D:1).

Ortega, Tony. 2000a. "Witness for the Persecution." *New Times Los Angeles*, April 20.

———. 2000b. "In the Hot Seat." *New Times Los Angeles*, May 25.

Passerini, Luisa. 1992. "Lacerations in the Memory: Women in the Italian Underground Organizations." *International Social Movement Research*, vol. 4: *Social Movements and Violence: Participation in Underground Organizations*, ed. Donatella della Porta. London: JAI Press. (161–212).

———. 1987. *Fascism in Popular Memory: The Cultural Experience of the Turin Working Class*. Cambridge, UK: Cambridge University Press.

Payne, Stanley G. 1995. *A History of Fascism, 1914–45*. Madison, WI: University of Wisconsin Press.

Perry, Barbara. "'White Genocide': White Supremacists and the Politics of Reproduction." In this volume.

———. 2001. *In the Name of Hate: Understanding Hate Crimes*. New York: Routlege.

———. 2000. "'Button-Down Terror': The Metamorphosis of the Hate Movement." *Sociological Focus* 33:2 May (113–131).

———. 1999. "Defenders of the Faith: Hate Groups and Ideologies of Power." *Patterns of Prejudice* 32:3 (32–54).

Pharr, Suzanne. 1996a. *In the Time of the Right: Reflections on Liberation*. Berkeley, CA: Chardon Press.

———. 1996b. "A Match Made in Heaven: Lesbian Leftie Chats with a Promise Keeper." *Progressive*, August (28–29).

Phillips, Scott, and Ryken Grattet. 2000. "Judicial Rhetoric, Meaning-Making, and the Institutionalization of Hate Crime Law." *Law and Society Review* 34 (567–606).

Phoenix, Ann, and Ann Woollett. 1991. "Motherhood: Social Construction, Politics, and Psychology." *Meanings, Practices, and Ideologies*, eds. Ann Phoenix, Ann Woollett, and Eva Lloyd. London: Sage Publications.

Pierce, William. 1978. *The Turner Diaries*. Hillsboro, VA: National Vanguard Books.

Postone, Moishe. 1986. "Anti-Semitism and National Socialism." *Germans and Jews since the Holocaust: The Changing Situation in West Germany*, ed. Anson Rabinbach and Jack Zipes. New York: Homes & Meier.

Potok, Mark. 1999. Southern Poverty Law Center researcher. Telephone interviews, July 16, 19, and 21 and December 23, 2002.

Preston, June. 1999. "Women Emerging as White Supremacist Leaders." *Reuters News Service*, September 12.

Quinby, Lee. 1999. *Millennial Seduction: A Skeptic Confronts Apocalyptic Culture*. Ithaca, NY: Cornell University Press.

———. 1997. "Coercive Purity: The Dangerous Promise of Apocalyptic Masculinity." *The Year 2000: Essays on the End*, ed. Charles B. Strozier and Michael Flynn. New York: New York University Press.

———. 1994. *Anti-Apocalypse: Exercises in Genealogical Criticism*. Minneapolis: University of Minnesota Press.

Rand, Kristen. 1996. *Gun Shows in America*. Washington, DC: Violence Policy Center.

Rape Abuse Incest National Network. 2002. "RAINN Statistics." Available at http://www.rainn.org/statistics.html.

Reinharz, Shulamit. 1992. *Feminist Methods in Social Research*. New York: Oxford University Press.

Richardson, James T., Jans van der Lans, and Frans Derks. 1986. "Leaving and Labeling: Voluntary and Coerced Disaffiliation from Religious Social Movements." *Research in Social Movements, Conflicts and Change* 9 (97–126).

Ridgeway, James. 2001. "Osama's New Recruits" in the *Village Voice*, November 6.

Ridgeway, James. 1995. *Blood in the Face*. rev. 2nd ed. New York: Thunder's Mouth Press.

Robb, James H. 1954. *Working-Class Anti-Semite: A Psychological Study in a London Borough.* London: Tavistock Publisher.

Robbins, Thomas. 1997. "Religious Movements and Violence: A Friendly Critique of the Interpretive Approach." *Nova Religio* 1:1 (13–29).

Robertson, Ian. 1987. *Sociology.* New York: Worth.

Robnett, Belinda. 1997. *How Long? How Long? African-American Women in the Struggle for Civil Rights.* New York: Oxford University Press.

Roches, The (Maggie Roche, Terre Roche, and Suzzy Roche). 1985. "Weeded Out." *Another World.* Warner Brothers. Lyrics copyright 1985, DeShufflin Inc., ASCAP.

Roediger, David R. 1991. *The Wages of Whiteness: Race and the Making of the American Working Class.* New York: Verso.

Ronson, J. 2002. *Them: Adventures with Extremists.* New York: Simon and Schuster.

Rose, Susan D. 1987. "Women Warriors: The Negotiation of Gender in a Charismatic Community." *Sociological Analysis* 48 (245–258).

Rosenblum, Karen E., and Toni-Michelle C. Travis. 2000. *The Meaning of Difference.* Boston: McGraw Hill.

Ross, Alfred, and Lee Cokorinos. 1996. "The Promise Keepers Are Coming: The Third Wave of the Religious Right." *Report.* New York: Sterling Research Associates.

Rothenberg, Paula S. 2001. *Race, Class, and Gender in the United States,* 5th ed. New York: Worth Publishers.

Rountree, Pamela Wilcox. 1998. "A Reexamination of the Crime-Fear Linkage." *Journal of Research in Crime and Delinquency* 35:3 (41–372).

Rupert, Mary. 1997. "The Patriot Movement and the Roots of Fascism." *Windows to Conflict Analysis and Resolution: Framing Our Field,* eds. Susan Allen Nan, Dwight Bashir-Elahi, Jayne Docherty, Larissa Fast, Robert Harris, Karen Hobart, Dan McFarland, Vicki Rast, Ilana Shapiro. Fairfax, VA: Institute for Conflict Analysis and Resolution.

Sachs, Wolfgang, ed. 1992. *The Development Dictionary.* London: Zed Books.

Sampson, Robert J., and Laub, John H. 1993. *Crime in the Making: Pathways and Turning Points through Life.* Cambridge, MA: Harvard University Press.

Sandilands, Catriona. 2002. "Lesbian Separatist Communities and the Experience of Nature." *Organization and Environment* 15 (131–163).

Sapp, Allen, Richard Holden, and Michael Wiggins. 1993. "Value and Belief Systems of Right-Wing Extremists: Rationale and Motivation of Bias-Motivated Crimes." *Bias Crime: American Law Enforcement and Legal Responses,* ed. Robert Kelly. Chicago: Office of International Criminal Justice.

Scher, Abby. 2001. "The Crackdown on Dissent," *Nation,* February 5 (23–26).

Schindler, Amy. 1998. "Power, Patriarchy, and the Promise Keepers: The Pleasure of Religious Ecstasy." Paper presented at the annual meeting of the American Sociological Association, Toronto.

Schneider, Alison. 2000. "A California State Professor Is Attacked for His Defense of a Holocaust Denier." *Chronicle of Higher Education* 46:42, June 23 (A19).

Schor, Juliet. 1998. *The Overspent American: Upscaling, Downshifting, and the New Consumer.* New York: Basic Books.

Schroer, Todd J. 2001. "Issue and Identity Framing within the White Racialist Movement: Internet Dynamics." *Research in Political Sociology* 9: *The Politics of Social Inequality,* eds. Betty A. Dobratz, Lisa K. Walder, and Timothy Buzzell. Amsterdam: JAI/Elsevier.

Scotch, Richard. K. 1984. *From Good Will to Civil Rights: Transforming Federal Disability Policy.* Philadelphia: Temple University Press.

Seltzer, William. September 1998. "Population Statistics, the Holocaust, and the Nuremberg Trials." *Population and Development Review* 24:3 (511–552).

Serrano, Richard. 1990. "Civil Suit Seeks to Bring Down Metzger Empire." *Los Angeles Times,* February 18.

Shanks-Meile, Stephanie L., and Betty A. Dobratz. No date. "Linkages of Hatred: Hierarchies of Oppression and Violence among Contemporary White Supremacists." Unpublished paper on file at Political Research Associates.

Shapiro, Joseph P. 1993. *No Pity: People with Disabilities Forging a New Civil Rights Movement.* New York: Random House.

Shariatmadar, Azi. 2002. "Anti-Immigrant Alert!" *Political Environments: A Publication of the Committee on Women, Population and the Environment* 9 (8–9).

Sheffield, Carole J. 1992. "Hate Violence." *Race, Class, and Gender in the United States,* ed. Paula Rothenberg. New York: St. Martin's Press.

Shulevitz, Judith. 2000. "Evolutionary Psychology's Anti-Semite." *Slate,* January 24. Available at slate.msn.com/Code/Culturebox/Culturebox.asp?Show=1/24/00&idMessage=4446.

Skorzeny, Mrs. R. G. 1993. "I Am the Wife of a Warrior." *The Code of the Skinhead,* 57.

Smith, Andrea. 2002. "Devil's in the Details." *Color Lines,* Spring, 4–6.

Smith, Christian. 2000. *Christian America? What Evangelicals Really Want.* Berkeley, CA: University of California Press.

———, with Sally Gallagher, Michael Emerson, Paul Kennedy, and David Sikkink. 1998. *American Evangelicalism: Embattled and Thriving.* Chicago: University of Chicago Press.

Snipp, C. Matthew. 1996. "Understanding Race and Ethnicity in Rural America." *Rural Sociology* 61:1 (125–142).

Snow, David A., and Robert D. Benford. 1992. "Master Frames and Cycles of Protest." *Frontiers in Social Movement Theory,* ed. Aldon D. Morris and Carol McClurg Mueller. New Haven, CT: Yale University Press.

———. 1988. "Ideology, Frame Resonance, and Participant Mobilization." *From Structure to Action: Comparing Social Movements across Cultures,* ed. Bert Klandermans, Hanspeter Kriesi, and Sidney G. Tarrow. Greenwich, CT: JAI Press.

Snow, David A., E. Burke Rochford, Jr., Steven K. Worden, and Robert D. Benford. [1986] 1997. "Frame Alignment Process, Micromobilization, and Movement Participation." Reprinted in *Social Movements: Perspectives and Issues,* eds. Steven M. Buechler and F. Kurt Cylke, Jr., Mountain View, CA: Mayfield Publishing.

Soule, Sarah, and Jennifer Earl. 1999. "All Men Are Created Equal: The Differential Protection of Minority Groups in Hate Crime Legislation." Paper presented at the annual meeting of the American Sociological Association, Chicago, Illinois.

Southern Poverty Law Center. 2003. Available at www.splcenter.org/intelligenceproject.

Southern Poverty Law Center. 2002. "The Puppeteer: The Organized Anti-Immigration 'Movement,' Increasingly in Bed with Racist Hate Groups, Is Dominated by One Man." *Intelligence Report* 106 Summer (44).

———. 2001a. "The Rise and Decline of the 'Patriots.'" *Intelligence Report* 102 Summer (6–8).

———. 2001b. "False Patriots" *Intelligence Report* 102 Summer (9–38).

———. 2000. "Church of the Creator: A History." Available at www.splcenter.org/intelligenceproject/ip-4k4.html.

———. 1999. *Intelligence Report* Spring. Montgomery: SPLC.

———. 1997. *False Patriots: The Threat of Antigovernment Extremists.* Montgomery: SPLC.

"Special Investigative Report." 1995. *Metro Times.* Detroit, April 26–May 2, 46.

Spelman, Elizabeth V. 1988. *Inessential Woman: Problems of Exclusion in Feminist Thought.* Boston: Beacon Press.

Spokane Spokesman Review. 1986. "Bigotry or Brotherhood?" December 31.

Stacey, Judith. 1987. "Sexism by a Subtler Name?" *Socialist Review* 17 (7–28).

Staggenborg, Suzanne. 1998. "Social Movement Communities and Cycles of Protest: The Emergence and Maintenance of a Local Women's Movement." *Social Problems* 45 (180–204).

Staudenmaier, Peter. 1995. "Fascist Ideology: The 'Green Wing' of the Nazi Party and Its Historical Antecedents." *Ecofascism: Lessons from the German Experience,* eds. Janet Biehl and Peter Staudenmaier. San Francisco: AK Press.

Stephenson, June. 1991. *Men Are Not Cost-Effective: Male Crime in America.* New York: Diemer Smith.

Stern, Kenneth S. 1996a. *A Force upon the Plain: The American Militia Movement and the Politics of Hate.* New York: Simon & Schuster.

———. 1996b. "Militias and the Religious Right." *Freedom Writer,* October (3–7). Institute for First Amendment Studies.

Stock, Catherine McNicol. 1996. *Rural Radicals: Righteous Rage in the American Grain.* Ithaca, NY: Cornell University Press.

Stormfront. 2002. Available at www.stormfront.org/crusader/texts/wau/wau5.html.

Strozier, Charles B. 1994. *Apocalypse: On the Psychology of Fundamentalism in America.* Boston: Beacon Press.

Swidler, Ann. 1986. "Culture in Action: Symbols and Strategies." *American Sociological Review* 51 (273–286).

Tanton, John. 1986. "Witan Memos," Available at www.splcenter.org/intelligenceproject/ip-index.html.

Taylor, Carl S. 1990. *Dangerous Society.* East Lansing, MI: Michigan State University Press.

Taylor, Verta. 1999. "Gender and Social Movements: Gender Processes in Women's Self-Help Movements." *Gender and Society* 13 (8–33).

———, Nancy Whittier, and Cynthia Fabrizio Pelak. 2001. "The Women's Movement." *Feminist Frontiers,* eds. Laurel Richardson, Verta Taylor, and Nancy Whittier. Boston: McGraw Hill.

Thompson, Al. 1995. Affidavit dated January 19, 1995, filed in *Thompson v. Carto,* Marion County, IN, Case No. 49D019410 CT 1178. Available at www2.ca.nizkor.org/ftp.cgi/people/c/carto.willis/thompson-vrs-carto. January 29, 2002.

Thompson, Damian. [1996] 1998. *The End of Time: Faith and Fear in the Shadow of the Millennium.* Hanover, NH: University Press of New England.

Tilly, Charles. 1978. *From Mobilization to Revolution.* Reading, MA: Addison-Wesley.

Tolchin, Susan J. 1996. *The Angry American: How Voter Rage Is Changing the Nation.* Boulder, CO: Westview.

Toler, Deborah. 1995. "Black Conservatives." *Eyes Right! Challenging the Right Wing Backlash,* ed. Chip Berlet. Boston: South End Press.

Tong, Rosemarie Putnam. 1998. *Feminist Thought.* Boulder, CO: Westview Press.

Tuveson, Ernest Lee. 1968. *Redeemer Nation: The Idea of America's Millennial Role.* Chicago: University of Chicago Press.

U.S. Congress. House. 1985. "Crimes against Religious Practices and Practices and Property." Hearings before the Subcommittee on Criminal Justice of the Committee on the Judiciary. 99th Cong., 1st sess. May 16 and June 19. Serial 134. Washington, DC: U.S. Government Printing Office.

U.S. Congress. 1992. "Hate Crimes Sentencing Enhancement Act of 1992." Hearing before the Subcommittee on the Constitution of the Committee the Judiciary. 102th Cong., 2nd sess. August 5. Serial 42. Washington, DC: U.S. Government Printing Office.

U.S. Congress. 1990. "The Violence against Women Act of 1991." Washington, DC: Government Printing Office.

U.S. Department of Justice. 2001. "News Conference with USA John Brownlee: Indictment of Darrell David Rice." April 10. DOJ Conference Center, Washington, DC.

———. 1996. *Training Guide for Hate Crime Data Collection.* Washington, DC: Government Printing Office.

Vaid, Urvashi. 1995. *Virtual Equality: The Mainstreaming of Gay and Lesbian Liberation.* New York: Anchor Books.

Van Dyke, Nella, and Sarah A. Soule. 2000. "The Mobilizing Effect of Social Strain: Explaining the Variation in Levels of Patriot and Militia Organizing." Paper presented at the annual meeting of the American Sociological Association, Washington, DC.

Wallace, Anthony F. C. 1956. "Revitalization Movements." *American Anthropologist* 58:2 April (264–281).

Walter, Gerry, and Suzanne Wilson. 1996. "Silent Partners: Women in Farm Magazine Success Stories, 1934–1991." *Rural Sociology* 61:2 (227–248).

Warr, Mark 1985. "Fear of Rape among Urban Women." *Social Problems* 32:3 February (238–250).

Weigman, Robyn. 1993. "The Anatomy of Lynching." *American Sexual Politics,* eds. John Fout and Maura Shaw Tantillo. Chicago: University of Chicago Press.

Weis, Lois. 1993. "White Male Working Class Youth: An Exploration of Relative Privilege and Loss." *Beyond Silenced Voices: Class, Race and Gender in United States Schools,* eds. L. Weis and M. Fine. Albany, NY: SUNY Press.

———, Amira Proweller, and Craig Centri. 1997. "Re-Examining 'A Moment in History': Loss of Privilege inside White Working Class Masculinity in the 1990s." *Off White: Readings on Race, Power and Society,* eds. Michelle Fine, Lois Weis, Linda Powell, and L. Mun Wong. New York: Routledge.

Weisberg, D. Kelly, ed., 1993. *Feminist Legal Theory: Foundations.* Philadelphia: Temple University Press.

West, Cornel. 1993. "Learning to Talk Race." *Reading Rodney King, Reading Urban Uprisings,* ed. Robert Gooding-Williams. New York: Routledge.

Wexler, Chuck, and Gary T. Marx. 1986. "When Law and Order Works: Boston's Innovative Approach to the Problem of Racial Violence." *Crime and Delinquency* 32:2 (205–223).

Williams, Loretta. 1997. "Some Promises Not to Keep." *Unity First*, August 9 (6).

Williams, Rhys H. 2001. "Introduction: Promise Keepers: A Comment on Religion and Social Movements." *Promise Keepers and the New Masculinity: Private Lives and Public Morality*, ed. Rhys H. Williams. Lanham, MD: Lexington Books.

———. 1995. "Constructing the Public Good: Social Movement and Cultural Resources." *Social Problems* 42 (124–44).

———, and J. N. Blackburn. 1996. "Many Are Called but Few Obey: Ideological Commitment and Activism in Operation Rescue." *Disruptive Religion: The Force of Faith in Social-Movement Activism*, ed. Christian Smith. New York: Routledge.

Wilson, James Q., and Richard Herrnstein. 1985. *Crime and Human Nature*. New York: Simon and Schuster.

Wing, Adrien Katherine. 2000. *Global Critical Race Feminism: An International Reader*. New York: New York University Press.

Wood, Julia T. 2001. *Gendered Lives*. Belmont, CA: Wadsworth.

Wright, Stuart A. 1999. "Radical Religion in America: Millenarian Movements from the Far Right to the Children of Noah." Review of Kaplan, 1997. *Sociology of Religion* Summer. Available at http://www.findarticles.com/cf_o/mOSOR/2_60/55208526/p1/article.jhtml?te

Yardley, J. 2001. "A Portrait of the Terrorist: From Shy Child to Single-Minded Killer," *New York Times*, October 10.

Young, Iris Marion. 1990. *Justice and the Politics of Difference*. Princeton NJ: Princeton University Press.

Young, Thomas J. 1990. "Violent Hate Groups in Rural America." *International Journal of Offender Therapy and Comparative Criminology* 34:1 April (15–21).

Young-Bruehl, Elisabeth. 1996. *The Anatomy of Prejudices*. Cambridge, MA: Harvard University Press.

Zald, Mayer. N. 1996. "Culture, Ideology, and Strategic Framing." *Comparative Perspectives on Social Movements: Political Opportunities, Mobilizing Structures, and Cultural Framings*, eds. Doug McAdam, John D. McCarthy, and Mayer N. Zald. Cambridge, UK: Cambridge University Press.

Zeskind, Leonard. 1999. "From Compounds to Congress." *Searchlight* May (20–23).

Zuckerman, Ben. 1999. "The Sierra Club Immigration Debate: National Implications." *Population and Environment: A Journal of Interdisciplinary Studies* 20:5 (401–412).

Zwerman, Gilda. 1994. "Mothering on the Lam: Politics, Gender Fantasies and Maternal Thinking in Women associated with Armed, Clandestine Organizations in the United States." *Feminist Review* 47 (33–56).

Statutes Cited

California Penal Code §422.6.
730 ILCS §5/5-5-3.2.
N.D. Cent Code §12.1-14-04.
Pub. L. §101-275.
Pub. L. §103-322.
R.I. Gen. Laws §12-19-38.
W.V. ST §61-6-21.

Contributors

Chip Berlet is Senior Analyst at Political Research Associates (PRA), a progressive think tank near Boston. He is coauthor, with Matthew N. Lyons, of *Right-Wing Populism in America* (2000) and editor of *Eyes Right!* (1995). Both books received the Gustavus Myers Center award for the study of bigotry and human rights in North America. Berlet has studied and written about the U.S. political right for over twenty-five years, with articles appearing in academic books and journals; popular magazines, including the *Progressive* and the *Nation;* and daily newspapers, such as the *New York Times,* the *Boston Globe,* and the *Chicago Sun-Times.* From 1977 to 1987 he worked in a multiracial community group organizing against a neo-Nazi/Ku Klux Klan movement that sought to block the integration of a southwest Chicago neighborhood. Berlet is the Webmaster of PRA's site, www.publiceye.org.

Rajani Bhatia is Coordinator of the Committee on Women, Population, and the Environment (CWPE). She is active in the reproductive rights and justice community. She has been involved in women's health research and activism internationally in partnership with the Forum for Women's Health (Mumbai) and the Feminist International Network of Resistance to Reproductive Technology and Genetic Engineering, based in Germany. She lives in Baltimore, Maryland.

Randy Blazak is an Associate Professor of Sociology at Portland State University in Portland, Oregon. He is the director of the Hate Crimes Research Network (www.hatecrime.net), which connects academic work on bias criminality. He is also the cofounder of Oregon Spotlight, which monitors hate groups in the state of Oregon. He has published his research on youth and hate in journals, book chapters, and books, including his text with Wayne S. Wooden entitled *Renegade Kids, Suburban Outlaws: From Youth Culture to Delinquency* (Wadsworth, 2001) and an upcoming text for Wadsworth on the sociology of hate activism. His most recent work appears in *The Encyclopedia of Terrorism* (Sage, 2002), *The Gang Reader* (Waveland, 2003), and *General Strain Theory: Essential Readings* (Wadsworth, 2003). Dr. Blazak is currently researching prison Odinism among white supremacists.

Kathleen M. Blee is a Professor of Sociology at the University of Pittsburgh. Her books include *Inside Organized Racism: Women in the Hate Movement* (2002), *Feminism and Antiracism: International Struggles for Justice* (coedited with France Winddance Twine, 2001), and *Women of the Klan: Racism and Gender in the 1920s* (1991).

Betty A. Dobratz is Professor of Sociology at Iowa State University. Her coauthored book *"White Power, White Pride!": The White Separatist Movement in the U.S.* with Stephanie Shanks-Meile received two sociology awards, one from a section of the American Sociological Association (ASA) and the other the North Central Sociological Association Scholarly Achievement Award. Dobratz edits *Research in Political Sociology,* including "The Politics of Social Inequality" (with Lisa K. Waldner and Timothy Buzzell, 2001). She has published widely, with articles appearing in *Symbolic Interaction, Journal for the Scientific Study of Religion, Sociology and Social Research,* and *Sociological Inquiry,* among others.

Abby L. Ferber is Associate Professor of Sociology and Director of Women's Studies at the University of Colorado at Colorado Springs. She is the author of *White Man Falling: Race, Gender and White Supremacy* (1998) and coauthor of the American Sociological Associations' *Hate Crime in America: What Do We Know?* (2000). Ferber is widely recognized as a leading scholar of the far right, and her articles have been widely published in academic journals (including *Ethnic and Racial Studies, Rural Sociology, Sociological Perspectives, Social Identities, Men and Masculinities, Sociological Focus* and *Teaching Sociology*) as well as news outlets, including the *Denver Post* and the *Chronicle of Higher Education.* Ferber is a frequent presenter at the meetings of the American Sociological Association and the Society for the Study of Social Problems. Ferber has also conducted many workshops on the far right, hate crime, and teaching about hate. She is also coauthor of *Making a Difference: University Students of Color Speak Out* (2002) and coeditor of *Privilege: A Reader* (2003).

Valerie Jenness is Chair of the Department of Criminology, Law and Society and an Associate Professor in the Department of Criminology, Law and Society and in the Department of Sociology at the University of California, Irvine. Her research focuses on the links between deviance and social control (especially law), gender, and social change (especially social movements). She is the author of three books: *Making Hate a Crime: From Social Movement to Law Enforcement Practice* (with Ryken Grattet, 2001), *Hate Crimes: New Social Movements and the Politics of Violence* (with Kendal Broad, 1997), and *Making it Work: The Prostitutes' Rights Movement in Perspective* (1993). Her work has been recognized with awards from the Gustavus Myers Center for the Study of Bigotry and Human Rights in North America, the Society for the Study of Social Problems, the Pacific Sociological Association, and the University of California.

Michael S. Kimmel is Professor of Sociology at SUNY at Stony Brook. His books include *Changing Men* (1987), *Men Confront Pornography* (1990), *Men's Lives* (5th ed. 2000), *Against the Tide: Profeminist Men in the United States, 1776–1990* (1992), *The Politics of Manhood* (1996), *Manhood: A Cultural History* (1996), and *The Gendered Society* (2000). He edits *Men and Masculinities,* an interdisciplinary scholarly journal, a book series on Men and Masculinity at the University of California Press, and the Sage Series on Men and Masculinities. He is the Spokesperson for the National Organization for Men Against Sexism (NOMAS) and lectures extensively on campuses in the United States and abroad.

Jacquelyn S. Litt is Associate Professor of Sociology and Women's Studies and Associate Director of Women's Studies at Iowa State University. She is the author of *Medicalized Motherhood: Perspectives from the Lives of African American and Jewish Women* (Rutgers) and numerous articles on care work and motherhood.

Peggy McIntosh is Associate Director of the Wellesley College Center for Research on Women. She is founder and Codirector of the United States S.E.E.D. (Seeking Educational Equity and Diversity) Project on Inclusive Curriculum. In 1988, she published the groundbreaking "White Privilege and Male Privilege: A Personal Account of Coming to See Correspondences through Work in Women's Studies." This analysis and its shorter form, "White Privilege: Unpacking the Invisible Knapsack" (1989), have been instrumental in putting the dimension of privilege into discussions of gender, race, sexuality, and class in the United States and throughout the world. McIntosh has taught at the Brearley School, Harvard University, Trinity College (Washington, D.C.), the University of Denver, the University of

Durham (England), and Wellesley College. She is cofounder of the Rocky Mountain Women's Institute and has been consulting editor to *Sage: A Scholarly Journal on Black Women.*

Barbara Perry is Associate Professor of Criminal Justice at Northern Arizona University. Her work emphasizes issues of inequality and (in)justice. Specifically, she has published in the area of hate crime, enthnoviolence, and hate groups in journals such as *Sociological Focus, American Behavioral Scientist,* and *Sociology of Crime, Law, and Deviance.* Her book entitled *In the Name of Hate: Understanding Hate Crimes* (Routledge) is a theoretical exploration of hate crimes as a mechanism for constructing difference. That book will soon be followed by another, *Hate and Bias Crime: A Reader* (2003). With Dr. Marianne Nielsen, Dr. Perry is the coeditor of *Investigating Difference: Human and Cultural Relations in Criminal Justice.*

JoAnn Rogers is a Ph.D. student in Sociology at Iowa State University. Her areas of concentration are family and social inequality with a focus on gender. She has presented papers at the Care Work Conference as well as the MidWest History Conference.

Stephanie L. Shanks-Meile is a Professor of Sociology at Indiana University Northwest. She has been researching the white separatist movement with Betty A. Dobratz since the early 1980s, culminating in the publication of articles and a monograph entitled *White Power, White Pride!: The White Separatist Movement in the United States,* published in 1997 by Simon and Schuster in the Twayne Social Movements Series, with the paperback edition published in 2000 by Johns Hopkins University. The book won several academic awards: *Choice* Award for Outstanding Academic Book, the North Central Sociological Association Scholarly Achievement Award, and the Distinguished Scholarship Award from the American Sociological Association Section on Marxist Sociology. She was a coeditor, with Susan Archer Mann and Michael D. Grimes, of a special issue of the *Journal of Race, Gender and Class on Marxism: Race, Gender and Class* (2001).

Index

CPSIA information can be obtained at www.ICGtesting.com
Printed in the USA
BVOW030450310112

281787BV00005B/32/P